QUEER ATTACHMENTS

Queer Interventions

Series editors:
Noreen Giffney and Michael O'Rourke
University College Dublin, Ireland

Queer Interventions is an exciting, fresh and unique new series designed to publish innovative, experimental and theoretically engaged work in the burgeoning field of queer studies.

The aim of the series is to interrogate, develop and challenge queer theory, publishing queer work which intersects with other theoretical schools and is accessible whilst valuing difficulty; empirical work which is metatheoretical in focus; ethical and political projects and most importantly work which is self-reflexive about methodological and geographical location.

The series is interdisciplinary in focus and publishes monographs and collections of essays by new and established scholars. The editors intend the series to promote and maintain high scholarly standards of research and to be attentive to queer theory's shortcomings, silences, hegemonies and exclusions. They aim to encourage independence, creativity and experimentation: to make a queer theory that matters and to recreate it as something important; a space where new and exciting things can happen

Forthcoming titles

Queering the Non/Human
Noreen Giffney and Myra J. Hird
ISBN: 978-0-7546-7128-2

Cinesexuality
Patricia MacCormack
ISBN: 978-0-7546-7175-6

Gay Men and Form(s) of Contemporary US Culture
Richard Cante
ISBN: 978-0-7546-7230-2

Lesbian Dames: Sapphism in Eighteenth-Century England
John Benyon and Caroline Gonda

The Ashgate Research Companion to Queer Theory
Noreen Giffney and Michael O'Rourke

Critical Intersex
Morgan Holmes

Queer Attachments
The Cultural Politics of Shame

SALLY R. MUNT
University of Sussex, UK

ASHGATE

Published by
Ashgate Publishing Limited
Wey Court East
Union Road
Farnham
Surrey GU9 7PT
England

Ashgate Publishing Company
Suite 420
101 Cherry Street
Burlington, VT 05401-4405
USA

Ashgate website: http://www.ashgate.com

British Library Cataloguing in Publication Data
Munt, Sally
  Queer attachments : the cultural politics of shame. -
  (Queer interventions)
  1. Homosexuality - Public opinion 2. Stigma (Social
  psychology) 3. Homophobia 4. Gays in popular culture
  I. Title
  306.7'66

Library of Congress Cataloging-in-Publication Data
Munt, Sally.
Queer attachments : the cultural politics of shame / by Sally R. Munt.
    p. cm. -- (Series: queer interventions)
Includes bibliographical references and index.
ISBN 978-0-7546-4921-2 (hdbk)
1. Homosexuality. 2. Sexual minorities. 3. Politics and culture. 4. Sex--Social aspects. 5. Shame.
I. Title.
HQ75.15.M86 2007
306.76'6091821--dc22

ISBN: 978-0-7546-4921-2 (hbk)
ISBN: 978-0-7546-4923-6 (pbk)

Reprinted 2009

Mixed Sources
Product group from well-managed forests and other controlled sources
www.fsc.org Cert no. SGS-COC-2482
© 1996 Forest Stewardship Council

Printed and bound in Great Britain by TJI Digital, Padstow, Cornwall.

Contents

List of Figures   vii
Series Editors' Preface: After Shame   ix
Foreword by Donald L. Nathanson   xiii
Acknowledgements   xvii

The Cultural Politics of Shame: An Introduction   1

Chapter 1   Queer Irish Sodomites: The Shameful Histories of Edmund
             Burke, William Smith, Theodosius Reed, the Earl of
             Castlehaven and Diverse Servants – Among Others   31

Chapter 2   Shove the Queer: Irish/American Shame in New York's
             Annual St Patrick's Day Parades   55

Chapter 3   Expulsion: The Queer Turn of Shame   79

Chapter 4   Queering the Pitch: Contagious Acts of Shame in
             Organisations   105

Chapter 5   Shameless in Queer Street   133

Chapter 6   A Queer Undertaking: Uncanny Attachments in the HBO
             Television Drama Series Six Feet Under   161

Chapter 7   After the Fall: Queer Heterotopias in Philip Pullman's
             His Dark Materials Trilogy   181

Chapter 8   A Queer Feeling When I Look at You: Tracey Emin's
             Aesthetics of the Self   203

Bibliography   229
Index   243

List of Figures

I.1 Radclyffe Hall, author of *The Well of Loneliness* with her beloved daschunds and Una Tronbridge 10

I.2 Woodcut. 'Sins of the Father' 1884. The caption reads: 'The sins of the drunken father are visited on the heads of the children – a thief and woman of shame visit their lunatic father in the criminal lunatic asylum 24

1.1 Stone of Shame in the Palazzo della Ragione, Padua 33

1.2 Stone of Shame (detail), Palazzo della Ragione, Padua 34

1.3 Earl of Castlehaven, contemporary sketch 35

1.4 'Cincinnatus in Retirement', published by E. D'Archery in 1782 (hand-coloured etching) by Gillray, James (1757–1815) 48

2.1 St Patrick's Day Parade in New York, 3 February 2003 57

2.2 St Parick's Day Parade in New York, 3 February 2003 66

2.3 Protesters at St Patrick's Day Parade, New York, 1996 69

3.1 Faces of Adam and Eve, from Masaccio, 'The Expulsion from the Garden of Eden' (1427), Brancacci Chapel, Florence 79

3.2 Stuart and Vince from *Queer as Folk* (Channel 4, 2000) 99

4.1 David Brent (Ricky Gervais) in 'The Office' 127

5.1 Frank Gallagher (David Threlfall) from 'Shameless' 135

5.2 Woodcut. 'The Ale Wife' circa 1810. A woman proffers a jug of ale to a man in the street from her 'house of shame' 140

6.1 From left to right: David Fisher, Ruth Fisher, Nate Fisher 165

7.1 Philip Pullman with a monkey-daemon, London Zoo 189

8.1 Tracey Emin, 'Everyone I Have Ever Slept With 1963–1995' (1995) 205

8.2 Tracey Emin, 'My Bed'. Installation Turner Prize Exhibition, Tate Gallery, London, 20 October 1999–23 January 2000 206

8.3 Tracey Emin, 'Why I Never Became a Dancer' (1995) 208

After Shame

Does shame have a history? Sally R. Munt's *Queer Attachments: The Cultural Politics of Shame* does for shame what Judith Butler did for gender in *Gender Trouble*; the kind of historicising work Michel Foucault carried out in relation to sexuality. She presents shame as a socially constructed and historically contingent entity, system or psychic process that in turn constructs us as subjects. Shame is, for Munt, an embodied emotion, one in which the body functions as an 'archive of feelings' in the words of Ann Cvetkovich. For Munt as for Butler, we are not our shame but rather are constituted as subjects by it in the acting out of its psychic processes. If Melanie Klein's work points to the 'memories in feelings', *Queer Attachments* encourages readers to uncover the memories *of* feelings and the feelings in memories. Munt calls on readers to explore the cultural vicissitudes of shame with her by traversing temporal locations, geographical regions, disciplinary formations and theoretical alignments in an effort to unpick shame's latent intricacies.

Queer Attachments is a mature work, one that has been in gestation for many years and shows evidence of Munt's considerable knowledge of lesbian and gay studies, queer theory, cultural studies, psychoanalysis, feminism, critical theory, class, space and textual analysis, all of which she brings to bear on this project. Munt is an accomplished thinker, one who makes productive use of a range of, what at first glance might appear to be, conflicting theories and approaches in the service of her analysis. She draws on a wide variety of scholars, including Raymond Williams, Charles Darwin, Erving Goffman, Pierre Bourdieu, Wendy Brown, Judith Butler, Silvan Tomkins, Melanie Klein, Benedict Anderson, William Meissner, Adriana Caverero, Eve Kosofsky Sedgwick, Michel Foucault, Jacques Lacan, Sigmund Freud, Luce Irigaray, Gilles Deleuze and Elizabeth Grosz. From historical speeches to film, academia to performance art, lesbian classics to children's literature, television to the Internet, normative politics to queer activism, Munt employs 'text' in its widest sense as she deftly traces the twists and turns of shame through time and space, presenting us with both its harmful effects and transformative potential.

Queer Attachments is an exercise in object relations. In this, Munt examines not just how individuals become shamed but also how shame facilitates the formation of those same individuals in the first place. The author asks readers not so much to enter shame because we are as social beings already thoroughly imbued with it, but instead encourages us to become self-reflexive about our relationship with shame and its role in the formation of the self and the attachments we forge, in addition to those we are unable to pursue, with others. The emphasis here is on shame both as an object and a process. In this, Munt examines not just how spaces become loci of shame but also how shame itself enacts a space, a system that facilitates the formation of identity while also regulating it, thus locating the force of its control in and on the body itself.

Masaccio's fresco 'The Explulsion of Adam and Eve from Eden', the cover image for *Queer Attachments*, illustrates how it is shame that is one of the guiding principles of Christianity. Munt writes in the shadow of shame because it is within that shadow that the human takes shape. It is through the myth of the Garden of Eden and the notion of Original Sin that shame becomes soldered to normativity in that everything that takes place within a Christian frame of reference then transpires *after* shame. In this way, heteronormativity as a concept to describe the mythology that has come to dominate what gets to count as proper modes of (sexual) relating is one that is awash with the tears of its own shameful genesis. If pride comes before a fall, Munt's book suggests that it is shame that precedes the formation of identity, *all* identity; a suave universalising move that shifts the responsibility of shame from the shamed queer, colonised or classed subject onto all parties in the transaction. Shame, for Munt, is performative. Through baptism, Christian subjects are interpellated by religious representatives through shame, called into community through the burden of Original Sin, into a system that both controls them while providing in a Foucauldian move the methods by which that regulatory apparatus can be resisted.

Queer Attachments is also temporally situated *after* the importance of shame has been recognised. Munt is interested, not in wallowing in the shamed subject as victim, but in harnessing that space as an analytical framework for working through the experience of shame, both as a mechanism for thinking about identity, desire, embodiment, relationships and social inclusion/exclusion and also as a catalyst that has the potential for catharsis. In this, Munt asks what it might mean to move *beyond* shame. The failure to successfully recognise and mourn shame leaves the split subject in a melancholic state, projecting much of what is uncomfortable onto Others or else turning those feelings inwards in an effort to punish the self for one's failure to achieve what one perceives as an inability to connect. Pride as the inverse of shame is facilitated by shame at the same time that it operates as a defence mechanism employed by the subject to protect itself from recognising shame's all-pervasiveness. *Queer Attachments* urges us to reconsider shame and accept its role in our self-identifications and attachments. By extension, Munt insists that we cease denying shame's presence, which merely transforms our feelings of vulnerability and fear into disgust and hate, in the process simply abjecting them onto those marked out as Other. Instead of rejecting or repressing shame, *Queer Attachments* confronts us with it as a primary object and asks us to reclaim, embrace and possibly transgress or move beyond shame in a reparative gesture towards self-healing.

Queer Attachments showcases queer praxis at its best. It is an example of how theory can be used to effect change. The Queer Interventions book series publishes theoretical work that situates itself within current debates about identity, desire, pleasure and politics in an effort to rethink the critical landscape of academia; efforts which think critically about what it means to put forward such challenges; and writings which bring about a queer praxis in the process of interrogating existing norms. Queer Interventions seeks out scholarship that invents as well as intervenes, putting the 'invention' back into 'in(ter)vention'. This book is a difficult one to read, not because of its language but because of the emotional demands it places on the reader. To engage with the subject of this book is risky because it is to engage not merely in an academic exercise in knowledge but to embark on an interrogative relationship with the self and the processes through which one interacts with others. It is an ethical book, one with a commitment to bringing about movement from denial to acceptance to transcendence for readers willing to give themselves over to it. *Queer Attachments*, like the performance art of Tracey Emin, 'brings forth into public culture an ethical challenge to think otherwise about shame, inciting us to risk entering shame and make insanely joyful, dancing sodomites of us all'.

Noreen Giffney

The Cambridge Dictionary defines 'intervention' as an 'intention to become involved in a difficult situation in order to improve it or prevent it from getting worse' and a thesaurus entry for the word collocates it with interference, interposition or insinuation; a mediation, intermission or obtrusion. The project of queer theory from its very beginnings has been to interfere, to interpose or insinuate itself (into texts, institutions, disciplines) and to interrupt and dis-locate the normative and the regulatory. In short, to get involved in messy situations in order to improve them and to turn things around, to mediate between the normative and the counter-normative and to obstruct the status quo so that things do not get any worse (and hopefully will get better).

Sally R. Munt's *Queer Attachments: The Cultural Politics of Shame* is interventionist in all these senses on both a practical and everyday level. The focus on the everyday should remind us of the political intentions of British cultural studies , which in Stuart Hall's definition was passionately moved by a desire to connect, to transform, to make a difference. Not unlike shame, cultural studies has an adhesive quality in that it gets itself into sticky situations in order to try to alter them, renegotiate them, and to make an ethical intervention into them. *Queer Attachments* re-connects queer theory and cultural studies by recognising how the two border on each other and are as porously open to one another as they are both to difference. Munt's 'architecture of affect', her queer politics of affectivity, queers cultural studies by resurrecting the signally vital cultural materialist critique one associates with British cultural studies particularly, but most obviously, with Raymond Williams. Despite all of the recent work in queer studies on public affect, mourning, melancholia, grief and shame, Williams and his 'structure of feeling' are rarely to be found. Yet, throughout this book the influence of Williams' ideas across *Culture and Society*, *Keywords* and *The Country and the City* about community, culture, class, the individual and intersubjectivity can be palpably felt. The effect of this intervention is not only to alter the intellectual and critical landscape of cultural studies but also to urgently suggest that the project of a queered cultural studies is precisely to intervene in the political situations it is entangled in. As we approach the 50th anniversary of *Culture and Society*, Munt's book reminds us how Williams' writings on space, selfhood and affect are still so crucially important.

There has been significant attention paid to affect and emotion by queer theorists in recent years. *Queer Attachments* makes a number of much needed alterations and interventions into this dispersive field. Firstly, this book engages with the *materiality* of affect, asking not just what a body can do (in the case of Tracey Emin and others) but what a *body politic* can do (in the chapters on nation), bringing about a queerly immanent politics of affect which is keenly attentive to questions of spatiality. It is also attuned, via a subtle negotiation of Michel Foucault, Louis Althusser and Friedrich Nietzsche, to how a cultural politics of shame reconfigures our thinking about the subject, and how one can turn the constitutive, interpellating moment of subjectivation around, so that the unwilled or unwanted shaming interpellation can lead to more positive locations in which to think about identity. This encourages a transformative political response and responsibility, opening up the ethical and political as such.

Queer Attachments not only works to extend our understanding of the ways in which affect shapes (as well as problematises) the subject and practices of the self, but also how affects are relational, how affects like shame, envy and hate circulate among and between bodies in what Sara Ahmed calls an 'affective economy'. Affect is felt and flows between bodies, between subjects, making us responsible for, obligated towards, as Cavarero shows, the other. The ethics and politics of affect sketched here draws on the ethology of Baruch Spinoza and its take up by Gilles Deleuze and Elizabeth Grosz, but with the added and novel twist of Foucault's later writings on ethics and the art of existence. For Deleuze following Spinoza, the body is capable of affecting and being affected, Munt's cartography of affect draws out this body's capacity for movement, its ability to act on other bodies, perceiving affect not just as a feeling but also a performative force. This circulation of bodily energies, for Foucault, influences a body's modes of existence, allowing for new modes of subjectivation that emphasises relationality and becoming. Following a tradition of Deleuze, Foucault and Grosz, for Munt a body is not defined by what it is (*esse*) but by its possibility (*posse*); what it is capable of doing affectively.

This Deleuzian critical politics of affect allows Munt to turn the negative, painful and de-formative scene of shame into an affirmative one. This reparative reading emphasising connectivity, love, and hope shares much with the later Foucault on friendship when he spoke about the art of existence or the art of life. Foucault's aesthetics of existence has been viewed as asocial, passive and apolitical but Munt's sublimely queer aesthetics of shame is consistent with all of the key ethical and political values Foucault endorses throughout his work: invention, innovation, creativity, and transformation. Above all, the impetus of Foucault's life as a work of art was to intervene into and resist normalising social practices and institutions. In Munt's equally resistant recovery of shame (one of the Indo-European etymological roots of the word is 'to cover'), *Queer Attachments* shows us that out of the wounded attachments of shame can emerge an energizing and life affirming, even redemptive, queer politics of hope.

Michael O'Rourke

Foreword

Best guess is that the year was 1983 — some time during the period I was shifting away from the sex based theories taken for granted during my training, toward the work on emotion that has come to dominate my daily life. A generation earlier I'd been taught that homosexuality was only a small step away from madness, and assured that formal psychoanalysis was required if any ordinary sinner were to become a healthy adult. "Even though you are only doing psychotherapy, there are still some things you can do for your patient," cautioned one influential teacher. Everybody's favorite writer about sexual matters was Robert J. Stoller, a legendary psychoanalytic theorist whose revelatory 1979 book *Sexual Excitement* poked fun at the very idea that there was a proper, normal, and intrinsically healthy way to be sexual. My work on shame had caught his fancy, and we'd chat now and again; he gave me a lovely chapter for *The Many Faces of Shame*. But this day I was truly perplexed about something that I was sure he understood thoroughly.

Knowing he saw his first analytic session at precisely 8am in Los Angeles, I timed my call to give us the few minutes my simple question would require. "Oh, hello, Donald." "Bob, explain to me how the sex drive knows whether it has been aroused by a male or a female." From the full minute or more of silence I thought the connection had gone dead. "Bob?" "No, I'm still here. It's not just that I don't know the answer. I was trying to figure out whether anybody ever asked that question before." He accepted easily my contention that the most powerful sexual stimulus was the presence of an aroused other, and that much or most of homophobia could be traced to our helplessness/ shame at unexpected and unwanted arousal. Subtle and complex negotiations are required if we are to accept arousal in any public or private situation.

Most people protect themselves from "improper" arousal by carrying an invisible sheath of disgust that flicks on when they're caught unawares and feel the slightest tremor of unexpected arousal. Disgust, said Tomkins, evolved as a built-in protector of the hunger drive that makes us omnivores; from infancy through senescence it promotes forceful expectoration of substances outside a genetically programmed range of acceptable taste. As we mature, disgust becomes the affective core of a system through which we reject people or ideas that no longer "taste good"; it can power divorce and "new brooms sweep clean" political movements. And disgust is shame's partner in the repudiation of sexual arousal.

I'm long ago outed as a straight American psychiatrist who believes that homosexuality is a normal variant of sexual behavior, as I've explained at some length in *Shame and Pride: Affect, Sex, and the Birth of the Self*. And until I read the book that opens a few pages from here, I thought I knew a thing or two about what it meant to "be homosexual." Professor Munt adopts a premise so logical, so fascinating and clear, that one is led on a path of queer studies that forces entirely new views of the ordinary and normal. Our personal worlds are filled with invisible/unconscious equations: If "heterosexual" is defined as "normal," then anything considered normal is also expected to be heterosexual, and anything abnormal may thus be thought of as "queer." The outsider is by designation marginalized but also stigmatized.

As a psychiatrist, I'd focused on the role of shame in the formation of individual identity. There rarely occurs a more powerful stigma, says Sally Munt, than assignment of the disgusting and shameful label of homosexuality. Simply stated, she extends the logic of stigmatization as queer, and notes that people group as cultures on the basis of specific patterns of affect management. Each religion legislates acceptance of shame within rituals rehearsed or phrases uttered so often that we perform them with pride. ("O Lord, thy sea is so vast and my ship is so small.") Thus, intrinsic to "being Irish" is the requirement to negotiate a general belief that all Irishmen are lazy drunkards, despite that reliable research demonstrates only a statistically average level of alcoholism in that culture. Historically, much of public and private homosexual behavior may be seen as a defense against analogous discourses of shame. For the American Christian Right, "gay rights" has become a cliché through which the public presentations of self exhibited by individual men and women are scripted to trigger maximal degrees of repugnance in their audience.

As individuals we wear our identity as both a costume and a body, the former varied as systems of presentation and the far more secret body thereby cloaked to protect us from shame. The secret name of a future ruler might be encrypted as a grove of trees, mystics trafficked in magic words and incantations meaningless to outsiders; secrets were always linked with power and the fear of its loss through discovery. Social form often reverses the polarity of this highly charged energy system, for the current culture of our entertainments rewards public display of bodies as sexual and surgical anatomies. Religious practice, for centuries held as deeply personal and private, is often now displayed on giant television screens that encourage public performance. Yet for each of us in every era, something is held back as intensely private no matter what is shown the outsider. *Queer Attachments: The Cultural Politics of Shame* asks that we uncover with respect the private role of shame in each and every person, society, subculture, movement, and language we encounter.

Tomkins taught us that the shame affect, the basic physiological mechanism underlying the experience we feel as shame, is triggered when we're interrupted whilst thinking/feeling/doing something pleasant. The associated period of blush, cognitive shock, incoherence, and confusion lasts only moments until we seek freedom from this discomfort through the compass of interpersonal manoeuvers I've described as withdrawal, submission, distraction, or attack on whomever we deem responsible for our discomfort. You'll see all of these in her book, and come to know shame as both public and private discomfort. Yet pause a moment at this image of a puppy in the throes of shame, clearly

'Reconnection' – source unknown [public domain]

begging to reconnect with his human companion. Wherever you see shame (no matter how vigorously defended against), someone is hoping for reconnection. It would be wonderful were the reader of this remarkable book to come away not so much drenched with contempt and disgust for the offences of modern society, but rather with a renewed desire to soothe the afflicted and heal the broken interpersonal bond, wherever found. Much is wrong with today, and much can be done to make it more right.

Donald L. Nathanson, MD
Executive Director, The Silvan S. Tomkins Institute
Clinical Professor of Psychiatry, Jefferson Medical College
Philadelphia, Pennsylvania, USA

Acknowledgements

Eight years ago I submitted a proposal for this book and sent it to 20 publishers, all of whom rejected it (I'm not bitter!). Since then there has been a resurgence of critical interest in shame. I am grateful to Katherine O'Donnell who encouraged me to dust off the proposal, not lose my faith in the project, and write the book I wanted to write. I am also grateful to Noreen Giffney and Michael O'Rourke for asking me to contribute a book to their first-rate new series, and for being so positive about this one. John Rignell spent many years thinking about the personal effects of shame with me, and I am indebted to his loving regard. The UK Arts and Humanities Research Council funded three months of sabbatical leave during 2005–2006, as did also the University of Sussex, making the writing up possible. I am grateful to my colleagues in the Department of Media and Film for covering this leave. I thank the referees who kindly supported my application for this funding: Maureen McNeil, Angela McRobbie, Beverley Skeggs, and Tim O'Sullivan. Conversations about shame take varied forms; I would like to thank the following people for their rich contributions, social and intellectual, in support of me completing the project: Dora, Anita Biressi and Heather Nunn, Rev. Kit Gray, Elizabeth Grosz and Nicole Fermon, Stuart Laing, Kate O'Riordan, Barbara Bush, Sue Thornham and Mike O'Neill, Jasmine Uddin, Jac Matthews, Chris Kibbey Newman, Karen McMullen, Rex Brangwen, colleagues from the MSc. in Cognitive Psychotherapy at the University of Brighton, the Brighton Unitarian Church, and my brothers Richard Munt and Nicholas Firth.

Copyright Information

'Shame/Pride Dichotomies in *Queer as Folk*' in *Textual Practice* **14**:3, 531–546; 'The Well of Shame' in Doan, Laura and Prosser, Jay (eds) (2001) *Palatable Poison: Critical Perspectives on The Well of Loneliness Past and Present* (Columbia University Press: New York) 199–215.

The Cultural Politics of Shame: An Introduction

Shameful thoughts

Thinking about shame over the past 15 years was not so much an intellectual choice as a survival strategy. Spending years as a butch lesbian had taught me much about different kinds of shame, as I began to consider how the homophobia I experienced daily was imbricated with other prejudices. Because of the nested quality of emotions within experience, the homosexual sensibility through which I live my adult life in Britain was instrinsically dyed with the rest of my own life-story, summarily including: my White working-class childhood in Yorkshire, my Protestant Christian (misspent) youth, and my uncomfortable and partial assimilation into the middle class as a career academic. I have found the ivory tower more of a looming prison really: pity the poor elephants. Encarta's second meaning for *tow er* is 'a building designed to withstand attack', and its fourth is 'to be considerably superior to somebody or something',[1] which can be lamentably fitting for academia. Growing up with divorced and warring parents in a draughty boarding house meant that I wasn't a typical grammar school girl; the second-hand school uniform my Mum got for me was too baggy, too shiny from other girls' arses. School trips – whether ski-ing in Winter or a cruise in Summer – were ridiculously far beyond our household's means. At 13 I embraced Jesus and became an Evangelical, but trying to be a good Christian whilst also having an abortion at 16 wasn't uncomplicated, nor being abruptly evicted from the Christian commune I'd joined at the age of 22. I suspect this might have been from a closeted affair. I just never seemed to fit: I was in constant unease, I was even the wrong sort of lesbian – according to many lesbians – too noticeable. Numerous times, nice middle-class lesbians would put serious effort into avoiding being seen, stood or sat next to me, as my visible homosexuality disturbed the closeted equilibrium of their own. I'm a Northerner living in the South, still noticing their strangely restricted ways, their deferred dinnertimes that seem to extend ever hungrily into the night. I knew where I'd come from: my Mum used to sing to me the Gracie Fields song 'Sally, Sally, Pride of our Alley!'[2], and my Yorkshire accent never seems to dim despite 30 years away. South Coast acquaintances consider it amusing to comment on my charming, dulcet tones. Some people find their social disparity a source of delight and distinction, but if truth be told I longed to be normal; I used to fantasise about life in suburbia, and being the quiet girl at the back of the class nobody noticed, instead of the clown. Ever since I was a child reading by torch under the bedclothes, books have become my escape from a diffuse sense of shame. School helped, studying brought respectability, even though I was 'odd', being clever seemed to mitigate it: reading became my rehabilitation.

Shame is an emotion that can occur momentarily, and intensely, in moments of acute embarrassment and humiliation, it is often a transitory feeling experienced intensely in, and on, the body as flushing. Memories of such experiences linger heavily in the thoughts. This is shame operating as a transitional affect, although the accumulation of such experiences can deposit compelling traces within the psyche, psychologists call this the difference between 'felt' and 'bypassed' shame. Shame can become embedded in the self like a succubus;[3] an incubus being the male demon believed to have sexual intercourse with women whilst they slept, but in classical thought shame is a woman, and I think she is too. She caused me much worry, like a nightmare she hovered on the edge of consciousness, I knew she was there but couldn't grasp her, her presence slippery and formless, but her touch stained my awareness. Shame is a very sticky emotion, when it brushes you it tends to leave a residue to which other emotions are easily attached, namely envy, hate, contempt, apathy, painful self-absorption, humiliation, rage, mortification and disgust, the inventory of related and subsequent feelings is substantial. Shame becomes embodied, and the body begins to speak for itself, in specific ways, as the editors of *BodyShame* Paul Gilbert and Jeremy Miles (2002) make clear in arguing that shame needs to be contextualised within what they call biopsychosocial models. The body itself can be the source of shame, such as in defigurement, ageing, or chronic illness, and suffused with shame in such cases of body dysmorphic disorder, and in eating disorders. It is important for medical sociology to remember that these sites of shame are only brought into being *because* of the cultural, because of what dominant ideas of health and physical wellbeing dictate, through the idealisation of norms. Sufferers of psoriasis, acne, bowel disorders and prostate cancer can experience the supplementary sickness of shame; diagnosis of cause and effect are complicated issues. A distinction between what is written on the body, what erupts from the body, and the visualisation of bodily activity from another's point of view, is a compound shame entanglement subject to much scholarly conjecture; unfortunately the answers to questions of origin depend largely upon the disciplinary subject boundaries the researcher happens to be trained in. Investigating shame needs to be from an interdisciplinary approach, so knotted are its messages. The fleshly intransigence of shame means that it can take an unusual grasp of a person's whole organism, in their body, soul and mind, sometimes in eccentric ways. I have suffered episodically from the disease Myalgic Encephalomyelitis [ME] for over 20 years now, and I suspect the cause of this to be lodged within the anxiety of my childhood, forever high on stress hormones the organism just cracked with disease, from carrying the shame of non-conformity. Although psychologically healed (and proud of my origins) this malady is like my soul's memory of what it is to feel estrangement and hindrance from your own life.

It is my contention in this book that shame, working at different levels, performs culturally to mark out certain groups. The political effects of shame can be observed on a national and global stage. Some nations can be notoriously shame averse in their cultural psyches, for example China, or Israel. Other nations, such as ex-Empires Japan and Germany have had to spend decades rebuilding a national imaginary out of the ruins of war, for them the shame of defeat and widespread moral ignominy that followed has had its own role to play in the subsequent challenge of national reconstruction. Sara Ahmed illustrates how Australia has dealt with – or rather not dealt with, even repressed – the national shame of how the White settlers brutalised the aboriginal peoples (Ahmed 2004, 101–121). Thomas Scheff and Suzanne Retzinger's work is essential to understanding the role of shame in destructive conflicts and their model is readily extendible to national disputes.[4] Diplomacy, of course, is the expensive international pastime of 'saving face'. Shame operates more visibly within nation states to single out particular groups and stigmatise them; many of these groups are common targets whose victimisation remains historically long-lasting, typically: the underclass and the urban poor, rural labourers and peasants, 'gypsies' or Travellers, homosexuals, sex-workers, and racial enmities enacted by ancient colonial dictat, for example between the Turks and the Kurds, the Greeks and the Albanians, Sri Lanka and the Tamils, China and Tibetans, citizens of the USA and Mexico, and the British and the Irish. Histories of violent domination and occupation are found frequently lurking behind these dynamics of shame, and the shame, although directly aimed at the minoritised group, also implicates the bestower. Shame is an emotion that travels quickly, it has an infective, contagious property that means it can circulate and be exchanged with intensity. Shame is peculiarly intrapsychic: it exceeds the bodily vessel of its containment – groups that are shamed contain individuals who internalise the stigma of shame into the tapestry of their lives, each reproduce discrete, shamed subjectivities, all with their own specific pathologies. Patterns can be detected as shared shame scripts emerge that enable us to analyse shame's idiosyncrasies. But no-one is ever just a case, a symptom, an example of a type: in categorising shame's energy and its effects it is important to recall that shame is not an isolated emotion working upon clean, pure slates within the psyche, it is enmeshed within the self, and therefore it is always co-implicated with existing states. Shame has a compound materiality, including a compound mentality, and its effects therefore can be unpredictable. Shame is also an emotion that can flow unrecognisably through the subject, it can saturate a person and s/he may yet remain oblivious to its results, merely experiencing a diffuse unyielding sadness.

Nonetheless, it is essential to my argument in *Queer Attachments* that shame is understood as a variegated emotion with effects and practices that are not necessarily negative. Shame is popularly perceived to be an affliction, a toxin to be avoided by good behaviour or to be 'processed' out of existence into an ideally shame-free future. This view has been propagated by the North American Recovery Movements within their ubiquitous 12-Step Programmes. But shame is more interesting than that; we require a degree of shame, as we do guilt, once a moral transgression has been perceived. As societies we require evidence of remorse from the supposed wrongdoer. There are a variety of opinions on the distinction between guilt and shame, and often the two are confused. In it simplest form the distinction is an epistemological/ontological one, that in the former one *knows* one has committed a wrong (guilt) and, because of it, one has entered a state of disgrace (shame).[5] We expect convicted criminals to exhibit corporeal shame, we feel morally entitled to their repentance, evidence for which is anticipated via behaviour modification. If a wrongdoer doesn't display appropriate levels of shame, then that lends public permission for more righteous punishment to follow. Sometimes there is no reason or justification for being stigmatised by shame, and shame is transmuted into pride as part of a strategy by individuals and groups to reverse the discourse, think of Foucault's famous example of such in *The History of Sexuality Vol.1* in which the pathologised homosexual turns himself into the out, proud gay man (Foucault 1977).

The binary opposition of pride/shame is one model for understanding contemporary social liberation movements since the 1960s, as we begin to understand the labyrinthine corridors of shame that bore into particular cultures, we also begin to understand that shame can incorporate some latent, positive effects. Shame has political potential as it can provoke a separation between the social convention demarcated within hegemonic ideals, enabling a re-inscription of social intelligibility. The outcome of this can be radical, instigating social, political and cultural agency amongst the formerly disenfranchised. When you no longer care that you are being shamed, particularly when horizontal bonds formed through communities of shame can be transmuted into collective desires to claim a political presence and a legitimate self, that new sense of identity can forge ahead and gain rights and protection. There is also a certain joy that can be liberated by slipping out from underneath shame that was expressed historically in the early eras of the Black Civil Rights Movement, Gay Liberation Front, and the Women's Liberation Movement in the 1970s. It is hard to recall their euphoria and optimism now; we may scoff and call it naïve, but collective emotions *do* instigate social change, and we need further and superior understanding of this. To be released from shame can produce elation, but even shame itself can be experienced as pleasurable, for example in sado-masochism. Shame may be relinquished *reluctantly*, shame can provide a frisson of excitement in both participants, the one who shames and the one whom is shamed. Ritualised shame is rather taken up with gratification, evincing an intense regard for customs that their due phases are respected. Parts of Anglo-Catholic mass concerned with reinvigorating a sense of shame and sinfulness before the Almighty in order that the supplicant be cleansed and renewed are deeply satisfying rites, sacraments even. What this book intends to explore is some of these intricacies of shame, exposing the queer latency of shame, and the attachments forged there.

Emotional creatures

What is an emotion? Reason and emotion have been considered binary oppositions since the Enlightenment, but research now considers this division too absolute. Robert Masters makes these following distinctions between affect, feeling and emotion, which are bare working classifications:

> As I define them, affect is an innately structured, non-cognitive evaluative sensation that may or may not register in consciousness; feeling is affect made conscious, possessing an evaluative capacity that is not only physiologically based, but that is often also psychologically (and sometimes relationally) oriented; and emotion is psychosocially constructed, dramatized feeling. (Masters 2000)

Crucially, an affect may not necessarily be registered as a 'feeling', for example shame often goes unrecognised and unacknowledged. The critical literature on emotion is enormous and unfortunately I do not have the opportunity to do a thorough review of it here. For those readers interested in gaining an impression of current philosophical debates on emotion though, I would recommend the useful collection of essays *Thinking About Feeling: Contemporary Philosophers on Emotions* (Solomon 2004). Our ideas on emotions come out of long forgotten principles. The eighteenth century philosopher Adam Smith wrote about feelings that drive a market society, including 'self-love' and sympathy. In *The Theory of Moral Sentiments* Smith (1759) wrote about envy and emulation, claiming that its destructiveness would be undermined by shame, which would promote social order since the 'looking-glass effect' of the regard of others will stimulate social conformity. Here we see an early link between shame, social conformity, and the organisation of a self. There have been major schools of thought on what constitutes an emotion, including those following perspectives first articulated by Charles Darwin concerning animal behaviour and expression. Darwin entitles his relevant chapter 'Self-Attention-Shame-Shyness', so we see in this primary text on shame already an intense concern with the relationship between self, and other:

> Under a keen sense of shame there is a strong desire for concealment. We turn away the whole body, more especially the face, which we endeavour in some manner to hide. An ashamed person can hardly endure to meet the gaze of those present, so that he almost invariably casts down his eyes or looks askant... (Darwin 1999, 319)

Darwin describes the break in connection that is central to my thesis on shame and self-formation, however he is also keen to draw attention to the tension embodied in the twisted torque of shame:

> ... As there generally exists at the same time a strong wish to avoid the appearance of shame, a vain attempt is made to look direct at the person who causes this feeling; and the antagonism between these opposite tendencies leads to various restless movements in the eyes. (Darwin 1999, 319–20)

Darwin equates shame with blushing (he is most interested in the physiology of emotions); he also identifies the social and cultural aspects of shame:

> *The nature of the mental states which induce blushing.* These consist of shyness, shame, and modesty; the essential element in all being self-attention. Many reasons can be

assigned for believing that originally self-attention directed to personal appearance, in relation to the opinion of others, was the exciting cause; the same effect being subsequently produced, through the force of association, by self-attention in relation to moral conduct. It is not the simple act of reflecting on our appearance, but the thinking what others think of us, which excites a blush. (Darwin 1999, 324)

Darwin's many examples of persons in the grip of shame are principally women, over-sensitive men, idiots, half-castes, albinos, and a myriad of racial and ethnic examples taken from the far-reaching British Empire, from the Hindoos, the Lepchas of Sikhim, the young squaws from wild Indian tribes, the Kafirs of South Africa, to the 'barbarians of Tierra del Fuego' (Darwin 1999, 325). Perhaps this is because Darwin interviewed missionaries in order to gain a – or rather their – global perspective. We see illustrated the cultural politics of shame, for example in his instances of shamed European women that are generally taken up with their nakedness. This moving example is reminiscent of the precocious gaze of the newly invented sexologist, his prurient, possibly abusive gaze is something I have noted before (Munt 1998), but this is Darwin's own story:

> [Dr J. Crichton-Browne] gives me the case of a married woman, aged twenty-seven, who suffered from epilepsy. On the morning after her arrival in the Asylum, Dr. Browne, together with his assistants, visited her whilst she was in bed. The moment that he approached, she blushed deeply over her cheeks and temples; and the blush spread quickly to her ears. She was much agitated and tremulous. He unfastened the collar of her chemise in order to examine the state of her lungs; and then a brilliant blush rushed over her chest, in an arched line over the upper third of each breast, and extended downwards between the breasts nearly to the ensiform cartilage of the sternum. (Darwin 1999, 313)

Note the style of writing in this extract: it has the unfolding narrative quality of soft pornography until that final jump into medical terminology in the last sentence; I suspect that this sudden change in authorial perspective reveals Darwin's own moment of shameful retelling, as he retreats into scientific objectification. He concludes by saying '[t]his case is interesting, as the blush did not thus extend downwards until it became intense by her attention being drawn to this part of her person.' Shame indeed is written on her body. Dr Browne is later described as causing blushing deliberately in his patients by the administration of amyl nitrite ('poppers').[6] This patient was installed (for epilepsy!) in the first West Riding Pauper Lunatic Asylum, built at Stanley Royd, Wakefield, Yorkshire, in 1818 to hold 1600 patients. My own grandmother, Annie Firth, was incarcerated by her husband Albert in 1927 a few miles away within the fourth West Riding Pauper Lunatic Asylum, Storthes Hall, Huddersfield. The building opened in 1904 and was built for 2,500 patients, Annie remained there for 60 years until her death. Having a member of the family committed to the asylum in the 1920s and for decades after was, of course, conventionally a matter of shame and disgrace. It is a credit to my parents, especially my Mother, that I recall no shameful memories of visiting Grandma, only (to my present chagrin) recollections of feeling really bored. My mother, my brother and myself would track the endless, sloping Victorian corridors of burnished, pale green linoleum every other Saturday, to enter the locked wards of the women's wing of the hospital. Tactfully it was explained to me that Grandma preferred being 'elsewhere' in her mind. This gentle, mild old lady who liked grapes and Milky Ways never remembered who I was, only my eldest brother, Richard, whom she used to call 'Eric'.

Darwin's approach is still very influential, a contemporary much influenced by him is Paul Ekman who has argued that specific facial expressions for anger, fear, sadness and enjoyment are universal, although their *display rules* are predominantly cultural (Ekman and Friesen 1975). Darwin's successors are many: the late twentieth century resurgence of socio-biology – arguably a crude simplification of his ideas – has had many fans. One minor string is the interest in evolutionary psychiatry, a largely functionalist science concerned with 'disorders' such as paedophilia, sado-masochism and schizophrenia. Homosexuality, discussed under the section 'Reproductive Disorders', is argued in *Evolutionary Psychiatry* to offer evolutionary advantage, as it is an 'adaptive mechanism' for subdominate males who have incomplete pre-natal masculinisations. The authors' assumptions are based largely on old-fashioned sexology and the doubtful 'gay brain' theory of Simon Le Vay (1991). On the other hand, homosexuals tend to be *nicer* and hence 'those who share this orientation have little cause for shame' (Stevens and Price 2000, 186). For note, I would disagree with the founding precept of socio-biology that the biological determines the social, the social, cultural and the biological are interactive matrices with unpredictable outcomes on the self, they act together to form what Darwin would have thought of as a creative eruption, or interruption.[7] Other cognitive and social constructivist perspectives followed on from Darwin, the neurological traditions all advanced. Based on discoveries made through neural mapping of the limbic system, the neurobiological explanation of human emotion is that emotion is a pleasant or unpleasant mental state organised in the limbic system of the mammalian brain. Contemporary work on the neurophysiology of emotions is best exemplified by the work of Antonio Damasio, whose *Descartes' Error* (1996), *The Feeling of What Happens* (1999) and *Looking for Spinoza: Joy, Sorrow, and the Feeling Brain* (2003) have made an enormous impact on the way the body, emotion and consciousness are now co-envisaged.[8] Damasio argues that self-consciousness arose out of the development of emotion, so that human consciousness itself is generated from the consciousness of the feeling, experiencing self, 'the very thought of' oneself. Damasio differentiates between 'three distinct although very closely related phenomena: an emotion, the feeling of that emotion, and knowing that we have a feeling of that emotion' (Damasio 1999, 8). Damasio explains consciousness:

... the presence of you is the feeling of what happens when your being is modified by the acts of apprehending something. The presence never quits, from the moment of awakening to the moment sleep begins. The presence must be there or there is no you. (Damasio 1999, 10)

There is an inter-subjectivity or a mindful reflexivity in this self that is reminiscent of the dependency relationship in shame, that comes into being within the subject because of self-attention, induced by another, in this case the 'something' being apprehended. His research has helped to elucidate the neural basis for the emotions and has shown that emotions play a central role in social cognition and decision-making. His latest work on emotion has turned toward interests in ethics and creativity, in a Spinozan mood he explores what emotions can do, what they are capable of, as energies or intensities. This is in common with an optimistic move in feminist philosophy, following Gilles Deleuze and exemplified in the work of Elizabeth Grosz (2004, 2005).[9] It is in this same spirit that I approach shame, as a potential, as a change agent for the self.

Occasionally emotions are studied in order to be synthesised. A stint of recent work in modeling emotional circuitry and recognition has come out of computer science, engineering, psychology and neuroscience, called affective computing, it is concerned with the neural network models of emotion recognition. The term 'Affective Computing' was invented by Professor Rosalind Picard at the MIT Media Lab in 1995. It has various applications in e-learning, and can be used to adjust the presentation of a computerised tutor when a learner is bored, interested, frustrated, or pleased; health services such as counseling can benefit by affective computing; robots with emotions can also work in complex and uncertain environments. Affective computing can be used in human computer interaction, the 'affective mirror' enables a user to see how s/he performs in front of others, it is a kind of personal computer monitoring agent that sounds an alert before you send negative or angry emails, or it can be a music player that selects tunes based on the user's current mood. Affective computing has applications in society, for example a car can scrutinise the driver's emotions, overriding her to avoid car accidents when s/he is angry, distracted or upset. Companion devices such as digital pets may also model the emotion of real pets, and even 'understand' the pet owner's emotion. These electronic affinities charge up the Internet, with its promise of new social nodes, cyber-communities and mediated emotion we need to invent new definitions for digital or virtual passions. Not all are enamoured, skeptic Mark Slouka portends:

[Cyberspace] is in danger of 'homo-genizing' or 'narrowing down' the rich plurality of emotionally embodied experience, eroding our autonomy along the way, and turning us all into mere (Baudrillardian) spectators of our own disembodied demise. (Slouka 1995, 134–5)

There is a growing literature on animals and emotions, and queer animal love, which was stimulated in mass culture by the substantial popularity in the 1990s of Jeffrey Masson's writing, commencing with his first lay study *When Elephants Weep*. Shame may not merely be a human emotion, recent work on the emotional lives of non-human animals suggests they can express a whole range of 'higher' emotions such as pleasure, playful joy, and grief, that are related to and recognisably familiar to human forms of affect. Shame can easily be conjured as an image by that phrase 'hang-dog', and who hasn't lived closely with a dog and endured feeling manipulated by its apparent culpability, especially when it slings its 'tail between its legs'? My own dear 16-year-old familiar, Dora, a mackerel tabby, has a singular expression seen only when she has been sick on the carpet (in the garden doesn't count); the emotion she shows can be interpreted as a rendition of shame – if we want to take current research on the human-animal continuum of affect to be true – or indeed, she could just be feeling queasy. Jeffrey Masson is very Manichean – dogs feel shame (they are social/hierarchical), cats (narcissists) do not (Masson 2003). His essay on 'Shame, Blushing and Hidden Secrets' is anecdotal but throws up some useful considerations for thinking about non-human shame; he is wrong, though, to attribute the following episode with a chimpanzee to guilt, I think it is shame:

> Washoe's adopted son Loulis was teasing Roger Fouts one day, 'just being a pill', and poked him harder than usual, cutting Fouts with his nail. 'I made a big deal of it, crying and so on. Later, whenever I showed him that, to make him feel guilty, if you will, to use it to exploit that, he would squeeze his eyes tight and turn away. He would refuse to look at me whenever I tried to show him or talk about this old old scratch that he had given me.' (Masson 1996, 186)

Inter-species shame between different animals is the eloquent theme of Jacques Derrida's essay 'The Animal That Therefore I am (More to Follow)', in which he talks of appearing naked before the evaluative stare of his 'little cat', the cat an emblem for the unfathomable gaze of the other. He describes how:

> Something happens there that shouldn't take place – like everything that happens in the end, a lapsus, a fall, a failure, a fault, a symptom (and *symptom*, as you know, also means 'fall'... it is as if, at that instant, I had said or were going to say the forbidden, something that shouldn't be said, as if I were going to admit what cannot be admitted in a symptom and, as one says, wanted to bite my tongue. (2002, 373)

Jacques sees his own nakedness through the eyes of his cat, the knowledge of this nakedness is what makes him ashamed, and it is what causes Jacques to know himself. It is through the eerie gaze of this cat that he gains insight of the 'absolute alterity' of the other, remarking that his own shame and self-consciousness separate and intensify these perceptions. His concomitant sensation of 'falling' into the beyond induces a guilty aporia, it presages the forbidden, insinuating that which lies shamefully outside legitimate discourse. Derrida mentions more than once in this essay that his sex is exposed, and that his cat is female. We are witnessing in this story his strange re-enactment of the Biblical Fall, a narrative that frames my present work on shame, as a foundational myth. Whereas Derrida conjures up the castrating, silencing force of this fall, though, my own approach to shame incorporates optimism.

9

Animal-human intimacy is teeming with affect, regrettably it is also subject to specious human classificatory systems. In a recent essay, 'Disciplined Affections', which studies foxhunting in England, I encountered intriguing evidence of status rituals. The packs of trained hunting dogs are always called 'hounds', they must have an elite pedigree to qualify for the sport which has always been associated with royalty, emperors, and the nobility. All other canines are bagged together as non-hounds with the name 'cur-dogs', imposing a highly classed ecosystem, as the author Garry Marvin comments '[t]he quickest way for an outsider to show their ignorance of the event or to denigrate it, is to ask about, or talk about, "the dogs" (Marvin 2005, 64). Hounds are always named with the same first letter of the name of their sire or dam, and the Masters of Foxhounds Association regulates that it must be a name of more than one syllable. Hounds are bred and trained (like elocution lessons for the class aspirant), for 'voice', as it is crucial that they can bay effectively and meaningfully to each other in the pack and the huntsman. Hounds are liminal because they are neither livestock nor pets, and the human-animal intimacy engendered is *collective*, a group relationship rather than an exclusive one-to-one closeness. This is achieved through the disciplined control of the hounds as a 'class', a cluster, a set. The huntsman, in order to excite the appropriate

Figure I.1   Radclyffe Hall (right), author of 'The Well of Loneliness' with her beloved daschunds and Una Tronbridge
Source: Getty Images/Hulton Archive, with permission

emotions in the hounds, must be deliberately enthusiastic, confident, and trusting, he is the role model, the 'top dog'. What this new kind of work subtly observes is the cultural politics of animal-human emotion. Our paradigms for emotional creatures need to be expanded to include considering the axes of the human-ecological, the post-human and the non-human, these are huge fields yet to be fully opened up.[10]

The cultural politics of emotion

New academic texts on emotion are appearing all the time as the field of what has been popularly dubbed 'the new intimacy' is expanding quickly. I do not think that this is unrelated to the focused and purposeful feminist scholarly activism of the 1970s and 1980s, throughout all disciplines, that challenged dominant epistemological frameworks of disinterested truth, reason and fact, totems that had held sway for hundreds of years, really since the inauguration of Western universities and the birth of modern institutionalised knowledge practices. Work on feeling, passion, sensation, experience, and emotion has acquired new intellectual respectability over the past decade as part of the aforementioned postmodernity. This must also be related demographically to the exponential growth of personal psychotherapy amongst the middle classes, and the concomitant self-reflexivity it can inspire. In recent years there has been a flurry of more popular science and psychology concerned with emotions, most famously perhaps Daniel P. Goldman's (1995) *Emotional Intelligence*, which gained global appeal extending well outside of its core readership of MBA students, middle managers, and those in organisational studies. Together with *Emotional Intelligence* came the growing popularisation of Arlie Russell Hochschild's (1985) *The Managed Heart*, a critique of the commercialisation of human feeling, the 'affect economy', and her call to recognise 'emotional labour'; both of these terms – emotional intelligence and emotional labour – have entered mass consciousness.

J.M. Barbalet's *Emotion, Social Theory, and Social Structure* (1998) provides a good overview of the sociology of routine, non-pathological emotions.[11] There has been a welcome intellectual shift toward feeling in what I can perhaps misnomer 'damp sociology', but this might disparage a discipline that has become successfully permeated by a feminist epistemological agenda drawn toward theorising the complexity of experience. Perhaps the better term then, is Ann Game's and Andrew Metcalfe's eponymous *Passionate Sociology* (1996). Barbalet is right when he states that 'what is needed in sociology is not another general theory of emotion but a deeper understanding of particular emotions, and especially those central to social processes' (Barbalet 1998, 2). His chapters on 'Class and Resentment' and 'Conformity and Shame' form a useful background to the themes I will explore in *Queer Attachments*. Barbalet draws attention to the current impasse in class analysis, despite a Nietzschian understanding of *ressentiment*. This is something I addressed in my own previous collection *Subject to Change: Cultural Studies and the Working Class* in which I argued that Cultural Studies needed to better integrate modalities of class analysis that are informed by identity and difference theory (Munt 2001). Barbalet argues that 'emotions have a macro-sociological presence in their own right... Emotion arises in the pattern of structured relationships' (Barbalet 1998, 65). He goes on to argue that the fundamental distinction drawn between culture and social structure is not viable once the analysis of emotion is engaged, a precept that I have tried to integrate here. This is because of the conventional disciplinary division between studying emotion as an internal state, as the 'psychology model', *or* as an external state, contained within cultural practices, the 'sociology model'. Broadly speaking Film and Literary Studies has tended to follow the former, whereas Media and Cultural Studies has concerned itself mainly with the latter.

Investigating the cultural politics of emotion has already been cogently shaped by Sara Ahmed (2004). Ahmed, tracing the Latin, describes emotions as kinds of movements, from *emovere* to move, or to move out. She states 'of course, emotions are not only about movement, they are also about attachments, or about what connects us to this or that' (Ahmed 2004, 11). Emotions are produced by attachments, they are effects, they also make us seek attachments and refuse attachments, and sometimes they are disparate energies that drive us, take us in, to become attached, ideologically, somatically, and unconsciously, within a circulation of emotion that we barely perceive. The agency of emotions is not to be found in one place, within the self, or within the social. Ahmed describes the transference of emotions as 'sticky', an effect of histories of contact, an impression, a relationship of 'withness' in which things can get bound together, or blocked (Ahmed 2004, 89–95). She defines this analogy further:

> Stickiness then is about what objects do to other objects – it involves a transference of affect – but it is a relation of 'doing' in which there is not a distinction between passive or active, even though the stickiness of one object might come before the stickiness of the other, so that the other seems to cling to it. (Ahmed, 2004, 91)

Ahmed talks about sticky signs that bind associations and affects that interpellate subjects, such as the racist epithet 'Paki', that conceals other silent concepts within it such as outsider, dirty, immigrant and such. Ahmed's work focuses on the cultural politics of emotion as they pertain to race hierarchies and ethnicity in contemporary Britain; her excellent study analyses the symbolic axis between White and non-White, a crucible for emotions of all kinds to circulate. However, my own book examines White ethnicity and considers how its internal dynamics become racialised, through poverty, and filtered through a symbolic and real Irishness. We also might consider how much the epithet 'queer' is sticky in multiple senses: a sticky wicket for some to negotiate intellectually or politically, recalling the dual significance of 'tacky' as in gummy and cheap, and even the accusation/appellation 'Queer!' sticks...

Emotions are not so much contagious, elemental entities but less pure 'sticky' transmissions, something that Teresa Brennan explored in her last book

The Transmission of Affect (2004). She takes issue with the taken-for-grantedness of 'affective self-containment', the presupposition that an individual owns their feelings, she calls it 'a residual bastion of Eurocentrism' (Brennan 2004, 2). Brennan starts from the commonsense experience of 'soaking up an atmosphere', an environmental transmission that she reminds us is also biological, and neurological. She is concerned to remind us that the projection or introjection of an emotional transmission involves momentary judgement, she claims 'affects are judgements, or, as a new vernacular has it, attitudes' (Brennan 2004, 5); that the communication of emotion involves discernment and evaluation, that there is a distance between what I feel and what I feel with. I think this can be best conceived of in the concept of orientation in that the emotion that is moving within us causes attitudinal perspectives, toward or away. Brennan identifies two types of transmission of affect, '[t]here is transmission by which people become alike and transmission in which they take up opposing positions in relation to a common affective thread' (Brennan 2004, 9). What we shall see in my examination of the cultural politics of shame is a Newtonian model of shame that articulates the 'turn of shame', away or back toward. Emotions are *not* neutral, they are charged with consequences. Not all theories abide by an ensuing model (X follows Y), within Chinese medicine for example, there is no distinction between a bodily symptom and an affect, they are integrative, one thing; recent science has also been attracted to this simultaneity of emotion in the 'mind' and in the body. There is a sense of instantaneity in emotional transmission that has yet to be understood in terms of spatial/temporal energies and change. The disparate ways in which an affect may be registered are multiple, cumulative, emotions are highly permeable, they intrude and extrude and like magnetic particles, cling.

Within Western traditions of psychology and psychoanalysis a healthy person is one that knows how to manage and contain 'their' emotions within the individual self. This masculine bounded self has become ubiquitously aspirational, its reverse is found in the feminine, and in extreme the stigmatised personality 'disorders', or psychotic 'disorders' such as paranoid schizophrenia (the diagnostic condemnation for poor Annie). Whilst medical diagnosis can make someone socially intelligible in a pragmatic sense there is no doubt that this labelling has ignominious effects. There is a vicious cycle in operation in which a subject learns that it must be inviolate, yet its everyday experience is one of extreme permeability. The human psyche is a leaky sponge fanatically absorbing all the affects in its environment; some are better able to cope with this than others, individuals may carry 'loads' like 'viral loads', they are the pack donkeys of the affect economy. Brennan argues that these folks are the ones who succumb to conditions like Chronic Fatigue or Attention Deficit and Hyperactivity Disorder; these specific syndromes are suspiciously gendered that is to say that more women suffer from the first, more men and boys from the second; surely there are cultural indicators to be isolated here? Emotional transmissions vary in speed, moving through one person very slowly over years, and in others passing through in a flash, 'shedding' onto/into one body rather than another, more resistant receptor. Wilfred Trotter called this 'susceptibility'. Brennan discusses the transmission of emotions within and between groups, in the specific waves of affects generated by different cultural constellations that do not even have to be together in one place. This phenomenon must depend upon empirical cultural structures we can hope to detect. A large body of work exists on group behaviour, and Brennan reminds us that a group can be quite mad and yet apparently stable and purposeful in its outward form: 'the group can be apparently sane (a university department for instance) and yet occasionally irrational or persecutory in its dynamics' – a topic I elaborate on in my chapter on organisations (Brennan 2004, 66). She does start to address the cultural politics of emotion, take this statement about British football crowds of the 1980s:

> Rather than ignoring these crowds it might do more service to class politics to note that from the perspective of the theory of energetic transmission many of the working-class participants are carrying the affective refuse of a social order that positions them on the receiving end of an endless stream of minor and major humiliations, from economic and physical degradations in the workplace to the weight of the negative affects discarded by those in power. (Brennan 2004, 67)

This book is a journey into the cultural politics of such refuse, except that whereas Brennan's position is one of evoking sympathy for the exploited, degraded recipients 'dumped upon' by a society that excretes its negative psychic energy downward, I am more interested in delineating the *refusal* of that load, as Andrew Sayer has described it:

> To the extent that the working class refuse what they are refused... they avoid the shame that accompanies lack, indeed this may be a motive for their refusal, though of course this involves refusing what may be valuable, and hence increasing their others' disdain for them. (Sayer 2005, 955)

Structures of feeling

British Cultural Studies has concerned itself for 40 years with the practices of everyday life, meaning, and the circulation of power. Since its inception in the late 1960s it has studied culture and cultural politics as an object, and encouraged political criticism of those objects as a practice of ethical intervention. Our discipline has underlined the different ways people read, receive, and interpret cultural texts as agentic consumers, as distinctive participators in cultural production. Work on identities and subcultures has much shifted, enabling 'the masses' to become distinguishable as social actors; to some extent this 'cultural turn' ended up romanticising resistance, but this approach has now matured, and incorporates a more variegated model that accounts for tones of ambiguity, complacency and ambivalence. The rhetoric of victimisation that tinged early identity-based scholarship has become largely subsumed by advanced methodologies based upon the exchanges of meaning distributed within complex social matrices. Clearly, though, 'class [still] matters', vast structural inequalities remain, indeed flourish, social stratification and stigmatisation may mutate over the decades, but they are apparatuses of supreme intransigence. Under the terms of the 1697 English statute the 'deserving' poor were required to wear a badge of shame. Steve Hindle has commented that:

> ... any pauper who refused the badge was either to have their relief withdrawn or to be whipped and committed to bridewell for three weeks hard labour. (Hindle 2004, 10)

He argues that this was 'the single most decisive moment in the creation of social identity in early modern England' (ibid), but that it was also probably responsible for encouraging the development of a collective identity amongst the poor, and the consolidation of them as a class.

We don't require red or blue patches to be sewn onto clothing anymore, but enormous millions of people still 'languish' (think about the cruel prejudice in that word) at the bottom of the social hierarchy, and are even now organised into categories of the 'deserving' and the 'undeserving'. In this book I am specifically concerned with three inter-related groups that in the hegemonic model of oppression constitute communities of injury: the poor, the queer, and the Irish Catholic. People rarely live their lives as categorically as these typologies imply, they are much more immersed, and overlap at the level of experience; this book therefore interweaves case studies of class, sexuality, and ethnicity, attempting to demonstrate a feminist epistemology of exploring 'rich texts' of cultural density, similar to what Clifford Geertz intended for ethnography in 'thick description' (1973).

The book aims to analyse the context of these intricate identities as they have formed historically within composite cultural narratives lodged in representation, and in doing so, it also necessarily strays into examining the qualifying, normative and privileged categories of middle class, Protestant, and heterosexual as well. This study centres on the distribution, circulation and refusal of the emotion of shame at 'satellite' sites, showing how the poor, the queer and the Irish Catholic, though woven together indiscriminately and thrown under a 'shame shawl', can be unpicked. In doing so I will be emulating Raymond Williams' model of the 'structure of feeling', which is the closest thing to a method in this inquiry. It has been the aim of Cultural Studies to introduce *ostranenie* – defamiliarisation – to disturb the unspoken suppositions which determine our daily entities, to make us look again at the natural, the normal, the taken-for-grantedness of life. It may not be Queer Theory, but perhaps Cultural Studies can be a 'queer discipline' with its emphasis on collectivity, collaboration and mutuality, its focus on understanding cultural attrition from the perspectives of the marginalised, and its principle of ethical, public intervention. Emotions disturb us, they intrude upon the most 'rational' aspects of academic scholarship and their very acknowledgment or recognition is conditioned upon what they are perceived to be *a priori* within discourse. The attempt here is, with Williams, to 'bring to light' how our sentient selves are classed, and ask how they are constructed within powerful frames of determination, often below consciousness. So, as long as classed experience exists, it predetermines the meanings we can make and the feelings we can feel. The argument here is not to reify 'class' and deselect other paradigms, but to return to sites of classed experience and theorise out of them, as Foucault once instructed us:

> We must return therefore, to formulations that have long been disparaged; we must say that there is a bourgeois sexuality, and there are class sexualities. Or rather, that sexuality is originally, historically bourgeois, and that, in its successive shifts and transposition, it induces specific class effects. (Foucault 1984, 127)

Intellectual work in Queer Theory has largely neglected this firm injunction from its most famous pioneer. Cultural Studies analysis on the other hand, should not pose an attempt to proselytise working class, or any class cultural aesthetic, as intrinsically authentic or defiant. However, it should contain a premise: that cultural participation is delineated and characterised by powerful, structural social relations of production and consumption, and that those relations are classed, sexualised and *felt*.

The famous critical aphorism 'the structure of feeling' is taken from *The Long Revolution* (1961). The implicit premise of much of Raymond Williams' writing is that the structural organisation of class *produces* structurally organised experience, and hence feeling, or emotion. His most thorough description of the 'structure of feeling' occurs in his essay 'The Analysis of Culture', which begins by offering three general categories of culture: the 'ideal', the 'documentary', and thirdly the 'social':

> ... in which culture is a description of a particular way of life, which expresses certain meanings and values not only in art and learning but also in institutions and ordinary behaviour. The analysis of culture, from such a definition, is the clarification of the meanings and values implicit and explicit in a particular way of life, a particular culture. (1975, 57)

Williams is describing a kind of sensibility, negotiated in the conjunction between ideology and practice. It conveys a notion of embedded experience not unlike Pierre Bourdieu's near contemporary (1967) concept of the 'habitus', another Marxist who is concerned to emphasise that social life cannot be properly understood as just the aggregate of individual experience. Both these writers tried to introduce concepts that bridge the superstructural and the individual, that help us grasp how social meanings are made manifest in bodies and practices – *lived*.[12] Habitus includes what Bourdieu describes as 'dispositions'; it is a combination of thinking and feeling, cognition and affect, a range of conscious and unconscious phenomena that act upon, within, and are acted by the person in their ordinary life. Like Williams, Bourdieu also stresses how experience, in his case embodied in the habitus, is subject to time: 'The habitus, a product of history, produces individual and collective practices – more history – in accordance with the schemes generated by history' (1990, 54). What follows in *Queer Attachments* might be described as a study of the shame habitus, embodied in the specific subcultural histories of the poor, the queer, and the Irish Catholic diaspora, as they are represented to themselves, and in public discourse.

Whereas Bourdieu can be read (rather dismissively) as presenting history, or indeed any aspect of hegemony, as a uni-directional force stamping itself irredeemably upon the subject, the tenor of Williams work is more intent on discovering and representing the presence of agency. This is one reason I think why Williams' work makes a more cheering read. Returning to him then, he is keen to stress the 'genuine complexity' of the task of cultural analysis:

> To study the relations adequately we must study them actively, seeing all the activities as particular and contemporary forms of human energy. If we take any one of these activities, we can see how many of the others are reflected in it, in various ways according to the nature of the whole organisation. (1975, 61)

He qualifies and cautions the kinds of transformations of affect that are possible:

> ... since the particular activities will be serving varying and sometimes conflicting ends, the sort of change we must look for will rarely be of a simple kind: elements of persistence, adjustment, unconscious assimilation, active resistance, alternative effort, will all normally be present, in particular activities, and in the whole organisation. (1975, 62)

Williams' definition of the theory of culture as 'the study of the relationship between elements in a whole way of life', is inclusive, a pattern in which,

> ... certain elements, it seems to me, will always be irrecoverable. Even those that can be recovered are recovered in abstraction, and this is of crucial importance. We can learn each element as a precipitate, but in the living experience of the time every element was in solution, an inseparable part of a complex whole. The most difficult thing to get hold of, in studying any past period, is this *felt* sense of the quality of life at a particular place and time: a sense of the ways in which the particular activities combined into a way of thinking and living. (1975, 63) [My italics]

He is modest enough to realise that not everything can be grasped analytically, an awareness I shall echo in regarding the work of artist Tracey Emin in the final chapter. The 'actual experience' through which the social is lived is:

> ...as firm and definite as 'structure' suggests, yet it operates in the most delicate and least tangible parts of our activity... I do not mean that the structure of feeling, any more than the social character, is possessed in the same way as the many individuals in the community. But I think it is a very deep and very wide possession, in all actual communities, precisely because it is on it that communication depends. And what is particularly interesting is that it does not seem to be, in any formal sense, learned. (1975, 65)

In Part II of his essay Williams goes on to illustrate his concept of the 'selective tradition' by examining the culture of 1840s England; particularly he focuses upon the rise of a self-conscious, politically aware, working class. Williams breaks down the dominant social character into class fractions, noting how different class positions complicate the picture. He argues that the structure of feeling will relate to the dominant social character, but that it also corresponds to divergent, classed manifestations of it. Although the structure of feeling is evident in the dominant productive group (in this instance, the middle class), it is also distinguishable by the absences and omissions from representation and discourse, that is to say by silences and gaps, consequentially the things that cannot be spoken. Here, I think that Williams is gesturing toward the influence of the unconscious. As I will also do in my study, he looks to fictional narrative to illustrate structure of feeling; Williams identifies how the emotional cost of the dominant social character is signified within the popular prose of the time, and he explicates the strategies used to manage the damage of that cost through imaginative expression. Significantly, the structure of feeling is subtle, both a synthesis and a transformation, which, whilst not intrinsically radical, does indicate movement and agency on the part of the affected class.

The ethnic 'Irish' underclass

Queer Attachments reads class, sexuality and ethnicity as co-implicated paradigms, the book benefits from the rich exposition of whiteness that has already strengthened our understanding of class since Raymond Williams wrote from a Marxist perspective in the 1960s and 1970s, and several of my case studies, from public cultures epitomised by Edmund Burke, the Castlehaven case, and St Patrick's Day marches, to fictional characters in popular culture such as *The Well of Loneliness, Queer as Folk*, and *Shameless*, emphasise Irish Catholicism and its queering effect upon ethnic norms. In contemporary Britain the largest ethnic minority in the white British lower classes is made up of the Irish diaspora. There has been a lack of statistical data on the presence of the Irish and their descendants in the UK mainland, only in the 2001 census was there a tick-box category for 'White – Irish', which is an increasing trend. However, for second generation Irish subjects who see themselves as British this category may not be desirable. Máirtín Mac an Ghaill writes of the historical under-estimation of the Irish in population surveys, commenting that after the 1971 census:

> Without including populations originating from Northern Ireland, the community was seen as reaching almost two million. This figure placed the Irish as the single biggest minority ethnic group in the country. According to the 1991 census, 1.5% of the population in Britain was born in Ireland, north or south. Taking people born in Ireland and their children, it is estimated that they form 4.6% of the population in Britain and 11.5% of the population in Greater London. (Mac an GHaill 2000, 142)

Traditional social research of the twentieth century has failed to recognise Irish ethnicity in race-relations theory, and hence the presence of anti-Irish racism in British culture. This omission has been called the 'colour paradigm' wherein race and non-whiteness are seen as coterminous, so the Black and Asian face posseses 'race', whereas the homogenous white face does not. The liberal Left fares little better, often fetishising visible racial difference, practicing policies that see certain authentic 'heritages' as needing protection for sustainability, whilst remaining utterly unaware of an Irish upbringing. Breda Gray has introduced Alison Bailey's concept of 'whitely scripts' into her study of the racialisation of Irish women in Britain, she remarks that whiteness means 'Englishness'; 'manners', 'reasonableness', and 'ladylike behaviour' which has a moral force that endows both respectability and national belonging. For Irish women this denotation is an impossible one, she calls the Irish subjects she interviews 'cultural 'outsiders' and racial 'insiders', suggesting that Irish women in Britain, in order to avoid discrimination, participate in a strategy of 'cultural bleaching' (Gray, 2002).[13]

It has not always been thus; the experience of the Irish Catholic in Britain has been structured by an 800-year-old history of English colonisation, which only partly ended in the twentieth century with independence in 1922. The racialisation of Irish immigrants and labour migrants on mainland Britain has a long and ignominious tradition. R.M. Douglas writing on the racialisation of the Irish between the two World Wars declares that 'The Irish were [viewed as] living fossils, representatives of an atavistic or primitive human strain that the more intense struggle for existence elsewhere in Europe had rendered extinct' (Douglas R.M. 2002, 44). He provides sources of arguments concerning the aboriginal origins of the Celts, of their simian skulls, their cannibalism, their barbarous ferocity and 'noted antipathy to soap and water', they have 'beady eyes, low foreheads, dark, coarse and often kinky hair, a strain of negro blood, and an abnormal fondness for destruction' (Alfred, Lord Douglas, 1922, quoted in Douglas R.M. 2002, 46). Infamously Dr John Beddoe was a founding member of the Ethnological Society of the nineteenth century, spending 30 years on his 'Index of Negrescence', as Anne McClintock comments, 'great efforts were made to liken the Irish physiognomy to those of apes' (McClintock 1995, 53). R.M. Douglas writes of the historical linkage between negroes and the Irish, then the Jews and the Irish. Fears of miscegenation were expressed by among others, the President of the Scottish Anthropological Society G.R. Gair who argued in 1934:

> ... that it was in fact the *mischling* Irish, rather than their pure-bred counterparts, that represented the greatest threat to the integrity of the Anglo-Saxon race. (Douglas 2002, 49)

Arguing for their segregation and sterilisation, Gair saw the over-breeding of the Irish as a threat to overwhelm native Anglo-Saxons. He is in sympathy with fellow writer Professor Ernest William MacBride (F.R.S.), a Belfast born Professor of Zoology at Imperial College London writing in *Eugenics Review*, who saw classes as equivalent to races:

> The slums of Liverpool and Glasgow are being filled with a stunted population of so-called Celts from Wales and Ireland, really belonging to the Mediterranean race. They have a low standard of life and breed like rabbits, and under the sentimental notions now in fashion the Nordic element is called on to support them and thus indirectly to contribute to its own undoing. The great problem of eugenics, in my

opinion, is fundamentally racial: the breeding of mental defectives, deaf-mutes, etc., is bad, but such mutations at worst form a small proportion of the population – and tends in the long run to die out. The real problem is to seek means to prevent the higher racial elements from being swamped by the lower. (Macbride 1929, quoted in Douglas 2000, 51)

Other hibernophobes such as R.L. Cassie maintained that the Irish were 'hopelessly unassimilable, maintaining their exotic characteristics for generations' (R.M. Douglas 2000, 53). Lord Alfred Douglas claimed in *Plain English* in 1920 that 'crime is a feature of Ireland, because it's people are Irish' (quoted in Douglas R.M. 2000, 56). A delegate at the General Assembly of the Church of Scotland in 1933 argued for sympathy toward the Nazi persecution of the Jews as the Jewish problem in Germany was so similar to the Irish problem in Scotland (R.M. Douglas 2000, 55). And, in another example of the racialisation of the Irish as non-White, Douglas comments on how the term 'toasted Irish' was used to describe Caribbean immigrants to Britain in the 1960s.

Máirtín Mac an Ghaill argues how the Protestant British consolidated a collective racial identity as a superior race that was defined against an Irish Catholic inferior race with markers of difference that juxtaposed:

... dirtiness, drunkenness, laziness and violence of the alien Irish with the purity, industriousness and civilization of the English. (Mac an Ghaill 2000, 145)

Paul Michael Garrett calls it 'a more rooted failure to *recognise* Irish people', further, that there is a 'willful ignorance' at work, particularly at the hands of social and family services who have 'been subjected to discrimination and multiple forms of disadvantage' (Garrett 2005, 1359, 1365). He talks of Irish users of welfare services being 'stigmatised or penalised' (Garrett 2005, 1372, 1374n). Anne McClintock has discussed how English racism in the nineteenth century took the form of inventing the *domestic* barbarism of the Irish as being a marker of racial difference. She argues that the iconography of domestic degeneracy was widely used against 'white negroes': Jews, prostitutes, the working class and the 'Celtic Calibans', the Irish (McClintock 1995, 53). The Irish are perhaps Britain's invisible internal Other, it is the simultaneous doubling structure of racism that makes the case of the Irish ethnic status in Britain particularly fraught. At the same time as invoking a discourse of the presence of the inferior savage, the skin colour of the Irish makes 'passing' possible, and thus incurring the symbolic 'absence' of the oppressed. Handwritten signs in the window of boarding houses 50 years ago ruling 'No Blacks, no dogs, no Irish' are missing now, and the popular discourse around race and racism seems to be silent on Irishness. Similarly, we have had the first actively closeted Catholic British Prime Minister, his affilation constantly played down by the premier as irrelevant.[14] There are still pub jokes circulating about, but they tend to be the old ones I already heard as a child about the token triumvirate 'the Englishman, the Scotsman, and the Irishman'. The era of open racism about Irishness, which peaked in the 1970s around the time of the bombings by the IRA, has been superceded by a covert set of stereotypes that persist within mainstream representation.

The largest Irish-born community in the world outside of Ireland itself, lives in Britain. Until the 1980s Irish immigration to Britain was conceptualised as a male phenomenon, focussing largely upon the mobility of male workers and their economic labour, Irish migrants were popularly characterised by the racist epithet of 'Paddy' or 'Mick'. In migration studies, right until the 1980s and 1990s men's employment trends were dominant, it was assumed that women accompanied them as wives and mothers. Due to a global shift in economic migration in the late twentieth century toward women in service industries, though, this emphasis has changed. Transnational migration, like poverty, has become feminised. Louise Ryan outlines the history of Irish women's migration to Britain, she points out that women had made up the majority of migrants for much of the nineteenth and early twentieth centuries, peaking in the inter-war years, and they came as single, independent workers. This was in part due to Irish men having greater ties to the land, often their work at home was agricultural labour and males traditionally inherited the farm. Irish women were 'spare' and thus freer to travel, indeed many families in Ireland depended upon the income sent back to them from their female members employed abroad in domestic or factory work. Established strong familial networks in England meant that Irish women could travel to pre-existing communities, and have a safe bed to sleep in. Ryan discusses how Irish migration in Britain is seen as invisible and inevitable, 'their processes of migration are simplified and their processes of adaptation or acculturation are taken from granted' (Ryan 2004, 354). She argues that:

> Irish people have been simultaneously viewed as insiders and outsiders. Variously depicted as inferior, stupid, backward, lazy, drunken, violent, and threatening, Irish people have been inscribed within a repertoire of stereotypes that have become so common place as to be almost taken for granted, invisible and virtually unrecognised for what they are. The very word 'Irish' has been incorporated into British vocabulary as a byword for anything that does not make sense. (Ryan 2004, 354)

Chambers Twentieth Century Dictionary defines queer as 'odd, singular, quaint, open to suspicion, counterfeit, slightly mad'. It is that specific sense of the fake, bogus, phony sham(rock) that I propose that 'Irishness' can function discursively to queer white British identity, it is 'off-white'.

Britain's largest immigrant and ethnic minority group are made culturally invisible in discourses of racism (pro- and anti-); but they resurface in the codification of the underclass as a racially inferior group. The logic of this semiotic collapse lies partly in the historical demography, the Irish did form distinct underclass communities in Victorian towns and cities, they were a source of cheap labour for the Industrial Revolution, and in terms of class mobility they were remaindered there. Irish men today are still disproportionately employed in unskilled labouring jobs, and similarly Irish women stay in low paid public sector service industries. This has to be understood in the light of the global feminisation of poverty. It has been pointed out to me that in other predominantly white countries such as the USA or Australia, the Irish migrants quickly worked themselves up through the powerful professions, often into government.[15] However in Britain, the old colonial home, the Irish diaspora are still overwhelmingly represented statistically in the poorer classes. Typically, this has had an effect on quality of life, as high levels of deprivation characterise the Irish experience of living in contemporary Britain:

> People born in Ireland [and living in the UK] suffer disproportionately from accidents, illness and suicide and Irish men have been shown to die younger in Britain then in Ireland, with their overall health standards being lower. In the field of mental health, Irish people are over-represented in figures for psychiatric hospital admission. However, psychiatry does not incorporate trans-cultural elements with an Irish perspective, resulting in misdiagnosis and mistreatment – notably of schizophrenia, which is frequently diagnosed as alcohol psychosis. (Mac and Ghaill 2000, 143)

This factor cannot be disassociated from the stereotype of the drunk Irishman. The Irish have been portrayed as routinely hard-living, and hard-drinking, the 'soft' side of this stereotype is of the Irish as humourous, sociable, convivial, and always up for the 'craic'. A key research project published in the journal *Addiction* in 1996 found the link between Irish ethnicity and alcoholism or heavy drinking to be unproven. Taking Scots of Irish descent and other Scots as two comparative groups, the authors found that heavy drinking and smoking patters were related to social-economic (class), religious and migratory stress factors, and that images of the ethnic Irish as extraordinarily heavy drinkers and smokers were 'essentially false' (Mullen et al. 1996, 253). Think also, of the descriptor 'thick', as applied indiscriminately and often to the Irish and the underclass. Given this picture of experience, it is perhaps unsurprising that second-generation Irish in Britain may be keen to renunciate their ethnicity, to disattach themselves from this stigma.

Queer attachments

It will become clear in the pages ahead how shame is peculiarly organised around issues of attachment and disattachment. Encarta Thesaurus lists synonyms for 'queer' that include the rather benign: 'perplexing, odd, curious, unexpected, remarkable', and it is that spirit that I am using queer to describe shame's attachments here.[16] Chambers Dictionary continues with more sinister definitions for 'queer': 'having a sensation of coming sickness, sick, ill, homosexual, to quiz, to cheat, to spoil', so queer can be rephrased as a kind of sick, criminal interrogation, a threat of impurity to the social body, a dread of ruin. I am also using queer in the specific sense of a political title for dissident sexualities, and hence these qualities will come in useful. Queer is being used as a verb and a noun, 'queer' in Chambers also provides these colloquial uses for the word:

> *Queer Street*, the feigned abode of persons in debt or other difficulties. *Queer the pitch*, to make the place of performance unavailable, to spoil one's chances. *Shove the queer*, to pass bad money cf. thwart.[17]

All these uses imply a wilful action, they communicate a sense of agency within a pre-existing relationship. Queer, performativity and shame are linked, as Eve Kosofsky Sedgwick pointed out in *Epistemology of the Closet* (1990). She argued in her next book that 'queer' doesn't just signify homosexual, here is Sedgwick's more inclusive definition in *Tendencies* as:

> ... the open mesh of possibilities, gaps, overlaps, dissonances and resonances, lapses and excesses of meaning when the constituent elements of anyone's gender, of anyone's sexuality aren't made (or *can't be* made) to signify monolithically. (1993, 8)

– I am intentionally placing a stronger emphasis on class and ethnicity in this project, in order to renew its critical viability. We might want to consider how 'queer' as a label for non-normative sexualities has itself become assimilated, I am reminded of a 2002 episode of *The Simpsons* 'Jaws Wired Shut' in which a Gay Pride March passes through Springfield shouting the obligatory 'We're here! We're queer! Get used to it!' to which Lisa's terse response is 'You do this every year – we *are* used to it'. Baby Maggie is even holding a pink balloon in the shape of a triangle.[18] Queer can be understood more broadly as a project of defamiliarisation, a sexed-up version of the Russian Formalists' conception of ostranenie. Simply put, the historical emergence of queer activism in the late 1980s has led to the development of a critical perspective, typified perhaps in the academy by Queer Theory, but not contained by it as such. This more attitudinal, diffuse use of queer can be traced back to its original political impetus to problematise identity, so that in the last 20 years or so queer has been itself queered, it has been opened up as a critical tool, so that it is possible to reconceive queer as a prism of perversity i.e. the intention to wilfully deviate 'from what is good, proper and reasonable' (Encarta). The queer attachments that I present here are thus reworkings of norms, attempts to create livable lives on the wrong side of the blanket.

I am keen to witness shame's sedimentation into the social, to observe the kinds of attachments forged by its effects, especially those that pass as undetectable, as opposed to those that are visibly marked. Erving Goffman's work needs integrating within an understanding of shame, for his insight upon embodied emotions and social roles, particularly his (1963) volume *Stigma – Notes on the Management of Spoiled Identity* (1990). Goffman starts his book by drawing attention to the genealogy of the term 'stigma', noting that its origin in Ancient Greek referred to the signs burnt upon the body to denote a morally polluted person. He then explains how stigmata have come to have metaphorical force in contemporary labelling in identifying a disgraced person; his link between the physical and the ideational is instructive. Goffman's work, like Raymond Williams', includes compassionate attempts to conceptualise how agency emerges in spite of the cruel consequences of repression. Goffman, by presenting us with some of the most stigmatised, disqualified, abject and 'deviant' persons, still formulates a picture of an individual able to manage the social information by which s/he is delimited, to construct a self. The critical principle here is important, it concerned to find what escapes, what persists, what perseveres and endures.

Shame is an emotion that is particularly attaching, it is gluey, with a revolving cycle of separation-attachment-disattachment. I search in public culture and popular culture to find the way shame's energy can be shaped into loops and spirals, waxing and waning as it moves. Wendy Brown's work on 'wounded attachments' is very relevant (Brown 1995). She starts her analysis with a story about Stuart Hall, the founder of British Cultural Studies, and some comments he made about the postcolonial return of the SS Empire Windrush Generation. She explains:

> ... just as the mantle of abstract personhood is formally tendered to a whole panoply of those historically excluded from it by humanism's privileging of a single race, gender, and organization of sexuality, the marginalized reject the rubric of humanist inclusion and turn, at least in part, against its very premises... Just when polite liberal

THE SINS OF THE DRUNKEN FATHER ARE VISITED ON THE
HEADS OF THE CHILDREN.—A THIEF AND WOMAN OF SHAME VISIT THEIR LUNATIC
FATHER IN THE CRIMINAL LUNATIC ASYLUM.

Figure I.2 Woodcut. 'Sins of the Father' 1884. The caption reads: 'The sins of the drunken father are visited on the heads of the children – a thief and woman of shame visit their lunatic father in the criminal lunatic asylum. Source: Getty Images (not to mention correct leftist) discourse ceased speaking of us as dykes, faggot, colored girls, or natives, we begin speaking of ourselves this way. (Brown 1995, 53)

I think the 'turn' she is speaking about here is an oscillation of shame; these shamed groups turned away with/from shame, produce autonomous statements, and turn back with a two-fingered 'salute'. This is the political retort of insult, something that Didier Eribon (2004) has cogently investigated in relation to homosexuality. He boldly claims '[i]t all begins with an insult' a performative utterance that:

> ... is more than a word that describes. It is not satisfied with simply telling me what I am. If someone calls me a 'dirty faggot' (or 'dirty nigger' or 'dirty kike'), that person is not trying to tell me something about myself. That person is letting me know that he or she has something on me, has power over me. First and foremost the power to hurt me, to mark my consciousness with that hurt, inscribing shame in the deepest levels of my mind. This wounded, shamed consciousness becomes a formative part of my personality. (Eribon 2004, 16)

Judith Butler has eloquently explored the effects of these injurious speech acts, but the paradox of recreating a subversive identity out of one that has been violently prescribed is claimed by Brown to not be without pleasurable irony, and she goes on: 'The question here is not *whether* denaturalizing political strategies subvert the subjugating force of our naturalised identity formation, but *what kind* of politicalisation, produced out of and inserted into *what kind* of political context, might perform such subversion' (Brown 1995, 55).[19] Containing or subverting this subject formation comes with its own 'logic of pain', and Brown offers here a foundational one: *ressentiment*, 'the moralizing revenge of the powerless' (Brown 1995, 66). She continues:

> ... identity politics may be partly configured by a peculiarly shaped and peculiarly disguised form of class resentment, a resentment that is displaced onto discourses of injustice other than class, but a resentment, like all resentments, that retains the real or imagined holdings of its reviled subject as objects of desire. (Brown 1995, 60)

The argument is convincing, but subtle, it maintains that in order to argue for 'rights', minority groups must make the bourgeoisie their aspirational model, they must 'talk the talk and walk the walk', assimilate those values and proselytise those norms, in order that their claim gains credibility:

> In other words, the enunciation of politicized identities through race, gender and sexuality may require... abjuring a critique of class power and class norms precisely insofar as these identities are established vis-à-vis a bourgeois norm of social acceptance, legal protection, and relative material comfort.
>
> [And so] ...without recourse to the white masculine middle-class ideal, politicised identities would forfeit a good deal of their claims to injury and exclusion... Could we have stumbled upon one reason why class is invariably named but rarely theorized

or developed in the multiculturalist mantra 'race, class, gender, sexuality'? (Brown 1995, 61)

If gay rights=bourgeois rights, and queer activism is based on an antagonistic sense of inferiority, fuelling an acquisitive thrust for the purchase of norms, then it is not surprising that the poor and 'other' excluded become consolidated by a double abjection, once over again, this time by a rancorous jury of peers. 'Starkly accountable yet dramatically impotent, the late modern liberal subject quite literally seethes with ressentiment' (Brown 1995, 70), s/he is consumed with blame and the need for revenge, punishment and reproach. Explaining how subjects become resolutely attached to their own exclusion, she uses Nietzsche to explain how, steeped in the slave morality, s/he reinfects the narcissistic wound of exclusion by seeking an unredeemable injury, by investing in revenge, and the politics of recrimination. Brown turns to Nietzsche's counsel of 'forgetting' for the solution to this bind, this *shame* bind, and she sees relinquishment of self-interest and openness to collectivity as a major possible route to its healing.

What Brown so eloquently figures in her explanation of wounded attachments is that impulse to revile and reject categorisations that are not in that small and diminishing band of playground pals we call 'us'. This impulse comes from the emotional impoverishment of shame and its allied affects, envy, disgust and contempt, it is a wounded 'dis'attachment. In fact it is a knowing suppression of empathy, this momentum is encapsulated in such offensive statements as 'I'm not a racist, but...', or equally 'I feel sorry for pregnant teenagers [insert various synonyms such as drug addicts/'Gypsies'/ the homeless/obese], but...'. Shame can incite a wilful disintegration of collectivity, it can cause fragmentation, splitting and dissolution in all levels of the social body, the community, and within the psyche itself. Unexamined shame can also fall like a mist, obscuring vital political connections, sourced from injury it unwittingly seeks to reproduce injury to others, as a positive energy through direct attack or a more negativising denial and obliviousness. We have seen this phenomenon of competition enacted within the academy, in the internecine battles amongst and between minoritarian subjects and their named disciplinary fields, as one 'hot topic' after another is appropriated by universities, lauded, then discarded by educational economies. Later in the book, I examine one of these cases, in the vicissitudes of Lesbian Studies.

Much published research in Television Studies can be seen as an elaborate and sophisticated declaration of dislike. Representations of working and under- class people on the mass media are heavily denigrating, and academics themselves fall uncritically into a related unquestioned condescension when it comes to commenting upon popular programmes like The 'X' Factor, with its relentlessly working-class contestants 'tastelessly' seeking fame. This is not simply about a 'backlash' of injured and shamed white men staking retaliatory claims. The fevered output in British television of the twentieth century of programmes that are narratively organised around the inadequacy of working-class families and homes (Wife Swap, What Not to Wear, Supernanny, Honey, We're Killing the Kids, DIY SOS, A Life of Grime, World's Filthiest Human, Would

Like to Meet, How Clean is Your House?, You Are What You Eat and many, many more...) is frightening. But the academics and journalists who critique these programmes don't actually watch them: it's shocking, but true! Or, often, they watch them only to confirm their preconceived opinions of 'waste'. These series are not simply digital homonyms of the marriage manuals from 100 years ago telling women to lie back and think of England, these texts offer articulations of distinctiveness despite the framing and gatekeeping of affluent television producers, *because working and underclass persons get to speak for themselves.* The texts' meanings are not proscribed by the form, they are unpredictable, and there is much honesty, integrity and humour to be found there. There is an analogy with watching images of homosexuality on television before direct gay and lesbian programming; in the 1960s, 1970s and even the 1980s audiences learned to gain pleasure from leaning into a plethora of queer representations (Munt 1992).[20] Inevitably those readings depended upon what needs audiences projected into them, but they could be rich with possibility. Classed affects are organised tele-thematically and become whole series, so that we have middle-class envy (*Nighty Night*), working-class disgust and repudiation (*The Royle Family*), petit bourgeois/suburban hate, dissolution, nostalgia (*The Sopranos*), and underclass contempt (*Little Britain*). I hope to unravel each of these case studies in subsequent work.

The book could have done with more on middle-class affects; I confess that I had a whole chapter planned on the phenomenon of popular grammar and Englishness guides that appeared in the past five years that intend to shame people into linguistic 'correctness' (*Eats Shoots and Leaves* and that ilk). Their condescension wound me up so much I couldn't complete the primary reading, I felt constantly apathetic toward the research, and in final acceptance of these ugly feelings I abandoned the job to someone else. In terms of queering class ('odd, singular, quaint, counterfeit, slightly mad, to quiz, to cheat, to spoil') the most fascinating text on TV at the moment is the Australian situation comedy *Kath and Kim*. The comedy centres around two petit bourgeois ('nouveau riche') women, a mother and a daughter, living in the Melbourne neighbourhood of Fountain Lakes.[21] Currently three series and a tele-movie *Da Kath and Kim Code*, written by Jane Turner, Gina Riley and brilliantly acted with Magda Szubanski, Glenn Robbins and Peter Rowsthorn, *Kath and Kim* queers suburban sexuality, gender, respectability and aspiration. It is affectionate satire – its content is entirely concerned with parodying normative heterosexuality – it is biting without being cruel, it tickles the sensibilities of suburban prejudice in the most gentle, and sophisticated manner, unpeeling the ridiculous. *Kath and Kim* is the female, Antipodean equivalent of *The Office*, in that the British comedy I analyse in Chapter Four renders a humane comedy of the routine male office worker, mirrored by a similarly empathetic teasing of the ladies who lunch in *Kath and Kim*. It cultivates a fellow feeling – cathartic pity – for the maligned middlebrow suburban Australian, as for the Slough bureacrat with his burned out dreams. Academic commentary is a diminished form of social criticism in comparison to these two shows.[22]

This book begins with the eighteenth century, with the Irish politician Edmund Burke and his plea for moderation following the pillory and murder of two men convicted for sodomy. This early example of public shaming involves queerness, sodomy, shame, Catholicism, Irishness and class transgression, all related themes that I go on to build further upon in each subsequent chapter. Beginning here is significant, because it is in the eighteenth century, illustrated in Burke's speech, we encounter the discursive coalescence of the 'sodomitical sublime', a trope that attaches queerness, sodomy, shame, the 'residual poor' and Irish Catholicism together in an alliance of meaning that has prevailed over centuries. My succession of case studies, drawn geographically across British, USA and Irish cultures, present thematic convergences that flow in and out of these conjunctions of the sodomitical, manifesting grammars of shame. Equally I have tried to indicate disparate inflections in each chapter by portraying the structures of feeling that characterise each milieux. I have addressed underclass, working class and middle-class cultures, and the aristocracy make a minor appearance. In my research I have found that the dynamics of shame were consistent across historical periods, genres, forms, social structures and subcultures, that patterns of shame were disturbingly long-lived, and that cultures retain far-reaching memories for continued and renewed use upon stigmatised groups. I found that there are 'shame traps' for people to fall into, and that shame loops around and around, recruiting subjectivities, consolidating discourses, attaching and disattaching new selves as it circles. Shame is an adaptive emotion across times and between spaces. But in researching the material effects of shame upon various habitus, I became tremendously moved to discover the riches of what shame stimulated, to wonder at why it sometimes 'didn't take', to take notice of its resistances, and to marvel at the enduring human aptitude to mutate shame into joy.

Notes

1   'Tower'. Encarta® World English Dictionary © 1999 Microsoft Corporation. All rights reserved. Developed for Microsoft by Bloomsbury Publishing Plc.

2   Interestingly, if you Google the song the very first hit is the gay and lesbian 'Seattle Men's and Seattle Women's Chorus Pride Concert'. Perhaps Mum knew a thing or two... http://www.flyinghouse.org/publications/pdf/magazine/fhm-2006summer.pdf#search=%22Developed%20for%20Microsoft%20b%20Sally%2C%20Sally%2C%20Pride%20of%20our%20Alley%22. Accessed 10 September 2006.

    Gracie Fields was a Lancashire mill girl born over a fish and chip shop who became famous as a singer of northern working-class songs. I would love to have been called after her, however, I am happy to be named for a friend of my mother's, and ex-lover of George Orwell's, a weaver, painter and communist called Sally Jerome (born Sadie Hertzberg).

3   'Suc·cu·bus' *n* a woman demon that was believed in medieval times to have sexual intercourse with men while they were asleep. See also incubus. Encarta® World

English Dictionary © 1999 Microsoft Corporation. All rights reserved. Developed for Microsoft by Bloomsbury Publishing Plc.

4   See Scheff and Retzinger (1991) for a fascinating study of the sociology of apology see Tavuchis (1991).

5   See further Lewis (1971), Morris (1971), and Piers and Singer (1971).

6   'The patients are at first pleasantly stimulated, but, as the flushing increases, they become confused and bewildered' (Darwin 1999, 323).

7   See further Grosz (2004, 2005).

8   It is delightful that his website states that in 1995 Damasio received the 'Golden Brain Award'.

9   How emotions are corporealised as libidinal energies that interact with and animate the social was taken up in Elizabeth Grosz's work *Volatile Bodies: Toward a Corporeal Feminism*. In her later work on Darwin, Grosz goes further, following Alphonso Lingis, who challenges anthropomorphism and contends that ethical imperatives come not only from other humans, but also from animals, plants, and even inanimate objects (Lingis 2000, see also Grosz 1994, 2004, 2005).

10 Those interested in the psychoanalytic elements of social reflexivity and emotion would do well to start with *Civilisation and Its Discontents* (Freud 1930), although all of Freud's previous work is centrally concerned with the psycho-somatic mapping of emotions on and within the body in some way, following the nineteenth century medical obsession with hysteria, or 'wandering womb'. For a feminist history of hysteria see Showalter (1985). She also followed up this train of thought in the rather more controversial *Hystories: hysterical epidemics and modern media* (1997). Ending the Victorian dualisms of mind/body, reason/emotion, self/society, conscious/unconscious has been perhaps *the* agenda of late twentieth century thought, what has been called the 'postmodern'.

11 I recommend this one and Simon J. Williams' *Emotion and Social Theory* (2001) for an introduction to the field.

12 'Habitus' first appeared in an appendix of Bourdieu's translation into French of E. Panofsky *Architecture Gothique et Pensée Scholastique* Paris, éditions de Minuit, 1967.

13 How this limited paradigm copes with non-White Irish ethnicity, as contemporary Ireland further experiences non-White racial heterogeneity, stimulated by 'Celtic Tiger' immigration, has yet to be explored.

14 'Tony Blair today is effectively a Roman Catholic, though he has not yet, to our knowledge, been formally received into the church. The odd thing is not that he has embraced the Catholic church, but that he chooses to hide it. When asked directly, he replies evasively: 'Surely being a Christian is what is important?' Beckett, Francis and Hencke, David (2004).

15 O'Donnell, Katherine, University College Dublin. Personal conversation, February 2006.

16 'shame' Encarta® World English Dictionary © 1999 Microsoft Corporation. All rights reserved. Developed for Microsoft by Bloomsbury Publishing Plc.

17 'queer' Chambers Twentieth Century Dictionary, Edinburgh, 1982.

18 'Jaws Wired Shut' (2002) Episode 9, Series 13. *The Simpsons* episode 278. Written by Mike Scully. Directed by Nancy Kruse.

19   On injurious speech see also Butler, J. (1997).
20   For a typology of homosexual stereotypes in British television see Munt, S.R. (1992).
21   http://www.kathandkim.com/
22   Happily there is growing concern to produce work on class, culture and affect within an inclusive, intellectually blended paradigm, feminist scholars such as Beverley Skeggs, Angela McRobbie, Stephanie Lawler, bell hooks, Yvonne Tasker, Valerie Walkerdine, Lisa Adkins, Sherry B. Ortner, Sherrie A. Inness and several others such as Kevin Glynn, Stuart Laing, Roger Silverstone, Robert Beuka, geographer David Harvey and historian Jonathan Rose. Similarly there has been a small but significant work on shame and culture, including by Bernard Williams, Donald L. Nathanson, Joseph Adamson, Arlene Stein and Elspeth Probyn. Pamela Fox's (1994) excellent literary study *Class Fictions: Shame and Resistance in the British Working Class Novel, 1890–1945* was an inspiration when I first read it 12 years ago. Readers wishing to gain a firm background in shame theory would be advised to turn first to the writings of Helen Block Lewis, Donald L. Nathanson, Helen Merrell Lynd, Michael Lewis, Gershen Kaufman, Francis Broucek and Carl Goldberg. Within Queer Theory, affect and emotion have been a constant theme, of course unparalleled in the work of Eve Kosofsky Sedgwick, but also Ann Cvetkovich, Sue Golding, Lynda Hart and Lauren Berlant have engaged brilliantly with its cultural dimensions, and Didier Eribon's book on *Insult* is a must for understanding how homosexuality is interpellated.

Chapter 1

Queer Irish Sodomites: The Shameful Histories of Edmund Burke, William Smith, Theodosius Reed, the Earl of Castlehaven and Diverse Servants – Among Others

This chapter seeks to illustrate that the discursively connected histories of queerness, sodomy, shame, Catholicism, Irishness and class transgression have a pedigree stretching, at least, right back into the seventeenth and eighteenth centuries. The approach suggests reconstructing the structures of feeling of that era, and my inclusion of these fascinating early cases is tactical, to give us pause at the beginning of the book to consider the trenchant associations of sodomitical shame that inform our cultural politics today. Shame has been central in the making of the modern homosexual. The chapter will examine a speech by Irish politician Edmund Burke, made in the British House of Commons on 12 April 1780, on the punishment of two men, a 'plaisterer' named William Smith and a coachman named Theodosius Reed, for 'the commission of sodomitical practices'.[1] Burke would have been very cogniscent of a preceding case of sodomy, the scandal of the Lord of Castlehaven, from the previous century. This important cultural backdrop is introduced first to help us contextualise Burke's position. Burke, in pleading for Smith and Reed to be shamed rather than murdered, effects a split between the private and public in which the future homosexual's individuation – via the mechanism of shame – lies. Reading Burke's speech now shows us how the category 'sodomitical practices' had fluctuating implications for the prospective male homosexual identity of later centuries. I chart the foetal specter of the male-identified homosexual from the early modern era, via his prism of public shame, and speculate on its unintended consequences. Hence, what Burke's speech portends is the rhetoric of the sodomitical practice, which then solidifies into the sodomite, ultimately the homosexual, and becomes an identity (also community) formed by, within and against shame.

Edmund Burke's measured plea for choosing pillory (rather than execution) for these men's sodomitical crimes would have been made with his full knowledge of the ignoble history of violent retribution that the state had already enacted against those it deemed shameful offenders, such as Castlehaven. Being pilloried on the stocks was selected by the courts for its ritualised humiliation as well as torture, it was a public punishment intended to shame that has had a long history in Western societies. For example, if one visits the Palazzo della Ragione built in 1218, in Padova (Padua), Italy, today, on entering the vast hall on the first floor in the north-eastern corner one can still see the large 'Stone of Shame'. This granite, chalice shaped figure is about one metre high, settled on a plinth, it was placed there in 1231, supposedly at St Anthony's request. Used to punish insolvent debtors, guilty men, wearing only their underwear, had to sit on the stone three times and utter the words 'cedo bonis' ('I renounce my worldly goods'). They were then banished from the city, and if they returned and were caught, they had to go through the same procedure again but this time three buckets of cold water were poured over their heads. The shape of the stone is such that it would be hard for a man's near-naked bottom to straddle the top, he is bound to fall into the rim of the cup, and hence appear ridiculous (on the second visit – drenched and ridiculous).

Shame, suffering and banishment are close-coupled together in the Judeo-Christian traditions of social control and legal enforcement, following the ur-text of Genesis. There is clearly a spatialisation operating, in the sense that traditionally the shamed persons are excreted from the social body. Pillorying enacts this by imprisoning the perpetrator's body, removing his right of free mobility as a citizen, removing his right to isolation or seclusion, and then inciting the mob to throw excrement at him/her. The pilloried body is thus subjected to a number of spatial twists around the dichotomy of inside/outside; we are reminded that the sodomite criminal is revealed in court only to be rapidly repressed. But this social death is presumably preferable to the state-sanctioned murder of sodomites that preceded Burke's victims, and one case in particular would have been very familiar to him.

Shame, banishment and death: The Earl of Castlehaven

Mervin Touchet, the second Earl of Castlehaven, was executed in 1631 for abetting in the rape of his wife and committing sodomy with his male servants. Five weeks after Castlehaven's capital punishment by beheading, his male servants Giles Broadway and Florence (sometimes 'Lawrence') Fitzpatrick were hanged at Tyburn. This case from early Stuart England was the most notorious sodomy case in British history until Oscar Wilde's prosecution in 1895, 164 years later. As Cynthia B. Herrup's excellent book *A House in Gross Disorder: Sex, Law, and the 2nd Earl of Castlehaven* makes clear, versions of the case have been continuously in print for almost 300 years, and it has served as a filter for debates about tyranny, redemption, marriage and the patriarchal model, homosexuality, deviance and degeneracy ever since. Mervin Touchet was a minor aristocrat who took a debauched turn, in that he is not so unusual, but his case has had intense symbolic significance for the future confluence of gender, class, and ethnicity in the cultural politics of shame.

**Figure 1.1   Stone of Shame in the Palazzo della Ragione, Padua
            (Photo: author)**

**Figure 1.2   Stone of Shame (detail), Palazzo della Ragione, Padua
(Photo: author)**

Briefly, the story is that the second Earl of Castlehaven lived in the great house of Fonthill Gifford, Wiltshire, in the 1620s. As the head of a household, he was the putative father and patriarch of a powerful Norman family, the Touchets, that had recently gained lands in Ireland by the gift of James I as a result of loyal service to the King's army. The Touchets had been landowners in Ireland since the thirteenth century. In 1612 Mervin's grandfather George Touchet owned more than 200,000 acres in Ireland, he was a member of the Irish Privy Council, and was a member of the Irish House of Lords. He took his title from where the Spanish had landed their troops before the battle of Kinsale, Castlehaven, a small cove in County Cork. Mervin Touchet was his heir, born in 1593, he inherited a large household of staff over which he had spiritual, moral and economic authority.

The true por-
traiture of:

the Earle of
Castlehaven.

The Lords that were his Peeres sate on each side of a great Table covered with greene, whose names are as followeth.

1. *The Lord* Weston, *Lord Treasurer.* 2. *Earle of Manchester, Lord Privy Seale.* 3. *Earle of Arundel and Surrey, Marshall.* 4. *Earle of Pembroke and Montgomery, Lord Chamberleyn.* 5. *Earle of Kent.* 6. *Earle of Worcester.* 7. *Earle of Bedford.* 8. *Earle of Essex.* 9. *Earle of Dorset.* 10. *Earle of Leicester.* 11. *Earle of Salisbury.* 12. *Earle of Warwicke.* 13. *Earle of Carlisle.* 14. *Earle of Holland.* 15. *Earle of Danby.* 16 *Viscount Wimbleton.* 17. *Viscount Conaway.* 18.*Viscount Wentworth.* 19. *Viscount Dorchester.* 20. *Lord Piercy.* 21. *L: Strange.* 22. *Lord Clifford.* 23. *Lord Peter.* 24. *Lord North.* 25. *L: Howard.* 26. *Lord Craven.*

Figure 1.3   Earl of Castlehaven, contemporary sketch

In early Stuart England there were perceived to be few worse dangers than the Irish or the Catholics, both were associated with corruption, anarchism, barbarism, and treachery. Castlehaven, through his Irish and Catholic associations, despite a public conversion to Protestantism and his rare enough visits to Ireland, remained tainted by Popery. He had openly Catholic relatives, including his brother, his father, brother, and eldest daughter who still lived in Ireland. 1730 began with Castlehaven's brother Sir Fernando being arrested in Dover for traveling in disguise with foreign servants, the implication being that he was a risk to the Crown. Castlehaven also had Irish servants. In short, despite being a minor aristocrat, he was felt to be an outsider, as Herrup comments:

> Castlehaven was a peer who stood apart from many of the conventions of the peerage: he had no ancient seat, no friends at court, no political involvement. His siblings were refractory; his subordinates dissatisfied; his spouse's relations distrustful. He was associated with the bugbears of both Catholicism and Irishness... the accusations against Castlehaven seemed far from preposterous. (Herrup 1999, 24)[2]

Sodomy was at the time considered a 'foreign' crime, perpetrated by those uncivilised, un-English races (such as Italy, Turkey, etc.) who had escaped the noble rationality and self-control that defined the national Protestant character. It was a crime of dissemination, of lack of control, of unconstrained and lascivious desires.

The legal case was initiated by Castlehaven's own son and heir, Lord Audley. In 1631 Audley was 17, and married – extremely unhappily – to his 15-year-old stepsister Elizabeth Brydges. They had been married by family arrangement for three years, something that in our era would perhaps be considered sexually inapt. According to Herrup 'this couple loathed each other' (Herrup 1999, 17). His young wife Lady Audley was having a sexual relationship with one of the servants, the Earl's former lover, Henry Skipwith. The Countess of Castlehaven herself, Elisabeth Barnham, was 12 years older than her husband, richer, and his social superior. On 6th April Castlehaven was indicted for three felonies: two sodomies originally committed on 1st June and 10th June of the previous year with Catholic servant Florence Fitzpatrick, and the rape of the Countess allegedly committed ten days later, with the assistance of servant Giles Broadway. In court the testimony of servants and his wife contended that the household suffered from a lack of moral compass, correct governance, and failed honour. The family seat was disrupted by malice, envy, financial opportunism, favouritism, sexual voyeurism, and moral equivocation, it was 'putrid with sexual impropriety' (Herrup 1999, 32). The court's view of the Earl was that he had not just failed his own household as paternal governor, but by implication breached the natural order, he was a traitor to Charles I, the King, then as now, being the symbolic head of the 'family' of the nation.

Sodomy was a shadowy crime: in early modern England it was difficult to 'see', and thus it conveniently allowed a certain plasticity of definition, and therefore proof. Sodomy and buggery, like Irishness and Catholicism, were concepts that were linked to huge fears of disorder and excess, and thus they invoked cruel and unusually violent punishments, such as that meted out later under the observation of Burke. Sodomy was seen as an act of corruption clearly marked by asymmetric class binaries, the sodomitical pairings of masters and servants, identified this crime as being particularly entangled with power and its abuse. Sodomy itself was seen 'as an invading force; born not in English hearts, but carried to the English shores to be left as a corrosive legacy... John Marston wrote that it had entered the country with the Jesuits' (Herrup 1999, 33–4). The 1534 Act for the Punishment for the Vice of Buggery is widely taken to be the root of anti-sodomy laws, it is best understood as part of Henry VIII's attack on the authority of the Catholic Church, as it was aimed at priests. What is interesting about the national psychology of such fears is that it positions England, and the English, as the *sodomised*, it is a fear about losing corporeal integrity, and being polluted. Herrup describes how the sodomite is feared because his unrestricted appetites have no focus, they contravene all boundaries, and thus 'Sodomy was less about desiring men than about desiring everything' (Herrup, 1999, 33). Thus sodomitical acts were about intemperance, loss of the Protestant Godly self, a cataclysmic failure of self-governance. Necessarily, then, we might conjecture that such fears precisely underlined the ubiquity of such desires. Herrup goes on to claim that:

> ... sodomy was a charge more potent as an organizing principle for other fears than as a focus for solitary prosecution. Intuiting whether sodomitical acts inspired these accusations or were convenient, even disingenuous, afterthoughts to other suspicions is less important than recognizing the social utility of sodomy as an accusation... Sodomitical behaviour never appeared alone in charges against elite defendants. On occasion, sodomitical acts may have raised suspicions, but like a quark, sodomy was known primarily by its effusions. (Herrup, 1999, 37)

It is instructive to pause and consider here that Oscar Wilde was of course the only other aristocrat prosecuted for sodomy, but he, of course, was an Irishman who infamously converted to Catholicism on his deathbed.[3]

In 'Can the Sodomite Speak?' Nicholas F. Radel joins the list of those looking once again at the Castlehaven case. He discusses the scapegoating of the servant, Lawrence Fitzpatrick, and understands his execution as being the outcome of his own testimony that made visible the accepted – but highly secretive – homoeroticism that circulated amongst gentlemen and servants in the Tudor and Stuart periods. Blame for this behaviour could be legitimately leveled at a servant because he could be interpreted as a minion intending to undermine the social order with his unnatural desires. Radel comments how sodomy is primarily associated with the lower born, and it is imagined to be linked to a transgression of status or hierarchy. So, what is occurring here is somewhat of a transference – the sexual traffic between masters and servants is more frequently enacted by the former onto the latter, but this would contravene belief in the master as temperate protector of his household. The blame must be transferred to the willful servant, the *class manqué*, linking him to an aberrant desire that threatens social stability. Radel concludes that:

Perhaps the question to raise in this context is not 'can the sodomite speak?' but 'can the servant'. Class or status issues are clearly inherent in the problem of 'voluntary' sodomy as I have described it. One might go as far as to say that voluntary sodomy, sodomitical subjectivity, is located in the place of service, even as it reflects back onto the master. (Radel 2003, 162)

This argument was previously taken up by Jonathan Goldberg in his wonderfully titled book *Sodometries* in which he says 'Accusations of sodomy in seventeenth-century New England are ways of policing emerging social and class relations'; in his analysis of William Bradford's *Of Plymouth Plantation 1620–1647*. Bradford firmly locates the sodomite as the lower class interloper (Goldberg 1992, 24). Labelling a man as a sodomite meant he lost class status, he was considered to have sunk into a filthy bestial pit, his soul irredeemably stained. Whether 'active' or 'passive' the sodomite was associated with the loss of status that was attached to femininity, the misogyny of gender hierarchy was mapped onto class. One anonymous author of an eighteenth century pamphlet 'Plain Reasons for the Growth of Sodomy', quoted in Cameron McFarlane's *The Sodomite in Fiction and Satire 1660–1750* expresses that:

I am confident no Age can produce any thing so preposterous as the present Dress of those Gentlemen who call themselves pretty Fellows... 'Tis a Difficulty to know a Gentleman from a Footman by their present Habits: The low-heel'd Pump is an Emblem of their low Spirits.. the Silk Wascoat all belac'd, with a scurvy blue Coat like a Livery Frock... I blush to see 'em Aping the Running Footmen, and poising a great Oaken Plant fitter for a Bailiff's Follower than a Gentleman. (Anon 1730, 10–11. Quoted in McFarlane 1997, 49)

As McFarlane says 'To slide down the scale of gender and become a "pretty Fellow" is to slide down the scale of class and become a servant rather than a master' (McFarlane 1997, 49). Crucially, the author's choice of verb for this sodomitical fellow is 'to ape', and the one recognizing and categorizing this transgression will *blush*. Locating aberrant, excessive, heretical or profane desires in the bodies of the working classes, (most especially the Irish and/or Catholic varieties), created a paradigm of queerness that was ineluctably related to shame.

Same-sex intimacy

In seventeenth-century England (and indeed in Europe more generally) expressions of passionate love between men were to be found in abundance. Ironically, the bodily expression of this love seems to have been enabled by that shadowy figure, the sodomite. Following Michel Foucault (1977a) and Alan Bray (2003), most historians of this period point to the fact that there were in fact scarcely any prosecutions for sodomy in this period, and those few prosecutions that did take place constructed the sodomite as a discursive concept, a symbol of the political traitor, heretic, foreigner, or corruptor of domestic order, rather than as a specific desiring individual. Foucault famously describes sodomy as 'that utterly confused category' and Bray gives his assent to the statement that 'one cannot write a history of sodomites' (Bray 2003, 275). Thus there was no name for passionate love and desire between men, such as the love that Shakespeare expressed in his sonnets, other than 'friendship'. The sexual terminology of the day such as pederasty and sodomy were equated with sin, corruption and inequality, by contrast most of the love expressed between gentlemen celebrated this friendship love as leading to a higher self. Bray has more recently explored how rites and expressions of such male friendships such as the kiss of peace, or taking communion together in a Catholic mass, sending personal passionate letters, sharing of food and beds and humour and co-burial memorials are testimony to the particular kinship of such friendships, and how '...the language of "sodomy" could be suspended from the physical intimacy that pervaded the culture of sixteenth-and seventeenth-century England' (Bray 2003, 272). Perversely, through the circulation of knowledge in the public sphere, it could be argued that the abstraction of the 'sodomite sublime' virtually legitimated the real practice of sworn friendships, which were so rich in signification and reference, being constantly reiterated, affirmed and verified.

Over the course of the eighteenth century, with the spread of capitalism, the development of urban centers and the rise of the middle-class, there was a shift in British society which transitioned from an older regime of social order based on what Foucault termed 'alliance', which had subordinated all men, women, and boys to higher ranked males, to one founded in sexuality, through which men and women have since emboldened their claims to personal and political privacy. The traditional formulations of same-sex friendship with their socially recognised kinship and ethical functions were downgraded, becoming less significant than familial and heterosexual bonds. Over the course of the century such passionate friendships were even understood as potentially inimical to these now socially vital bonds. In the eighteenth century we can see the ground shift under passionate male friendships. The seventeenth century looks strange to us with the license allowed to eroticism between men but as the eighteenth century progressed we recognise how this passion is increasingly restricted, denied a public function or open expression, it becomes denaturalised and more recognizably queer. Sodomy becomes increasingly to be seen as a transgression of social and gender roles, and the perpetrator becomes more clearly defined by the processes of criminal law, and later by medical pathology, as ever incurring the condemnation of the churches.

One of the more cogent contemporary discussions of the figure of the sodomite is David Halperin's (2004). Halperin refines and revises his earlier work in *One Hundred Years of Homosexuality* to argue that there are 'genealogies' of homosexuality that show continuities over time and space. While he still maintains a historicist approach to the construction of sexuality, and cautions us to be aware of our own pre-conceptions of what sexuality is or ought to be, he provides a schema that explains the relation between the category of our modern homosexuality and four distinct categories from the ancient and pre-modern worlds. The categories he discusses are: effeminacy, sodomy, friendship, and inversion and he shows the irreducibility of each one to the other by arguing that our modern understanding of homosexual identity is not capable of explaining every instance of male-to-male intimate encounters (then or now).

There has been a relatively recent move among historians of this period in turning from a focus on sexual behaviour and the figure of the sodomite to study affect, love and friendship between men. George E. Haggerty (1999) might be seen as heralding this move in arguing that the concepts of love and emotional intimacy offer a more useful perspective for understanding late eighteenth-century male-male relations. Haggerty focuses on the ways in which ideologies of sensibility, friendship, and masculinity enabled startlingly public, yet potentially subversive, avowals of same-sex love. However, in the case of Burke's speech, it is his invocation of the traditional figure of the sodomite that is at the crux of his argument for leniency in the punishment of those convicted of sodomitical practices. Burke is at pains to hold at bay the moves to define sodomites as the clearly recognised antithetical 'other' to normal (hetero)sexuality. He argues, using the historical consensus, that sodomitical practices are difficult to delineate succinctly, and therefore we might all imagine how such desires arise and hence perhaps maybe have empathy for such offenders. Despite this, his argument slips ineluctably into the Enlightenment project of giving definition to the sodomite in that he proposes public shaming as a fit punishment for such practices.

An analysis of Burke's speech

In literary terms, Edmund Burke (1729–1797) is chiefly known as the author of the extremely influential aesthetics treatise entitled *A Philosophical Enquiry Into the Origin of Our Ideas of the Sublime and Beautiful* (1756), the Romantics and Victorians hailed Burke as one of the greatest prose writers in the English language. In Eighteenth-Century Studies he holds a pivotal position in British politics at the time. Over the course of the last three decades of that century he was a cogent defender of the American revolution, a passionate foe of British colonial policy in India, a severe, if surreptitious, critic of that 'Junto of Jobbers'; the Protestant Ascendancy in Ireland, and, perhaps most (in)famously, he was the foremost adversary of the French Revolution. The speech, made by Burke is reprinted from the 1780 Annual Register in full at the end of this chapter.

Throughout his speech Burke seeks to deploy the epistemological vagueness that traditionally accompanied sodomy, the sodomite, and the sodomitical; he argues that the lack of precision and ability in recognising sodomitical practices ought to render us unable to punish. Burke begins his speech by drawing the attention of the members of the House to their role as legislators: 'to make laws for the subject'. The word 'subject' carries two distinct valences: the subject in a sentence is the being that performs the action, but to be a subject can also mean to be under the scrutiny of one who has the power to describe, inscribe, conscript or proscribe another. To spell out their differences: the first subject is constituted by their own actions, the second subject is constituted by the actions of another. Both senses of the word are conveyed by Burke's phrase 'to make laws for the subject'. Burke's words can be seen to be referring to the individual agent who required that Government make laws to safeguard and further his interests, and we can also see the subject who is being controlled, as it is being produced, simultaneously investigated and regulated.[4]

Burke makes a distinction between 'the laws of civil polity' and 'the criminal laws'. 'The first only regarded men's property, criminal laws affected men's lives.' In his elaboration on this statement Burke makes it clear that he understands that criminal laws affect men's lives in how the laws punish those who are deemed criminal. The criminal is a subject who is brought into effect solely through the focused discussion of others, if he himself has made a denial or a defense this has not been considered adequate in deferring the criminal sentence. The criminal is the target and anchorage for the gaze, and the object of the spoken and written pronouncements of others. The *a-priori* assumption of the process of the law in the case of the two men who are at the center of Burke's speech is that the sodomitical touch is by definition a criminal assault. Nobody can consent to be assaulted; conversely to assent to be assaulted is to become Nobody, to be without subjectivity. In defining sodomitical touch to be a criminal assault, it is the very desire of the men for this touch that allows the law to appropriate their subject position. It is the men's actions in expressing their will, their desire and their consent to being sodomitical (subjects in the first instance) that perversely enables the law to define their subjectivity as criminal (becoming subjects in the second instance). These men's bodies are not their own private property, through the enactment of legal processes of gaze, discussion and pronouncement their bodies become property of the state, which they are then guilty of assaulting due to their sodomitical desire. He follows his terse condemnation with the declaration: 'The crime was however of all other crimes a crime of the most equivocal nature, and the most difficult to prove.'

In the late eighteenth century, and indeed even to the present day, when sodomitical practices and nature are mentioned in the same sentence, the word 'against' generally comes between them. Gibbon (1776) was neither the first nor the last writer to describe those practices as 'a sin against nature'. Burke describes the nature of sodomitical practices, their ontology and epistemology, as 'equivocal', in other words, as containing voices that cancel each other out. In his treatise on the *Sublime and Beautiful*, Burke wrote: 'To make any thing very terrible, obscurity seems in general to be necessary' (Burke 1756, Part Two, Section III, OBSCURITY). In this instance, he leaves aside the fact that the obscurity that surrounds the concept of 'sodomitical practices' allows it to be a malleable category, which can be exploited to terrorise. Instead, he makes a brilliant rhetorical move where he uses the integral obscurity – the 'equivocal nature' of the concept – to deconstruct sodomy and thus its enactment as a crime. 'Difficult to prove' is a phrase that carries with it the suggestion that it is opaque for even the practitioner of sodomitical practices to realise, in both sense of the word, his actions. Burke asserts that the precise lack of definition in 'sodomitical practices' means that we can't claim to recognise the crime, as the definition collapses, and by extension the law can't claim to recognise the sodomite either (of course, this does not mean that sodomites don't exist). Burke is caught in a quandary: he is reminding his audience of the traditional deployment of the term 'sodomitical', which was a vague 'utterly confused' category, but his use of the term is on the cusp of being *reinscribed* to refer to a species of men who might habitually behave sodomitically. Burke finds himself also arguing for leniency, and even acceptance, for this more recent understanding of the sodomitical as a desiring subject.

The main point of Burke's speech is that in making criminal laws the punishment ought to be 'more calculated to operate as an example and prevent crimes, than to oppress and torment the convicted criminal.' Burke enacts plasterer William Smith's death for the reader in typically Burkean gruesome detail; he gives a vivid account of Smith's torture and the violence of the mob which both men endured as they stood in the pillory.[5] The effect of Burke's retelling of Smith's torment has the effect of making the reader a witness to his horrible death. In his 1756 treatise, Burke himself wrote of the fascination excited in witnesses when faced with the sublime event of a public execution (Burke 1756, Part One, Section XV, Of the effects of TRAGEDY). Burke reasons that we are attracted to the suffering of others because it causes us 'delight'. By 'delight' Burke means the awareness that the spectator by contrast is out of danger and free from pain. Burke focuses his audience's gaze on Smith's black face with the blood forcing itself out of his nostrils, his eyes, and his ears, but Burke's intention is to awaken our sympathy via our revulsion. The Oxford English Dictionary quotes from Burke's treatise in its definition of sympathy: 'Sympathy must be considered as a sort of substitution by which we are put into the place of another man and affected in many respects as he is affected.' According to Burke's world view:

> ... as our Creator has designed we should be united by the bond of sympathy, he has strengthened that bond by a proportionable delight; and there most where our sympathy is most wanted, in the distresses of others... This is not an unmixed delight, but blended with no small uneasiness. The delight we have in such things, hinders us from shunning scenes of misery; and the pain we feel, prompts us to relieve ourselves in relieving those who suffer. (Burke 1756 Part One, Section XIV, The effects of SYMPATHY in the distresses of others)

Burke's central argument depends on our identification with Smith the sodomitical, we experience 'delight' that we are not being tormented, but this delight depends on an acknowledgement that it is possible that we could be in the place of the sodomitical through sympathetic identification.

This awareness that we might be 'affected in many respects' in the same manner as the sodomitical is crucial to Burke's position. What Burke so correctly invokes is the pleasure of being in close proximity to the perverse – the thrill of the forbidden – and he draws attention to it in order to reveal voyeuristic enjoyment, making explicit the sadistic pleasure of vicarious, public punishment. There is an intriguing juxtaposition here of 'public' and 'popular': 'public reproach and contempt' still allows for a private space where we might be 'affected in many respects', just as those convicted of sodomitical practices.[6] To receive the reactions of the 'popular', of the people's, 'fury, assault and cruelty', implies that the sodomitical is not popular, nor of the people. There is no place where the sodomitical can be a public person (a social identity, a self), but crucially though, the sodomite might be a *representation*, a figure of popular projection. Burke's implicit plea for a private sodomitical territory that we can all access, if only in our imagination, mitigates against the establishment of the concept of a personal identity based on sexual orientation, wherever that sexual orientation be directed. This structure of substitution is fascinating because it heralds the *symbolic* function of the sodomite to embody repudiated desires, to act as a vehicle, a figure, perhaps even a mask, for feelings that are prohibited from integration with the self. Thus we can argue that the sodomitical is a synecdochal projection for those inchoate feelings of same-sex desire. The 'sodomitical' hence becomes a condensed sign for the generalised inchoate mass of private, shameful desires that are forbidden explicit expression in the public realm. Those desires then coalesce around the sign of the 'sodomitical', but crucially for Burke this is a collective symbol for unacceptable sexualities that exist in everyone, a commonality that can be recognised through the process of identification and familiarity that is empathy. So we can see that Burke is using the older definitions of sodomy to resist the new logic whereby the habitually sodomitical – the homosexual – is signified as the monstrous queer who has abnormal, unnatural desires.

Burke breaks from arguing about the punishment of the pillory to comment on the crime of those 'poor wretches', Smith and Reed: 'The crime for which the poor wretches had been condemned, was such as could scarcely be mentioned, much less defended or extenuated. The commission of sodomitical practices.' Burke's declaration that 'The crime... was such as could scarcely be mentioned' was the tight-lipped euphemism, a requisite rhetorical trope for all those who were compelled to allude to sodomitical practices, used for centuries in English culture.[7] Even in the nineteenth and twentieth centuries we can find a trace of the early English jurists in the origin of that phrase: 'The love that dare not speak its name'.[8] Silence about sodomitical practices could only be broken by the clerisy, those lawyers, medics, churchmen, who were working towards its eradication. But of course as they described and debated those practices they publically developed the discourses through which the homosexual could come into view, be represented. It is crucial to notice here that Smith and Reed are not gentlemen. Despite being a plasterer and a coachman, they are not 'working class' in the contemporary, post-Industrial sense of the term; although they may themselves have had servants they are most certainly not of the same class as Edmund Burke himself, nor of his audience, his aristocratic peers in the House. Smith and Reed would be classified at the time as common people, much of the same general public as the members of the crowd who punished them by shaming them. Both men are denied the power to name or legitimate themselves, or to label their practice, for this is the secure business of the Parliament and courts.

Burke fulfils the requirement to be silent about the crime that 'could scarcely be mentioned' in the use of the phrase: 'The commission of sodomitical practices'. The phrase is in the passive voice, it cannot be decided if the definition of 'sodomitical' is either an adjective or an adverb, 'practices' are a range of possible behaviors and contains the connotation of approximate rehearsals, preparations for an actual performance, but not the performance itself. The phrase has been recorded as a complete sentence though grammatically it is not a sentence; we are left to supply our own interpretation as to how the 'poor wretches' might be related to 'the commission of sodomitical practices'. The reader is left to (thrillingly?) imagine what the 'commission of sodomitical practices' might entail. There is a tremendous possibility for the enactment of power in having such a vague phrase with the potential to mean so much. In giving definition to such a phrase one is enabled to make a treatment of the subject – the action and the actors – according to one's own terms.

The imposition of this grid of definition on the possibilities of the body, on the possibilities of *all* bodies, was in April 1780 a relatively new phenomenon in Britain. It was throughout the 1780s that there was an upsurge in prosecutions for attempted sodomy. Unlike the first half of the century, when most such prosecutions were actions taken by injured parties for attempted rape, most of the cases were now the state prosecuting consenting adults. Legal standards for conviction were often ignored in practice, so that acts bearing no obvious relationship to the statutory definitions of sodomy were being prosecuted successfully as 'sodomitical practices' (Greenberg 1988, 342). The *Public Advertiser* of Tuesday April 11 1780 reported that it was for 'Sodomitical Practices at the Magdalen Coffee House' that Smith and Reed were convicted. The phrase 'Sodomitical Practices' stands in place of sodomy, in other words the desire for same-sex touch (in whatever manner it was perceived by the legal judiciary) is what renders the men criminal.

Burke next makes a rather perfunctory gesture towards a public condemnation of sodomitical practices: 'A crime of all others the most detestable, because it tended to vitiate the morals of the whole community, and to defeat the first and chief end of society.' Burke's routine phraseology does not fit logically with his argument that the pillory is too harsh a punishment for the 'poor wretches' convicted of sodomitical practices, but his condemnation does allow him to speak from a 'popular' position, as one of 'the people', and to evade being accused of being too conciliatory. What makes this sentence interesting is the positioning of sodomitical practices in an adversarial role to the 'first and chief end of society', by which he presumably means the reproduction of humanity through the birth of children. In the logic of this argument heterosexuality is linked to the production and care of children whereas sodomitical practices put children, and hence society's future, under threat. Hence the replication of compulsory heterosexuality is necessary for the survival of the world. What can be seen here is an early example of the rhetorical strategies by which the homosexual and heterosexual were defined in relation to each other. The definition and existence of the sober heterosexual is brought to light with the appearance of the shadowy homosexual. The condition of the assertion of this heterosexual is its obliteration of the homosexual.[9] Even as we see Burke make a courageous and intellectually adept argument in favor of asserting that sodomy is a shadowy practice with which we might all empathise, he loses his footing in his battle with the new wor(l)d order by trying to make common ground. His definition of homosexuality is that which puts heterosexuality in danger, it supports the emerging discourse of the homosexual as abject.

Shame and contagion

Burke argues that the punishment of the pillory was designed to be: '... a punishment of shame rather than of personal severity ... When criminals convicted of sodomitical practices were sentenced to the pillory, they were adjudged that punishment with a view to expose them to public reproach and contempt, not to popular fury, assault and cruelty.' Burke sees the action of being shamed as intrinsic to the crime being punished, he presciently connects the emotion and practice of shaming to a public/private split, and he also intuitively links shame, homosexuality, and contagion, to *pleasure*, according shame this frisson via the structure of empathy and its concomitant 'delight'. The Old Testament Book of Hosea chapter 4, verse 18 – 'Their drink has become bitter; they are completely false; her rulers take pleasure in shame' – illustrates how the association of shame with pleasure is intrinsic to the Judeo-Christian tradition. Different translations of the Bible relate forms of sexual pleasure to shame, typically prostitution, harlotry, whoredom and lewd deeds.[10]

In the Authorised King James Version of the Holy Bible (the edition familiar to Burke), Chapter 2 ends with the creation of Eve from Adam's rib 'And they were both naked, the man and his wife, and were not ashamed' (v.25), the Fall of Adam is then described in Genesis chapter 3. In the Creation Myth the origin of human experience, individuation and desire resides in a locus of shame, and it is out of that shame, separation and loss via Adam and Eve's expulsion from Eden, that sexual differentiation occurs, and hence, gender regulation. Burke seems to be reaching for this interpretation in his speech, for the crime of Smith and Reed takes place in that popular centre for eighteenth century male recreation, the coffee house (the heterosexual pun on 'making coffee' is unavoidable). It is a garden for growing unique species, a limit-site separated from the world in which new forms can materialise that can challenge the dominant (godly) hegemony, the 'natural order'. This source of individuation for the later 'homosexual', the development of his subjectivity through separation and shame, comes through the two men's sodomitical touch in this room. It is at once shunning the ruling parameters of sexual practice, and through that rejection of the norm opening up new possibilities for articulation. The café space scene of the crime is designated neither wholly private nor wholly public, café spaces at that time were liminal, tavern-like rooms filled with intense wordmongers, sensuous gossips, scandals and innuendo, where men would congregate for fevered intellectual amusement. From the point of view of the public, these cafés would seem to offer a tantalizing heterotopia of indecipherability and potentially transgressive leisure.

In 1785 the Utilitarian philosopher and law reformer Jeremy Bentham (1748–1832) wrote an extensive argument against punishing sodomitical practices (the manuscript runs to over 60 pages). It might be described as the first known argument for homosexual law reform in England except for the fact that it was not published until 1978 when it was edited by Louis Crompton for the Summer and Fall issues of *Journal of Homosexuality*.[11] Bentham's tract is a cogent argument against the positions adopted by Montesquieu and Voltaire who argued for continued punishment of those who committed sodomy: Voltaire because he felt it was a threat to population, and Montesquieu because its effeminising influence would weaken a nation's military strength. Bentham argues that homosexual acts do not weaken men, or threaten population or marriage, or lead to women-hating, and documents their prevalence in ancient Greece and Rome. He opposes punishment on utilitarian grounds and attacks ascetic sexual morality, but did not publish his essay for fear of being branded a sodomite himself; as he noted in marginal jottings: 'To other subjects it is expected that you sit down cool: but on this subject if you let it be seen that you have not sat down in a rage you have betrayed yourself at once' (Crompton 1978).

In this exposition there are at least three sites of shame: the pleasurable shame of the onlooker who sees the forbidden practices; the pleasurable shame of one who chooses to re-enact shame in controlled circumstances, and the far less pleasurable shame of one (the juridical subject) who has no control over the violent consequences of his practices. Darwin, in *The Expression of Emotion in Man and Animals* (1872) described how shame is the most social and reflective of emotions, as it is always concerned with the viewing of the self, both from the point of view of the other, and as a kind of internal theatre. Blushing is a key indicator of that shame – Silvan Tomkins has suggested how shame is peculiarly written on the body, specifically the face (Tomkins 1995, 134). Tomkins memorably stated how 'shame strikes deepest into the heart of man' (Tomkins 1995, 133). Shame is personified as a weapon that cleaves asunder, that renders and splits the self from itself, and all others, through loss of face, through mortification. Shame 'thereby generates the torment of self-consciousness' (Tomkins 1995, 136). Critically, this self-consciousness is an act of existential emergence. By invoking shame as the punishment for the sodomitical men (and notably describing the horror of the shamed, sodomitical *face* of a dying man), Burke is consolidating their existence – and by extension bringing to light – facing the public with – the potential for this transformation in all those who have felt the stirring of same-sex affection. Shame can read nihilistically as a ritual of self-sacrifice, but it is also frequently possible to detect a discursive reinscription of shame. Shame, as we know from its pervasive presence in sadomasochism, is a script that can be rewritten. In a sense, it is possible to *enjoy* shame, perversely, it is also possible to be shamelessly shameful, to be put into the psychic location of shame, and languish there. In part this may be because shame is a pungently intransigent affect, one that requires re-experiencing in order to relinquish it. For this reason too, then, we may glimpse a pleasurable inflection for the call 'for shame', that queer frisson of delight that hovers over the crowd.

Shame's voyeur

The day after Burke's speech the *Morning Post* contained the following comment:

> Every *man* applauds the spirit of the spectators, and every *woman* thinks their conduct right. It remained only for the patriotic Mr Burke to insinuate that the crime these men committed should not be held in the highest detestation, and that it deserved a milder chastisement than ignominious death.

The division of roles according to gender is noteworthy, not least because in a neat inversion of norms, the men are associated with the emotion of the crowd, and the women, the reason of the law. In the early decades of the eighteenth century there were sporadic raids on the Molly houses; taverns and homes where cross-dressing men, 'mollies'; and their admirers might gather. Mollies were regarded as 'women haters' and contemporary cartoons and woodcuts show the mollies being pelted at the pillory by 'real' women (Bray 1982). Towards the end of the eighteenth century we can see how 'heterosexuality' is beginning to be defined in its opposition to 'sodomitical practices'.

Burke filed an affidavit at the King's Bench on 31 May 1780, maintaining that the attack on him in the *Morning Post* was published 'for the purpose of defaming, calumniating and injuring this Deponent in the opinion of the Public.'[12] Burke is trying to wage a battle on two fronts: that to be associated with being soft on the sodomitical was to have the estimation of one's character lowered in the public perception, but still Burke tries the argument that it is wrong that 'the people' murder the sodomitical. While Burke was successful in this particular court case, his speech on behalf of Smith and Reed did him no favours in his political career.[13] When he was leading the case to impeach Warren Hastings for misrule and corruption in India, he was routinely depicted as sodomitical in political caricatures of the day.[14] He also faced a second libel case in the 1780s 'when the old whispers against him were revived' and that time he was not as successful.[15] Burke's bravery in speaking out on behalf of leniency in the case of sodomitical practices is also highlighted by the decision of Jeremy Bentham not to publish his essay arguing for the abolition of punishment of sodomy when he completed his tract in 1785. Although Burke's father was a convert to Protestantism under pressure from the Penal Laws, whispers of allegiance to Catholicism undermined the Irish born Burke throughout his career as a Member of Parliament. His mother and his sister remained strong and loyal to the Church of Rome. His support for free trade with Ireland and his advocacy of Catholic emancipation were unpopular with his constituents and caused him to lose his seat in 1780. Burke, who was considered by Karl Marx in *Das Capital* (1867) to be 'an out and out vulgar bourgeois', has always remained an independent, even quixotic figure of Anglo-Irish political history, and to many remains a shameful figure.[16]

The Public Advertiser of Tuesday 11 April 1780 contains a curious statement that: 'A Maid-Servant of Reed, who stood yesterday in the pillory at St-Margaret's-Hill, is now suffering a Sentence of Imprisonment in Bridewell

Figure 1.4   'Cincinnatus in Retirement', published by E. D'Archery in 1782 (hand-coloured etching) by Gillray, James (1757–1815) © Courtesy of the Warden and Scholars of New College, Oxford/The Bridgeman Art Library

Note: Nicholas K. Robinson writes of this scurrilous image of Edmund Burke as a Jesuit: 'Seated at his impoverished table he fastidiously peels a steaming potato, symbol of the penurious Irish, which he has taken from the chamber pot' (1996, 40). Note also the dancing devils under the table.

for accusing him of the practice of which he was convicted and sentenced to that Punishment.' It seems that the nameless maid's claim that she was able to recognise sodomitical practices was imputed to be a knowledge that could not have been learned without participation in the guilt of the crime. Her guilt might seem to be altogether more damnable if she did not take the initiative in reporting her employer to the authorities and her admission that she knew of her employer's sodomitical practices came about due to the inquiries of the constables. An analogy can be made in the death sentence that was given at this time to women who witnessed the rape of other women but did not intervene to save the victim (Henry 1994). To recognise, to see, to know and acknowledge the homosexual touch or homosexual desire in others seems to have been in itself a punishable offence, a sodomitical practice, as in the legal case of this unnamed, and significantly lower class maid. We see here a clear pattern in class terms of who gets to declaim sodomitical shame, and who is judged to be guilty of participation.

This lack of distinction between the public and private realms became intrinsic to the public discourse on private sexual practices, prefiguring the subsequent

British prosecutions for sodomy, lewdness, licentious behaviour and gross indecency that haunted the lives of men until the present day. Shame goes hand in hand with the axis of public/private. The perverse recognition by the maid prefigures the reception of the narrative. The contagious act (the corruption of the onlooker through her collusion, implied by the secret knowledge she is suspected of owning) is connected to the paranoid association of homosexual desires as a contagious touch. An implicating gaze – a performative speech if you like – is why sodomy cannot be named, because to name is to enact and to bring to public language and view and thus to generate, to fashion and form. We are reminded that homosexual men are still not allowed free access to a private realm, as contemporary infamous legal battles such as Bowers and Hardwick (USA), and Operation Spanner (UK), have shown.[17]

Sodomitical practices are 'the secret shame' that is simultaneously a pervasive knowledge, crucially a private and *subjugated* knowledge, a thing that is known of but not spoken. Shame is the key to understanding Burke's speech, shame is acutely tied to recognition, to the face/seeing, to acts of perception that must be acknowledged in order to be repudiated. So, the crucial appeal that Burke is making in his speech is that William Smith and Theodosius Reed should be shamed, for taking something that should have remained private and relocating it to the public. Of course this is a transference (or indeed a substitution), in actuality it is the state, not the men, that is guilty of this act, through the men's prosecution. Burke's appeal for their public shame and castigation is intended as a compassionate substitute for their obliteration. Burke appeals for this lesser chastisement so as to spare the men's lives. He persuades his audience to have sympathy for the men in an implicit acknowledgement that the private realm of sodomitical desires are a recognised internal territory that all intuit and share.

This also accounts for the conjunction of shame with paranoia. The Greek meaning of paranoia is to be 'beside oneself', in a relationship to oneself rather as a public subjectivity purviews and surveys a private one. This is psychoanalytically the policing role of the super-ego, an activity of internalised repression that is of course a reproduction of social law, integrating the public within the private. The proximity of sodomitical desires to the conscious mind ensures that there is a heightened fear of touch, a terror of the leprous, scabrous, diseased touch of homosexuality, of those unspeakable desires that lurk so close to the surface of the self. The paranoia is intensely present in the public agora, where the accidental touch of strangers might lead to the emergence of contagious desires. Shame is contagious; we are ashamed of our shame, and when those around us catch it, they flush and blush in awkward sympathy. To be within the law, the ordering/ signifying system, to have a place, we must be put into place, by shame. Shame has consolidated the existence of sodomitical men: shame happens when one's private life is made public, when sodomitical men not allowed a private life are violently dragged *into* the public, within which the contagious effects of shame ensure sodomitical desires are communicated. The emergence of the shamed and ambiguous figure of the sodomite consolidated diffuse same-sex desires into a representation – a sign – into which those desires could then be drawn. Burke, in pleading for shame rather than obliteration, effects the split between the private and public in which individuation, via the mechanism of shame, can occur.

The sodomitical representation depicted here is a synecdochal substitution for the glorious contradictory turmoil that is human sexual desire, therefore it is a frontier. What Burke's speech prefigures is the rhetoric of this sodomitical practice later solidifying into the spectral figure of the sodomite, and then the homosexual, an identity (then community) formed by, within, and against shame. Ironically that route of individuation meant the formation of the homosexual (rather than the sodomite), which is precisely what Burke did not want to see, since the homosexual by definition does not share the feelings of the heterosexual, and so is excluded from the very public sympathy that Burke saw as so crucial to justice. Whereas Foucault infamously claimed in *History of Sexuality* that sodomy was an 'utterly confused category', and that the sodomite was 'a temporary aberration', tracing the etymological significance of this term has to be more than an exercise in antiquarian eccentricity. Despite running the risk of scandalous dehistoricising, I hope to have introduced a symbolic nexus of related structures inflected by shame that is ripe for further deconstruction.

* * * *

Text of Edmund Burke's Speech to the House of Commons on 12th April 1780

Mr Burke called the attention of the House to a very particular matter. He said, they sat there to make laws for the subject; that the laws which chiefly came under their consideration were laws of civil polity, but those which most claimed their attention and care were the criminal laws. The first only regarded men's property, criminal laws affected men's lives, a consideration infinitely superior to the former. In making criminal laws, it behoved them materially to consider how they proceeded, to take care wisely and nicely to proportion that punishment so that it should not exceed the extent of the crime, and to provide that it should be of that kind, which was more calculated to operate as an example and prevent crimes, than to oppress and torment the convicted criminal. If this was not properly attended to in the criminal laws which passed that House, they forced his Majesty to violate his coronation oath and commit perjury, because his Majesty, when he was crowned, and invested with the executive government, had solemnly sworn to temper justice with mercy, which it was impossible for him to do if that House suffered any penal laws to pass on principles repugnant to this idea, and in which justice, rigid justice, was solely attended to, and all sight of mercy lost, and foregone. He said, the matter which had induced him to make these reflections, was the perusal of a melancholy circumstance stated in the newspapers of that morning. He hoped to God the fact was mis-stated, and that the whole relation had no foundation in truth. It had, however, made a very strong impression on his mind, and he conceived it of a nature sufficiently interesting to merit the attention of that House, because if it should turn out to be true, he thought it would be incumbent on that House to take some measure in consequence of it. The relation he alluded to was that of the unhappy and horrid murder of a poor wretch, condemned to stand in the pillory the preceding day. The account stated that two men (Reed and Smith) had been doomed to this punishment; that one of them being short of stature, and remarkably short-necked, he could not reach the hole made for the admission of the head, in the awkward and ugly instrument used in this mode of punishment; that the officers of justice, nevertheless, forced his head through the hole, and the poor wretch hung rather than walked as the pillory turned around; that previous to his being put in, he had deprecated the vengeance of the mob, and begged that mercy, which from their exasperation at his crime, and their want of considering the consequences of their cruelty, they seemed very little to bestow. That he soon grew black in the face, and the blood forced itself out of his nostrils, his eyes, and his ears. That the officers seeing his situation, opened the pillory, and the poor wretch fell down dead on the stand of the instrument. The other man, he understood, was likewise so maimed and hurt by what had been thrown at him, that he now lay without hope of recovery.

Having stated this to the House, Mr Burke proceeded to remark, that the Punishment of the Pillory had always struck him as a punishment of shame rather than of personal severity. In the present instance it had been rendered as instrument of death, and that of the worst kind, a death of torment. The crime for which the poor wretches had been condemned, was such as could scarcely be mentioned, much less defended or extenuated. The commission of sodomitical practices. A crime of all others the most detestable, because it tended to vitiate the morals of the whole community, and to defeat the first and chief end of society. The crime was however of all other crimes, a crime of the most equivocal nature, and the most difficult to prove. When criminals convicted of sodomitical practices were sentenced to the pillory, they were adjudged that punishment with a view to expose them to public reproach and contempt, not to popular fury, assault and cruelty. To condemn to the pillory with such ideas, would be to make it a capital punishment, and as much more severe than execution at Tyburn, as to die in torment, was more dreadful than momentary death, almost without sensation of pain. He submitted it, therefore, to the consideration of the House, whether, if the facts turned out as they were stated in the newspapers, and as he had reported them to the House on newspaper authority, it would not be right to abolish the punishment of the pillory, since it was liable to such violent perversion, to be rendered not the instrument of reproach and shame, but of death and murder. If no man would take the matter in hand, he would bring in a Bill for this purpose; he saw, however, a learned gentleman in the House, [the Attorney General] from whose high character and distinguished place, it was fair to infer that the matter would be better lodged in his hands, and would be more properly conducted than it could be by him. He hoped that learned gentleman would take it up, and that the House, if the facts should turn out to be true, as he had mentioned, would direct the learned gentleman to proceed against those to whose neglect, or cruelty, the murder was ascribable.

Notes

1   The work on Edmund Burke in this chapter was jointly undertaken with Katherine O'Donnell at University College Dublin, and I am immensely grateful to her for bringing it to my attention at the 'Sexuality After Foucault' Conference at the University of Manchester UK, 28–30th November 2003, and for our ensuing collaboration on his speech.

2   Much of my subsequent discussion is indebted to Herrup's scholarship, as a case study of legal and social history this book is brilliant in its careful unraveling of the Castlehaven saga.

3   On Wilde's deathbed conversion see http://www.poetrymagazines.org.uk/magazine/record.asp?id=9404 Accessed August 31st 2006.

4   Most men in England were not franchised to elect or otherwise influence government and no women had such franchise.

5   Throughout his career Burke used rhetorical accounts of tortured bodies to create emblematic images of systematic injustice. In the manner of the Gaelic Aisling, the stripped and mutilated Princesses of Oudh become conflated with India and the naked and fleeing Marie Antoinette is France.

6   Burke did establish sympathy in some influential quarters; the editors of his correspondence tell us that he secured an annual pension of £36 for Smith's widow.

7   By the time that the influential jurist William Blackstone published his *Commentaries on the English Law* (1765–1769) sodomy was routinely described in English law '…in its very indictments as a crime not fit to be named; *"peccatum illud horribile, inter christianos non nominandum"* (that horrible crime not to be named among Christians).' Another typical example can be found in Edward Gibbon's *Decline and Fall of the Roman Empire* (1776): 'I touch with reluctance and dispatch with impatience, a more odious vice, of which modesty rejects the name, and nature abominates the idea.' This is the introductory sentence to two paragraphs, very lengthy paragraphs, even by Gibbon's standard, which abound in florid expressions of disgust.

8   In the summer of 1894, John Francis Bloxam, a homosexual undergraduate at Oxford, asked Alfred Douglas for a contribution to a new periodical called *The Chameleon*. Alfred Douglas contributed two poems. These were quoted at Oscar Wilde's trial for homosexual offences on 30th April 1895. The last line of the poem *Two Loves*: 'I am the Love that dare not speak its name' has become a trope for alluding to homosexual love. Re-published in Stephen Coote (1983, 262–4).

9   See further katz Jonathan Ned (1995).

10   See http://bible.cc/hosea/4-18.htm.

11   See Vol. 3:4, 383–388 and Vol.4:1, 389–405.

12   As his biographer, Sir Philip Magnus puts it: 'It was characteristic of Burke that

he should have laid himself open to the grossest charges by his imprudent zeal in taking up cases of homosexual offenders' (Magnus 1939, 55).

13   The work of King (2004) *The Gendering of Men, 1600–1750, Vol. I: The English Phallus* is useful in thinking through Burke's brave stance on behalf of the despised Smith and Reed.

14   For a discussion of one of Burke's own unconventional love affairs see O'Donnell, K. (2006).

15   In 1784 Burke again went to court to sue for libel, this time against the publisher of the *Public Advertiser.*

16   http://en.wikipedia.org/wiki/Edmund_Burke, accessed 30th August 2006.

17   *Bowers v. Hardwick*, 478 U.S. 186 (1986), was a United States Supreme Court decision that upheld the constitutionality of a Georgia sodomy law that criminalised oral and anal sex in private between consenting adults. Seventeen years later the Supreme Court directly overruled *Bowers* in the *Lawrence v. Texas*, 539 U.S. 558 (2003) decision and held that such laws are unconstitutional. *Operation Spanner* was the name of an operation carried out by police in Manchester in the United Kingdom in 1987. The police had obtained a video which they believed depicted acts of sadistic torture, and they launched a murder investigation, convinced that the people in the video were being tortured before being killed. This resulted in raids on a number of properties, and a number of arrests. The apparent 'victims' were alive and well, and soon told the police that they were participating in private activities. Although all of those seen in the videos stated that they were willing participants, the police and Crown Prosecution Service insisted on pressing charges. Sixteen men were charged with various offences, including 'assault with actual bodily harm' (ABH). The trial judge ruled that consent was not a valid defence to ABH, and the defendants pleaded guilty. The case was appealed first to the High Court, then to the House of Lords. In March 1993, the appeal was dismissed (*Regina v Brown* (1993) 2 All ER 75) by a 3–2 majority of the Lords. An attempt to overturn the convictions in the European Court of Human Rights in 1997 failed.

Chapter 2

Shove the Queer: Irish/American Shame in New York's Annual St Patrick's Day Parades

Imagined communities

As I hinted at in the Introduction, shame can colour the way whole countries are thought of, and how citizens think of themselves. Contrary to the commonsense view, nationalisms are not invested solely in pride, sometimes they are intractably linked to feelings of shame. Nationalist ideology is sustained by shaming those it considers to be external to its real and imagined borders, but it saves special regard for the repudiation of its internal others, those who are considered to be supplementary to the nation's needs, that it would prefer to make invisible or expulse. On those groups and individuals nationalism casts a particular stigma. This chapter considers one case, turning its attention to the way shame inflects ethnicity and class and produces specific kinds of narratives. Here I examine Irish-Americanism in order to unpack links between different kinds of prejudice, class hatred and homophobia, explaining how the roots of such are embedded in forms of shame.

The seduction of nationalism lies in Benedict Anderson's promise of an 'imagined community', 'conceived as a deep, horizontal comradeship', a mental image of communion powerful in evoking 'love, and often [a] profoundly self-sacrificing love' (Anderson 1991, 141). As postcolonial critic Homi Bhabha points out, though, whereas it is possible to bind people together in nationalism in the name of love, 'the ambivalent identifications of love and hate occupy the same psychic space', and hence there must be other people left to target with latent aggression: 'the paranoid projections outwards return to haunt and split the place from which they are made' (Bhabha 1994, 149). Of course, the nationalism of Irish-Americanism is impossible to separate from the desire for an ethnic identity within a country that insists on imposing such subcategories of citizenship upon its people. However, the call is to be an 'American' – it is in the transcendence of the American constitution that Irish-Americans invest. Americans are required to find a hyphenated self in order to experience a place in that world and a community. Inverting this pressure into pride then causes a number of crises in its protagonists, as there is no straightforward 'home' for the American Irish diaspora to inhabit.

If national identity is a fantasy for the Irish in Ireland, how much more so for those, and piquantly their descendants, historically forced out during the trauma of famine, and subject to shameful discrimination in their chosen land of exile and opportunity. In Edward Said's essay 'Reflections on Exile' he describes the heroic literature of exile as merely an effort to overcome the crippling sorrow of estrangement, and loss. These are the very conditions of nationalism. But exile is a solitary experience, a sense of being outside a group predominates and hence a condition of *shamefulness*:

> Exiles feel therefore, an urgent need to reconstitute their broken lives, usually by choosing to see themselves as part of a triumphant ideology or a restored people... (Said, 2000, 185)

A pride/shame dichotomy is in evidence here, and we are reminded that in classical literature heroes *suffer* from pride. The exile is in the position of being banished, s/he becomes 'eccentric' – out of place – and s/he then seeks to compensate for this exclusion:

> ... because *nothing* is secure. Exile is a jealous state. What you achieve is precisely what you have no wish to share. (Said 2000, 186)

Conditions of exile thus create envy and destructiveness in its injured parties, and a defensive retrenchment into pride. The full implications of these nationalist feelings need better clarification, so that the injurious effects of pride and prejudice, and the vicious spatial re-enactment of these passions, be mollified.

Political history of New York's St Patrick's Day Parade

When the Irish Lesbian and Gay Organization [ILGO] applied to march in the New York St Patrick's Day Parade of 1991, they were told that there was no room by the organisers of the parade, the Ancient Order of Hibernians. ILGO's on-going struggle for inclusion in the world's largest celebration of Irish ethnicity became a major news item that has rumbled on seasonally for a number of years across the USA, in Ireland, in the international gay community and amongst the international Irish diaspora. Fifteen years after its first application to join the parade, ILGO is not only still prohibited from marching – remarkably, in the land of the 'brave and the free' – ILGO is even legally prohibited from holding a protest at its own exclusion.[1]

This chapter begins with establishing the claim that the concept or figure of a nation demands social homogeneity and blocks ambiguity. Its idea of uniformity depends upon an account of 'oneness' that requires by default compulsory heterosexuality. Because heterosexuality is naturalised and assumed, accordingly homosexuality is read as antithetical to the nation and its political embodiment within nationalism. In this case study, Irish-American nationalism = heterosexual, the logical corollary of which justified the homophobic exclusion of gay and lesbian Irish-Americans from the St Patrick's Day Parades. This premise was successfully argued through the USA courts, even defended by the respected American Civil Liberties Union: that being homosexual is antithetical to being Irish, and the Irish Lesbian and Gay Organization is a violent, obscene enemy bent on the destruction of Irish ethnicity and Irish communities.

The Irish diaspora in the United States endures a collective memory of discrimination that is articulated via nostalgia for a lost or denied sense of 'Ireland'. The US St Patrick's Day Parades (in particular the ones in East Coast cities) are ritualised occasions for expressing this denied sense of national belonging. The marches in cities like New York and Boston expose aspects of nationalistic sentiment that emphatically render its phantasmatic quality: the Ireland being celebrated in the parades is a historical sentiment, a nation made static in the minds of its ethnic descendants by exile and loss. What identity-based marches such as the Annual St Patrick's Day make abundantly clear is that the traditional segmentation of the urban space, visualised and auralised through the compartments of the protest march with flags, banners, and bands, is not so much a performative sign of strategic inclusion (as with Gay Pride marches), but a very moving and vital force of exclusion. The case study of the St Patrick's Day Parades is an illustration of how much homophobia is linked with a historical and discursive association of nationalisms with *homophilia*, and that the virulent reaction from organisers (AOH) coupled with the spontaneous aggression from the crowds lining the marches, lends proof to this proximity. Irish-American nationalism can thus be read as illustrative of the heterosexualisation of nationalism, a move illustrating the disjunction between the homogenised, idealised semiotic nation, and the complex, heterogenous lived experience of its natives.[2]

Figure 2.1   St Patrick's Day Parade in New York, 3 February 2003
Source: Getty Images/Getty Images News

Nations and nationalism

In 1882 Ernest Renan gave his now famous lecture 'What Is A Nation?' in which he observed:

> ... the essence of a nation is that all individuals have many things in common, and also that they have forgotten many things. (Renan 1882, reprinted in Bhabha 1994, 11)

Nationalism is defined by Ernest Gellner as primarily 'a principle which holds that the political and national unit should be congruent' (Gellner 1983, 1).

> Nations as a natural God-given way of classifying men, as an inherent... political destiny, are a myth; nationalism, which sometimes takes pre-existing cultures and turns them into nations, sometimes invents them, and often obliterates pre-existing cultures. (Gellner 1983, 48–9)

For a nationalist ideology to form there must be some general functional prerequisites: firstly there must be an emergent 'specialised clerical class', as Gellner called it, 'a clerisy' (Gellner 1983, 8), which forms an intellectual culture. Nationalism is thus dependent upon the stratification of a society or state through imposing class allegiances. Education is key to this development, producing a shared culture and technological skills of communication, depending on the establishment of a common culture, one that is then proselytised by the middle class. This culture is one appropriated in the name of the 'folk', i.e. the putative working class, its symbolism draws heavily from a selective and idealised representation of the working class or, as in Ireland's case the peasant folk.[3] It is repackaged and delivered back to 'the people' in a stylised and romanticised summons to authenticity. Secondly, despite the fact that nationalism preaches a historical continuity with the past, paying homage to the 'folk culture' it has bowdlerised, it operates using a form of nostalgia, which is intrinsically new and commensurate with the demands to amalgamate and reformulate 'the nation' according to contemporary criteria.

Ernest Gellner defines nationalism as a *sentiment* produced when the political and national unit is incongruent:

> ...the feeling of anger aroused by the violation of the principle, or the feeling of satisfaction aroused by its fulfilment. A nationalist *movement* is one actuated by a sentiment of this kind. (Gellner 1983, 1)

If we understand nationalism as a sentiment, then, as a feeling of exclusion which is articulated as a protest for inclusion, we must necessarily examine that feeling and the ways in which it is echoed and reproduced as an act of language, becoming in Foucault's words a 'discursive formation', a political structure, inventing the 'nation' where one previously did not exist. We also need to conceive of how nationalism appears as a narrative, a story, which inscribes its readers through a mechanism of emotional identification, through interpolating sentiment. Nations are imaginary constructs that depend on a range of cultural fictions to maintain their mythic existence. Geoffrey Bennington highlights this connection:

> ... we undoubtedly find narration at the centre of nation: stories of national origins, myths of founding fathers, genealogies of heroes. At the origin of the nation, we find a story of the nation's origin. Which should be enough to inspire suspicion. (Bennington in Bhabha 1994, 121)

He continues to stress that 'the idea of the nation is inseparable from its narration' (Bennington 1994, 132). Nationalism therefore depends upon a homogenising, idealising process that tells a proud story of origins dependent upon selective denial, or repression.

Nation space

It seems axiomatic to claim that 'nation' is a spatial metaphor. The borders of a nation are best perceived as membranes, permeable boundaries, which permit communication with and sometimes infusion by, the Other.[4] The nation has to have something to delineate itself against, meaning is created by a process of differentiation, and 'nation' as a concept contains its own degeneration, as those boundaries bleed. In considering the nation as a space from the point of view of the Other, the most cogent theorisation appears in Homi Bhabha's work, specifically in his (1994) essay 'Dissemination: Time, Narrative, and the Margins of the Modern Nation'. Firstly, Bhabha speaks movingly of the gathering of scattered peoples:

> The nation fills the void left in the uprooting of communities and kin, and turns that loss into the language of metaphor. (Bhabha 1994, 141)

Here we have the sense of nation as an expression of grief for something that has been lost, and is consequently longed for.[5] The nation also embodies the desire of the exile – Bhabha lyrically invokes us to realise 'how fully the shadow of the nation falls on the condition of exile' (Bhabha 1994, 141). The nation from this perspective is not 'here', but 'there', not 'now' but 'then', a desired object, representing a projected yearning for a perfectly consolidated self, paradoxically beyond the self. Perhaps we might think of this nation as externalising a dream of integration.[6] The profundity of this yearning can only be revealed metaphorically, in a 'figure of speech'. So, the grief of unbelonging, of migrancy, is fixated by its own antithesis, a fantasy of transcendence and immanence. In relation to Irish Americans these elements are intensified because they are diasporic, for the country they mourn for and desire is not of course the solid ground they are walking upon; the Ireland they love is 2000 miles away. National belonging is a homogenous cultural formation that doesn't need to specify its conditions of exclusion, it is (as Benedict Anderson so famously said) a 'deep horizontal comradeship'

(Anderson 1991, 7) in which affectional ties and identifications are naturalised and mutually unquestioned. It is a keenly felt phallic imaginary. Bhabha argues that 'from the liminal movement of the culture of the nation... minority discourse emerges... minority discourses that speak betwixt and between times and places' (Bhabha 1994, 155/158). A nation is ineluctably comprised and shaped by what it defines itself against from its own inside. 'Irishness' as an ethnicity is a neutral space of historical descent, a claim on ethnic inheritance that can be made legitimately whether one is straight or gay; to participate in the formal ritual of performing the national, though, creates a distinction between formal and informal agency. The imagined nation of nationalism is fantasised as intact, impregnable, unitary, constant and monolithic; as a material entity the nation space is ruptured, it is mutable, temporal, limited, and precarious, haunted by its own division.

Thus, we need to approach any examination of the occasion of nationalist sentiment typically manifest in the annual Irish St Patrick's Day Parades with the tools of narrative analysis, to see how nations, as fictions, involve the curiosity and evoke the commitment of a reader, and asking why this particular story captures her/his intricate social imagination, at this specific fork in history. Historians remark on the fact that the narratives of identity of the Irish of east coast America differ from the Irish diaspora who went to Chicago, St Louis, Cinncinnati and the other new cities of the American West (O'Connor 1995, 61). Irish-Americans' story of origin is one of enforced exile due to English greed and misrule, finding solace in fidelity to their Catholic religion, Irish culture and allegiance to America. In the land of open economic opportunity, the identity of the Irish-Americans in the major cities of the east coast USA such as New York, has an added dimension. The memory of surviving systematic severe sectarian oppression, enacted by the ultra Protestant Nativists or Know Nothing gangs of those cities, is fundamental to the formation of their identity. The Irish-Americans of the east coast USA remember how employment advertisements routinely closed with the phrase: 'No Irish need apply'.[7] Irish-American ethnicity in New York became characterised by being obedient to the Catholic clergy and in maintaining an organised Irish labour brotherhood that was kept in place by their block vote for the local and national Democratic Party; this discipline was allied to a cultural memory of surviving systematic persecution by the English in Ireland, and now the Ultra-Protestants of the USA. The persistence of this characterisation is remarkable in its enduring legacy; the stigmatised underside of it has also persisted, in the violent, slovenly, maudlin, racist, drunk Irish-American man tied into the corruption of local and city politics.

The Ancient Order of Hibernians, the organisation that runs the New York St Patrick's Day Parade is a fraternal [men and boys only] organisation who claim origin from the sixteenth century when the members were needed, in the words of their official historian: 'to protect the lives of priests who risked immediate death to keep the Catholic Faith alive in occupied Ireland after the reign of England's King Henry VIII'. The evidence of the existence and impact of this Ancient Order in Ireland is slight to say the least, but the

AOH was founded in America in 1836 at New York's St James Church, to protect the clergy, and church property from the 'Know Nothings' and their followers. While its origins in the USA lay in 'the purpose of defending Gaelic values, and protecting Church and clergy', its role became crystallised with the influx of Irish immigration following the famines of the 1840s when it sought '... to aid the newly arrived Irish, both socially and politically'. It is now the largest Irish society in the USA and, as its website declares, it sees its role as welcoming 'new Irish Americans', fostering and preserving Irish culture, and being at: 'the political forefront for issues concerning the Irish, such as; Immigration Reform; economic incentives both here and in Ireland; the human rights issues addressed in the MacBride Legislation; Right-To-Life; and a peaceful and just solution to the issues that divide Ireland.'[8]

At the forefront of the activities of the AOH is the organisation of The New York St Patrick's Day Parade. St Patrick's Day in Ireland was traditionally marked by wearing fresh shamrock pinned to your coat, going to Mass, having a break from the Lenten fast, braving the showers to watch a local parade and certain sporting fixtures, and was a tame affair indeed to St Patrick's Day celebrations in the USA. St Patrick's Day falls neatly halfway through the American college students' second semester, and is beloved by generations of American students as a riotous drink-fest. The commercialisation of the day is long established in America: green beer, maudlin songs, the traditional fare of corned beef, cabbage and potatoes, gaudy green decorations for the body, the ubiquity of 'Kiss Me, I'm Irish' buttons, plastic leprechauns and Made-in-China shamrocks further increases its appeal as a national party day on the streets. Even by the summer of 2005 there were nearly 120 St Patrick's Day Parades advertised to take place across the USA in March 2006 on the website SaintPatricksDayParade.com. In the memory of the AOH their New York St Patrick's Day Parade still bears the hallmarks of its roots in the troubled 1850s. By 1854 the Irish were on red alert from violent attacks by the Know Nothings and as the AOH's Deputy National Historian, Gerry Curran puts it, the St Patrick's Day Parade of that year contained an:

> ... unusually large number of Irish units of the state militia... Protection of their community in general, and of the marchers in particular, motivated these men (many of whom were AOH members). Their demeanor stood in striking contrast to the proverbial Irish faults of violence, indolence, and intemperance with which the popular media of the time portrayed them. The inclusion of these military units helped transform the St Patrick's Day procession into the parade we recognize today.[9]

Curran goes on to describe how in 1856 the AOH president led the Father Mathew Total Abstinence and Benevolent Society in the parade: 'This famous Irish temperance organisation helped bring a new dimension of order to the line of march and deflated the myth that the Irish were, as suggested by Henry Cabot Lodge: "...a hard-drinking, idle, quarrelsome, and disorderly class, always at odds with the government".' The association of St Patrick's Day with drunken debauchery clearly embarrassed the AOH officials, and they still suffer from the stigmatised identification of Irish Americans with alcoholism. The AOH has been the prime organiser of the New York parade since this time, it quickly grew in size and the AOH spread rapidly into the cities wherever the Irish were to be found. Soon both the AOH and St Patrick's Day parades became a feature of every substantial North American city. So the parade demonstrated the pride and unity of Irish Catholics, in their ancestral heritage and but also their American citizenship. In Curran's words: 'The celebration of St. Patrick's Day has become a symbol not only of devotion to our patron saint and ancestral home but also of our constitutional right to freely assemble in our streets as respected American citizens.'[10]

Parade rituals

Many histories intersect at the horizon of the bad encounter of American queer and Irish parade-making, involving complex metropolitan politics of ethnicity, and the anti-racist and anti-homophobic histories of taking to the street to perform as yet unachieved rights, or to memorialise rights recently hard-won, but still vulnerable. There are strong analogies to be made between St Patrick's Day parades, (particularly as it is understood by the AOH organisers of the New York Parade) and Gay Pride Parades, which are part of a Summer festival or ceremony held by the Lesbian, Gay, Bisexual and Transgender [LGBT] community, usually of a city, to commemorate the political struggle for lesbian and gay rights. Taking place annually in June, they commemorate the Stonewall riots which were a series of violent conflicts between working-class homosexuals and police officers in New York City. The first night of rioting began on Friday, 28th June 1969 when police raided the Stonewall Inn, a gay bar in Greenwich Village. 'Stonewall', as the raids are often referred to, was generally considered a turning point for the modern gay rights movement worldwide, as it is one of the first times in history a significant body of homosexual people resisted arrest, and protested against their persecution.[11] Many parades still retain a political or activist character, especially in less gay-positive settings. The term 'parade' has replaced an earlier nomination, the 'march', whose military and narrowly Leftist (perhaps even Maoist) connotations signalled the political rights agenda more clearly. However, recently and in more gay-positive cities, the parades take on a festive or Mardi Gras-like character. Large parades of tens of thousands often involve floats, dancers, drag queens and music; but, even such celebratory parades customarily include political and educational contingents, typically local politicians, marching groups from gay and queer institutions of various kinds, local gay-friendly churches, gay employee associations from large businesses and trade unions, and representatives from state services such as the police, ambulance and fire brigades. For many lesbian, gay, bisexual or transgender people, attending their first 'Pride' remains a significant rite of passage. In that place, in that moment, the queer nation, and their full citizenship of it, seems to exist.

Pride and protest marches by self-identified groups who are temporarily bonded by ties of perceived disenfranchisment have been a feature of civil society since 'rights' were there to be claimed.[12] There is a growing body of published research on gay and lesbian pride marches. In *Queering Tourism: Paradoxical Performances of Gay Pride Parades* Lynda Johnston analyses the paradoxes of gay pride parades as tourist events, exploring how the public display of queer bodies – the way they look, what they do, who watches them, and under what regulations – is profoundly important in constructing sexualised subjectivities of bodies and cities (Johnston 2005). Pride parades are annual arenas of queer public culture, where embodied notions of subjectivity are sold, enacted, transgressed and debated. Michael Luongo's analysis of World Pride in Rome in July 2000 is particularly useful for drawing attention to the idea of the axis of the globalised gay-local activist model, particularly as Rome was chosen for this event in order to send strong gay positive signals to the Vatican, and the Catholic Church.[13] Whilst the Italian authorities were obstructive, Luongo reports that the Italian media were largely supportive of the event, mirroring the experience in New York (Luongo 2002).[14] St Patrick's Day Parades also happen on a large world-wide scale, it is the one national holiday that is celebrated in more countries around the world than any other, and like Gay Pride Parades they are a mixture of a disenfranchised people claiming a civic and cultural space whilst celebrating their brand identity. It is challenging to make coherence from the multiply determined story of clashing utopianisms that crash down upon the heads of minoritised communities. Whilst the original impetus might have been outrage, thousands of marches continue through ritualised repetition, year after year, to make an appearance to expressly mark their unchanging identity, to be present in urban space to make a retrospective and highly nostalgic claim of tradition, and consistency. 'Sameness' is highly regulated: routes, music, dress, and the order of participation, must remain unchanged.

The heterosexual nation

Nation/bodies have lives – they are born, get old, and die. Corporeal metaphors are unavoidable, as the nation is often depicted as a vital body, with a heart, lungs, mind, and extremities, concomitant with the fantasy of the bounded sealed body. Nations can be 'healthy' or 'diseased', depending on one's rhetorical viewpoint. Metaphors of contagion assail the nation/body. Nations, like bodies, are also sexed. 'Nationalisms', as Anne McClintock underscores 'are from the outset constituted in gender power' (Parker et. al. 1992, 17 fn19). Despite the fact that citizenship has historically been denied to women, who in law have paradoxically been rendered stateless, as the editors of *Nationalisms and Sexualities* have pointed out, in the rhetoric of war there is a deeply ingrained 'depiction of the homeland as the female body whose violation by foreigners requires its citizens and allies to rush to her defence' (Parker et. al. 1992, 6). This rape analogy depends on the trope of nation-as-woman, but more specifically the patriarchal construction of the nation as Mother, the dutiful angel who nurtures and protects the propagation of the national culture. This structure can be read back through British colonial rule in Ireland as Irish men were repeatedly denigrated as feminine; it is there in older form in the Irish nationalist construction of Mother Ireland. By implication then, nations are metaphorically incestuous, for who if not 'men' impregnate the Mother – who is at once the ground (grammatically) and the figure; the rape metaphor, which invokes not so much loss as incorporation, produces melancholia. In this heterosexist and perverse construct, then, the men queerly impregnate the 'soil' of the nation with their potent seed. Critics have observed how often liberation movements also employ this same predicate, 'women's bodies can become cyphers in the imaginings of male resistance fighters' (Parker et. al. 1992, 366–46). In the erotic fervour of nationalism, heterosexual desire foments the ardour of the activist.

The AOH has an oft-remembered origin as a military protector of the Church, clergy and the beleaguered Irish in New York. We can describe them as heterosexist and perhaps by extension then panicked about homosexuality. However, their anti-colonial imagination just does not clearly fit with the Anglo-Germanic Imperial fantasies usually exemplified in nationalist theory – and there is also a marked difference between the conception of Irish American masculinity and Irish masculinity. The Irish men in the States are supposedly infamous for their fighting spirit and readiness to brawl (perhaps most aptly symbolised in the football team: The Fighting Irish of Notre Dame). Irish men in Ireland throughout the nineteenth century were stereotyped, most famously by Matthew Arnold, as 'Celtic' romantic, mystical, emotional, and infantile. The rhetoric of the Irish Republican Brotherhood (IRB) of 1916 was the ideology of martyrdom – self-immolation to light a spark of revolution, a blood sacrifice for Mother Ireland to rejuvenate her. The rhetoric of Mother Ireland needing her sons to rescue her from (sexual) bondage has a long and potent genealogy and the fey non-macho, shamed masculinity of Irish masculinity is only just recovering from colonisation. To illustrate: it may help to see the Irish Americans' 'nationalism' as a veneration of the Mother Church as much as Mother Ireland – we can think of the 'England [male] get out of Ireland [female]' banner (which ironically is the only political slogan the AOH allow in the Parade).

The homosexual nation

In mapping out the field of nationalism there is crucial research that posits the homoerotic, rather than heterosexual, affiliations of nationhood. George Mosse's history of sexual norms in modern Europe, *Nationalism and Sexuality*, argues that our present notions of middle-class morality and 'respectability' are rooted in nineteenth and twentieth century ideologies of nation. Mosse argues how nineteenth century bourgeois idealisations of virility came to be sublimated as nationalist virtue, manliness and male beauty symbolising the nation's spiritual and material vitality. The 'back-to-nature' movement in England and

Germany depended on the neo-classicist romantic revival of Greek models of (male) citizenship, and the naturalisation of nudity. The covert homoeroticism abeyant in this cult of the body was made explicit by figures such as Edward Carpenter in England, and the poet Stefan George in Germany.[15] It is Nazi Germany that provides Mosse with an example of established homoerotic nationalism. The naked Greek youth distilled the aspirant imagery of the Third Reich, clearly a raced symbol, as well as sexed. As Mosse comments: 'a beautiful Jew was a contradiction in terms' (Mosse 1988, 139). The Nazis built upon the nineteenth century concept of the *Männerbund*, passionate male friendship formed primarily among élite youth, emphasising nature and physical strength grounded in a brotherhood of leaders. According to the historian Hans Blüher, homosexuality in the *Männerbund* represented spiritual principles – heroism, leadership and communality. Mosse comments on how the distinction between homoeroticism and homosexuality became blurred:

> The rediscovery of the human body combined with the exclusively male nature of the early youth movement did raise the spectre of homoeroticism, even homosexuality. Those who tried to recapture their own bodies as well as nature from the hypocrisy as well as artificiality of bourgeois life, as they saw it, also wanted to find refuge in a true community of affinity. They began to perceive the nation as such a community. Moreover the nation helped spiritualise their new sensuality... (Mosse 1988, 57)[16]

Within the intellectual Stefan George's circle, homoeroticism was seen as the principal agent of national renewal. Mosse concludes:

> The dynamic of modern nationalism was built upon the ideal of manliness. Nationalism also put forward a feminine ideal, but it was largely passive, symbolising the immutable forces which the nation reflected. As a living organism, filled with energy, nationalism tended to encourage male bonding, the *Männerbund*, which by its very nature presented a danger to that respectability the nation was supposed to preserve. Such bonding had been reinvigorated by the rediscovery of the human body at the *fin de siècle*. The male eros tended to haunt modern nationalism.

Such formulations are redolent of the works of critics such as Eve Kosofsky Sedgwick (1991), Jonathan Dollimore (1991), and Terry Castle (1993), all of whom locate homosexuality spatially as proximate, even central to Western culture. Sedgwick's claim that gay proximity leads to gay panic is vital to our understanding in this context:

> I argue that the historically shifting, and precisely the arbitrary and self-contradictory, nature of the way *homosexuality* (along with its predecessor terms) has been defined in relation to the rest of the male homosocial spectrum has been an exceedingly potent and embattled locus of power over the entire range of male bonds, and perhaps especially over those that define themselves not *as* homosexual, but *as against* the homosexual. Because the paths of male entitlement, especially in the nineteenth century, required certain intense male bonds that were not readily distinguishable from the most reprobated bonds, an endemic and ineradicable state of what I am

calling male homosexual panic became the normal condition of male heterosexual entitlement. (Sedgwick 1991, 185)

The central component of the argument here is that if this model is interpreted in relation to nationalism, it is feasible to argue that it is a queer attachment: the pervasive, visceral heterosexuality of most nationalisms is the manifestation of a kind of panicked response to the elemental structure of homoeroticism it is compelled towards and concomitantly desperate to repudiate.

Queer Nation

Queer Nation was first started in New York in April 1990 primarily by people involved in HIV and AIDS activism who also wanted to respond politically to a number of bashings of lesbians and gay men in the East Village. So, its origin in part was in the desire to defend space. Queer Nation coalesced around a new generation who were both angry and ironic, it assembled around

Figure 2.2 St Parick's Day Parade in New York, 3 February 2003
Source: Getty Images/ Getty Images News

an anarchist aesthetic which mobilised a 'cultural happening', a momentary incursion into the domain of representation. Queer Nation practised a form of cultural terrorism on the American nation by incursions into the public realm of sexuality that attempted to 'queer' the nation body. This had the effect of disclosing the heteronormative hegemony at the same time as it attempted to camp it up. Its intent was to make the nation a space safe for queers, not just in the sense of being tolerated, 'but safe for demonstration, in the mode of patriotic ritual' (Berlant and Freeman, 1993, 198).[17] In that sense, then, Queer Nation was a logical expansion of the marching cultures of Gay and Lesbian Liberation, it was a temporal intervention in urban space intended to intervene with a 'queer bubble', its bodily progress down wide avenues of the city intending to provoke the public realisation that spaces were simultaneously sexed/queer.

Queer Nation was a deliberately spatial politics of queer embodiment, as Lauren Berlant and Elizabeth Freeman argued:

This emphasis on safe spaces, secured for bodies by capital and everyday life practices, also finally, constitutes a refusal of the terms national discourse uses to frame the issue of sexuality: being queer is not about the right to privacy: it is about the freedom to be public. (Berlant and Freeman 1993, 201)

Queer Nation inverted the liberal division of society into public/private space to which lesbians in particular had been confined. Crucially, the public spectacle of queer sexualities being performed was also intended to make heterosexuality estranged, to displace it to the margins, and centre the formerly deviant queer. As a strategy of inversion it was risky, but the desire to aggressively territorialise was a reverse colonisation and a response to what felt like 100 years of restraint: 'queers are thus using exhibitionism to make public space psychically unsafe for unexamined heterosexuality'.[18] Urban activism – such as highly visual participation in street ritual – was essential to the Queer Nation project.

Queer identity was fixed in a romantic undifferentiation – that compulsion to sameness would not relent – but the present reality of inequality and regret kept breaking through. In a piece on 'Women as Queer Nationals' in Out/Look Maria Maggenti bemoans the loss of the agency of the Lesbian Nation first articulated by Jill Johnstone in the 1970s (Johnston 1974). She attends a Queer Nation meeting sensing:

... an underlying desire, an unspoken yearning it seems, to be accepted instead of liberated. I go home that night worried. How are lesbians ever going to be able to define ourselves in this group, in this decade, in this world? (Maggenti 1991, 23)

In expressing the need for a young lesbian participant to find her home, she concludes with a fantasy refrain for the new nation:

And I want to tell her to grab her female friends and run, run out into the rainy street shouting with power and anger and glee, shouting and dancing her way to some unknown place, some undiscovered continent, some still-unnamed territory. (Maggenti 1991, 23)

American lesbians are still, just like Huckleberry, 'lighting out for the territory'.[19]

In many ways we can read the 1990s campaigns by the Lesbian Avengers as an outcome of the felt exclusion of women from Queer Nation. The Avengers icon – a cartoon bomb – and their street actions, were explicitly anti-national. They were coded ironically as urban guerrillas, and the movement, via cell groups, rejected any hint of nostalgia for statist intervention:

The Lesbian Avengers is a direct action group using grassroots activism to fight for lesbian survival and visibility. Our purpose is to identify and promote lesbian issues and perspectives while empowering lesbians to become experienced organisers who can participate in political rebellion. Learning skills and strategizing together are the core of our existence. (Schulman et. al 1993)

Their zaps combined humour with the exigency of a pressure group, the image responded to a nostalgic desire to return to the effective vanguard politics of earlier counter-cultural movements. The Lesbian Avengers performed urban warfare as an attempt to colonise urban space through direct action, they were 'space guerillas' that drew from the Happenings Art movement of the 1960s. The Lesbian Avengers was created in Spring 1992 by six New York women: Anne-Christine D'Adesky, Marie Honan, Ann Maguire, Sarah Schulman, Ana Maria Simo, and Maxine Wolfe, all of whom had previous experience in building counter-cultural protest movements. The six founding members of the Avengers had met through their ILGO activism in New York City.

The precursor to Queer Nation, both ideologically and more precisely in terms of membership was the direct action group, Aids Coalition to Unleash Power, known better by its acronym ACT UP, which by its astute and spectacular protests made strategic symbolic interventions into American cultural politics which had material effects in changing both discourse and policy on what became known as 'AIDS awareness' and treatment (Signorile 2003). On December 10, 1989 ACT UP and WHAM! (Women's Health Action and Mobilization) had their first 'Stop the Church' demonstration. 4,500 protesters gathered outside St Patrick's Cathedral to protest the Church and specifically New York's John Cardinal O'Connor's opposition to safer sex education, violent homophobia, and attempts to block access to safe and legal abortions. Although 111 people were arrested, the news media focused on and distorted a single Catholic demonstrator's personal protest involving a communion wafer.[20] The protestor, Tom Keane, refused the Eucharist when presented it by the Cardinal but his action was represented as a desecration.[21] Roman Catholics receive the consecrated host as being the actual body of Christ, it is this understanding of the sacrament, more than any other theological difference, that is understood by Catholics to differentiate their Christianity from Protestantism. For many Irish-Americans, the protest of ACT UP, was read as a pollution of the most sacred rite of communion in their beloved St Patrick's Cathedral, and was felt deeply as a personal and communal injury, their memory of being victims of sectarian violence was aggravated. This memory was still fresh and raw when ILGO applied to march in the parade.

Irish Lesbian and Gay Organization [ILGO]

Judith Raiskin has drawn attention to the twin Victorian doctrines of evolution and degeneration to remind us how those 'hybrids' who crossed so-called 'natural' boundaries of race or sex were classified and reviled as deviant and regressive (Parker et al. 1992). A healthy nation, according to the ideology of eugenics, is racially and sexually homologous. However, there are queer fissures within nations and nationalism, as Eric Hobsbawm points out:

> First, official ideologies of states and movements are not guides to what is in the minds of even the most loyal citizens or supporters. Second, and more specifically, we cannot assume that for most people national identification – when it exists –

Figure 2.3   Protesters at St Patrick's Day Parade, New York, 1996
Source: Getty Images/Getty Images News

excludes or is always or ever superior to, the remainder of the set of identifications which constitute the social being. In fact it is always combined with identifications of another kind, even when it is felt to be superior to them. Thirdly, national identification and what it is believed to imply, can change and shift in time, even in the course of quite short periods. (Hobsbawm 1990, 11)

The 'remainder', those identifications of an/other kind, creates precisely the faultline between the identities of being citizens of Irish and gay worlds that ILGO sought to address. When ILGO marched in the New York Gay Pride parade in 1990 the reaction from the onlookers was one of surprise and a certain hilarity that there were lesbians and gays who were – of all things – Irish. However, the difficulty that many in ILGO experienced of expressing being both Irish and (also at the same time, in the same place) gay was to be solidified as an impossibility in the public discourse from the earliest days of the parade controversy.

ILGO did get to march in the 230th New York St Patrick's Day parade in 1991 at the invitation of the Manhattan-based Division 7 of the AOH. As guests of AOH Division 7 they were not allowed to carry their own banner, but ILGO reasoned that their visibility would be ensured as the first, and as yet, only African American Mayor of New York, David Dinkins, was marching in solidarity with them. The Division 7 contingent was isolated from the rest of the parade up Fifth Avenue, which was clear for blocks ahead and behind the group. The screams of hatred for ILGO accompanied their procession up the Avenue. People shouted 'AIDS! AIDS!' as if they could wish the disease on the group. The shouting hatred was echoed in placards: 'Die Faggots,' 'Beware the AIDS of March', 'We're going to get you, We know who you are' and prophetically: 'Dinkins – One term Mayor'. Beer cans were the items most frequently thrown. Keith Moore, a gay man from Donegal describes the experience of standing amongst the crowd of on-lookers at St Patrick's cathedral when ILGO arrived:

> They were shouting, 'Faggots. Queers. You're not Irish. Your parents must be English.' People were standing beside me shouting and screaming and then looking at me and smiling. They would've wanted to kill me if they'd known I was gay. (Maguire 2006, 17)

At the end of the parade the Mayor held a brief press conference where he was visibly shaken. He had in fact just walked a few blocks with ILGO, joining them before they came to St Patrick's Cathedral but he compared marching with ILGO to the 1960s civil rights marches in Alabama, he told TV reporters: 'It was like marching in Birmingham. I knew there would be deep emotions, but I did not anticipate the cowards in the crowd. There was far, far too much negative comment.' John Cardinal O'Connor was outspoken in his denunciation of ILGO's participation in the parade. His opposition was to prove to be the greatest barrier to ILGO's inclusion and his power and influence and dogged hard work was ultimately to prove to be supremely effective in barring the lesbians and gay men from the party on Fifth Avenue. As the parade reached St Patrick's Cathedral the Cardinal did not come down the steps to greet the mayor, who would traditionally have led the parade. Dinkins, in a Kelly-green jacket made his way up the steps to the Cardinal who coldly received his handshake (Maguire 2006, 19).

In the run up to the parade of the following year *The Irish Voice* newspaper, a weekly newspaper read by tens of thousands of the 'New Irish' immigrants to the USA, ran with an op-ed piece by ILGO who wanted to make clear that contrary to what the AOH were saying, ILGO had not been established specifically to disrupt the parade. Marching in the St Patrick's Day Parade was regarded by ILGO as:

... an appropriate cultural activity for the group to celebrate its Irish heritage ... We see this as a fight for the full participation of all Irish people in the annual celebration of our heritage. The Parade Committee shouldn't be trying to determine who is Irish enough to celebrate St Patrick's Day. (Maguire 2006, 79)

ILGO recognised that a fundamental ground on which their exclusion was sought was that they were not representative of Ireland or Irish identity, and that it was the AOH who were claiming the right to determine what that identity might be. The unusual virulence of AOH's homophobia, and the concomitant delegitimisation of LGBT Irish ethnicity through the courts, can only be understood via the peculiar pain of the exile, in her/his struggle for taking pride in the supposed purity and authenticity of the vaunted, idealised and lost object. This idealisation inevitably contains the unspoken shame of non-belonging, hence it is a queer attachment.

Enshrining homophobia in the legal status of the parades

The fallout from the 1991 parade also included a legal hearing by the Human Rights Commission of New York to determine if ILGO was being discriminated against by the AOH. An unsolicited amicus brief was filed on behalf of the AOH from the New York Civil Liberties Union (NYCLU).[22] They describe themselves as working 'also to extend rights to segments of our population that have traditionally been denied their rights, including Native Americans and other people of color; lesbians, gay men, bisexuals and transgendered people; women; mental-health patients; prisoners; people with disabilities; and the poor.'[23] The brief of the NYCLU, written by lawyer Norman Segal, supported ILGO's exclusion from the Parade. The grounds on which this exclusion was sought was by portraying ILGO as being, by definition, anti-Irish − antithetical to being Irish − not just the opposite but a violent self-defined enemy of the Irish:

> Could the organizers of the Israel Day Parade be compelled to accept German born neo-Nazis to its ranks? Would the Gay Pride Committee be required to accept heterosexual homophobes and skinheads to its contingency? Can the AOH exclude on the grounds of national origin an English born group which wishes to march with the banner 'England Stay In Ireland'? Must the AOH include non-Catholic groups who wish to express their anti-Papal beliefs? (Maguire 2006, 94)

The ACLU describes itself, without irony, as America's 'guardian of liberty'.

A major victory of the Civil Rights Movement in the USA was the ending of the segregated school system beloved in the Southern States, the legal argument accepted by the Supreme Court which led to desegregation was that separate systems could not be equal.[24] Remarkably the brief of the NYCLU argued that ILGO be awarded a permit for a separate parade on St Patrick's Day − separate but equal. NYCLU would go on to make this same argument against ILGO in other courts and the ACLU would eventually be on the

71

winning side in the American Supreme Court which successfully overturned lesbians' and gays' right to be included in the Boston St Patrick's Day Parade.[25] Perhaps it was the support of the African American Mayor for ILGO in the teeth of the opposition from the Cardinal that led Segal to the assumption that ILGO were not quite Irish. Certainly it was the unarticulated assumption by the NYCLU that an intrinsic expression of Irish identity was homophobia, therefore a proud claiming of homosexual identity could not be performed as an Irish identity, the two discourses were adversative. The battle as to who really was Irish continued in the hearings of the Human Rights Commission. Jacob Fuchsberg who was the legal representative of the parade organiser, Frank Beirne, questioned his client only to assert the genuine credentials of Beirne's Irish identity. Beirne, who had left Ireland in the 1950s did not demur when Fuchsberg said: 'Perhaps everybody will agree with me, you have a kind of a charming Gaelic accent. Now, I want to ask you did you get any education in the United States in English after you came here?' (Maguire 2006, 99). Beirne, who like the vast majority of Irish people spoke only English and who would have whatever knowledge he had of the Gaelic language as a subject learned in school, colluded with his attorney's attempt to establish him as the genuine Irish native.

The Human Rights Commission judgement, written by Judge Rosemary Maldonado, rejected the AOH argument that the parade was a private affair. Attended by hundreds of thousands of people and costing millions of dollars to the taxpayer, the Commission ruled that the parade was a public accommodation. The judgement also ruled that the AOH's claim that they had ILGO on a 'waiting-list' of would-be participants was a sham and that the AOH had discriminated against ILGO. Despite this, Judge Maldonado's final analysis was that as the parade was a celebration of Irish ethnicity, the AOH had a right to discriminate against ILGO, based on the tacit acceptance that an *a-priori* condition of being Irish was an active intolerance of homosexuals and therefore there could be no expression of an identity that was simultaneously Irish and homosexual. The effect being that the AOH's right to be homophobic because they are Irish outweighs Irish people's right to define themselves as gay.

When a three-judge panel at the New York City Commission on Human Rights overturned Moldonado's original recommendation concluding that given the secular nature of the annual Irish celebration on Fifth Avenue, that ILGO should march, the media echoed the argument of the NYCLU and the analogy between ILGO and the Ku Klux Klan was welded into a short-hand trope. New York Newsday asked: 'Would anyone force a civil rights group to let David Duke [of the KKK] march in a parade honoring Martin Luther King Jr.?' (Maguire 2006, 130). Such is the power and danger of analogies that they can so readily slip from being a comparison to being an aphorism that can be substituted for the truth. Though ILGO can hardly be said to resemble the KKK except for the fact that they are a largely white group, this idea that ILGO were a mimicry of the KKK came to characterise public and media commentary. For instance, the New York Times gave right-wing conservative Pat Buchanan the column inches to fulminate that: 'Martin Luther King Jr. could not have been compelled to let the Ku Klux Klansmen march with him' (Maguire 2006, 130), while the President of the New York County AOH, Timothy Hartnett, filed an affidavit to reverse the Human Rights Commission decision, exploiting the same rhetorical tactic: 'Constitutional protection is not reserved for zealots. It is not only the Nazis and the KKK and the gay groups that have the right to shape their message' (Maguire 2006, 133). In fact court rulings eventually decreed that ILGO was not allowed to march in 1992 but did grant permission to stage a protest at the sidelines. This was to be the last time that ILGO were allowed the right to protest. Since 1993 ILGO has been put in the position where organising any kind of protest on Fifth Avenue is interpreted as civil disobedience and results in mass arrests. The USA media took an extraordinary interest in the controversy and were largely very sympathetic to the Irish Lesbian and Gay Organization: 'mild mannered' became the epithet most associated with ILGO.[26] However, while expressing 'genuine sadness' for ILGO's plight most media commentators and print editorials were happy that ILGO had not been ordered into the 1992 parade by a court decision, as *The New York Times* put it that would have been the cure 'that looked worse than the disease'. Fifteen years after the first parade controversy the 2006 New York parade chairman, John Dunleavy, of the AOH, in an interview with *s*, again recycles the analogy of ILGO and the KKK in *The Irish Times*, declaring that an African American parade could hardly be expected to have the KKK march with them, therefore why should New York's St Patrick's Day Parade include ILGO? (*The Irish Times* 16 March, 2006, p. 6).

Stereotypying and class prejudice in representations of the Irish-American

Irish-Americans have had a long struggle to be included in the white and middle classes of the east coast USA.[27] The Irish in Boston and New York are still negotiating the negative portrayal of the Irishmen as a brawling, racist working class, with their leaders depicted as network of corrupt union officials, crooked cops, tribal politicians and elected officials, all ultimately ruled by creepy, secretive and reactionary Catholic clergy. This typology renders in its subjects a state of shame and disavowal, it may not be unrelated to the phenomenal aspirational success of the Irish-Americans in the twentieth century in terms of attaining conventional professional, and political achievements. Despite the collective triumph of the Irish in American society as an immigrant ethnic group, the spectre of its 'white trash', peasant stereotype still troubles. It is perhaps no surprise then that the American courts and media were most comfortable in maintaining the status quo representation of the Irish AOH as intrinsically bigoted and homophobic and ILGO, ironically, as having a racist potency, a representation expressed through the media associations of ILGO with the KKK. The ethnic Irish were again depicted as bigots: the comfort that New York liberals found in their own ethnic and heterosexist supremacy had once again found a self-confirming foil in the Irish.

The American courts and media seemed most comfortable in maintaining the representative status quo of the Irish/AOH as homophobic, plus ILGO, perversely as having a racist potency through the press routinely quoting figures associating ILGO with the KKK, reinforcing that conjunction. Irish ethnic pride in these cities is articulated within the context of these negative stereotypes, and within the realities of an active participation in trade unionism, policing, pub culture, white racism, class shame, Democratic party politics, and Catholicism.

Modernity, tolerance, and the new Irish Republic

A key touchstone for Irish identity in Boston and New York (cross-class) is founded on the status of being the descendents of exiled victims of the Famine and refugee survivors of the British Empire. Irish America takes seriously its role in keeping this memory alive. It is this backward looking aspect of Irish America and its concomitant fund-raising for the IRA that most embarrasses the Irish living in the Republic of Ireland. In the early 1990s, pre-economic boom Ireland was still a country desperate to 'modernise', to join Europe, to repress and to disavow kinship with Northern Irish Catholics, in a complex struggle to remove the influence of the Catholic church from state affairs. However the ideological aspiration of the country as enshrined in law and constitution (no contraceptives, abortion or divorce, homosexuality illegal, claiming the territorial right to the whole island) was patently at odds with the growing liberalisation of the country. In Ernest Gellner's formulation '[the nation's] self-image and its true nature are inversely related' (Gellner 1983, 125), and whereas modern Ireland's mixed idea of itself can seem to tolerate its 'remainder', (Hobsbawm 1990, 11) the 'narcissism of self-generation' (Bhabha 1990, 1) that is required of the marching Irish-American seemingly cannot. Based on their own experience then, Irish born people in Ireland did not necessarily believe that the pieties expressed by the Irish Americans were 'for real', and a temporal fissure can be seen to emerge across the geographic space, tinted with shame.

Irish gays politically and symbolically constructed themselves as totems of 'modernity', harbingers of Irish modernisation – although only in 1993 was the expression of a gay male sexual identity decriminalised in the Irish Republic. The Celtic Tiger has led to a broader national secularisation and concomitant social liberalisation, particularly in attitudes to sexuality. With the migration of the ILGO/AOH controversy to Ireland in 1992 a group of lesbians in Cork decided to apply to march in the St Patrick's Day Parade which was organised by the Chamber of Commerce in that city. Thirty-two lesbians marched as a contingent behind the banner that read 'Hello New York' and were awarded a prize as 'best new entry'. Kieran Murphy, of the Cork Chamber of Commerce, told *The Washington Post*, 'I guess you could say we are pretty progressive here in Cork'. The following year, lesbians and gay men (still criminalised until June of that year) paraded in Galway and Dublin, and the Dublin St Patrick's Day Parade expressly announced itself as an inclusive multi-cultural festival, an expression funded by the City Council that has been re-iterated since 1993. Signifying postmodernity through the spectacle of cultural diversity has been part of a recent global trend in the commodification of urban space. An entrepreneurial approach to tourism that demands cosmopolitan flavour has enabled what the *Economist* magazine has called a 'geography of cool' to be adopted by cities keen to promote themselves. Dereka Rushbrook (2002) has written about how queer spaces are used as *prima facie* indicators of this 'coolness' for entrepreneurial cities, and Cork – European city of culture 2005 – could be one example of Irish lesbian and gay claims for political reform acting in strategic alliance with a smart attempt to link the Celtic Tiger with the perceived inclusive demographics of a liberal, future-oriented European economy. Whilst this could herald a sharp move for reform, Wendy Brown's words of caution may yet come back to haunt: 'the marginalised reject the rubric of humanist inclusion and turn, at least in part, against its very premises' (1995, 53). The turned away and shamed all too often required to take the role of conscience.

The Irish state is in the midst of reforming laws that criminalise homosexuality, bringing in legal recognition for sexual equality against a fulminating background of the Catholic Church's long-term abuse of children in Ireland, and its continuing outrage at this liberalisation. The twists and turns of the sodomitical sublime continue to recycle: recently, Kildare-based poet Desmond Egan, winner of the American National Poetry Foundation Award, wrote a poem entitled 'Understanding God Too Quickly in Topeka'. It ridicules the Kansas Church that had been encouraging members to 'celebrate' deaths of US soldiers in Iraq, congregation members picket the funerals of soldiers killed in Iraq, to protest that these troops died to save the 'homosexual nations' of Afghanistan and Iraq. The Kansas Church is the home of the notorious and regrettably longstanding webpage godhatesfags.com. A journalist from the *Irish Independent*, Tom Lyons, interviewed the church's minister Preacher Fred Phelps, who had harsh words for Egan: 'The Bible says that the only thing worse than a fag is a fag enabler,' he claimed. 'He is pushing the fag agenda in his poems and he is on his way to hell.' Phelps continued: 'Ireland is a land of sodomite dandies since it joined the EU.'[28]

Notes

1   The historical research in this chapter was the work of Katherine O'Donnell of University College Dublin, who was a member of ILGO and participated in the protests and group arrests. This chapter could not have been written without her input, it is a truly collaborative effort and my own ideas in it are a direct result of our conversations.

2   For a discussion of how the Irish American construction of identity locates homosexuality as 'elsewhere' see Conrad (2004, 63–68).

3   Concepts of the folk pre-exist the modern industrial working class, and in some ways are contradistinct. However, in nationalisms 'the folk' is often deployed

as a rhetorical trope to indicate a pastoral or rural sense of collectivity and authenticity.

4 Something that mobile phone reception makes starkly clear. When standing just inside the borders of one country a text message welcoming the user to a neighbouring state is all too common, and one assumes unwelcome in many contested national boundaries.

5 Interestingly, the nation is for Bhabha what heterosexuality is for Butler – the site of loss and melancholia. See Butler, Judith (1990).

6 In practice this desire for integration is often manifest in compulsory assimilation, with cultural examinations being set as a condition of citizenship.

7 Though as Theodore Allen points out these notices have been '... more effective in discrediting anti-Irish bigotry than in reducing the entry of Irish workers into domestic service employment.' Allen, Theodore W. (1994, 139). See also Dooley, Brian (1998).

8 www.aoh.com, accessed 29 April 2006.

9 Curran, Gerry Saint Patrick's Day www.aoh.com, accessed 29 April, 2006.

10 www.aoh.com, accessed 29 April, 2006. See also Cronin, Mike and Adair, Daryl (2002, 37).

11 Undoubtedly there is a certain amount of Americo-centrism in this portrayal, as Lesbian and Gay Rights Movements were nascent simultaneously in a number of countries at the same time. There has been contestation over the cultural history of Stonewall being the defining moment of gay identity politics in the West, see for example Erebon, Didier (2004) and Myers, Joanne (2003).

12 For further clarification on the distinctions between pride, shame and guilt see Taylor (1985).

13 Readers may wish to know that the Italian national airline Alitalia refused to assist World Pride.

14 Luongo ends with a now poignant hope: 'As for changes in the Vatican's stance on gay and lesbian issues, the gay and lesbian rights movement may indeed have to wait until the next pope is elected.' (2002, 179).

15 Both men inspired a following, one from the political Left, the other from the Right. Edward Carpenter was a utopian socialist who espoused a return through nature to a true community of men. A reformist homosexual, he believed that nudity, 'the gospel of individual regeneration', would abolish discrimination. Carpenter was particularly interesting for his romanticisation of land and working-class labour, both factors that will reoccur in the lesbian nationalism of the 1970s.

16 This middle-class rebellion from middle-class life also has parallels with Sexual Liberation and the (white) student resistance cultures of the 1960s and 1970s.

17 See also Berlant, Lauren (1997) for a discussion of how the image of the nuclear heterosexual family is projected as an image of the United States' nation and repeatedly invoked in the public sphere as a straightforward articulation and as the object of attack.

18 Ibid. p. 207. Its assertiveness in taking up public space gave Queer Nation an incipient masculinity it was never able to shake.

19 For example the women who set up Camp Sister Spirit in Mississippi in the early

1990s as women's land based on lesbian feminist ideals. Camp Sister Spirit has been continuously harassed by locals since its inception.

20 See the archive of actions at www.actupny.org, accessed 29 April, 2006.

21 See the interview by Sarah Schulman with Emily Nahmansun in the ACT-UP Oral History Project: a collection of interviews with surviving members of the AIDS Coalition to Unleash Power, New York. www.actuporalhistory.org, accessed 29 April, 2006.

22 The NYCLU are a regional branch of the influential American Civil Liberties Union ACLU who have a membership of over 400,000 and who prosecute over 6,000 cases a year in the USA.

23 http://www.aclu.org/about/aboutmain.cfm, accessed 29 April, 2006.

24 The Civil Rights Movement ended school segregation, but rather saw a shift from formal to regulative and informal exclusions on the basis of race in the USA. However, recently in Nebraska school segregation seems to be back on the map. See further Dillon, Sam (2006).

25 Also in 1992 – United States District Court ILGO's lawsuit against the AOH and NYPD. The NYCLU again argued that there was a constitutional guarantee of any private organisation to define its message (the import being that AOH's right to be homophobic because they are Irish outweighs Irish people's right to define themselves as gay). For a discussion of homosexuality and American identity in the St Patrick's Day parades in Boston see: Stychin, Carl F. (1998, 21–51); Yalda, Christine A. (1999, 25–45).

26 ILGO came under increasing pressure leading up to the parade in 1993 to publically distance themselves from the 'bad gays' of ACT-UP, the carrot being inclusion in the parade. See Maguire 2006, 138–139.

27 See Ignatiev, Noel (1996) and Jacobson, Matthew Frye (1999).

28 Lyons, Tom (2006) Text available online at http://www.unison.ie/irish_independent/stories.php3?ca=9andsi=1604202andissue_id=13963

Chapter 3

Expulsion:
The Queer Turn of Shame

The Fall

Masaccio's 'Expulsion from the Garden of Eden' (1424–1428) is a fresco to be found high up on the left side of the altar wall in the Brancacci Chapel, Sta. Maria del Carmine, Florence. His figures of Adam and Eve stride away from Paradise stricken with grief. Exiled from God, the Angel above them banishes them, chasing and tormenting with his terrifying sword. Alone, they turn away from spiritual union, they are blinded by tears. The woman covers her genitals, the man covers his face, in shame. Their bodies, however, uphold a classical naked beauty, and Masaccio has chosen to paint the light source reflecting upon them as coming directly from the world, not from the dark gate of Eden behind. Although this painting has been interpreted as the epitome of universal suffering and exile – as Adam and Eve turned from God, so He has

Figure 3.1   Faces of Adam and Eve, from Masaccio, 'The Expulsion from the Garden of Eden' (1427), Brancacci Chapel, Florence (Source: Scala: London)

turned them away and turned from them – I find in it a strange, almost uncanny hopefulness, that intimations of beauty can be seen amongst such anguish.

In the Authorised King James Version of the Holy Bible, the Fall of Adam is described in Genesis chapter 3. Chapter 2 has ended with the creation of Eve from Adam's rib 'And they were both naked, the man and his wife, and were not ashamed' (v.25). They are now on probation; God has warned them not to disobey Him and eat the fruit of the forbidden tree, so the serpent tries to tempt Eve: 'For God doth know that in the day ye eat thereof, then your eyes shall be opened, and ye shall be as gods, knowing good and evil' (3 v.5). So of course they eat it, 'And the eyes of them both were opened, and they knew that they were naked' (v.7); they clothe themselves and try and hide. In theological terms, the Fall is densely symbolic, the consequences for disobeying are that humankind will experience firstly spiritual death, as sin separates us from God, and secondly physical death, which is the punishment for this original, mortal sin. The original traumatic separation, the expulsion from Eden, ensues. We need to notice that this is the foremost shame narrative of Western culture, and it has a number of elements: sexual desire disrupts the bond of spiritual connection; the ensuing rejection by God instigates Man's individuation; his self-consciousness occurs because of separation. This is the vacillation of subjection and individuation, and it is locked into the dynamics of shame, an affect that pulls towards and against its source. What we see in the Creation Myth is that the origin of human experience, individuation and desire resides in a locus of shame, and it is out of that shame, separation and loss that sexual differentiation occurs.

Shame is fundamental to the originary myth of Judeo-Christian societies, as Adam and Eve were shamefully expelled from Eden to discover their fallen humanity, in the world. Shame is also a powerfully spatial emotion, effecting displacement, and effacement in its subjects. It is important to understand this motion of shame in that it is characterised by a *fall* from a higher status to a perceived lower, adverse one. This descent is of prime concern as it involves a loss and a degradation, undeserved or not. There is a gravitational logic to shame that includes within it a compensating fantasy of reparation, of re-ascent to former glory. Minority groups are shamed in this way because they are compelled to feel inferior to a social ideal, the loss of the idea of possibility of which is experienced as humiliating, for example internalised homophobia causes us to suffer (rightly) in the belief that we are not absolute citizens, that the entitlement to participate in the fully human has been denied. Others are born into shame, such as women, knowing that they are incompletely human in the eyes of the law. In this chapter I will bring together two differently gendered examples of popular cultural material on shame, one lesbian and one gay, using first the English novel *The Well of Loneliness* (1928), and second the British television drama series from the late twentieth century *Queer as Folk*. I will explain how shame produces shamed subjectivities, however it is an aspect of the dynamism of shame that it also can produce a reactive, new self to form that has a liberatory energy.

The Well of Loneliness

Catharine Stimpson (1981) identified two types of lesbian novel, the 'dying fall' and the 'enabling escape', illustrating the former with a critical treatise on the most famous lesbian novel of all, *The Well of Loneliness* (1928). Stimpson evocatively described *The Well* as a narrative of damnation, and rereading *The Well* in the twenty-first century, it is impossible not to be struck by the novel's religiosity. Hall was known to be a committed Catholic, and Joanne Glasgow has explained this apparently irregular connection:

> ... the erasure of lesbian existence and the phallocentric ontology of sex that Catholicism presents actually provided... the necessary space and lack of intrusion or control that allowed Hall to find her place in a radically alien universe. She did not have to fight a church or a God to be a lesbian. (Glasgow 1990, 252)

There is a long discursive history linking sodomitical practices to Catholicism, and although most of the prosecutions for sodomy involved men, some indeed were women. Fears concerning the monstrous desires of nuns have circulated for centuries, producing a whole subgenre of sexually titillating manuscripts, for example the fictional 'Venus in the Cloister; or, the Nun in her Smock' (1683/1725), taking place as a dialogue between an older and younger nun that reproduces the typical hierarchy of sodomitical pairs, and allows the reader to relish the voyeuristic pleasures of its *faux ingénue*. Sister Angelica espies Sister Agnes (the 'Lamb') through the 'crevice' of her cell:

> Dost thou not know, my little fool, what it was I could see? Why I saw thee in an action, in which I will serve thee myself, if thou wilt, and in which my hand shall now perform that office which thine did just now so charitably to another part of thy body. This is that grand crime which I discovered, and which my Lady Abbess * of **** practises, as she says, in her most innocent diversions, which the Prioress does not reject, and which the Mistress of the *Novices* called *The Ecstatic Intromission*. (Barrin 1683, in McCormick 1997, 190)

Although Sister Agnes, when obliged to speak to her confessor claims she will 'die with shame', this comes across as coquettish rather than theological, awarding the reader another scene of erotic anticipation. Nun pornography is of course one aspect of the vast, diffuse eroticisation of Catholicism enjoyed throughout Western culture, from common parody to the literature of high moral seriousness. *The Well*, of course, to most, is of the latter. Hall deploys the figure of Stephen to great messianic effect in the novel. She reads Havelock Ellis' sexual inversion *through* the lens of Christian martyrdom and agency. The two are not exclusive: to exist in the communion of saints, we are impelled to die to the self, to be 'born again' as a new, shining creature, laundered by Christ. Held deep within the promise of cleansing is a reinvention of a self in which pain and degradation are eliminated, implying an unspoiled signifying space in which to conceive a new beginning, a new belonging. The parallel between religious conversion and contemporary lesbian identity politics is too tempting.

In my analysis I will explore a number of thematic conjunctions between shame and subjection, sexuality and class, starting with *The Well of Loneliness*, as Jane Rule once said 'either a bible or a horror story for any lesbian that reads at all'. (Rule 1975, reprinted in Doan and Prosser 2001, 78)

Stephen Gordon is the upper-class hero of *The Well of Loneliness*. Stephen's ancestral home is the country seat of the Gordons of Morton Hall. Morton is Eden, and to it comes Lady Anna, 'the archetype of the very perfect woman' (8), to marry Sir Philip the romantic knight, 'a dreamer and a lover' (8–9).[1] The novel starts by establishing this ideal and aristocratic gender conformity, expressed in the courtly heterosexuality of an echoed Creation Story. But the dream is corrupted by shame's antithesis, pride:

> It never seemed to cross his mind for a moment that Anna might very well give him a daughter; he saw her only as a mother of sons, nor could her warnings disturb him. He christened the unborn infant Stephen. (9)

We know from classical literature that heroes must *suffer* from pride, and that proverbially pride must come before a fall. Hence, Stephen is born on Christmas Eve, 'a narrow-hipped, wide-shouldered little tadpole of a baby' who yells with outrage, without ceasing, in the face of all those predetermining desires. Stephen remains 'cock of the roost' (11), as no other child is forthcoming. It is Lady Anna's discomfort with Stephen that mars her childhood. Hall describes with cutting detail the estrangement – 'that queer antagonism' between them:

> But her eyes would look cold... The hand would be making an effort to fondle, and Stephen would be conscious of that effort. Then looking up at the calm, lovely face, Stephen would be filled with a sudden contrition, with a sudden deep sense of her own shortcomings; she would long to blurt all this out to her mother, yet would stand there tongue-tied, saying nothing at all. (12)

It would seem to Anna that 'Stephen were in some way a caricature of Sir Philip; a blemished, unworthy, maimed reproduction' (13).

Stephen's sexual development is painstakingly described through a series of religious epiphanies. The first test on this prepubescent pilgrim's progress is the 'florid, full-lipped and full-bosomed' (15) maid, Collins. Stephen strokes Collins' sleeve, and:

> Collins picked up the hand and stared at it. 'Oh, my!' she exclaimed, 'what very dirty nails!' Whereupon their owner flushed painfully crimson and dashed upstairs to repair them. (15)

Stephen's desire is inflamed by this shame scenario – hands, of course, are powerful signifiers of lesbian desire. She indulges in heroic delusions of herself as William Tell, Nelson, and more pertinently 'to dream that in some queer way she was Jesus' (21). In an orgy of prayer, she beseeches 'I'd like to be awfully hurt for you, Collins, the way Jesus was hurt for sinners' (20), and she begs 'I would like to wash Collins in my blood' (21). This may read to us now as so much sado-masochistic schlock-fiction, but it is a juvenile foreshadowing of

Hall's brazen, blasphemous, future figuration of Stephen as Christ. Collins is dismissed, the shame of Stephen's attachment being displaced onto the maid. In this episode, as we have already observed of sodomitical desire, the working-class servant woman is blamed for stimulating Stephen's inappropriately sexual excitation, and so she is sent away. Anna and Stephen try to achieve rapprochement. Walking through the woods one day, with Stephen clinging to Anna with 'anxious fingers', this curiously sexual scene occurs:

> The scents of the meadows would move those two strangely – the queer, pungent smell from the hearts of dog-daisies; the buttercup smell, faintly green like the grass; and then meadow-sweet that grew close by the hedges. Sometimes Stephen must tug at her mother's sleeve sharply – intolerable to bear that thick fragrance alone!

> One day she had said: 'Stand still or you'll hurt it – it's all round us – it's a white smell, it reminds me of you!' And then she had flushed, and had glanced up quickly, rather frightened in case she should find Anna laughing. (33)

The extract clearly articulates Stephen's sexualised dissmell/disgust.[2] Indeed the colour white, and unpleasant smells recur in the novel to connote sexual disgust (this is repeated *ad nauseam* in the descriptions of Brockett's queenly white hands). In this extract, Stephen recognises the sexual potency of Anna as something disgusting and dangerous to her, which later she will recast as all femininity. As in Genesis, knowledge of sexual difference emerges here from sexual shame, and Stephen begins to experience consciousness of herself as a thing apart (from femininity).

There are several instances where Stephen gazes at her mother, and Anna responds by shaming her, averting her own gaze. Darwin, in *The Expression of Emotion in Man and Animals* (1872) described how shame is the most reflexive of emotions, as it is always concerned with the viewing of the self from the point of view of the other. Shame is marked on the body, facial blushing indicates its occurrence, and it produces a kind of internal theatre:

> The shame response is an act which reduces facial communication... By dropping his eyes, his eyelids, his head, and sometimes the whole upper part of his body, the individual calls a halt to looking at another person, particularly the other person's face, and to the other person's looking at him, particularly at his face. (Tomkins 1995, 134)

Shame is personified as a weapon that cleaves asunder, that renders and splits the self from itself, and all others. Tomkins enquires:

> Why are shame and pride such central motives? How can loss of face be more intolerable than loss of life? How can hanging the head in shame so mortify the spirit? In contrast to all other affects, shame is an experience of the self by the self. At that moment when the self feels ashamed, it is felt as a sickness within the self. Shame is the most reflexive of affects in that the phenomenological distinction between the subject and object is lost. Why is shame so close to the experienced self? It is because the self lives in the face, and within the face the self burns

brightest in the eyes. Shame turns the attention of the self and others away from other objects to this most visible residence of the self, increases its visibility, and thereby generates the torment of self-consciousness. (Tomkins 1995, 136)

Critically, this self-consciousness is an act of lonely individuation, perhaps of existential isolation, cast adrift from all relational options. No wonder then, that 'the soul' yearns for God, made manifest through Christ on the Cross, as an escape from that very material life of pain, grief, and mourning. God can become the one and only perfect mirror, a utopian projection of wholeness, a sublime.

Stephen is transubstantiating into this very imago, into the crucified Christ, the compensatory, transitional figure who brings us to God, by banishing sin. Next in Stephen's Stations of the Cross is tea with Roger, the child who is later to humiliate her sexually with Angela *Cross*by. Stephen is already internalising the paranoidal sensibility of someone who is by now living in a state of shame:

She would think that the children were whispering about her, whispering and laughing for no apparent reason. (49)

This is of course further intensified by dominant class tradition, and the Gordons (the 'Gay Gordons'?), epitomise the propertied classes' enthralment, at that time, with their own image of themselves as conforming to strictly conservative social norms. Roger is incredibly cruel, exposing Stephen's momentary masculinity on the hunting field as a foolish sham – 'What about a fat leg on each side of her horse like a monkey on a stick, and everybody laughing!' (55). Roger has the real (erect, not flaccid) penis, and Stephen knows this is the source of her envy. Hall returns Stephen to her father, the one with the honourable phallus, who imputes to Stephen the idealised masculinity she is to pursue through the rest of the novel. Existing in this wilderness of gender indeterminacy, this 'no-man's-land of sex' (89), Stephen is wandering through Eden, wearing the mantle of shame: 'I'm lost, where am I? Where am I? I'm nothing – yes I am, I'm Stephen – but that's being nothing ----' (79). She searches for herself:

Staring at her own reflection in the glass, Stephen would feel just a little uneasy: 'Am I queer looking or not?' she would wonder... Came a day when Stephen was suddenly outspoken: 'It's my face,' she announced, 'something's wrong with my face.'

'Nonsense!' exclaimed Anna, and her cheeks flushed a little, as though the girl's words had been an offence, then she turned away quickly to hide her expression. (82–3)

Read upon the face, shame segues into contagious blushing, as the parent turns away from her offensive child she ensures Stephen's spiritual torment.

Stephen's first adult affair is with the shallow, *nouveau riche* Angela Crossby.[3] Stephen, 'a little grotesque in her pitiful passion' (172), is reduced to begging for 'schoolgirlish', 'crude' and 'sterile' kisses. Angela's crushing question 'Could you marry me, Stephen?' (172) is delivered to inflict the keenest sexual humiliation. Ralph Crossby reinforces it by regularly enquiring of his wife 'How's your freak getting on?' (174), and remarking '...that sort of thing wants putting down at birth' (175). This episode contains unrelenting passages on Stephen's shame, including the introjection of wounding, imputing that, as her father prophesied, she is maimed by God. Stephen is relentless:

> With head bowed by her mortification of spirit, Stephen rode once more to The Grange. And from time to time as she rode she flushed deeply because of the shame of what she was doing. (180)

Her perception is not all it could be, however. Travelling to Bond Street she buys Angela a precious pearl (symbol of clitoral love), 'Angela's colouring demanded whiteness' (191), in *The Well* the colour of sexual dissmell. Stephen ignores the portents:

> People stared at the masculine-looking girl who seemed so intent upon feminine adornments. And someone, a man, laughed and nudged his companion: 'Look at that! What is it?'

> 'My God! What indeed?' (191)

That the ungendered Stephen is displaced as Angela's lover by Roger is somewhat of a narrative inevitability. Angela aspires to aristocratic legitimacy through marriage, but her actual claim is inauthentic (a sham/e), compared to Stephen's birthright. This phase of the novel is the most arduous and agonising for the reader, as Stephen sinks into total abasement and solitude. On finding the two together sneaking out of The Grange at dawn, Stephen 'laughed and she laughed like a creature demented – laughed and laughed until she must gasp for breath and spit blood from her tongue' (227). She returns to Morton and writes a letter pleading to Angela 'I'm some awful mistake – God's mistake' (229). The letter has an important narrative function, which is that it allows Stephen to be totally repudiated by her mother:

> 'And this thing that you are is a *sin against creation*. Above all is this thing a *sin against the father* who bred you, the father whom you dare to resemble. You dare to look like your father, and *your face is a living insult* to his memory... I can only thank God that your father died before he was asked to endure *this great shame*. As for you, I would rather see you dead at my feet than standing before me with this thing upon you – this unspeakable outrage that you call love' (233–4). [my italics]

Stephen is now lost, she is an abomination, a depraved, corrupted unnatural grotesque, an animal. The shaming of Stephen is intensified by religious condemnation; with the whole weight of purgatorial suffering behind it, Stephen is cast into spiritual and psychological annihilation. She is expulsed from Eden. She is severed.

Hall has layered Stephen's shame like a thick shroud which should have silenced and even suffocated the bravest apologist. It is lesbian folklore that Radclyffe Hall's life with Una Troubridge was a happy one. Perhaps we tell ourselves this in order to mitigate the pain of her fictional protagonist, to reassure that no-one could experience such abuse, *and survive*. To me, this is the most powerful passage of the book. This scenario of Stephen's shame is a distillation of common experiences of homophobic rejection, even today. In Silvan Tomkins' typology of the 'total affect-shame bind' (Tomkins 1995, 163), and in Helen Block Lewis' description of the 'feedback loops' of shame, Stephen is in a state of near-ontological shame – shame is her being, and hence also, her non-being (Lewis 1971). Hall's oppressive layering of shame has the effect of finally reducing Stephen to nothing. From here, she can only disconnect, in order to survive. Her psychological environment is toxic, and she is displaying the symptoms of those shame binds. Her only chance is an enforced renunciation of the love object; she must leave behind both the bad mother (Anna) and the good mother (Morton), mourn, and then become the fantasy parent herself.

Shame and the Self

Shame, in the nineteenth century, became a code word for homosexuality and queerness. Alfred Douglas, Oscar Wilde's lover, wrote a poem entitled 'In Praise of Shame':[4]

> Last night unto my bed bethought there came
> Our lady of strange dreams, and from an urn
> She poured live fire, so that mine eyes did burn
> At the sight of it. Anon the floating flame
> Took many shapes, and one cried: 'I am shame
> That walks with Love, I am most wise to turn
> Cold lips and limbs to fire; therefore discern
> And see my loveliness, and praise my name.'
>
> And afterwords, in radiant garments dressed
> With sound of flutes and laughing of glad lips,
> A pomp of all the passions passed along
> All the night through; till the white phantom ships
> Of dawn sailed in. Whereat I said this song,
> 'Of all sweet passions Shame is the loveliest'.

Published in 1894, the poem was interpreted at the time for its implications to the Oscar Wilde trials, as shame, in common nineteenth-century parlance, was understood as a synonym for homosexuality. Reading the poem for these meanings is not brazen, it is difficult to imagine what else these passions could be. Although *The Well*, written 30 years later, can be read nihilistically as a ritual of self-sacrifice, it is also possible to detect in the novel a discursive reinscription of the shame of homosexuality, and a refutation of Wilde's era. Shame, as we know from its pervasive presence in sadomasochism, is a script that can be rewritten (Sedgwick 1993). However shame is a pungently intransigent affect, one that requires re-experiencing in order to relinquish it. There are clues to this in *The Well*, namely the sheer quantity of references to shame imply not just an invocation, but also an attempt to batter the reader with Hall's intention to commute shame into selfhood. In the episode with Collins, and her prosaic 'housemaid's knee', there is enough affection in Hall's description to suggest that Stephen's fervent masochistic tendencies are to be viewed with amusement. But it is the adult Stephen that makes the agenda unmistakably clear; in the book's pivotal drawing-room scene, Stephen confronts Anna:

> She held up her hand [in benediction or malediction?], commanding silence; commanding that slow, quiet voice to cease speaking, and she said: 'As my father loved you, I loved. As a man loves a woman, that was how I loved – protectively, like my father. I wanted to give all I had in me to give. It made me feel terribly strong... and gentle. It was good, good, *good*... I don't know what I am; no one's ever told me that I'm different and yet I know that I'm different – that's why, I suppose, you've felt as you have done. And for that I forgive you, though whatever it is, it was you and my father who made this body – but what I will never forgive is your daring to try to make me ashamed of my love. I'm not ashamed of it, there's no shame in me.' (234–5)

This is the moment of individuation for Stephen, for her to loosen the shackles of the shame bind. This is also a moment of semiotic vulnerability, for in her state of indecipherability, she does not know who or what she is. In that instant though – and this is shame's potential – she is a floating sign, disattached; she is all possibility. This is related to the radical uncertainty of shame, which has a double effect – to sever the connection between self and other and to annihilate the individuated self. This means therefore that unshame (i.e. pride), is an act of connection with another, something which *The Well* now seeks to demonstrate.

Book Three ensues, in which Stephen, like any sensible invert in this position, goes off to become a writer, to *write* the self, in a kind of Barthesian utopic impulse. Book Four brings war, and of course, Mary. By this time, Stephen has acquired her conspicuous scar, the 'mark of Cain'. I have discussed elsewhere (Munt 1998), through rereading Judith Butler and Teresa de Lauretis, how this scar can be interpreted as the lesbian fetish, that which always stands for the lost object of the female body. This loss is tempting to relate to the oft melancholic, wounded quality of lesbian love.[5] Scars, of course, are also signs of *pride*, they are the morphology of bravery, of privileged membership. Stephen's scar is her 'war wound' in more ways than one; it is the visible transmutation of her shame into pride – which, like shame, is always conferred by others. We read that the 'little French doctor' assures her that 'Mademoiselle will carry an honourable scar as a mark of her courage' (338), and shortly after Mary makes her move:

'All my life I've been waiting for something.'

'What was it, my dear?' Stephen asked her gently.

And Mary answered: 'I've been waiting for you, and it's seemed such a dreadful long time, Stephen.'

The barely healed wound across Stephen's cheek flushed darkly... (339)

Stephen then goes through her own dark night of the soul, pacing with anxious responsibility over the corruption of her 'child' Mary. That flush is the sign that she has re-entered shame: 'Then Stephen must tell her the cruel truth, she must say: "I am one of those whom God marked on the forehead. Like Cain I am marked and blemished. If you come to me, Mary, the world will abhor you, will persecute you, will call you unclean." (347) The sexual tension between them is finally addressed by Mary, who cries for Stephen, and explains:

'Do you think I'm crying because of what you've told me? I'm crying because of your dear, scarred face... the misery on it... Can't you understand that all that I am belongs to you, Stephen?' (361)

The few lines end with the most famous phrase in lesbian literature, 'and that night they were not divided'. Crucially, it is Mary who transmutes Stephen's shame, thus reforming the bonds of shame as love. As E.M. Forster would have put it, 'only connect'.

Shame, separation, and gender melancholy

Mary, the mother of Christ, gives birth to Stephen. Mary is the good love object, the only appropriately classed match for Stephen, who enables her to determine her selfhood. Conversely, Stephen aspires to be the ideal parent to Mary. At first, she gazes with the unflinching 'eyes of a mother' (376), but Stephen's mothering begins to misfire. She fails to read her child properly, infantilising Mary ('Go and have your luncheon, there's a good child' (392)), rather than provoking her agency. Interestingly, Hall explains this in the language of shame behaviour – '*blinded* by love... she erred towards Mary' (395). Shame is a very specular affect; shame is caused not just by gaze aversion, but also by misrecognition. The gradual attrition of their intimacy is stimulated by Stephen's steady interpolation back into her psychic environment of shame, upon which Stephen unwittingly puns when she claims 'real life must be *faced* once again' (390). The social rejection of the couple by Lady Massey provokes this lament:

She seemed to be striving to obliterate, not only herself, but the whole hostile world through some strange and agonised merging with Mary. (430)

Obliteration is not unlike the shame allusion, 'losing face'; in the code of the book, this 'merging' is a sexual encounter, in which shame has now entered, as *unheimlich* – the strange, the uncanny. Their union is now a loss of self, an unhoming. Stephen begins to exist in the place of shame; she sinks into the Parisian bars populated with that 'miserable army' of foreigners who are 'covered by shame' (450). To their ilk Stephen exhibits a violent antipathy and revulsion:

> He bent forward, this youth, until his face was almost on a level with Stephen's – a grey, drug-marred face with a mouth that trembled incessantly.
> 'Ma sœur,' he whispered.
> For a moment she wanted to strike that face with her naked fist, to obliterate it. (451)

Suicide, poverty and death are the endings promised for those inverts without the cultural capital of class. Stephen's inculcation into this new familial bond results in her returning to shame-humiliation and contempt-disgust. There is also ambivalence in this queer attachment, a prevarication, symptomatic of the push-pull dynamic of shame. Shame is ambivalent because it is founded upon the interruption of love, where the self is dependent upon the acceptance of the other, and yet the inception of identity is predicated upon separation from the other, even the renunciation of the other. Shame is a kind of imperative to the emergent self. It is only once Stephen has allowed herself identification with *others like her*, of her class, that she is able to gain herself an identity as 'invert'. She has reformed the bond, through shame, and commuted shame into love (with all its attendant aggression).

> 'Stephen Gordon was dead; she had died last night... No, assuredly this was not Stephen Gordon.' (507–8)

Stephen dies to Mary, and is resurrected as Stephen the martyr, the messiah. This Mary, though, unlike in the scenes of the piéta in Catholic iconography, does not hold the dying Christ in her arms. There is a childlike rage in the narrator's cry which echoes Stephen's impossible ranking as Christ to Sir Philip's God, with Anna's annihilating curse 'I would rather see you dead', with a re-enactment of the childish fantasy 'I wish I were dead, then they'd be sorry!' – what a perverse meshing. Righteous epiphany returns though, the loss of Mary enabling Stephen to extend into her calling as a pious intercessor. Remembering that sin separates us from God, an inverted heavenly host cries out from the shadows for spiritual restitution. Sin, in *The Well*, is located in the bars of Sodom, but only in the sense that those 'sinned against' have fallen into despair. Stephen incarnates their voices, she becomes shame's witness:

> 'Acknowledge us, oh God, before the whole world. Give us also the right to our existence!' (510).

It is often extreme loneliness that compels us to seek God, who is so much a projection of our own needs. Perhaps, for the shamed soul, He becomes the only safe repository for those angry, crushing, inexorable emotions that we dare not impose on another. The hope of that transcendence is itself shaming, for at the same time as we are reaching, we are also falling.

It would seem irrefutable that this text has constituted readers and reading communities in shame and through shame, and in its own significant way, 'made' new inverts/butches/lesbians or queer readers of us all. *The Well* figures highly in coming-out stories (O'Rourke 1989).[6] As a narrative of sexual evolution it continues to resonate with plastic identifications for diverse predilections. Which sexual community 'owns' *The Well* is a redundant question, reflecting the kind of competitive behaviour which is compulsive to marginal, shame-based identities. The logic of *The Well of Loneliness* is precisely this: to show the reader that in order to transcend shame, we have first to enter it and know its deleterious effects. We can then explore its capacity for mutation. *The Well of Loneliness* is a refractory, blasphemous polemic, its theological audacity is remarkably scandalous; the novel manages to shift the Church's biblical interpretation of homosexuality as a sin 'against nature' (in Paul's Epistle to the Romans ch.1 v.6–7), to an interpretation of inversion as itself a God-given, natural state. It is an audacious legitimation that has contributed significantly to the emergent twentieth-century rhetoric of homosexual rights.

Shame/pride dichotomies in *Queer As Folk*

> When Zeus fashioned man he gave him certain inclinations, but he forgot about shame. Not knowing how to introduce her, he ordered her to enter through the rectum. Shame baulked at this and was highly indignant. Finally, she said to Zeus:
> 'All right! I'll go in, but on the condition that Eros doesn't in the same way; if he does, I will leave immediately.'
> Ever since then, all homosexuals are without shame.
> *This fable shows that those who are prey to love lose all shame.* [original italics] (Aesop, 1998, 91)

My second example, of gay shame, is from *Queer As Folk*, an eight-part drama scheduled in February, March, and April 1999, which was seen by British Channel 4's then Chief Executive, Michael Jackson, as a signature show that would help to develop the channel's distinctive place in British broadcasting for radical, experimental, minority television. The programme subsequently developed iconic value for Channel 4, appearing on much of their publicity material and mission statements, signifying the sincerity of their liberal credentials. The shorter, two-part sequel, *Queer As Folk 2*, screened in February 2000, similarly received significant pre-exposure in a number of media domains. This section will explore the encoding of gay identity within the series. *Queer As Folk* was a huge hit with gay, lesbian, and straight women audiences; it functioned as a popular crossover text carrying complex enjoyment to some diverse viewing positions.

Queer As Folk follows the lives of three white, young and good-looking gay men, Stuart and Vince, stalwarts of the Manchester gay scene, and Nathan a new initiate. Stuart Jones is described in Russell T. Davies' script as 'what's called an A-Gay' (Davies 1999: 12). His is the most intricate character of the three, the focus of much of the series' scopophilic curiosity, he is represented as a super-spunky vaguely Nietzschean hero. Vince Tyler is his long-suffering best friend, the progenitor of unrequited love for Stuart, and the conduit for the prescribed viewer's desire. Into this unconsummated marriage enters Nathan, a 15-year-old schoolboy virgin who has sex with Stuart early in the first episode, prompting predictable (and queerly punned) complaints from the conservative press:

- From Lynda Lee Potter in the *Daily Mail,* 'QUEER AS FOLK proves that we need censorship. Year by year, the boundaries of what is deemed permissible are *pushed wider and wider apart.* Certainly we shouldn't be at liberty to watch naked actors having relentless homosexual sex. Any nation which allows this without any voices raised in dissent is lacking in both wisdom and self-respect. It's *hell-bent* on destruction.' [my emphasis]
- From *The Times* newspaper, 'IF IT didn't have the novelty of gay sex, would anyone have made a fuss about it? Or got excited about it in a positive way, rather than because of its depiction of under-age man-boy sex? Its cynicism could just be a *stab* at chic metropolitan knowingness, but *you can imagine it leaving a nasty taste in many viewer's mouths.'* [my emphasis][7]

The British Broadcasting Standards Commission, a state quango which reports on taste and decency, received 138 complaints, primarily about the portrayal of homosexuality. The Independent Television Commission, the regulating body for the commercial channels, received more than 160, making *Queer As Folk* second only in notoriety to the screening of Martin Scorsese's film *The Last Temptation of Christ.* The finding of the BSC's Standards Committee was to uphold three of the complaints: that it was troubled by the explicit and graphic nature of the sexual encounter involving an underage character in episode one; that the use of the phrase 'fucking bastard cunts' in episode two had exceeded acceptable boundaries; finally, in episode three, the Commission took the view that the portrayal of troilism (three-way sex) had exceeded acceptable boundaries.

The association of the programme with contention, controversy, and danger was intrinsic to its marketing and critical reception. In part this can be read as an intentional backlash against the flat fawning flunkeys that epitomise most of the 'acceptable' mainstream gay media stereotypes. These images, which most closely resemble public information shots, render the traditional gay man as a lone, desexualised helpmeet, primarily structured to service heterosexual plots. Instead, as *The Guardian* newspaper's television reviewer observed, 'the drama emerges from the premise that, ultimately, gays give good hedonism... "The main characters are best described as three fuckabouts," says Russell T. Davies, the writer of the series... "The most important thing in their life is going out and looking for a shag. Everything else in their lives is incidental. This is an image of gay characters that is never seen on TV".' (Collins 1999). The rhetoric of *Queer As Folk*'s marketing has been suffused with boundary-breaking, outrageous, cutting-edge attitude; advertising the series has been imbued with provocation, it being the antidote to 'Middle England', the scourge of sexual repression. The style of the show is repeatedly, emphatically 'contemporary' – as *The Guardian* journalist Michael Collins puts it – 'pink is the new black'. The iconography of *Queer As Folk* is coded with sexual modishness, as the US magazine *The Advocate* put it: 'It's the television series that made the *Ellen* coming-out episode look like *Teletubbies*.' (Bodhan 1999, 65). Simon Hoggart, writing in the conservative British *Spectator* magazine, takes up this theme in his review of the second series:

> *Queer as Folk* (Channel 4) returned this week, set in a Manchester which looked like a cross between Rio and the Upper East Side. It seems to be a very different city from the one in which I used to work. On the *Guardian* in those days was an elderly sub-editor, a nice inoffensive fellow in a mud-green cardigan. Once he said wistfully, 'This gay liberation business, you know, it's all come a bit late for me.' It was one of the saddest things I've ever heard.

> Of course, if he's still alive, he'll have cottoned on to the fact that he's no more welcome at the party now. There are few quietly desperate men in mud-green cardies cruising Canal Street. Everyone there is young, gorgeous and spends their time pouting, eyeing each other's backsides... The only time we see a real city... is when we're with the straights, who live in squalor. (Hoggart 2000, 52)

His veiled nostalgia for pre-Stonewall clostetry concludes: 'we are invited to gawp through the window and envy them.' Certainly the show capitalises on gay identity as a desirable (no longer shamed) commodity. Stuart's opulent apartment, his job as an account executive in a chic Manchester PR company, his rich, have-it-all lifestyle is a powerful designer fantasy. But whereas in *Friends* capitalism is comfortably humane, in this British product there is a cleft of irony. As the three celebrate gay utopia (find 'em/fuck 'em/forget 'em), there is a commingling of darker effects and displacements that I would now like to explore.

Queer As Folk invokes a pre-AIDS sexual cornucopia ('cornucopia: from the late Latin 'horn of plenty' – a mythical horn able to provide whatever is desired').[8] It is nostalgic for an era when gay sexuality was discursively associated with excessive, abundant pleasure and unconstrained, guilt-free licentiousness. Like most behaviours, gay sexual excess carries a double valence: on the one hand it contains a radical challenge to heteronormative coercion; on the other hand it is a reaction *to* that same repressed conservatism, thus continuing, in effect, to be inscribed within it. This may cause us to ask: 'what is too much sex – what is excess?'; the question reflects that limits are always desired to be known. Sexual excess is of course pathologised as nymphomania, and it has been part of the sexological project to abject this behaviour as abnormal. The reverse discourse of gay pride has sought to rebut sexual repression in favour of expression, indeed, the articulation, in word and deed, of gay sexuality as proud, liberated, has been the pivot of a political movement much influenced by Freudo-Marxism. Theories of repression have been powerful analytical tools in the search to understand how passive, authoritarian values perpetuate and create neurotic citizens. Orgiastic potency holds the promise of spontaneous sociality; libidinal energy is key to individuation, to autonomous selfhood. Sexuality has been proposed, as Foucault so smartly observed, as the vehicle to liberate the self (Foucault 1979).

As Michael Collins' review observes '... in *Queer As Folk*, the thrills, the spills and the tiller of the plot rely entirely on the sexuality of the characters.' More precisely, the characters of Stuart, Vince and Nathan are read *through* their sexuality, which confers on them identity; it is a stolidly Foucauldian formulation. There is a shift in traditional televisual terms however: the characters are not represented so much as stuck in an *ur-moment* of becoming gay – they are busy *doing* gay – the confession/conversion moment has been superseded. The series begs the adjectival description 'unapologetic'. The viewer is so accustomed to televisual gayness being qualified by the presence of explanatory or justificatory frames that their lack leaves a gap, the logic of which signifies 'excess'. Its brash confidence is highlighted by the intergenerational sex between Stuart and Nathan in episode one which invokes the spectres of gay paedophilia and corruption. This was a brave move in the Britain of 1999, as the Houses of Parliament voted once again on the equalisation of the homosexual age of consent (the motion failed). *Queer As Folk* was castigated by the Independent Television Commission for failing to 'provide educational back-up to the series on subjects such as safe-sex, and young people and sexuality. Further episodes of the series should be 'enhanced by such responsible messages'. The regulator had 'concerns about the celebratory tone... [that] left little room for any questions to be raised in viewers' minds about the rights and wrongs of the illegal under-age relationship' (Gibson 1999). The ITC demanded that clearer 'warnings' should have been given by the broadcaster. Within an appropriately gay discursive frame however, Channel 4's utterance in response to the judgment was to declare itself 'extremely proud'.

There were actually voices of ambivalence among gay viewers that only appeared in the alternative press coverage; for example, Angela Mason comments in the British *Pink Paper* 'It certainly didn't challenge any stereotypes. All the gay men wanted to have non-stop sex and all the lesbians wanted to have babies. I thought the explicit sex scenes with a youthful 15 year old did smack of sensationalism' (*Pink Paper* 5th March 1999, 4). These reservations illustrate the power of stereotypes to maintain hegemonic meanings despite efforts to redefine and re-encrypt them by minority discourses. However, even dominant stereotypes can provide pleasure for subcultural viewers by offering reassurance and knowingness; the consumption of them can also sometimes be satiric, even if the intention is not. The criticism also relates to an older feminist school of media analysis that engages with debates about realism, and positive and negative images; *Queer As Folk* became a paradigm break in gay representation because it was the first popular gay-authored text that played knowingly and self-consciously with realism and heroic intention, thus inscribing multiple readings (critical and favourable), within its gay and lesbian audiences. The dilemma circulates around the issue of symbolic legitimacy: if gays are to be represented, what conscious and unconscious mechanisms will structure and determine that sign, and what will secure an amenable reading?

In Judith Butler's *Bodies That Matter* she describes the unholy zone of the 'constitutive outside', the space outside the subject which nevertheless founds the subject through repudiation. She writes of the threat of the abjected outside, in that it cannot be completely directed or foreclosed because of its existence apart from symbolic legitimacy and intelligibility, thus affording a potential for collective sorts of disidentifications and queer disattachments:

> I suggest that the contentious practices of 'queerness' might be understood not only as an example of citational politics, but as a specific reworking of abjection into political agency that might explain why 'citationality' has contemporary political promise. The public assertion of 'queerness' enacts performativity as citationality for the purposes of resignifying the abjection of homosexuality into defiance and legitimacy. I argue that this does not need to be a 'reverse-discourse' in which the defiant affirmation of queer dialectically reinstalls the version it seeks to overcome. Rather, this is the politicization of abjection in an effort to rewrite the history of the term, and to force it into a demanding resignification. (Butler 1993, 21)

Later, she asks 'how is it that the abjected come to make their claim through and against the discourses that have sought their repudiation?' – reminding us that the 'outside' only exists because of the context 'inside' (Butler 1993, 224). But then she offers one kind of specific illustration that is relevant to my purpose here:

> The term 'queer' has operated as one linguistic practice whose purpose has been the shaming of the subject it names or, rather, the producing of a subject *through* that shaming interpellation. 'Queer' derives its force precisely through the repeated invocation by which it has become linked to accusation, pathologization, insult. This is an invocation by which a social bond among homophobic communities is formed... (Butler 1993, 226)

I am not suggesting that this is the end of the story, that 'the magic of the name' suddenly imputes legitimacy and restores agency, but there is an 'I' and a 'we' emerging here, from the double-valenced interstices of shame. Shame has a contradictory latency: on the one hand it can reinforce shrinking conformity, and on the other hand it can proudly bring into being new and expansive grammars of gender. For example, it is not until near the end of *Queer As Folk 2* that Nathan claims the name of 'Queer!' as his insolent answer to his homophobic classroom teacher's reading of the student register. Instead of responding with the predicted antiphon 'Here!', Nathan's rhyming intervention invokes Queer Nation's call 'We're here! We're Queer! Get used to it!'. Performing and citing shame carries the same implicit risk that identity summons, always open to that critical reinscription, of discursive thievery. My argument here, then, is that the excessive and 'proud' sexuality defiantly cited and mobilised in *Queer As Folk* is premised on an uncomfortable historically discursive shame. This shame erupts in certain textual displacements elsewhere within the narrative, some knowingly deployed for reinscription, some shifted, rewritten, and substituted over other forms of social abjection. This is why the homophobic teacher at Nathan's school, and the unpredictably violent lodger who tries to marry Romey for illegal immigration purposes, are both *black*.[9]

Can there be a homosexual subject who is *not* formed from shame? In any personal trajectory, the growing consciousness of same-sex desire must, in a Western context, give rise to feelings of difference and exclusion. An identity may be imposed, or it may be wished for, but there is ultimately no choice, if one wants to live out erotic attachment to one's own gender, in experiencing some form of ascribed exclusion/prohibition. The presence of shame has been repressed in the discourse of homosexual rights in an unhelpful way, in order to gain greater agency, we must learn to revisit its ambivalent effects.

Both series of *Queer As Folk* challenge homophobia directly. Indeed, the heroic rebuttal of homophobia by its central characters, principally Stuart and Nathan, provides a strong fantasy of agency for the gay viewer. There are two rather grim instances of this though, firstly when Stuart encounters his friend Alexander's mother after she has just made Alexander sign away his inheritance rights on his father's deathbed. To the background music of a slide guitar, Stuart makes the sign of a pointed gun, pretends to shoot and says 'Maybe next time'. His vigilante/cowboy role persists when, after Vince fails to stop him firebombing Alexander's mother's car, Vince tells him 'Just tell them to fuck off' and Stuart replies: 'It's not enough any more... You're just straight Vince, you're a straight man who fucks men, that's all.' Stuart's gay identity is premised on a violent indestructability and inflated sense of heroic justice that is unfortunately enough often vented on women. As he viciously observes of Nathan's schoolfriend Donna 'Remember that little friend of his, that girl – he didn't need her in the end – clever boy'; Donna is also subjected to much shaming in episode seven in respect of her lack of chic (cultural capital), and crucially, she is another *black* character. The character overall is sympathetically represented in the narrative, so this shaming has the effect of exposing Stuart's – and by extension many gay men's – misogynistic pretentiousness toward poorly dressed, often working and underclass women.

Let us examine more carefully one of the prime shame scenarios of the narrative, which centres on Stuart. At the beginning of *Queer As Folk 2*, Stuart's nephews are dropped off at the apartment by his single-parent sister. The eldest, Thomas, aged eight, disappears to play on the computer, whilst Stuart and the youngest boy play a game of Scalextrix. Stuart discovers that Thomas has logged onto 'Big Cock City'. After being told off by his uncle, the boy shouts at him 'You're a poof, and nana and grandad, they don't want to know. £25 or I'm telling!'. Stuart's response to this clumsy blackmail attempt is to pick up Thomas, carry him to the toilet, put his head down it and flush. Thomas then yells at him 'You're gonna pay, you're so gonna pay. I want £50 a week, every week. I'm telling Dad... cos he wants access... You touched me just then, you bloody touched me, you pervert!' Toilets, of course, are the principal shame spaces of Western culture, they are also traditionally associated with morality, punishment in the form of ritual chastisement, and sexual anxiety/indecipherability (Munt 1998). The significance of this scene is that it presages the soliloquy to come: shortly afterwards, Stuart and his parents are helping his sister move into her new house. Thomas starts to drop heavy hints concerning men coming round to Stuart's apartment. His parents aren't biting, but Stuart comprehends the implications immediately:

Stuart's Dad, Clive Jones: 'Stuart, come and give me a hand with these shelves, will you?'

Stuart: 'I can't.'

Dad: 'Course you can, I just need a hand, come on.'

Stuart: 'We don't do hammers, and nails or saws, we do joints and screws but that's different.'

Stuart's Mother, Margaret Jones: 'Who does?'

Stuart: 'Queers [pause] ... because I'm queer, I'm gay, I'm homosexual, I'm a poof, I'm a pufftah, I'm a ponce, I'm a bumboy, batty boy, backside artist, bugger. I'm bent, I am that arse bandit. I lift those shirts. I'm a faggot arsed fudge-packing shit-stabbing uphill gardener. I dine at the downstairs restaurant. I dance at the other end of the ballroom. I'm Moses and the parting of the red cheeks. I fuck and am fucked. I suck and am sucked. I rim them and wank them and every single man's had the fucking time of his life. And I'm not a pervert. If there's one twisted bastard in this family it's this little blackmailer here. So congratulations Thomas I've just officially outed you.'

This extraordinary coming-out speech is the most powerful shame rebuttal I have ever encountered. Brilliantly delivered by the actor Aidan Gillen with Shakespearean ironic levity, it is filmed in close-up on Stuart's face. It is an invocation to shame, a citation of shame that through its dramatic, confrontational momentum exceeds the confessional moment and becomes a statement of being. The shame is shifted off sexual perversion and onto the perpetrator. Agency is snatched back by Stuart through a discursive inversion causing the child Thomas himself to be shamed – he is the one that averts his eyes, he is the one who is subsequently sent outside, into the garden, by Stuart's mother. In a *coup de grâce*, Stuart adds one more radical twist: '... Oh, and one more thing – did I mention I've got a baby?' Stuart's parent's reaction to this outburst is interesting: his father's response to it is to go and see him in order to ask him not to turn up to a family function at which Stuart's nephews will be present, commenting 'I've told her... [Stuart's Mother] It just happens – some boys grow up to be... [pause] bastards.' Bastards being, presumably, synonymous with queers.

On the other hand, Margaret Jones then seeks out Hazel Tyler, Vince's mother, for sisterly reassurance. Nathan's mother is also present, also trying to come to terms with her son's new status. In a touching scene around the kitchen table Hazel Tyler advises Margaret Jones: 'Try not to think about the arse thing and you'll be fine.' To which Janice Maloney adds: 'Well... I'm not trying it again, the arse thing.' Hazel replies to this 'I quite like it myself, you can read a book, at the same time.' And Margaret adds a coda: 'Well don't look at me, it's a foreign language', invoking, of course, the sodomitical association of buggery with racial otherness. Three heterosexual women discussing experiences of anal sex on broadcast television drama – *Queer As Folk* lives up to its reputation as boundary breaking. Anality itself is classically related to shame, an alliance that is not necessarily unhappy. Take for example, Aesop's fable 'Zeus and Shame' that I cite at the beginning of this section: we are reminded that in classical Western culture shame is discursively linked to women, and to be 'passively' receptive in anal sex is associated with femininity and non-citizenship. The conjunction of shame with femininity is closely allied to the demasculinisation of gay men. Here we note that shame is a woman, yet that she is depicted in the fable as a woman with agency. Shame is connected to love, and in this context, significantly, heterosexual love. In Aesop's fable shame has destabilising properties that are not necessarily negative; the tone of it is one of humourous *possibility*. Similarly, the conversation in *Queer As Folk* manages to evoke symbolic complexity, whilst remaining humourous, normalising, and domestic.

Most of the action in *Queer As Folk* takes place in Manchester's post-industrial, cosmopolitan landscape of gentrified fetishism. Manchester city is marketed internationally as a gay mecca; gay tourism, endorsed by a historically Left-wing council, created an estimated wealth of £45 million per annum by the end of the twentieth century.[10] Gayness has been formulaically rebranded as attractive and aspirational, it has acquired cultural and symbolic capital, it has, through commodification, become *respectable* (Skeggs 1997). The perfect gay aesthetic is embodied by Stuart whose rendition of style, taste and distinction is contrasted to Vince's anorak 'sad-bastard' habits, exemplified by his archive of science-fiction videos, his petty-bourgeois aspirations to becoming Deputy Manager of Harlo's supermarket, and his fearful and unsuccessful attempts at getting laid. Here, sexual capital is linked to economic capital: whereas Vince is often seen working in the series, Stuart's labour is largely invisible; the only scenes of Stuart at work are when he is organising sex, in one way or another, notably in one scene shagging a client in the toilets. In this way, Stuart's production *is* his gay sexuality. It is 'new gayness' that makes Stuart rich, not productive labour. Thus, gay sexuality is powerfully resignified, but the cost of this resignification is to distinguish new forms of exclusion, around class, and money. His secretarial assistant, Sandra Docherty – a straight woman – actually does most of his ostensible work. Stuart is nouveau riche, not middle class, this is apparent from the interior of his loft apartment in which everything is new, the ambience highly 'designed'.[11] One radical aspect of the coding of Stuart is that it is his gayness that gives him class capital, through gay style. This is in contrast to the frequent references in the series to 'scallies', 'hen nights', 'Adidas suits' – all referents to working-class culture, all undesired in Canal Street's clubs. Vince's family often pose as the counterpoint to Stuart's effortless affluence; the stage directions in Davies' script describes Hazel Tyler's house as 'one of those faceless modern terraces along Brunswick Street... it's stacked with boxes of Christmas crackers' (Davies 1999, 58). The phrase is doubly apt: firstly because of the reading of shame as 'loss of face', and secondly because Hazel and Bernard's homeworking is obsolete, labour intensive, and economically unrewarding – they are 'crackers' to do it.[12] Stuart's casual 'shags' are almost always coded as working class, epitomised by the presumably eponymous 'Goodfuk', the 'dead hard' pick-up from the I.R.C. room (Internet Relay Chat) in episode two. We are reminded of the historical term for working-class sex as 'rough *trade*'. Agentic working-class sensibility is designed and organised out of the gay space of Canal Street, its presence is permitted only as objectified pleasure, as a temporary, truncated target of sexual consumption. In the gay marketplace, working-class *bodies*, not selves, are desired; the latter are excluded, banished and abjected to another space, where they languish with hostile intent.

The final scene of *Queer As Folk 2* is structured as science fictional, cleverly adopting Vince's *Dr Who* fantasies, and blending with them Stuart's codings as a cowboy vigilante. This cross-generic narrative shift away from realism indicates how the two men's desires might be harmonising, but this is achievable only within a fantasy space. Stuart's jeep – a central prop of his driving energy – accelerates down Canal Street, spins in a glow of light, and is surreally transported to a deserted Arizona highway ('go West, young man'), just like the Tardis.[13] To a banjo soundtrack, the two travellers pull into a gas station, and walk across the dusttrack together, holding hands. A severely stereotyped 'White Trash' man passes them, and slurs:[14]

White Trash Man [WTM] [strong regional accent]: Faggots.
Vince: Excuse me – what did you say?
WTM: You heard me.
Vince: 'Coz I'd better warn you, my friend here, he's got a hell of a temper, once he's off, so – what did you say?
WTM: I said... [spits on the ground] Faggots.
Vince [to Stuart]: What do you think?
Stuart: Blood. [pulls out a revolver from his pants and points it at WTM. CU of WTM looking horrified. Stuart unlocks safety guard. WTM backs away in terror.]
Vince [to WTM]: Hold on a tick. Bit deaf mate. Too many nights out clubbing. One more time. What did you say?
WTM: Nutthin'.
Vince: And one more word, beginning with 's'.
WTM: Sorry. [Stuart lowers gun, WTM runs off]
Vince: Maybe next time.
Stuart: Fuck off. [last line]

All codings in the narrative diegesis are upbeat at this point, allowing for the humiliation of this homophobic man to be read as a delightfully heroic gesture. The moment is intrinsically problematic, however. This is the third time that the trigger-happy Stuart has invoked guns as an answer to confrontation; it may not be entirely co-incidental that the actor playing Stuart is *Irish* – not a felicitous casting within the context of modern British/Irish politics, I would suggest. Whilst this might have sent a positive signal to the huge and usually pathologised Irish working-class community in Manchester, the racial structuring of the narrative vitiates this message. The casting can be read another way however: that the ur-Gay of *Queer As Folk* is an Irish Catholic is testimony to the cultural history of the sodomite. Stuart's simple allusion to 'Blood', though, echoes his earlier use of the term in which blood stands for a hard-on, for sexual excitement, which here is linked to violent revenge fantasies, and possibly, ethnicity. What is occurring here is a shame logic, in a primary instance of substitution, 'gay shame' has become 'class shame', and perhaps even 'race shame'.

Figure 3.2   Stuart (left) and Vince from 'Queer as Folk'

It is a cliché of white middle-class gay (and lesbian) existence that homophobia is the preserve of non-white and working-class cultures (Moran 2000). Violence is transposed onto these marginal spaces in a discursive shift that empties middle-class life of any accountability. It is my argument here that the violence done to Stuart (here functioning representationally for any gay man) – the internal violence of homophobia and shame – is reproduced externally and redirected – misfired – against structural affinities, misperceived as enemies. Dominant discourse has long conflated non-normative subjectivities with criminality and threat; indeed, there is a kind of discursive contagion operating in which shame is infectiously displaced. Shame is contagious, we are ashamed of our shame, and when those around us catch it, they flush and blush in awkward sympathy; vacillating, they turn their gaze upon another. In this melancholic state of loss, such is the desire to be homed, to salve the *unheimlich*, we reach a state of uncomfortable self-knowledge which is conscious of our differentiation. To be within the law, the ordering/signifying system, to have a place, we must be put into place, by shame. Shame, in this schemata, functions as a kind of originary myth, as Francis Broucek has described it, a 'keystone effect', which can substantiate a recursive moment of recognition, of our place in the world – with 'others' – something to be embraced or repudiated, depending on the quality of awareness that that shame has provoked (Broucek 1989, 369). The principle mechanism I'm suggesting remains consistent, which is that shame is based upon separation and loss. However, (like pride), it can also provide a subjectivity, and possibly a self, and therefore to illuminate this conjunction is to better understand shame and its unstable connection to other repudiations, or potential alliances.

In Butler's *The Psychic Life of Power* she describes this paradoxical dynamic within the production of subjectivity:

> ... power that at first appears as external, pressed upon the subject, pressing the subject into subordination, assumes a psychic form that constitutes the subject's self-identity.

> The form this power takes is relentlessly marked by a figure of turning, a turning back upon oneself or even. a turning *on* oneself... the turn appears to function as a tropological inauguration of the subject, a founding moment whose ontological status remains permanently uncertain. (Butler 1997, 34)

She comments upon the psychoanalytic tenet, that 'no subject emerges without a passionate attachment to those on whom he or she is fundamentally dependent', an attachment that cannot be clearly 'seen', that has to be at least in part denied, for the subject to properly form (Butler 1997, 7). How evocative is this turning, this *volte-face*, of the dynamics of shame: shame is not just laid upon the subject, delivered by a gaze which is then deflected ('cutting'), it sets in motion a double turn, it activates its recipient to turn also, to turn away from the source of shame, in doing so to be *lost from view*, and thus, to inaugurate a condition of uncertain possibility. Needfully, we must remain modest about the extent of this possibility; Butler cautions: 'Painful, dynamic, and promising, this dynamic between the already-there and the yet-to-come is a crossroads that rejoins every step by which it is traversed, a reiterated ambivalence at the heart of agency' (Butler 1997, 18). That inchoate figure turning at the crossroads, turning away from us, winding into itself, twisting against itself, doubling back, is a tormented one. Because its desires always outrun their fulfilment, it is also ashamed. Yet we are reminded that shame is predicated on the yearning for reconnection, for love, and that those in the most chronic state of shame will be amongst the most deeply loving, because they will not relinquish hope of restitution.[13] (As Stuart elatedly extols Canal Street 'This stupid little street. It's the middle of the world. Coz on a street like this every single night anyone can meet anyone and every single night someone meets someone.') The very last shot of *Queer As Folk* is fundamentally utopian for this reason: when Stuart and Vince drive into the sunset, the moment's indecipherability allows for all endings to be satisfied in love. Remembering that shame is an embodied emotion which primarily resides in the face, centred on the composition of the gaze, it is as though acknowledging the injurious effects of shame can free us to grasp the transformative moment and *look them right back in the eye*. Thus 'turning' is not so much 'to be turned' as the more agentic *to* turn, to rotate the axis of determination/signification in such a way as to deviate the terms.

But first we also have to mitigate the traumatic consequences of separation. In Freud's essay 'Mourning and Melancholia' he differentiates between two processes: firstly mourning, which is the regular reaction to the loss of a loved person, and secondly melancholia, which is a more extreme and pathological experience of loss in which the object-loss is in some way unconscious. Mourning has its own pace, during which the subject loses all interest in reality, and turns inward to a piecemeal processing of that loss, finding his/her own theatre for that sequence of reparation. In melancholia, the patient can be aware of *whom* he has lost but not *what* he has lost in him' (Freud 1991, 254). In this loss, it makes sense for the subject to compensate by searching out fantasies of ego-replacement, and, in looking to fiction, the subject can be said to be appropriating the vicarious satisfaction of the heroic figure *par excellence*. In his essay 'Creative Writers and Day-dreaming', Freud analysed popular novels whose indestructible heroes he compared to 'his majesty the ego' (Freud 1973, 142). The unconscious, like novels, is peopled by characters onto whom we project fierce identifications. Mechanisms of projection mark the melancholic condition: the melancholic becomes pulled into obsessional and narcissistic behaviour in which he acts out various violent and murderous impulses against himself and others that are expressions of hate and anger for the loved object he has lost. He is consumed by revenge fantasies – he projects his inner violence onto others. The melancholia exhibited in the one who mourns can also transmute into mania, into triumphalism, elation, and a delight in movement and action. In Freud's analysis of melancholia we can see the considerable potential for readerly cathexis contained in the figure of Stuart Jones. His melancholy, which is interspersed with manic episodes, carries the sign of unspoken grief. One of the most complex moments in the text is the following interchange between Stuart and Hazel, Vince's mother:

[Background music: Patsy Cline singing *Crazy for Loving You*.]

Hazel: You'd've shagged a letterbox... but not him... are you saying my son's ugly?'

Stuart: You've got to fancy him... never mind love... love can fuck off... if you fancy him, there's blood, there's a hard on... if you just... if you just love him... [pause] [kisses Hazel] No blood.

[Hazel puts her hand on Stuart's crotch]

Hazel: Just checking.

[Stuart walks across to Vince and takes his hand. They dance, slow, loving, looking into each other's eyes.]

[Background music: 'Spanish Eyes' (camp). Stuart asks Vince to stay the night at the hotel. Stuart is seductive, for the first time acting like a lover; they walk upstairs holding hands. In the room they undress, mirroring each other]

Vince: Know what Phil used to say ... you're saving me for your old age.

Stuart: So the day I shag you... I'm old.

Vince: Better get some sleep – long day tomorrow.

[Scene ends with Vince lying awake – in a teeshirt, Stuart is fast asleep, naked. Another failed consummation.]

The promise of sex between Stuart and Vince constitutes the narrative drive, yet it is ultimately unrepresented, perhaps unrepresentable. Stuart splits off feelings of tenderness and respect from his sexual objects, instead he directs such emotions towards his 'real' lover, Vince, with whom sex is prohibited, or to be mediated/substituted through a third party. Just like in Aesop's Fable, Eros and Shame appear irreconcilable. To fuck Vince would be to become 'old', Stuart grieves for something, but it is unclear what (it is an unconscious loss, thus difficult to retrieve). Perhaps it is for the lost connections his shame substitution has caused, through that diverted shame which has produced his partial individuation, at the cost of the enemies his psyche must fashion. Stuart's displacement is of the one who has turned, has been severed from social belonging, but has not yet learned to turn back and reconnect. He has a *misrecognition*.

William Meissner has argued that within the process of individuation, the child defines itself through opposition (Meissner 1978). The need for an enemy, therefore, may be a necessary step towards a conception of self as a separate identity, indeed grief itself can become the enemy (and who hasn't, in grief, felt persecuted by it?). Certainly the anger produced by grief enables the subject to force a separation which ultimately, when it has played itself out, enables the subject to recover a coherent sense of selfhood. If mourning is to be successful, the anger will be replaced by a true acknowledgement of loss including a wish for reparation. The hero can embody these functions, he is a wish fulfilment fantasy of omnipotence and triumph – a hallucination, if you will. A narrative can represent a displaced arena in which we inhabit the split off characters of our inner life, and it is precisely because of this displacement that we can allow those disturbing phantoms to exist. Narratives become the performative force of grief, they represent the moment of death and they revise it, replay it, until the memory becomes de-cathected. They bring the two temporalities together – the original event, and our grieving present, and they can *move* us to restitution, through the passages of time that reading, and grief, requires. The logic is precisely this: to show the reader that in order to transcend shame, we have first to enter it and know its deletrious effects. Shame's capacity for mutation can be beheld through psychic rotations of incorporation and introjection. Its twists and turns can propel intense violence – witness, for example, the spate of school shootings in the USA in which teenagers, extant as they are in a phase of unstable subjectivity, developmentally caught between individuation and dependency, have murdered those perceived to have shamed them. Shame can spur brutal volatility. In order to properly understand shame's choreography then, we need to reanimate Butler's figure of the turn, via a reading of Newtonian motion:

> If one body A is acting on another B, the mutual action between them is a force. If we are considering only one of the bodies we say that this force is an *external* one, or an *impressed* force; if we are considering both bodies we say that the action is an *internal* force. When the bodies are in contact, their mutual action is called a *pressure* or a *tension*, when they are at a distance, the action is called a *repulsion* or *attraction* (e.g. the action between two electrified bodies). (Newton 1949, 57) [emphasis in original]

The mechanics of shame are rotational: the body that is shamed is compelled to change by the action of impressional force, it is metaphorically slapped. In applying Isaac Newton's most famous claim, that 'to every action there is always an equal and contrary reaction' (Newton 1949, 58) we note that this turning has a duration, during which the energy is internalised. To deploy this analogy within the sphere of discursive signification the moment is productive, in the sense of Foucauldian fields of force. The motion sustained is unstable and unpredictable, the body must vacillate between internal, psychic states of repulsion and attraction, in which the pressure or tension intensifies and reproduces its own demanding effects. Shame has momentum, but its effects on the subject cannot be foreclosed, it is not ontologically secure.

Shame puts us in our place, but the spaces of subjectivity are not wholly fixed or predetermined; shame's loss carries uncertainty, but it also presages a desire for reconnection. It is this desire for re-attachment that has the precarious potential for violence, or love. As we know from Butler's reading of Levinas on the face, the face is the vehicle for the self, an embodied metaphor for what it is to be human (2004). The face turned away – or in shame's case *both* faces turned away (that of the shamer and the shamed) – involves some loss of representability, that 'loss of face' invokes a risk of dehumanisation. This is the volatility of shame, that it allows the subject to momentarily step outside linguistic determinability; it can then fall into abjection, or it can unfix itself and rise, in radical unpredictability. This turn is Catholic in the sense of its historical associations with sodomitical threat, however it is also catholic in the sense that its potential is all-embracing. *The Well of Loneliness* and *Queer As Folk* are remarkable, popular texts that although released 70 years apart, broke boundaries for the public representation of queer desires in unpredictable ways. They forged ambivalent consequences for the reformulation of gay identity after shame, by making shame their principal momentum. These texts reinscript shame in order to teach us something about its plasticity, its peculiar, latent potential, and in doing so they open up a queer tapestry of shame to show us intricate threads of possibility for reattachment.

Notes

1　Hall, Radclyffe (1928) *The Well of Loneliness* (reprinted London: Corgi/Jonathan Cape 1968). All parenthetical page citations refer to this edition.

2　In Silvan Tomkins' work, dissmell and disgust are 'drive auxiliary responses' that have evolved to protect humans from ingesting harmful foods; they often manifest as contempt and are associated, like shame, with rejection. He argues that when shame shifts the self into hopeless despair, then contempt emerges as a defense. These feelings are often projected onto parents, so much so that one eventually renounces one's own love object and longs to become one's own fantasy parent. Tomkins, Silvan (1995) 'SHAME-HUMILIATION CONTEMPT-DISGUST' reprinted in Sedgwick, Eve Kosofsky and Frank, Adam (eds) (1995) 133–178.

3   The *nouveau riche* are universally reviled in both classic and popular culture as 'fake', the contempt reserved for them perhaps reminding us of the shameful aggrandisement of the rich.

4   *In Praise of Shame* Alfred, Lord Douglas 1894. See further Cohen (1994).

5   For a longer discussion of butch shame see Munt (1998) 200–209.

6   Despite the fact that O'Rourke's reader response survey is nearly 20 years old, the novel's notoriety is still strong and it remains a crossover text for those on the cusp of a queer life.

7   Both quotations are taken from *The Independent on Sunday* web page, accessed 28 February 1999: 'Debate: Queer as Folk has shocked TV audiences with its explicit portrayal of gay men. Great says James Sherwood, finally there's a TV show telling it like it is. Not so says Chas Newkey-Burden, *QAF* is a dangerous parody of gay life.' (p. 1169).

8   *New Shorter Oxford English Dictionary* (1993 edition). In some respects this description does embody Stuart Jones.

9   Romey is the lesbian mother of Alfred, Stuart's baby. The paradigm I am developing here, that the shame displacement operates racially/ethnically, is also mirrored in the negative representations of lesbians in the series.

10   Figure taken from the ESRC Sexuality and Violence Project day conference, University of Manchester 24th March 2000. It is important to remember that Manchester's rebranding and commodification as a gay mecca is not necessarily welcomed by local lesbians and gays themselves, who remain healthily cynical of international marketing. There is a distinction to be made between the representational and the experiential levels of the gay village, one which the project sought to explore. See also Binnie (2004).

11   In rewriting the nouveau riche stereotype it becomes a complex sign in which class fakery is queerly allied to the sodomitical sublime.

12   The term 'cracker' is of course offensive North American slang for poor and supposedly ignorant white working-class people.

13   Russell T. Davies went on to become Head Writer and Executive Producer of the new versions of the classic BBC series of *Dr Who*, starting in 2005 and ongoing. *Dr Who* currently has a gently queer subtext that can be read as gay positive.

14   'White Trash', like 'cracker', is a term used in the USA for underclass whites, commonly construing them as an ethnic, criminal class that are fat, dirty, slovenly, and hostile.

15   Nathanson (1997) credits this observation to a personal communication with Silvan Tompkins.

Chapter 4

Queering the Pitch: Contagious Acts of Shame in Organisations

This chapter investigates selected unpalatable thoughts on shame, envy and hate in organisations and institutional cultures. The first part of the chapter assesses the working environment of most of the readers of this book – the university. Then I open this out to describe the more generic white collar setting of *The Office*, through a reading of the British comedy series of that name. What is intended in these readings is to bring to the fore – to expose – the psychic contagion that can taint these organisations, and hence spoil the lives that embody them. Shamed cultures *infect* membership, drawing down practices of shame, and a glut of other emotions allied to shame; these shame patterns are spiralled, in the sense that they have the effect of magnetising other negative emotions and intensifying them. I illustrate how shame becomes institutionalised within groups, reproducing its own energies seemingly irrespective of any individual's intentions, or frequently, awareness. Thus, there seems to be free-floating culpability attached to shame, that individuals become complicit in reproducing damaging behaviour as though the shame that was 'outside', communicated to the group, becomes 'inside', in dynamics not dissimilar to Judith Butler's model of the 'constitutive outside' (1993). Whether shame works purely as an infectious agent, or whether there is an 'internal resonance' – a kind of DNA psychic key – is one of the unanswerable fascinations of working with shame.

A seat at the table – some unpalatable thoughts on shame, envy, and hate in lesbian studies

The unmentioned emotions that ghost this section include my own 20 year hurt, rage, loneliness and melancholia. It addresses pervasive and pernicious emotional dynamics among lesbians who work within the career structure of third-level institutions. These dynamics are like the elephant in the sitting room – we've all been to some extent a party or witness to these scenarios and hence are all implicated in the psychic life of these dramas, but we don't wish to describe or analyse these relationships or address their emotional impact. This is because universities are not therapeutic structures, they serve a different purpose, they are ostensibly dedicated to the pursuit of rationality. They are also – and importantly – very middle class, white environments in ethos – they are enculturated with liberal bourgeois principles of order, tolerance, evenness, and reasoned debate. Emotions are intrinsic to university life, but they are also frowned upon. The Enlightenment, with its denigration of non-rational modes, continues to frame the experience of teaching in universities, for better or for worse. This section uses object relations theory to better understand these dynamics in order that we may respond more reflectively, and hopefully ethically, to the damage they cause.[1]

In this short reflection I share some thoughts about the presence of destructive emotions such as shame, envy and hate, specifically within Lesbian Studies, and by extension, minoritarian subjects in general, and open up to question a commonsense about institutional life in Anglo-American universities. It is about high-achieving lesbians-who-study, teach and write Lesbian Studies at third-level institutions who become the target of envy and hate from their erstwhile colleagues. I enquire whether the institutionalisation of our scholarship has led to a crushing poverty of representation for both students and faculty alike, as both struggle with the psychic inevitability of shame, hatred and envy that the spectre of a few powerful women can provoke. For the purpose of this chapter I present a fairly one-dimensional focus on the related affects of shame, envy and hatred: the presence of lesbian (studies) stars on the horizon of academic life does not automatically and always result in this rather linear trajectory of feeling. There are indeed a whole host of other academic dyke dramas involving achievement, recognition, affirmation, fandom and fame. However I concentrate on what becomes repressed by institutionalisation, using primarily a framework from object-relations theory to identify what emotional costs might be incurred in our interpellation, our incorporation into *academentia*?[2]

In her essay 'What Makes an Analyst?' Jacqueline Rose discusses the institutionalisation, through formal training, of psychoanalysis[ts], tracing how even Jacques Lacan's radical refusal and opposition to traditional training eventually became incorporated into academe (Rose 2003, 167–197). She separates training from the process of the psychoanalytic experience, which she argues has failed to deliver Sigmund Freud's radical original vision: in his future for psychoanalysis, the process had a politically egalitarian, transformative agenda for society. As it became professionalised during the twentieth century, Rose argues that its radical potential became neutralised. The mechanism of cultural appropriation operates to aggressively neutralise the radical content of ideas that are generated by the critical edges of society. Fields of counter-cultural knowledge do become institutionalised, in an unavoidably conservative absorption by the ideological state apparatus of education. We must also consider this dilemma in all aspects of the lesbian dance in/around/of/against (use any preposition here, there is no escape!) the social, as we grapple with the disappointment that unfeasible visions for Lesbian Studies has provoked. Most minorities engender projective identifications, whether longing or aggressive, toward those spectral powers of academia. Whilst the cultural trope of the hegemonic lesbian ghost has been so eruditely explored by Terry Castle in *The Apparitional Lesbian*, perhaps we should delve deeper and lurk about amongst the shadows of our own camera obscurae; we might do well to wonder about some self-propagating lesbian phantoms in our collective disciplinary subconcious.

Whilst the institutionalisation of lesbian knowledge has indisputably created specific gains in such key academic objectives as funded research, archival collections, employment, and the bit-queering of the canon, there remains the question of what becomes repressed by these gains, and at what cost? In this harsher evaluation I am following a small tradition of fairly rueful writers who have asked similar questions.[3] Here is Sarah Chinn worrying a decade ago:

> ... we can't help but recognise the temptations and pleasures of belonging to any institution, the safety of the office, the paycheck, the name in print. For me at least, the minefield of queer studies is strewn with fragrant flowers as well as shattering mortars, and it's impossible to intuit which I'll step on at any given juncture. (Chinn 1994, 244)

The imaginings Chinn renders here are inescapably from the Great War, in which the petals crushed underfoot are presumably poppies, and she continues:

> ...When we cross the minefield do we leave it unchanged for those who follow behind us? Do we risk losing a limb, or dodge with our eyes closed, praying, or sprinkle more explosives behind us with the rationalization that the challenge of wading through bombs builds character? Do we drop the seeds for roses and hope they grow among the rubble, even as we leave them behind? (Chinn 1994, 244)

Fifteen years ago there was a strong sentiment of war, battle, and conflict felt by many of us entering the profession with a mindset for change.[4] To teach Lesbian Studies then was to be publically declarative, to perform a speech act, to *profess*. Being a soldier for Sappho was Stephen Gordon-like, embraced as a self-sacrificing heroic mission; however we know from speech act theory that all utterances contain unforeseen consequences. The reality of any war is that all parties become brutalised in the process, and it may be that we lack a proper understanding of how those wounds turned, over time, to scars.

In the 2003 annual British HESA return statistics there were about 14,000 full professors in our universities, of which 1,800 were women.[5] Since the growth of Women's and Feminist Studies in the past couple of decades, a small proportion of those high achievers are academics, most often to be found in the Humanities (though not exclusively) who have achieved success in some part *because of* rather than in spite of, the radical quality of their scholarship. Women 'of a certain age', who have maintained careers in the academy and eventually become powerful within the parameters of their home disciplines, have been raised up through a conjunction of their own efforts and a certain historical set of benevolent effects. A tiny proportion of these women work openly on non-normative sexualities, although most do not do this to the exclusiveness of other intellectual interests in their fields. In the educational economy, these women are rare creatures, predominantly to be found in Anglo-American contexts, although we know that isolated individuals do beaver away elsewhere. Nevertheless, it remains the unlikely case that their radical thought, embedded in the successful adoption of professional skills, has secured their passage to a permanent university elite.

Infective spirals

The PhD, now well established as the core qualification for a career in academia, instils within the learning process a certain anxiety of influence, producing student subjects who learn to emulate their supervisors in mental, written, and professional practices. Irrespective of their own personal position in the matrix, all academics do progress through a system of mentoring, and hence to an extent are destined to become agents with hagiographic tendencies. Education, right back to Plato and Socrates, has been particularly marked by models of identification and replication. The heroic individualism of contemporary academic cultures is conditioned by an oppositional impulse toward imitative and co-operative behaviours, if one is to profitably advance. Thus, to some extent an academic career has to move from emulation to individuation, through a classic psychoanalytic process of aggressive incorporation. This idea is based on the principle of introjection, which is the development, in the Kleinian tradition, of the internal world as a space in which external objects come and go, and are consumed and integrated as hostile or friendly parts of the self. The assimilation is more or less successful in creating an identity, through a process of *identification*. This dynamic in lesbian contexts is related to, but distinct from, T.S. Eliot's description of the relationships between (assumed to be male) poets and critics in *Tradition and the Individual Talent*, or Harold Bloom's depiction of (assumed to be male) critics and poets in *The Anxiety of Influence*, in which the psyches are being described as repressed, split and murderous and enmeshed in each other. The 'feminine' version circulates intensely – one might suggest shark-like – around the anxious boundaries of the ego, more permeable and thus more vulnerable in the female subject under patriarchy. This 'appetite' for intellectual recognition is commonly held to be an avaricious quality if displayed too openly, particularly in women. Hence, as the essential fuel for academic careers it must be tactically disguised if the subject is to achieve promotion. This requirement can lead, perhaps, to a surfeit of grace.

Surely we would do better to expose the repercussions of these negative emotions in our institutional lives, thus leading to a fuller or more mature understanding of them and our part in their proliferation? I want to suggest that having these few 'famous lesbians' in higher education ensures a hysterical identification that is destructive to both parties. Charismatic, special leaders unfortunately tend to be seduced into the belief of the myth of their own reproduction as exceptional. Worship is rooted in affectual mires of shame and envy; shame is tendentious in that an unstable rejection is invoked. In part this is an aim of the process, that the student, once sufficiently trained, is productively abandoned by mutual consent. However, the psychic child can seldom forgive its parent their limitations, and the parent can rarely quite relinquish its status, thus both parties can become trapped in a hopelessly undermining misrecognition.

Unfortunately, whilst mentoring remains the deep structure of academic training for students, it also continues to be a naturalised part of academic life post-qualification, as hierarchy in academic institutions is fundamental. I say 'unfortunately' because this guidance model is enacted permissively without wider consciousness of its predeterminations. To say that a degree of hurt is the essence of the student/mentor relationship is axiomatic, yet we do not seem to have found clear ways yet of articulating it.

Eve Kosofsky Sedgwick recently published a short essay on 'Teaching/ Depression' in which she charts pedagogical relationships amongst 'multiple positions within a densely innervated matrix of generational transmissions' (2006, 1). She reminds us that Silvan Tomkins, when writing about shame, labelled the educator as a 'depressive personality' (1995), commenting that:

> For Tomkins, the most notable feature of *the depressive*, on emerging from childhood, is that he or she combines a passion for relations of mimetic communion – ideally, two-way or mutual mimesis, based on the sweetness and anxiety for the child of imitating and being imitated by an intermittently attentive adult – with an intense susceptibility to shame when such relations fail. (Sedgwick 2006, 1)

Because developmentally the loving gaze of the parent cannot ever be constant, and must necessarily withdraw in order to attend to other demands, the child feels shamed. Positive regard has been removed because 'I have been bad and am not worth it', goes the internalisation, and unfortunately, it can form a narcissistic wound. In a Kleinian move Sedgwick segues from Silvan's account of the depressive person to Melanie Klein's more universal 'depressive position', and through that its partner, the paranoid/schizoid position, in which affective relations are intractably poisoned, this latter:

> ... is liable to propel circuits of interpersonal accusation that are explosive with the very forms of hatred that are under internal erasure. Thus for Klein's infant or adult, the paranoid/schizoid position – marked by hatred, envy and anxiety is a position of terrible alertness to the dangers posed by the hateful and envious part-objects that one defensively projects into the world around one. (2006, 1)

Sedgwick justly observes: 'It is the terrifying contagion of paranoid modes of thought [that]... seem[s] indispensable for a lot of political analysis and group dynamics' (2006, 2). The collective paranoidal position is very binding, it has deep investments, projections, and strong self-justifications 'driven by attributed motives, fearful contempt of opponents, collective fantasies of powerlessness and/or omnipotence, scapegoating, purism and schism' (2006, 2). Sedgwick concludes by explaining that the paradoid/schizoid position 'involves bad karma, lots of it' (2006, 3).

Envy is based upon the impulse to destroy the object of one's desire. Even more present in professional life than shame, envy seems to stalk one's university life as an inevitable consequence of formal success. Particularly virulent in its destructiveness, envy is produced when one person's progression is seen as a rejection of the collectivity of injury, in that former allies now 'raised up' are perceived to have become threats in their closer move toward power. This suspicion is correct, in that it can challenge another person's failure in conventional terms as being due to their own performance rather than a more unspecified generic oppression and victimhood. Previous expectations of collegiality or *a priori* loyalties are disappointed once power intervenes; as it does, as it will. In destroying former identifications, the betrayal of equivalence can lead to an angry expulsion on the part of the communal imaginary. This pungent disidentification could then be understood to produce an emotional disinvestment, but actually the opposite occurs, because of envy's close companionship with hate.

Hate is a vitally intimate force. Hate, like love, is a kind of paradoxical longing dependent upon cycles of connection. It is our own hate that forges a boundary against our fears, its presence in our inner life is so unacceptable that we externalise it as the malevolence of another, binding us to that person. There is pleasure in hatred, as well as torture. Hatred is determined to secure a relationship with someone, even if that aggression is marshalled for their destruction this is actually a false hope, as the hatred doesn't end there. Destroying one's object of hate means that one will live in an impoverished world, as the walls of the psyche relinquish a powerful representation of self. Hate is a preferable state to melancholy, in which we cannot identify what we have lost, and decline into depression, rather it is an externalised energy that at least superficially is not directed at the self. Hate is obviously not always 'bad' either, it is a clarifying stimulant. Hatred is infinitely preferable to being alone and facing oneself. Hatred is bristling with the energy of connective desires. Hatred is relishly conducted through wilfully maintained ignorance and projection, built upon the partial knowledge the unconscious generates. I have encountered much hate in academia, but it is rarely named as such, nor called to account. Jacques Lacan commented upon the current ubiquity of hate, arguing that the inability to see it or name it is a result of hate's greater perpetration or suffusion within contemporary societies:

> These days we know less about the feeling of hatred than in times when man was more open to his destiny... These days subjects do not have to shoulder the burden of the experience of hatred in its most consuming forms. And why? Because our civilization is itself sufficiently one of hatred. Isn't the path for the race to destruction really rather well marked out for us? Hatred is clothed in our everyday discourse under many guises, it meets with such extraordinarily easy rationalisations. (Lacan 1991, 67)

Linking by association – and remember that Lacan was the master at this – hatred with rationalisation and proliferation invokes a Weberian worldview of bureaucratisation. The implication here is that hate bears some relationship to the continuous fracturing, ordering and rationalisation of organisations and cultures occurring within late capitalism. Whilst this connection remained unexplored by Lacan, being merely inferred or hinted at, I think it is germane to my argument here. If hate has become undifferentiated and diffuse (so much so that it is unrecognisable), it may in part be due to a paradox of possibility, that there is at one and the same time too much, and too little.

Understanding the hugely emotional character of these relationships remains at a facile level precisely because of the devaluing of emotion in academic cultures. The popularity of Daniel Goleman's idea of emotional intelligence outside of academia and the concomitant trashing of such ideas within stands testament to its denial. We may be able to wax lyrical upon the emotional complexity of arts and literature, but we are unable or unwilling to refocus analytically on the emotions engendered through our personal and institutional practices. The Italian psychoanalyst Francesco Bisagni writing on envy has this to say on its transgenerational transmission:

> ... psychic nuclei are apparently transmitted through different generations. Sometimes they seem to remain dormant for years within a member of a group, then they erupt and become apparent in another member before becoming dormant again for a while, waiting to reappear somewhere else in a kind of endless poisonous movement. (Bisagni 2002, 189)

The pathology of envy is that it circulates within family cultures as though waiting for a target to fix upon – envy abhors a vacuum. Envy makes the environment we work in toxic, it makes many of us sick. A classic cycle of envy is enacted when a good object becomes a bad object, which the good object is predestined to become as it cannot fulfil the huge expectations placed upon it; it must fail, as all our loving is ultimately inadequate to the expectations laid upon it. Envy disavows the healing potential of empathy, as in spatial terms the former is distanciating, and the latter is intimate, it has a peculiar propensity to expand and grow as it travels, inculcating those whom it touches. Cultural change is needed to dispel the envious creep, replacing rivalry with acts of kindness does much to shrivel its progression. Envy is performative, and we can act to refute envious behaviours despite accepting that this indeed can be our private feeling. What this does is draw the envious object closer, thus dispelling the threat. This endeavour can also then realise a different set of feelings. If this seems too abstract, then consider how you felt when one of your peers gained promotion, when you didn't... a banal prickle fundamental to academic life. As ever, it is what is publicly said that is important – further – public statements can have the force to dissipate private resentments.

These issues have been raised before during the 1990s in two previous incidents in the USA – the major critical case of Professor Jane Gallop's infamous 'lesbian kiss', and the perhaps more subcultural, glamourous grad-student fanzine 'Judy', an irreverential pastiche on the fame of the feminist/queer scholar Judith Butler.[6] More prosaically, our community of Lesbian Studies is stippled with anecdotes of vengeful colleagues, jealous and destructive competitiveness, ambitious cowards, the all too common tale of 'sisters' whose real or perceived aggression has destroyed the progress of more deserving candidates. Righteously claiming the 'outside' becomes a more and more sticky project once one's subject is conceived as core to a number of academic objectives. The romantic outside (the outside as a projected ideal), is a very different realm indeed from the material or real outside that dictates the lives of most people, and outlawism has a tendency to produce a self-aggrandising stance that can produce more alienation than dialogue. States of injury are endemic to the perception of being outside, when often outsider status is claimed by a subject whom in other respects has an accumulation of cultural and/or material capital that has successfully enabled her self-determination. Fantasies of the inside/outside creates a violent oscillation, birthing an energy that perpetuates hostility, positionality, territorialism and rhetorical moves to claim space and authority.

The trajectory is not necessarily linear and predictive: in this sad economy of claims-making and breaking, those same powerful women are not always simply the victims of jealous, underachieving or up-and-coming mentees. They – or should I risk a 'we' – can frequently be patronising, condescending, autocratic, manipulative, wilfully oblique, bullying, and self-aggrandising in the most unattractive ways imaginable. We swear that *we shall be the one* to remain real and grounded, but it is not so easy. The embodiment of these emotions, whether one is complicit with its origin and source, or its reception, exacts unforeseen damage on all protagonists. True non-conformity produces a large amount of anxiety, indeed, one might say a field of anxiety, that intensifies and elaborates the hurt. This can induce the shame/contempt cycle, both of these emotions are peculiarly contagious, and implicate all of those touched. Whole groups then start reproducing these elemental emotions, they lock onto us in spite of our best intentions, with all parties anxiously denying their own part.

It is quite hard to accept that power is a chimera when you are injured, envy is driven by this delusion, and once you slide up the pole the realisation that there is no 'there' there, can produce trenchant disillusionment, coupled with deceptive nostalgia for the radical sisterhood left behind. One has to be careful not to inflict this epiphany on others. Academia is a micro-culture in which shame circulates powerfully, but is rarely recognised. To acknowledge shame is often to appeal to it, to become somehow stained by it. For example, to tell someone about an incidence of humiliation reinvigorates that original feeling, similarly, to speak about one's shame often makes us re-shamed. The inexorably stepped progression of an academic career means that the shame non-dominant identities were made to feel whilst occupying more 'junior' positions (undergraduate, postgraduate, temporary lecturer, tenure-track), is emblematic. Knowingly or unknowingly wearing the badge of shame causes us to be cruel to those perceived to be underneath us, and encourages us to pull up the ladder after ourselves. Paradoxically, shaming behaviour can also trap those who sustain a great belief in their own benevolent powers of patronage, their counsel and support can be dispensed to perceived (and often non-consensual) acolytes, in order to ward off feelings of their own performance as worthless or failed.

One root cause of profound disappointment is the chimera of 'Lesbian Studies'. Where is she, the 'real' lesbian of this project? Of course, she does not exist, yet she haunts our endeavours, she is our measuring post. Fixing an academic area of study upon an identity whose essence is lodged in injury is asking for trouble. Returning to her via reverse discourse can only ever be partially successful, as the lesbian abiding in shame, envy and hate lies suspended in our institutional/social unconscious (Foucault 1979). Idealisation is a problem for shamed identities; it functions compensatorily to reassure by providing aspirational figures and states, but paradoxically it also cruelly and simultaneously secures their own denigration. All lesbians, like all gay men, suffer to a greater or lesser degree from homophobia, the category and the experience of homosexuality is inescapably permeated with it. This is the 'double-bind' of identity that we are damned to repeat – in order to call upon pride and presence we also invoke the corollary of shame and annihilation – claiming of self entails loss of self, as making a self is predicated upon disavowal, even in its earliest, crudest forms. Thus our psychic life is always already infused by poignancy, melancholia, nostalgia, so we must necessarily inhabit the present with all our pasts and futures openly in mind, aiming to keep the balance between comprehending our subjection (loss) and temporal, future-driven narratives of possibility (hope).[7] Naming Lesbian Studies, and/or ourselves as lesbians-who-study, incurs queer schizophrenia.

This is the dynamic that Judith Butler addressed so cogently when she argued that injury cannot be cleanly and legalistically separated from recognition (1997). Butler turns her analysis to hate as it is embedded in speech, identifying the violence of enunciation, and the linguistic vulnerability that is its 'other' side. What is so inspirational about Butler's work is that it consistently refuses the victim position: the author ensures that we powerfully acknowledge the hate directed against us, then leads us into a moral comprehension of our own complicit reproduction of that affect. Simply put: if you hate me, then that hate harms you. Indeed, as a speech act your hate can be inefficient, misfire and 'fail'. Then, if I refuse to be inculcated by, and hold your hatred, that will have the delicious effect of making you hate me more. The consequence of your speech act may be more infelicitous for you than for me, despite your worst intention (so goes my revenge fantasy, anyhow). The mirrored scenes of hate wilfully occlude the need to hate, the satisfaction of hating, and the occasional necessity of hate. Hate can be pleasurable, as William Hazlitt demonstrated in his essay, first published in 1826:

> Nature seems (the more we look into it) made up of antipathies: without something to hate, we should lose the very spring of thought and action... The white streak in our own fortunes is brightened (or just rendered visible) by making all around it as dark as possible; so the rainbow paints its form upon the cloud. Is it pride? Is it envy? Is it the force of contrast? Is it weakness or malice? But so it is, that there is a secret affinity, a *hankering* after evil in the human mind, and that it takes a perverse, and yet a fortunate delight in mischief, since it is a never-failing source of satisfaction. (Hazlitt 2004, 108)

The vindictive, rankling and headstrong humours of hate seem in Hazlitt's understanding to be provoked by boredom, indifference, and malaise, and I do not think he is wrong. Hate, he reminds us, has a watchful compulsion, it begs to be recognised, and like shame, is potently embodied and exchanged in the face.

In reaching some understanding of my experience and that of my peers, envious professional attacks and the inflamed wounds they cause seem to come more often from within the queer community than from the predictable quarters of patriarchy, from whom I suppose a certain amount are rightly anticipated. Consider how or where lesbians are fair game for other lesbians in academia – and ask is there a difference between how we treat those whom we know to be lesbian and those whom we suspect to be lesbian? This competitiveness causes the mind to close rather than open, it engages with the spirit of intellectual enmity rather than co-operation. There is an indulgence of trashing in academic life, it provokes us to lift ourselves up by pouring scorn on another, for example implying or explicitly reporting that someone else's work is 'untheorised', 'derivative', or old-fashioned. These accusations are lazy indictments in the sense that the protagonist has often not bothered to consider the learning context in which they are presented, nor have they necessarily taken time to understand the nuance in the work that can offer the reader some new ways of understanding. It is a serene arrogance that assumes we have nothing to learn from another's consideration or perspective. Incidentally, this is not an argument for intellectual relativism, nor is it a defence of poor thought – I am drawing attention to the frequent occurrence of hasty judgements that drive down another's efforts in order to proselytise one's own cleverness.

Contempt is an emotion embodied in one's own shame that has enormous power to wound the giver and the receiver. Andrew P. Morrison (1989) suggests that contempt may be interpreted using Melanie Klein as the projective identification of shame, he argues that contempt is an attempt to rid the self of shame by relocating it in another. This recipient is pressured to take on the shame and treated scornfully as shame can intensify as it travels, s/he becomes interpellated by this shame, Francis Broucek calls it 'borrowed shame' (1991, 73). Fully understanding shame-humiliation and contempt-disgust models further takes us back again to the work of Silvan Tompkins (1995). Shame has ambivalent effects because it is founded upon the interruption of love, where the self is dependent upon the acceptance of the other, and yet the inception of identity is predicated upon separation from the other, even the renunciation of the other. Shame is a kind of imperative to the emergent self. It is however only once the lesbian makes identification with *others like her*, that she is able to gain herself an identity. She has reformed the bond, through shame, and commuted shame into love (with all of its attendant aggression!).

We must not be naïve concerning the institutionalisation of knowledge and its protagonists. The underlying structure of the academy is the same as any other hierarchical organisation under capital, and we need more awareness of the contract we have made and the function to which we are put. The poverty of these organisations reproduce a punishing range of angry identifications and disidentifications that have historical pathologies that intersect all too readily with our own unconscious wishes. For example, the logic of shame can be that we remain trapped in a cycle of ruthless competition. We cannot compensate adequately for these predispositions, they are always already in the life we have chosen, or had chosen for us. We need to find ways of preventing a passive sorority that represses our thoughts and our agency. To be crude – none of us can be the permanently good breast – the strain of maintaining, sustaining these emotions gives some of us cancer.[8]

The closet is the fundamental structure underpinning these dynamics. We perpetuate aggression for the reason of a colleague's real or suspected lesbianism, not in spite of it; we need to examine internalised homophobia, asking how it becomes channelled toward colleagues who are more openly (and embarrassingly) lesbian. We swallow huge discomfort whilst wearing the lesbian *straight*jacket, and sometimes yearn paradoxically for the anonymity of the suit. It is important to remember that the lesbian performance is temporal and thus a *duration* – meaning that some moments/movements are more constraining/ closeting than others. Emotions too are temporal, and involuntary, and as mutable states are subject to the vicissitudes of the organisational unconscious. This unconscious is the 'other-space' of the institution, since emotions are so generally closeted in academia, they are eviscerated from the public discourse of professional life. But the personal cannot be escaped in a political economy whose measure of exchange is reputation. Thus the homosexual-in-the-academy is always already angry, injured, and victimised, by the organisations we work for and by all levels within it. Both 'powerful' and 'weak' homosexuals are inextricably bound to anger in the university imaginary; with that imprint on our foreheads we share a level playing field, batting for the same team whether we like it or not, we endure (inwardly protesting), an angry affinity of low status based upon the adage 'my enemy's enemy is my friend'.[9] This is not to romanticise or reify our lesbian bonds however, as we may secure authoritative positions through other forms of financial or cultural capital.

We have – we owe – collective norms of obligation and relations of political affinity. To be successful these depend upon the candid recognition of the problematic motives that can drive us; we don't like to be confronted by our narcissistic or aggressive impulses, nor to be held responsible for nasty consequences that we have brokered by our wilful naivety, our spilled-over bad karma. We are unwilling to own how impatient we feel with the suffering of others, how irritated and withholding we can be, as Lauren Berlant describes:

> … we witness… someone's desire to not connect, sympathise, or recognise an obligation to the sufferer; to refuse engagement with the scene or to minimize its effects; to misread it conveniently; to snuff or drown it out with pedantically shaped phrases or carefully designed apartheids; not to rescue or help; to go on blithely without conscience; to feel bad for the sufferers, but only so that they will go away quickly. (Berlant 2004, 9)

The aversion we feel, and the structural and symbolic violence we can subsequently commit, is a response to the poverty of our own emotional imagination; with George Eliot we might then concur:

> If we had a keen vision and feeling of all ordinary human life, it would be like hearing the grass grow and the squirrel's heart beat, and we should die of that roar which lies on the other side of silence. As it is, the quickest of us walk about well wadded with stupidity. (Eliot 1986/1871, 226)

That 'stupidity' usefully insulates us against acknowledging our own deprivation, an insufficiency of love that results from the inevitable failure, in spiritual terms, of heroic individualism and its vaunted achievements. Rather, better to admit we are all scholars who in creatively intersubjective thus interdependent ways require the supportive empathy of others. We need therefore to find forms of altruism that are not enacted by the narcissism of the ego, beyond what Lacan described as 'what I want is the good of others provided that it remains in the image of my own.' (Lacan 1992, 187)

Does dialogue, mutual-appreciation, admiration, learning, friendship, collegiality, peer groups, academic freedom, tenure, retirement, superannuation… ever cut across the predeterminations of an academic life? Whilst hatred is conducted through wilfully maintained ignorance and projection, love seems to have more dimensions and variables and expressions and developmental periods. Love is not always, or even often, primitive – love is often reflectively tended, sophisticated – wisely/melancholically aware of its own vulnerabilities, complexities, contradictions, bitter impossibilities, limits and process of change. Isn't 'lesbian' also an identity created through dialogue, across differences, in a sense (however partial or unsuccessful or deluded) of creating a sustaining community, with at least a shadow of a sense of shared heritage, culture and history, an identity based in desire for each other and trying to find new models and practices of making communities, homes and love? Readers of this piece may have wished for a more constructive intervention based in 'thoughtful, positive, and reasoned alternatives' to shame, envy and hate, but I am writing against the impulse to make good, or to rationalise an exit, without fully mulling over the painful prolongation of these damaging emotions. Enacting this aspiration can only be realised if we are able to accept the limiting humanity of ourselves and our colleagues, daily rediscover empathy, and not confuse the laurels of academia with the loyalty due to those lesbians-who-study, and their friends.

Chancellor Denice Denton

I end this section pausing for a moment to think about the late Chancellor of the University of California at Santa Cruz, Professor Denice Dee Denton.[10] Professor Denton killed herself on 24th June 2006, at the age of 46, by jumping off her partner's 43-story luxury apartment building in San Francisco. Her partner, Gretchen Kalonji, was away in New York at the time, on university business according to press reports, but her mother was in the building. Denton's story is one of rare achievement: a relatively young woman who achieved high office and professional excellence, whilst insisting on being publicly open about her homosexuality. This story struck a chord with me not just because she was the same age as myself, and a lesbian also not from a middle-class home, but because I conject that she was shamed into suicide. Reading the media coverage of her appointment less than a year and a half before, and her brief tenureship at UCSC, there is sustained media outrage about her $600,000 campus residence refit, her alleged $30,000 dog run, and her spousal appointment, housing allowance, and $60,000 removals bill; it is impossible not to presuppose how a heterosexual male appointment would have been left alone to benefit rather noiselessly from the same economic incentives that are typical at this level of executive recruitment. I am struck by how much this negative media coverage mobilised public shaming of Denton and her partner, it must have eviscerated an extraordinarily powerful woman who was a national pioneer in Electrical Engineering and Higher Education leadership in the USA.

Initially, on reading the web-based obituaries from university presidents and such, the striking quality of repetition around her fight for diversity, her fairness and commitment to staff, leads us to presume that this was a woman who aspired to ethical professional standards and outspoken opinions on minorities in education. University of Washington President Mark Emmert, her former employer, where she was Dean of Engineering, had this to say on the day of her death:

> We mourn the loss of Denice Denton. She was a remarkable leader during her time at the University of Washington. She believed it was important to make academia a more humane place, where students and faculty could do important work and lead rich lives. She was also very committed to social justice issues – for ethnic minorities, gays and lesbians, immigrants, international students and faculty. She was truly a transformational leader at the UW, setting our College of Engineering on a path toward even greater achievement. Her many friends and colleagues here will miss her.[11]

University of California President Dynes had this to add:

> It was with profound sadness and shock that we learned this weekend of the death of UC Santa Cruz Chancellor Denice Denton. Her tragic passing on Saturday is a tremendous loss. Denice was an accomplished and passionate scholar whose life and work demonstrated a deep commitment to public service and to improving opportunity for the disadvantaged and underrepresented. She was a person of enthusiasm, of big ideas, of tremendous energy, and of great promise.[12]

She is perhaps most well recognised on the international stage of academe for objecting vigorously to the President of Harvard University, Lawrence Summers' infamous claim that men are just naturally better than women at Science and Maths, a claim made rather unwisely at a conference on women and minorities in Science and Engineering, in January 2005. As Denton commented tactfully and pointedly at the time 'Academic leaders in the United States, from Presidents to Professors, really should be in the business of creating environments where all minds are valued and encouraged to reach their full potential'.[13]

Despite this woman's attempts to show principled leadership in public discourse, it is clear that popular derision accumulated around the figure of the 'out' lesbian Chancellor, so much so that Paul Wagner, a local community housing advocate, posting a memory of chatting with her one evening at a function, describes how:

That future meeting, unfortunately, never took place. Travel schedules interfered. Communication slowed. And soon thereafter, the chancellor's staff found it necessary to tighten up, to close in, to literally circle the wagons, both physically and procedurally, to protect Denton from the increasing number of incidents involving invasion, harassment, physical obstruction, death threats, and ultimately, ever louder talk of resource cutoffs and legal hostilities...[14]

Denton was not a popular Chancellor, despite her attempts to make significant changes for the good at Santa Cruz, to make universities a 'more humane place' for others, she undoubtedly made mistakes, alienating a Left-oriented staff and student body that left her isolated. However, men rarely make these kinds of mistakes in leadership, because they have established networks of peers in place to protect, advise and guide. One feels the weight of all of that expectation on her isolated shoulders, and with hindsight the pity that she was unable to take that pressure, of exposure and attack. This is a story of an impressive figure, driven for her own reasons to achieve outstandingly in her field, perhaps even a tragic hero, murdered by public shaming and derision. Homophobia underpins this death, but we also need to understand its particular rendition here as shame.

In the baiting of Denice Denton there is also present shame's related affect: envy. In Melanie Klein's 'Envy and Gratitude' (1957) it is the idealised object that provokes envy. Thus, that which was formerly and briefly idealised as the 'good breast' is violently rejected via the child's envious aggression. This kind of primal envy, as we know from Klein, can be intensely brutal, even sadistic, and the child seeks to spoil and even destroy the source of its own sustenance and support as part of its own halting formation of self. In the Kleinian model, the idealised object becomes perceived as a source of persecution, in a psychic mechanism of projective (mis)identification. The persecution is clearly coming from 'below'. In the case of the public hostility toward Denton I speculate how much of it comes from women, working-class people or even lesbians, 'minorities' for whom Denton's success has a double valency. On the one hand Denton has attained social recognition and is representative of these groups, on the other hand the pressure to be exemplary, to offer a model for imitation, to be symbolic of a forced federation or alliance, can easily be reversed. One perceived deviation from the idealised totem can result in the full force of opprobrium descending, as Denton's failure to embody the ideal threatens to invalidate, and shame, whole subject groups.

One (of many) postings on Denice Denton from one of her own UCSC students will illustrate my point; she was known as an 'unusual' dresser who spent a lot of money on clothes.[15] Extravagance in dress for a major figure in public service is not unusual, but her taste seemed to run to the flamboyant (mention is made elsewhere of a silk purple trouser suit, and orange spectacles, for example). Denton was not elegant, a big-boned woman, her performance as Chancellor seemed gauchely over-stated. This is a classed error, to know how to dress for power with subtlety is a cultural capital not easy to acquire, especially perhaps for lesbian engineers. This made her a figure of fun, and the derision exemplified in these comments and the cartoon reproduced below, which appears on the web next to a posting that twins her with drag queen Dame Edna Everidge, links Denton to the 'ugly lesbian' caricature so unfailingly linked to failed femininity. Denton, then, was a Chancellor in bad drag, and let us not underestimate the extreme personal anxiety provoked in performing a social role that is commonly perceived to be a chimeric figment. The clothes didn't fit.

I wonder how many times Denice Denton saw herself humiliated in these kind of depictions, and what kind of inner feelings of lesbian and/or class shame it reverberated? The truth is that for many aspirant minorities, there is always an internal 'hook' to which these barbs can stick. The perpertrator herself is also caught up in shame, and usually in any manner of a range of feelings of powerlessness (or indeed, frustrated entitlement). This student web posting (below) has some uncanny elements:

****

Come on Folks, Why are we hurting Chancellor Denice Denton?
By Carolyn Baker

CHANCELLOR DENICE D. DENTON

You know, I listen to all these people speaking evil over Chancellor Denice Denton and I think, 'What kind of monsters would do such a thing?' Who are we? How can we live knowing that we're putting her down? Have you ever woken up in the morning, looked in the mirror, and saw Denice Denton staring back at you? Think about what that's like. What does that do to a person? She has to do it every day. Have you ever wanted to buy an orange blazer but couldn't unless you could find a pair of matching orange-rimmed glasses to go with it? I extremely doubt it! Chancellor Denton suffers from a disorder, and if she doesn't wear glasses that match her blazer, she loses it. I don't see any of you trying to help her out. Where's that support group? What's that? It doesn't exist? That's interesting.

I'm sure you've all seen Mary Poppins. There's a point in the story when Mary Poppins brainwashes the children, causing them to run away from their father. When Burt the Chimney Sweep finds them they whine that their dad doesn't look out for them and only cares about work and the bank. Burt tells the kids, 'But, who's looking out for your father? No one, that's who.' And so I ask: who's looking out for Denice Denton? Surely not her partner Gretchen Kalonji. Denice was the one who had to go out of her way to get Gretchen a job. You ever had to find your sweetheart a job? It's hard enough finding one for yourself. Plus, Denice can't feel comfortable knowing that her girlfriend is only making $192,000 a year. Think about it. What if you had to find your boyfriend/girlfriend/husband/wife/stalker a job and it was only paying a meager $192,000 a year?

119

Imagine the guilt. You add that to Denice's $275,000 and you don't even have half a million there. I can't even picture what kind of dump she has to live in. Breaks my heart, I swear it does.

The worst thing about this all is that Denice really loves us and we don't even know it. When she had the police show up at Tent University, I was like, 'She's out for my safety.' She wants what's best for us. Did you know that she went to M.I.T.? That's one of the best schools in the country. I bet she could turn UCSC into an M.I.T., except we'd call it S.C.I.T. or maybe D.D.I.T, where the D's stood for Denice Denton. If she could accomplish such a feat, then she would deserve to have the new UCSC named after her.

In closing, I just hope Denice finds it in her heart to forgive us of our wrongdoings. What kind of cowards and bullies are we to attack such a kind-hearted, fragile woman who stands for diversity, safety, career opportunities, and color coordination? I apologize and ask for forgiveness. God bless you, Chancellor... and shame on you UCSC students! [16]

Source: http:santacruz.indymedia.org/newswire/display/18040/index.php

*****

The author of this web comment Carolyn Baker first invokes the doubling effect of the narcissistic lesbian gaze, the idea of Denton looking in the mirror and 'seeing herself', a cliché of split subjectivity from film and literature that has structured the representation of the modern lesbian self. By association, the concept of 'monster' still rings from the previous sentence, reinforced by an opposition in the invocation of fairy tale/mythological figure Mary Poppins, in paragraph two. This is a classic hero/villain function as identified by Russian Formalist, Vladimir Propp. And so we have a lurking figure in the paragraph, effected through symbolic bricolage: Denton, the narcissistic lesbian monster. A woman who is intrinsically 'disordered', a woman (with ghastly prescience) who should be 'put down'. The surreal associations in the piece are intended to humiliate Denton by ridicule, and no doubt were effective in ritualistically shaming the Chancellor – the nightmare of the orange glasses is particularly potent – and queer (Sedgwick 1993). The grammar of the page is convoluted, the subject/agent/speaker of the sentence shifts constantly from being Denton, to Baker, to a collective 'us', meaning that not only do some very old tropes of lesbian ugliness appear, but also that the reader of this page is *inserted within them*. The writer even asks 'Who are we?' and ends with that strangely elliptical plea:

> In closing, I just hope Denice finds it in her heart to forgive us of our wrongdoings. What kind of cowards and bullies are we to attack such a kind-hearted, fragile woman who stands for diversity, safety, career opportunities, and color coordination? I apologize and ask for forgiveness. God bless you, Chancellor... and shame on you UCSC students!

As the posting from Arcticman Speaks! observed two days after her suicide: 'I didn't know Ms Denton well enough to know exactly why she took her own life. I'm doubtful it was to celebrate Gay Pride, though.'[17] Shame on her, shame on you, and perhaps also shame on us.

Having looked at what would be, for some readers, the specific, maybe even rarefied micro-subculture of Lesbian Studies, more widely lesbian academics, and indicated generally the hyper-competitive preconditions for an academic career and the damage this can cause, I want to turn to another institutionalised form of shame, what might be considered its banal opposite: the heterosexualised space of the archetypal office. Instead of continuing to use 'real world' examples of shame culture, I want to turn to this fictional representation because it has the peculiar ability to distil, or intensify, shame situations through the narrative construction of the joke. I want to consider shame-spaces, places that are imbued with shame, and think about how shame becomes constitutive – 'drills down' – in organisations. Within shame cultures, what happens to those people whom inhabit shamed subjectivities, and hence identities? How does shame spiral through to the heart of man? Having written a book previously concerned with the pride/shame dichotomy of the heroic, perhaps it is time to address briefly the unheroic, in the tragic-comic figure of David Brent.

A tragi-comedy of manners – the psychic life of *The Office*

The Office, a serial comedy that is set up as reality television, as a fictional crew go into document 'life in an office', first aired on July 9 2001, and since then it has been sold by BBC Worldwide to 33 national broadcasters, and shown in nearly 100 countries.[18] France's Canal Plus and, in the USA, NBC have made their own versions, screened in 2006 and 2005 respectively. *The Office* DVD collection has outsold any BBC product, Series One shifted 80,000 units in one week following its release in October 2002. This is extraordinary for a low-budget comedy series first screened as a gamble by BBC2, the middlebrow channel. Since its success, the BBC has been inundated with requests from companies' HR departments wanting to show clips for staff training. As a third of BBC Worldwide's £ 20M turnover in 2004 came from corporate e-learning, one wonders if the original scheduler foresaw a sweet opportunity for media synchronicity (Hoare 2004). *The Office* ran for two series, followed by a two-part Christmas special screened on BBC 1 on 26–27 December 2003. So far *The Office* has been more successful in Britain and France than in the USA where reception has been mixed, probably because it is the *ancién regimes* European countries that have still relatively fixed hierarchical cultures of failure and prestige.

The Office is written and directed by Ricky Dene Gervais and Stephen Merchant, who picked up two Golden Globes for it in 2004. Gervais is the working-class son of a French-Canadian labourer and English housewife. He grew up on a large post-war estate in Reading, a city fairly close to Slough, West of London, and co-incidentally birthplace of the first ever docu-soap,

The Family in the 1970s. Gervais, who also acts as David Brent in the series, was clever and got a place at prestigious University College London where he gained a 2:1 in Philosophy. As Gervais himself commented 'I did not realise I was working class until I got to university and everyone talked like Prince Charles' (Adams 2005). He distinguishes his own comedy from some of the classic English approaches to representing class sensibilities:

> I really like the social faux-pas [...] But I don't necessarily believe in that *Abigail's Party* thing, you know [that] someone having no grasp of art is embarrassing. It's a class snobbery. I loved *Abigail's Party* and Mike Leigh, but a part of me thought: that's my family. There's nothing wrong with being working class and aspiring to have a better life. And its sometimes too easy to take the piss without affection. (Adams 2005)

But Gervais himself goes on to comment 'The whole point of my family was taking the mickey out of the one sitting next to you. That seemed to be the Reading way. It was all a wind up. Everything was fine as long as you never got the hump.' This constant communal teasing or banter has its clear rules of play, when Gervais' mother saw him on the late night comedy programme *The 11 O'Clock Show*, he describes how 'She'd tell the neighbours I was on and they'd say, "Does he have to swear so much?", no doubt bringing him "down to size".' (Adams 2005) This tradition of English humour is contained within a comedy of manners in more than one respect, there are clear constraints acting upon 'going too far' that include trenchant disapproval of outright cruelty, or nastiness, and codes preventing offensive language or obscenity. There is in English working-class humour rules of etiquette that disapprove of 'going too far', both by the actor and the recipient of this humour, neither of whom should deviate from moderate teasing. Being sensitive to the recipient's ability to 'take it' should also pre-empt them 'getting the hump'. Ironic self-deprecation is approved, but too much defensive sulking is seen as mean-spirited, as the target must also enjoy the modest joke by countering with a witty riposte. All of these subtle skills are trained into children growing up in verbose working-class homes. Sadly Gervais' parents never lived to see their son's phenomenal success in *The Office*, but the affectionate working-class practice of 'taking the piss' frames the show's central aesthetic, and is presumably, their cultural legacy.

David Brent, the central character of *The Office* is the regional office manager of a Slough-based paper company Wernham Hogg. What they sell is blank paper, the salesmen are purveyors of the tools of expression, but they have 'nothing' to say or write upon it, it is form without content, the blandest product imaginable, it is vacant, bare, empty, plain, a void. The signature shot of each episode is the photocopying machine's automatic tray silently continuing to fill, one by one, blank sheets, this is the icon of this bleak marketplace. Wernham Hogg is *The Office* of 'Everyman', a kind of hell without the fire. The series is based in Slough, an English town in Berkshire famed for the invention of the chocolate Mars bar ('helps you work, rest and play'), a place evocative of bog, and dead skin. Evoking John Bunyan's allegorical novel *The Pilgrim's Progress* (1678):

This miry slough is such a place as cannot be mended: it is the descent whither the scum and filth that attends conviction for sin doth continually run, and therefore it is called the Slough of Despond.

– the town carries a heavy semantic burden. Slough is the urban hangdog of the bohemian imagination, as John Betjeman so ringingly put it in his 1937 poem *Slough*:

> Come, friendly bombs, and fall on Slough
> It isn't fit for humans now
> There is not grass to feed a cow
> Swarm over, death!

Ted Hughes has a go at Slough too in *Birthday Letters*

> I was sitting Youth away in an office near Slough
> Morning and evening between Slough and Holborn
> Hoarding wage to fund a leap to freedom.

Slough is a place to escape from, and only a destination as a joke – Spike Milligan posed Slough satirically as a holiday resort, which was taken up in the 1990s song 'Costa del Slough' written by the rock band Marillion, a sentiment echoed later by the band the Tiger Lilies who also repeated the Poet Laureate's refrain 'Drop a bomb on Slough! Drop a bomb on Slough!'. Slough vaunts the first and largest trading estate in Europe. It is a focal business centre due to its transport links and it is therefore a 'concrete' embodiment of that embarrassingly un-English habit – trade. Slough represents what the upper classes hate – petit bourgeois economy, coupled with working-class light industrial and suburban sprawl. Contempt for Slough is enshrined in English snobbery, as journalist Michael Hann observed 'People always need somewhere to look down upon and Slough has fulfilled that role for generations for the aspirant middle classes' (Hann 2001). However, it is one of the most ethnically diverse towns in the UK, including being home to the largest Sikh population in the country. Cheryl Coppell, Chief Executive of Slough Borough Council has this to say:

> People here think Betjeman is mad, for them Slough represents a dream. I think Betjeman's is a very white, middle-class view, and I think there are some overtones of racism in there. We've just done one of the surveys that the government insists we do on what people think of their town. And something like 85% think Slough is a nice place to live. But we are a working town, surrounded by very upper middle-class areas. (Hann 2001)[19]

To site *The Office* in Slough, then, was to incite multiple associations of desperation that are not, presumably, shared by its residents. Even Slough has its dreams, as Coppell adds somewhat wistfully: 'The council says it hopes that Slough could one day be Britain's Bilbao.' In spite of Sloughish loyality and ambition, the location communicated to most of the British public the silent frustration of the anonymous, generic office drone, the small man of English society, his endurance and his idiosyncratic dreams of escape.

Occasionally in popular culture a character can transfer from a minor series into the mass imaginary, because he encapsulates an essence, his character being a vehicle for the transference of certain cultural anxieties and expectations. Courtesy, oblique-ness, convolution, restraint, inhibition, reserve, physical awkwardness, a distaste for artificiality, pretension, self-promotion, all of these characteristics typify ordinary English behaviour, but perhaps none so much as the sentiment of embarrassment. English culture has a distinctive preoccupation with embarrassment, and it is focal aspect of our comedy tradition, as its potential eruption is so pervasive. The social inhibitions of the lower middle-class/upper working-class fractions are noticeably strong sites for this anxiety, but it is true to say that fear of embarrassment marks out all British social classes, we are a country of 'manners', according to our own (self-fulfilling) national imaginary. David Brent's behaviours are intensely embarrassing, there must be few regular television viewers who have not seen the clip of his improvised dancing for the annual British charity event Red Nose Day, and cringed with the comic awfulness of his routine, as his employees look on, falling silent in horror, and his boss Neil covers his mouth in reflected shame.[20] Brent's routines (in this instance 'Flashdance fused with MC Hammer shit'), his mannerisms, his trials are centrally concerned with shame, he is a figure of intense pathos. This is why reviews most commonly refer to *The Office* as so painful as to be unwatchable, but it is also compulsive. All of my subsequent examples are taken from this single episode, Number 5 of Series 2.

Ricky Gervais himself has the outsider-within perspective, he has an anxious hyperactivity that means he seems to be always maniacally 'on', performing in comedy mode, not at ease with himself. Stephen Merchant describes himself too as 'pathologically shy'; due to his early onset of growth, he is a very tall 6 feet 7 inches and is often portrayed as having 'bulging eyes', material that is appropriated in the script in a scene when Merchant casts himself as a minor character 'Oggy the Oggmonster', friend of Gareth's, who is reduced to tears on Red Nose Day by the lads' teasing of his ocular malformation. Brent makes predictable jokes along the lines of did his parents put him in a Gro-Bag when he was a kid, and calls him a 'goggle-eyed freak'. Merchant, playing Oggy gets suddenly serious and says he has a medical astygmatism. Brent tries to redeem the situation and asks him what his real name is – 'Nathan' – 'Well that's a nice name... ' he says, before Nathan runs out crying. Gareth averts his face throughout. It is an unusually raw moment in which Merchant, the scriptwriter, is presumably fictionalising his real-life bullying as a gag, but afficianados of the series will undoubtably 'get' the tender paradox. We are acquainted with the stereotype of the tragic-comic genius, with endless figures from Charlie Chaplin to Jerry Lewis, to Tony Hancock and Kenneth Williams, and it is tempting to reproduce that here. But I think what Gervais and Merchant do so cleverly in *The Office* is take up all the incidental minor mockery and mundane teasing of everyday workplaces and expose its cruelty. Comedy is famously 'all about timing', and it is the timing that enables a segue from tragedy into the comic. Gervais and Merchant's specific skill in *The Office* is this comedy of embarrassment, delivered sparsely and with physical observation, humdrum and inspired. David Brent, and sometimes the ambitious Gareth, the hysteric, with his daydreams of military savagery, are most often the butt of this quietly effective humiliation. Their mutually reinforcing capacity for self-delusion is captivating, because although they are continuously shamed, these two characters with dignity refuse to be crushed. As Simon Edge (2002) noticed in *The Express* newspaper David Brent bounces back from every knock 'like a baleful, goateed Weeble'. Brent is smug and insecure, pompous and childish, petty, platitudinous and gauche. He is a diabolical Shakesperean fool, he is the buffoon Malvolio, or more relevant for today's audiences he has become one of the luminaries of British television comedy alongside Captain Mainwaring, Basil Fawlty, Alan Partridge. As Andrew Anthony observed, Brent is like the long-suffering Oliver Hardy 'with his almost stoical inability to see his own flaws, and his hopeless giggles, grimaces and sighs' (Anthony 2003). What Brent's character does is externalise or intensify the sadness behind each of the employees' lives, lives of modest aspiration, even 'quiet desperation'.

Perhaps the most painful scene in this episode comes when David Brent is sacked. Brent has survived the merger of his branch with Swindon, and become manager of the combined teams. Over his head is his former peer, Neil, who manages to terrorise Brent with his smooth, good-looking and confident, securely middle-class charm, and effortless executive style. Whereas Brent's physicality is repellent, sweaty, flabby and awkward, Neil is the alpha male who glides with clean and blameless menace through *The Office* every week, banking sexual and social approval. It starts with David Brent face to camera saying 'It's just a normal day at *The Office* innit? It's just a [pause] normal day.' Then he turns away from the camera momentarily and then turns back wearing his plastic red nose. Receptionist Dawn looks at him with a face that's clearly thinking 'Oh no, please not that'. She looks away in embarrassment (a shame gesture). No-one around Brent is yet laughing, he giggles frenziedly to himself and directly to camera at his imagined docu-soap audience, until the parasitic, co-dependent Gareth hops over to support his boss. Brent then comments in a stagey portentous voice 'Its Comic Relief... We are raising money for people who are *starving to death*.' The episode, like many others of *The Office*, somersaults from one shaming scenario to another, first David's lonely and humiliating performance as master of ceremonies, which is upstaged as usual by the bully Chris Finch, who tries to get Dawn to kiss a plastic nose affixed to his penis, then follows a weak joke about lesbians, then one of the guys in *The Office* is ambushed by a gang of co-workers who rip off his trousers and underpants, much to the man's evident distress. This is intercut ironically with Tim trying to make a statement to camera about dignity and charitable giving. The series motif shot of the photocopier comes in next, a narrative device enabling the viewer to process the brutal act s/he has just seen amongst the tedium, the detritus of the overlooked banality of lower middle-class life. The direction in the series is superb; it is said that the difference between tragedy and comedy is in timing, and *The Office* avoids being slapstick by using these long pauses and silences, with intercut images for pacing. It flirts constantly close to pathos by deliberate exclusion, by focussing on what *not* is said, and by giving the viewer a moment to realise intensely the shock of what she has just seen. Gareth and David then pull out from her desk a worker in a wheelchair and point out judiciously that the Comic Relief fund goes to 'cripples' like her, only the 'worse off' since she's got a job. Gareth comments that this charity should be means-tested so that its not fraudently claimed, when challenged as to how practicable this would be, his response is: 'Well – stick pins in their legs, see if they react.' Tim tries to kiss Gareth for a £1 donation, this is not mild homosocial play however, it is Tim and Dawn's habitual office subversion to tease him relentlessly about being gay, usually through getting Gareth to say double entendres, the meaning of which he remains ignorant, a joke that hyper-masculinised and twiggy Gareth never gets.

Brent performs a piece direct to camera about his future plans for global mentorism, his delusional grandeur winding up the dramatic tension. After this there are more office skits including a memorable first kiss between Dawn and Tim, the painfully stalled romantic interest that provides the series with its dramatic momentum, and then Jennifer and Neil from Head Office come in to give David Brent a verbal warning. Not long afterward they return, to offer him instead a non-negotiable redundancy package. In shock, David steps from behind his desk, wearing a lurid yellow fluffy ostrich costume, and points out that cruelly, the suits have done this on, of all days, Red Nose Day. Brent asks them to leave; at this moment what comes across is his incredible dignity. He goes out to the open office floor and relates what has happened to his staff, his grammar broken up, halting, and resorting to cliché. David's emotions always exceed articulation, hence his speech snowballs with clumsy aphorisms. Stood there holding the faux-penis of the ostrich head on a stick in front of him, his phallus comically rendered for what it is, waving monstrously large, fluffy, comic in cartoon yellow. Brent gesticulates vigorously with it as he is talking, the other hand laid effeminately on his hip:

'I said... you lot are... go mental...' [pause, camera cuts to silent workers, one man surveys the collective stillness, as a witness to the resounding inaction]
'... And I've got to go and give laughter!' [Brent waves up ostrich head/penis]
'But...' [pause, plays with the fluffy hair on the costume's head. Then tuts, nods head, then half-salutes with hand.]
'See you.' [Tuts. Pause. Brent turns round, still waiting for response.]
'Huh?' [Nothing. Brent nods to Dawn, tuts, looks at Dawn again. Dawn, panicked, looks back at the room. Brent exits. Dawn looks back at him in reverse shot. Still no response.]

Brent's words fall into the void. Outside in the gloom, Brent, Tim and Dawn pose for a photograph of themselves holding a large novelty cheque in the car park for the local newspaper. The photographer asks Brent to 'make it peck' 'run around a bit', so unsmiling and deflated Brent dances around in the silly costume, absolutely humiliated. In a desperate end to a wretched day, the

Figure 4.1 David Brent (Ricky Gervais) in 'The Office' (BBC Productions, 2003), with permission

photographer tells them he didn't bring a flash so the shots will be unusable. Capitalism operates a vampiric system, an oedipal paradigm of sucking skills from your superiors in order to advance beyond them, something that *The Office's* Gareth understands well when he is made David Brent's replacement. Tactical deference is the sacrificial logic of capitalism, envy and rivalry are the drivers.

Feminism of course has not escaped this pattern, one Head of Womens' Studies told me recently that a helpful tip from a fellow Subject Chair was to read Sun Tzu's 'The Art of War', the 2,500-year-old Chinese text, not in fact with the aim of helping her with senior management, but with coping with her own platoon (Krause 1996, Sun Tzu 2005).[21] Feminism has done a lot of shaming of women and men, abuse has often been justified as legitimate strategy. Shame and envy are poisoned apples for feminism: they are part of the Creation Myth I described earlier in which Eve desires the very thing she has been told by God she cannot have. In biting the apple, Eve is understood to have succumbed to envy and hence sin and suffering enter Paradise, by her own hand. The Garden of Eden is destroyed by a woman's inappropriate desire. 'Penis envy' has of course become a sad old joke for feminists, but envy is a social emotion that has been feminised throughout its discursive history. This is why Gareth's envious hyper-masculinity is coded as gay and feminine in *The Office*. Envy is centrally concerned with 'lack', with the realisation of lack and the attempt to destroy what the other is seen to have. Woman is henceforward doomed to recycle impossible longings for a thing she cannot have, frustrated and trapped by her wishes for insubstantial substitutes. Soren Kierkegaard, after all, called envy 'concealed admiration', and it is closely linked to emulation.

Envy is deeply associated with class *ressentiment*, the nineteenth century Marxist expanded concept of class resentment introduced as a philosophical term by Friedrich Nietzsche. The concept came to form a key part of his ideas concerning the psychology of the 'master-slave' question (articulated in *Jenseits von Gut und Bose* (*Beyond Good and Evil* 1886]), and the resultant birth of Christian morality. Nietzsche's first use and chief development of ressentiment came in his book *Zur Genealogie der Moral* (*On The Genealogy of Morals* 1887). The term was also analysed by Max Scheler in his book *Ressentiment* (1912), which was later suppressed by the Nazis. Ressentiment is viewed within Existentialism as an effective force for the creation of identities, moral frameworks and value systems, it is connected to a profound sense of frustration and hostility, directed at that which one identifies as 'the cause', and generated by a sense of inferiority. In the Marxist model this can ultimately generate a new value-system or morality that exists as a means of attacking the perceived source of one's own sense of inferiority. What is interesting about envy that the writings on ressentiment make clear is that it is possible to *mobilise* around envy, to create communities of (angry) sympathy. Envy has a creative, innovative energy that can draw people into an active political critique (and clique), it is an emotion that is rhetorical and bonding. Feminism can be said to be a movement that was created as much toward women as against men, it has thus been impossible to untangle envy in its subsequent life, and we may not wish to.

In her book *Ugly Feelings* Sianne Ngai has a chapter on envy that is primarily concerned with envy between women, in which the field of difference is class (Ngai 2005, 126–173). She also addresses the conundrum of why groups such as feminism rely on dynamics of antagonism to fuel debate, and she asks what is at the root of the vicious conflicts between feminists. She identifies how the psychological threat of aggression has historically been associated with feminists of color, but this is a specifically American assertion, for in the UK academy the same can be observed in reaction to working- class feminists and lesbians, and in Ireland the reaction is against Traveller women. She reminds us that in *Group Psychology* Freud (1922) talked about a correlation between feminine exemplarity (an inducement to imitation), and transmissibility or infection, and that femininity, through a mechanism of emulation, desires a compound female subject, one that can be aggressively incorporated. This is evident when groups shame one of their members whom they consider to be 'getting above themselves'. For the new 'feminist men', more anger and resentment toward women is often the outcome: if you shame someone then they will react and their illegible rage becomes a nascent (and unforeseen) political text.[22]

The Office is inspired, it takes as its aesthetic the emotion of shame, and turns it around and around in an organisational context like a bird with a worm, investigating its every facet. The show exposes the scopophilic curiosity of shame, for we must consider its compulsive viewing pleasure as constitutive. The audience is shamed by its own spectatorship of such relentless shaming; this is why so much meta-commentary on the text refers to its unwatchability –

watching it makes the shamed viewer's body squirm with squeamish identification in a shamed vernacular, it is a shame dialogue, and it makes viewing the show uncomfortable. It is a queer text too – it is no great theoretical leap to apply Judith Butler's theory of performativity to it – David Brent is a manager in drag, his phallic ostrich costume adding a direly comic, Disneyesque twist. Like many tragic heroic failures, Brent has his head in the sand, yet the viewer predicts his downfall, admittedly with her own hands shamefully covering her face, her fingers parted over her eyes. The viewer continues compulsively to watch, relishing the unremitting, excruciating humiliation, it is a highly *predictable* pleasure inscribed within the story, the shame spreads out but in the viewer it becomes substituted. What is she laughing at? It is the laughter of embarrassed recognition, of culpability. Brent's management is also highly camp, its ineptitude constantly draws attention to the artifice and fragility of 'real' management, its peculiar bodily comportments, its props, scripts, and gestures. Brent is indeed melancholic, as wounded hero he has lost the phallus, and the plot, but typically he does not know what he has lost. The audience knows what he has lost, but is unable to tell him, or show him, only observe transfixed. His tragic self-ignorance is simultaneously painful and hilarious, his inept machinations like chalk scraping on blackboard. *The Office* was a huge televison success for all of these reasons, but also for one other elemental reason: the effervescent joy of the series, its overall optimism. The writers not only gave us the endearingly prattish Brent, but in the satisfying closure of the series in the final Christmas specials Brent tells the bully Finch to fuck off, upstages Neil, and gets a fabulous and funny girlfriend. Brent is a twit, a plastic Napoleon, seedy but not dangerous, and definitely not a hard malevolent bully like Finch. There is also the conventional resolution of the romance plot between the receptionist Dawn and the salesman Tim who finally rises from his inertia and makes his romantic claim, a moment that made most of the nation cry therapeutically in relief, one reviewer calling it 'blissfully satisfying'. (Flett 2003). What *The Office* got so right was the belief that shame could be transformed into joy.

Notes

1   An earlier version of this essay's first part was rewritten following conversations with Noreen Giffney and Katherine O'Donnell. With thanks also to Julie Applin of the University of Sussex Library for finding some crucial references. I am grateful to John Rignell for bringing *The Office* to my attention during our discussions on shame.

2   The neologism belongs to Mary Daly.

3   Examples include: Chinn, Sarah (1994); Hughes, Christina (2004); Valentine, Gill (1998); Smyth, Ailbhe (1995); Munt, Sally R. (1997); Munt, Sally R. (1999).

4   Chinn's metaphor is also derived from a seminal essay written in the 1970s by Kolodny, A. (1980).

5   UK Higher Education Statistics Agency annual report Summer 2004.

6   For useful discussions of these wider issues including the Gallop case see Roof J. and Weigman R. (1995). *Judy* Vol. 1, Number 1, Spring Fever 1993 was produced by Ingrid Sischy and Grace Mirabella as a spoof on the iconoclastic reaction to the writing/persona of Judith Butler.

7   Narratives of hope, in my opinion, are more easily located in the creative rather than critical genres of writing. Creative writers, artists, and activists such as Adrienne Rich, Barbara Smith, Jeanette Winterson, and Monique Wittig have played an important role in creating, developing, and maintaining Lesbian Studies. These writers' tangential relation to the academy often enriches their view.

8   The idea of the good breast is Melanie Klein's (1975).

9   Or, as Hazlitt so eloquently puts it:

> Does any one suppose that the love of country in an Englishman implies any friendly feeling or disposition to serve another, bearing the same name? No, it means only hatred to the French... (1826/2004, 109)

10   I am grateful to Jenny Reardon for bringing this sad event to my attention.

11   http://www.uwnews.org/article.asp?articleID=25234, accessed 7 July 2006.

12   http://www.lbl.gov/today/2006/Jun/27-Tue/dynes-statement.pdf, accessed 7 July 2006.

13   http://www.abc.net.au/worldtoday/content/2005/s1284885.htm, accessed 8 July 2006.

14   http://bohemian.com/metro-santa-cruz/06.28.06/denice-denton-0626.html, accessed 7th July 7, 2006.

15   For other negative postings see for example The American Thinker at http://www.americanthinker.com/comments.php?comments_id=4771

Perhaps most disturbing is the report that local newspapers received a great deal of reader response over the death of Denton, much of it allegedly unfit to print.

16   http://santacruz.indymedia.org/newswire/display/18040/index.php, accessed 7 July 2006.

17   http://www.moonbattery.com/archives/2006/06/death_of_a_moon.html

18   BBC Productions (2001–3) *The Office*. Producer: Ash Atalla. Executive Producer Anil Gupta. Written and Directed by Ricky Gervais and Stephen Merchant. David Brent is played by Ricky Gervais. Tim played by Martin Freeman. Gareth played by Mackenzie Crook. Dawn played by Lucy Davis. Neil played by Patrick Baladi. Chris Finch played by Ralph Ineson.

19   Similar emotions characterise the working-class town of Crawley, close to Gatwick airport, which is surrounded by the rich semi-rural villages of West Sussex. See 'Horsham and Distinction' Simon Stewart, PhD thesis University of Sussex 2006.

20   For the terminally uncool, the clip can be downloaded from the BBC website at http://66.102.9.104/search?q=cache:YIU5HECYgo8J:www.bbc.co.uk/comedy/theoffice/clips/brent/dancer.shtml+david+brent+dancingandhl=enandct=cln kandcd=2andlr=lang_enandclient=safari

Red Nose Day is bi-annual event in the UK, originally started by a group of Left wing comedians, Comic Relief, in 1985. The day is intended to raise funds for charity via local sponsorship; at the most simple level people are encouraged to pay £1 for a plastic red nose which is worn on the day itself, with all proceeds going to the fund. A television marathon of comedy is screened all night live on BBC 1, with many public figures agreeing to perform ridiculous acts for the 'good cause'. Audiences phone in with donations. The USA, Australia and Germany have followed this model with similar schemes.

21   The same Head commented to me that Tzu's book had its limitations, because she wasn't a general and she didn't have an army.

22   More thought is necessary concerning these energies and effects of expulsion, subjection, injury to the psyche, repudiation, and vilification. Some of this work has already existed in postcolonialism for years, for example in Homi Bhabha's meditations on the melancholy, rage, and subjection of the oppressed.

Chapter 5

Shameless in Queer Street

Shameless was first screened on independent British television (Channel 4) in January 2004. Made by Company Pictures, it instantly gained audiences of more than 2 million. In a conversation with a non-academic acquaintance its popularity was summed up rather piquantly when he had asked me what I was working on this week and I responded with '*Shameless* – do you watch it?'. 'Oh yes,' he said, '– It's brilliant. But it is class tourism though isn't it?'[1] This valenced and ubiquitous knowledge of class dynamics is known globally as 'the British obsession with class', although clearly other states have their own peculiar renditions. What makes British television and film distinctive is this classed fascination, or rather class voyeurism, with its added nod to eroticism. What I intend to explore in this chapter is how *Shameless* is a model for understanding how class is read through ethnicity, and how shame and shamelessness are projected onto a civil/savage binary.

Press coverage of the series has made much of the author/auteur, a 46 year-old Burnley man, Paul Abbott. Abbott's biography is usually featured in press coverage *apropos* his deprived Lancashire childhood, his absconded parents, his rape aged 11 and subsequent mental health problems and teenage suicide attempt. An interview with Abbott in the week preceding the first broadcast in 2004 mentions that *Shameless* is a seven part series that is a 'recreation of his childhood' (Adams 2003). It is this aura of authenticity that is crucial to framing the series' critical reception, it endows the viewing position with licence to watch the underclass caricatures represented here with an empathetic identification, through an authorial guide into a culture that is undoubtedly alien to the mass of the British public. Abbott is depicted as writing himself out of the Northern underclass, being the only child in his family who could read and write. In British culture since the Industrial Revolution poverty is read spatially, and 'northern' is a pseudonym for 'working-class poor' and a host of associated meanings. Abbott's story is of the self-made man of Northern grit, he became the youngest ever scriptwriter for *Coronation Street*, the world's longest running television soap opera, and still a beacon in the industry for quality, multi-layered scripts, he went on to write for shows such as *Cracker, Clocking Off, State of Play* and *Alibi*. In 2004, following *Shameless*, Abbott won the writer's prize at the Royal Television Society (RTS) awards, and the Dennis Potter award for outstanding television writing at the BAFTAS (the British equivalent of the Oscars). In the media section of the *Guardian* newspaper in July 2004 he was described as the 'undisputed King of TV drama'.[2] In 2005 at the RTS awards in London, Abbott gained the Judges Award, the Writer Award, again, and *Shameless* got the prize for Best Drama Series. Anne-Marie Duff, the series' female lead, got the Best

Actress award. Paul Abbott now has his own production company, Tightrope Pictures. In 2006 Abbot went to the USA to oversee an NBC version of the series, which will provide an interesting forthcoming cultural contrast in terms of North American broadcasting restrictions on sex, drugs, and cigarettes (but not, of course, violence).

'Nobody's saying the Chatsworth Estate is the Garden of Eden'

On Tuesday January 13th 2004 the first episode was screened on Channel 4 Television. Kathryn Flett, writing in *The Observer* newspaper reviewed it:

> Home to the Gallaghers is a cramped and chaotic semi on the Chatsworth Estate – the sort with burned out car-carcasses rather than crepuscular duchesses... [the family is] just this side of feral. As far as his motherless kids are concerned, Frank (dys)functions mostly as a labour-intensive pet rather than a close blood relative, as loveable and yet repellent as a wet dog. He is, for example, regularly to be found sprawled on the kitchen floor in a urine-stained alcoholic stupor while around him the offspring – Fiona ('a big elp', according to Frank), Philip (or 'Lip for his 'habit of talking gobshite'), Ian ('a lot like his mam'), Carl ('nits love him'), Debbie ('sent by God, total angel') and Liam ('gonna be a star once we've got the fits under control') marshall themselves into some semblance of domestic harmony, though *The Sound of Music* it isn't. (Flett 2004)

Popular culture has resonant Irish stereotypes, but the name of Gallagher is most associated with the band *Oasis*, two brothers of Irish descent known for their brilliance, fighting, drinking and drug-taking. Frank [Vernon Francis] Gallagher's opening line on the credit sequence for *Shameless*, 'Nobody's saying the Chatsworth Estate is the Garden of Eden' gives viewers the first four clues of the show's concerns: the Garden of Eden is the place where shame and humanity first erupted, as television critic Nancy Banks-Smith points out (presumably, in the pre-Fall Arcadia) 'No one felt shame in the Garden of Eden' (Banks Smith 2004); this will be a show about 'class' – the British joke being that Chatsworth House is one of the richest aristocratic estates in England belonging to the Duke and Duchess of Devonshire, and a top destination for class tourism of rather a different kind; thirdly that 'Frank' is the show's paternal anchor, an unreliable narrator who tells it like it is – as the actor who plays Frank, David Threlfall, comments 'The Gallaghers are like *The Simpsons* on acid' (Rampton 2005). Fourthly, this is a drama concerning ethnicity, Gallagher being an Irish name. This will be a central concern of this chapter, as I take up an argument concerning the discursive expression of *shamelessness*. What I shall develop in this chapter is a model of how class is read *through* ethnicity, in a disconcertingly effaced effect of whiteness. I will illustrate how to be without or beyond shame in the British underclass is a position that is ethnically – even tribally – marked as Irish, historically the British state's internal Other, and how that structure is naturalised, 'unseen' to the viewer. Irish Catholicism functions here as the queer

Figure 5.1   Frank Gallagher (David Threlfall) from 'Shameless'
© Company Pictures, 2006, with permission

uncanny in an ethnic context, as Nicholas Royle has summatively stated 'The uncanny *is* queer. And the queer is uncanny.' (2003, 43)

Paul Abbott describes writing Frank Gallagher's speeches as 'some of the best days of my life. He has this pristine, unassailable self-regard, even when he's stealing money from his kids to buy drugs' (Rampton 2005). Frank's six children are: Fiona, 'Lip, Ian, Carl, Debbie, and Liam. Within the first three minutes of episode one a teenage girl, Karen Jackson, is giving a blow job to Philip ('Lip), Frank's teenage son, under the neighbour's dining room table, whilst her agorophobic, dildo- and bondage-fan mother, Sheila, is in the kitchen. This is 'Lip's payment from Karen for doing her homework ('She's desperate to get Physics'). 'Lip is depicted as preternaturally bright, his economic sideline is filling in fake insurance claims for the illiterate on the estate. In the next scene 'Lip discovers his 15-year-old brother's gay pornography in their bedroom. Fiona and her Catholic neighbour Veronica (an ex-hospital cleaner who has a veritable pharmacy of semi-legal drugs) meet series hero Steve McBride, who thumps and then bares his arse to a bouncer at a nightclub. The theme continues with Steve and Fiona's noisy fucking in the kitchen being interrupted by the police bringing home drunk, incontinent Frank. Each of these moments are filled with 'rough' shocking incidents that are counterposed with comedic music, within ten minutes the programme has firmly established that it is all about family, fucking, class, and violence.

On the DVD version of *Shameless* the viewer can choose to display subtitles, as on a foreign language film. Presumably this is so that the Mancunian accents can be understood. Similarly, the *Shameless* website at Channel4.com has the following header:

> Shameless is packed with sex, drugs, gratuitous violence, love and scams. Venture, if you dare, on to Manchester's Chatsworth Estate and meet the locals...[3]

It is possible to read the estate as a visual zoo in which erotic creatures can be safely viewed. A pet is of course a non-threatening term for an animal, and the continued animalising of the Gallaghers by critics underlines a tendency to orientalise, dehumanise and spectacularise the family in a voyeuristic fashion. Besides Flett's use of the term 'pets' to describe the Gallaghers, another well established British critic Nancy Banks-Smith reviewing the same episode describes Frank as 'an old family dog' (Banks-Smith 2004). Journalist James Rampton describes Paul Abbott's childhood with his siblings as an 'almost feral existence' (Rampton 2005). This is language that is coded by a historical discourse on the savage underclasses, underpinned by a classism rooted in racism, in eugenics, a medieval Chain of Being and an evolutionary metaphor crudely adopted from Charles Darwin's 'survival of the fittest'. As the actress who plays Fiona, Ann-Marie Duff comments about the Gallaghers: 'they're like animals in the way they protect their own.' (Lane 2004)

Reading class as an ethnicity – or worse species – was firmly established under Victorian Anthropology.[4] The anthropological gaze continues to be a pleasurable one for television viewers, and it is of course, highly eroticised. As Flett commented 'There's a lot of unselfconscious shagging in *Shameless*' (Flett 2004). In episode 1, second son, teenager Ian Gallagher, and shopkeeper Kash Karib are having sex in the backroom of the local shop; his brother 'Lip later confronts Ian: 'Fake Muslim cheats on white fundamentalist wife with gutless gay boy. Says more about [Manchester] United fans than it does about the rest of us.' Later 'Lip tries confronting Ian again, showing him the porn 'How can that be good for you? Actually up the arse? Do you get used to that? Can you?' 'Lip asks all the sex questions non-gays want to know, and then they share a companionable cigarette and laugh and say 'we were only given lungs so we could fucking smoke'. Smoking is the current pariah of the British middle class, a habit expelled from its midst, now judged as vulgar and needy. The tight historical associations between shame, homosexuality and interracial sex were often conflated, particularly under the 'British Raj', here in multicultural urban Britain Kash and Ian are 'shameless' in their pursuit of pleasure even though Ian is 15 and Kash is twice his age. The cacophony of sex and its associated transgressions to be enjoyed by the *Shameless* viewer is counterposed with the family's own code of ironic but warm affection, loyality is the 'moral containment' for this queer transgression. The episode ends with Frank's voice-over:

> One thing I'll say about my lot, though, you know they've been raised to show respect. And I like that. It matters in our house.

– as Frank himself sprawls unconscious on the kitchen floor with the family eating a large fried breakfast above him.

Actress Anne-Marie Duff who played Margaret in Peter Mullan's Irish film *The Magdalene Sisters* – a film about being utterly sexually shamed and derogated, and yet finding a self to live by – plays Fiona Gallagher. The film won The Golden Lion for Best Picture at the Venice Film Festival in 2002. Later that year she filmed on the BBC's *Sinners*, another drama set in the Magdalene Laundries in Ireland. Duff's mother is from Donegal and her father is from Meath, Duff herself was born in London, part of the working-class Irish Diaspora. She comments though: 'I'm not the full Paddy... I'm a Londoner.' And yet the majority of Duff's parts have been ethnically coded as Irish, Duff seems to be exhibiting a kind of ethnic shame herself regarding her origins; this may be due to the derogatory British label for second- or third- generation Irish who want to claim ethnic belonging – the 'Plastic Paddy' – a twist on the very Catholic and sticky label: 'Plastic Saints'. Fiona has an on-screen quality of whiteness that is mesmerising; uncannily, visually the character has more in common with tantalising movie stars than is strictly convincing. She has the same luminescence that Richard Dyer so elaborately described in his excellent *White* (1997). Duff commented on Fiona, 'She's shiny. She glitters doesn't she?' In the ethnicising of *Shameless* we have therefore a representation of white trash that is unusually alluring. Flett describes how the Gallaghers are not 'your typical white trash clichés... they are far too lovingly drawn to be loathsome' (Flett 2004). In series 3 (2006) the drama continued without Fiona, arguably the lack of a central 'star' who is desired by the audience temporarily rendered thin its scopophilic pleasures, and supplementary characters, such as the Maguires, come to feature more.[5]

Duff commented in an early interview about playing Fiona: 'It was really odd, but at the beginning, we didn't see that it was a comedy. We thought it was quite a gritty drama.' She raises the conundrum of how to place the series in terms of established genre, keen to point out the 'seriousness' of representing poverty and the underclass communities in Northern Britain. Yet the show is repeatedly interpreted as comedy by viewers, that quintessential genre of parody, self-conscious or not. This fits with Abbott's comments on the generic location of *Shameless*:

> Abbott said he wanted *Shameless* to be 'upsetting and funny in the same breath' but had some harsh words for TV executives who, he claimed, were not as ambitious as viewers. 'The TV literacy of audiences is way beyond most executives,' he said. 'We should be able to have comedy and emotional truth in the same drama... I want to change the genres.'[6]

Amy McNulty, speaking at a conference on British Television Drama in 2005 has commented upon the multi-layered style of the series, involving comedic farce and slapstick, old-fashioned romance, 'must-see TV moments', catch phrases such as Frank's 'a pint and a couple of Es', social realism, fantasy, melodrama, situation comedy, soap opera and conventions of the Victorian novel via the reliable narrator (McNulty 2005).[7] She described how the fast visual production style of *Shameless*, involving rapid cut editing and camera mobility, encodes realism, 'life as lived', and connotes the intimacy of the family video. McNulty pointed out how the conventions of storytelling in the series are quite formulaic, and thus audience pleasure is predetermined according to expectations. She made key observations regarding how the issue of authenticity is talked up in media reception of the show, and that this tendency ignores the extent to which the representations are highly stylised, and hyper-real, reminding us of the professional production and firm industrial conventions that underpin the narrative. She argued that middle-class audiences enjoy *Shameless* precisely because of its predictability, and that the over-the-top performances are key to the viewer's delight and satisfaction. *Shameless* also parodies the stereotypes ('yes, we shag endlessly and only eat fish and chips or fried breakfasts'), the knowing wryness of its tone is simultaneously deconstructive and sentimental. The speed of the narrative, coupled with fast jump-cut editing, rhythmic bass soundtrack, and hand-held camera work, creates a buffeting effect on the viewer that can obscure the individual intensity of cruel and shocking incidents. The storylines are shock-jock TV, their net impression is of a ceaseless wave of ironic trauma. Within the first seven minutes of episode 2 we have two scenes of voyeurism, one of the milkman's giant erection following Veronica's shifting breasts pressed against her window, one of vigorous anal fucking between Veronica and Kev (which is witnessed by Fiona), a vision of gay prison sex for Ian, a reminder of Karen's blow jobs, and the queer incident of Carl tongueing his plate of fried eggs, upon which the other kids comment surreally: 'they're his tits. It's the only reason he does eggs. He just licked that one.'

Julia Hallam of Liverpool University, in response to McNulty's paper, pointed out that there are generic forebears to *Shameless* such as in Liverpool pioneering scriptwriter and animal rights activist Carla Lane's invention of 'situation tragedy' in the 1980s.[8] *Bread* (BBC, 1986–1991) is probably the closest precursor to *Shameless*; drawing upon her home city of Liverpool for its inspiration, *Bread* explores the hopes and dreams of a working-class Catholic family as they try to make ends meet amidst the poverty and unemployment that all but swamped Liverpool in the late 1980s. *Bread* became one of the UK's most popular sitcoms, competing at the top of the ratings by 1988. Other influences include Director Penny Woolcock's council-estate films *When the Dog Bites* (Consett, Newcastle), *Shakespeare on the Estate* (Birmingham), *Mad Passionate Dreams* (Rhondda Valley), *Macbeth on the Estate* and her docu-dramas *Tina Takes a Break* and *Tina Goes Shopping* (all Leeds), filmed using residents as actors. The success of *Shameless* lies therefore at least partly in it conforming to generic conventions in terms of its mode of production, its appropriation of televisual clichés and formal narrative imperatives, and in its knowing direction of audience response.[9] Generic competence is not necessary to the viewer's pleasure, it is a dramatic text that can be seen by younger student audiences with no familiarity, for example, or older more 'knowing' audiences that can self-reflexively follow a tradition of screen representations of poverty. From the breathless enthusiasm of the media commentatary though we might gather that watching *Shameless* for the critics functions like a David Attenborough nature documentary; the flavour communicates the irrepressible thrill of biologists discovering a new species.

Anthropological origins, class tourism and 'slumming'

Director Penny Woolcock gave the annual Forman Lecture in Visual Anthropology at the University of Manchester (the city where *Shameless* is shot), in 2004, entitled 'Stories from the Margins'. It primarily concerns her documentary *The Wet House* filmed inside a London shelter for alcoholics which allows them to continue drinking. She starts by talking about what she learned from reading two anthropology books as a young woman, Marcel Mauss' *The Gift* and E.E. Evans-Pritchard's *The Nuer*, a tribe of naked nomadic Sudanese who live with their cattle and drink their blood to communicate with their ancestors:[10]

> I was impressed by the whole notion of fieldwork – the idea of leaving home and setting off to find a small microcosm, trying to figure out how it works, and using this knowledge to cast light back onto the more complex metropolis in which we live.

She found these street alcoholics familiar and totally strange at the same time, she mentions that many of them were Irish, old soldiers from paramilitary units, both loyalist and Republican. Talking about gaining entrance to these 'underworlds' that are her films subjects Woolcock describes how:

> ... outsiders generally only go in on punitive missions, to take people's children away, accuse them of fiddling 'the social' or arrest them. Initially you are foisting yourself on people who just want you to piss off. You are shunned.

> I came across this in *The Nuer*.

> *When I entered a cattle camp it was not only as a stranger but as an enemy, and they seldom tried to conceal their disgust at my presence, refusing to answer my greetings and even turning away when I addressed them.*

She draws self-conscious lessons from the anthropologist E.E. Evans-Pritchard. To shun strangers is a way of maintaining dignity by a threatened group, so when asked why she goes into these 'underworlds', her answer is the stock documentary realist phrase 'to tell stories from the margins in a truthful and humane way. It's not The Truth, of course. Just the best truth I can tell' (Woolcock 2004). It is clear from reading about Woolcock that her intentions are to be empathetic and ethical, however established patterns of objectification are clear, like the rendition of Woolcock and her assistant 'going native' in timeless fashion as they travel home on the Tube stinking with urine and stained with vomit. Woolcock, although a middle-class middle-aged white woman, has spent time living as a poor single parent when younger, claiming now to remain living 'on the edge' of underclass urban enclaves. She explains that, 'what fascinates me about life on the edge is the carnivalesque, roller-coaster quality of life. Where people flout the rules, cock a snook and laugh like drains.' This rather Bakhtinian statement bears more analysis: rather like her claim that where 'we' live is a 'more complex' metropolis, she has fallen for primitivism, believing that the underclasses are residually more simple, their appetites more raw. The association with the carnivalesque is of course ripe with meaning, and it is also this same chaotic sensibility that runs through *Shameless*, whose camera movement and overall aesthetic can be described as 'roller-coaster'. Disadvantaged communities have their own rules, and their own complex systems; these formations may not be observable however by the interloper's camera, peering down the drain. To give this Director credit however, Woolcock seems more aware than most of the perils of spectatorship, admitting that her voyeurism brings her vicarious, liberating thrills.

Class tourism has a long and spatial history; generally it is the economic mobility of higher status classes that confers the freedom to wander socially downward and consume the visual spectacle, to enjoy the erotic/affective satisfaction to be found there. Less voluntaristically perhaps, the working

Figure 5.2 Woodcut. 'The Ale Wife' circa 1810. A woman proffers a jug of ale to a man in the street from her 'house of shame'
Source: Getty Images/Hulton Archive

classes have sashayed through upper- and middle-class spaces for centuries, cleaning and serving food to them, their children, and their animals. The great Victorian novel would be lost for subject matter without this armchair travel, think, for example of Elizabeth Gaskell's *North and South*, the writings of Jack London, Matthew Arnold, or even the complete works of Charles Dickens. George Orwell famously tripped through the lands of the poor in the twentieth century; although Orwell's writing was more sexually explicit, he encased his remarks in disgust. One fascinating study of the moral ambiguity of class tourism in the nineteenth century is Seth Koven's *Slumming: Sexual and Social Politics in Victorian London* (2004). Koven depicts the cultural history of the Victorian and Edwardian 'slummers', hundreds of men and women who – sometimes on an omnibus, sometimes on foot – visited the sites of London poverty to thrill to the sights of the 'wretched houses where they are huddled together like beasts' (Rev. Prebendary W. Rogers of Balliol College, quoted in Koven 2004, 9). The underclasses of London were described then in various ways: the residuum, the submerged tenth, as miserable paupers. An ethos of degeneracy and fears of miscegenation permeated Victorian public discourse on the underclasses, the growth of eugenics and a distorted Darwinism ensured that quasi-medieval attitudes toward social hierarchy persisted, although newly articulated via scientific, rather than religious statements.

Ideologically the leisure pursuit of class tourism has been deployed for a variety of educational purposes: to teach of the injustice of poverty, or to train in the absolute faith of social differentiation. The intention of the author-guide to such imaginary or real journeys does not (of course) manage to circumscribe its effects upon the audience. Visiting, or even taking up residence in the slums, could be pursued for philanthropic reasons, setting up charities for the poor to provide for their perceived moral, physical and spiritual needs; however, Koven's study is based around these questions:

> Was philanthropy a laudable form of self-denial, an expression of a deep human impulse to witness and enter sympathetically into the suffering of others in order to diminish it? Or was benevolence merely a cover for egoistic self-gratification, a means imaginatively and literally to enter otherwise forbidden spaces, places, and conversations, to satisfy otherwise forbidden desires? (Koven 2004, 14)

Koven examines some well-known cases of alleged class tourism. He describes how the 'New Man' worked philanthropically in the slums allowing middle-class masculinity to develop 'types', inventing new and distinct practices of manliness which were inscribed upon the bodies of the poor. The attraction and repulsion of contact with the poor was often relished, more often, however, the salacious activity of slumming was layered with disavowal. Many participated in that journey as though their face was turned aside, their vision obscured by their handkerchief. Perhaps they were ashamed, split between their scopophilic curiosity and an internal conscience. Perhaps it was just the smell: in Tomkins' shame vocabulary 'dissmell' is a characteristic of the depressive:

... [the] one who has forever lost his innocence. Though he has not been driven out of the Garden of Eden to live by the sweat of his brow in fear of his God, nonetheless he knows what it means to be driven into that corner of Eden which is hell; and having internalised disgust and dissmell, he is now capable of judging others as he has been judged. (Tomkins in Sedwick and Frank 1995, 224)

Slumming often involved the adoption of a disguise, and so the wealthy would occasionally masquerade as destitute in order to be admitted to the state-regulated workhouses. Hence the fascination reaped by the journalist James Greenwood's report of such a nightly escapade in 1866 published in the *Pall Mall Gazette*, in which the opportunity to enjoy a frisson of homo-eroticism via his 'horrified' reports of male nakedness and touch would delight the reader. As Greenwood comments: 'I could not help thinking of the fate of Sodom' (in Koven 2004, 43). A penny leaflet edition that retold the story of this heroic dandy becoming a tramp, trespassing in the dirt of the homeless, sold thousands of copies in the London streets. Koven's analysis unravels the fears of sodomitical contamination that suffused such texts, even health reformer Edwin Chadwick was not immune to its rhetorical power. The publication of 'A Night' galvanised John Addington Symonds to write 'John Morden' a cross-class love poem between men. The vice of homosexuality, according to commonsense and the trope of the 'sodomitical sublime', was more prevalent amongst low-class men, conflating economic marginality with sexual marginality. As Koven concludes, reading John Worby's tales of 'queer slumming' in the 1930s in conjunction with 'the truth that Greenwood has discovered: [that] extreme poverty among men was itself a form of sexual deviance' (Koven 2004, 86), he comments on George Orwell's note on London's 'dirt and its queer lives', that his account in *Down and Out in Paris and London* (1933):

... marked the culmination of a long history of Victorian and Edwardian social reporting in Britain that imagined the slums of London not only as sites of physical and social disorder – 'dirt' – but as spaces hospitable to 'queer' lives, and 'queer' sexual desires. (Koven 2004, 183)

'Going dirty' however was not only the provenance of men; elite women would also enter the slums presumptively, with the ostensible aim of a 'civilising' scheme of social purity that would also serve up a freeing effect upon their own queer desires (or more negatively 'morbid curiosity' as it was termed at the time).

Edward Carpenter was the radical socialist, utopian ruralist and vegetarian who most associated the 'urning' with a vision of philanthropic love. Whilst Edward Carpenter's ideas are universally recognised, one may also wonder to what extent they were also George Merrill's, his longterm working-class partner. Dissident male sexuality in the nineteenth century was often based upon a cross-class model, famously Oscar Wilde had a harem of rough boys with which to pleasure himself, but the practice was widespread, particularly amongst aristocratic gentlemen.[11] The Oxford University charity in Whitechapel, Toynbee Hall, was a centre for such lovers. Working and underclass men's sexuality was seen as more primitive, natural, and accessible than the refined, yet perhaps admittedly repressed modalities of the aesthete. Christian socialism grew out of the trade union movement, the fraternal student brotherhoods, the urban university settlements, and the non-conformist theologies of the nineteenth century. Koven describes how various denominations such as Methodists, Quakers, and Catholics established their slum outposts in the East End, each experimenting with their version of a muscular Christianity. Contemporaneous accounts relate the intense hyper-real quality of the participants' experience, that it is supposedly more real, more vibrant, more filled with atavistic and vital forces than its pallid bourgeois circles of origin. Henry Scott Holland, an Oxford House man, describes with relish the spectacle of the slums:

> You must see actual living, actual dying, actual sinning, real good hearty vice, naked sin: drunkenness, murder, reveling and such like. (Holland, 1871, quoted in Koven 2004, 253)

Finding the sacred amongst the squalor is a Christian ritual, and a spatial narrative, based upon Christ's travails walking the world among the sinners. There can be seen here a masochistic, sensory joy that is both wallowing and redemptive at the same time, something that can also be perceived in Christian liturgy. Historian Karen Halttunen has commented upon what she calls the 'pornography of pain' contained within the humanitarian appeals of the past two centuries, emphasising the erotic charge of watching cruelty and deprivation (Haltunnen, Karen 1995, 324–5). Photographs of barely clad, ragged children were used by philanthropic organisations in the nineteenth century to raise charitable funds, their appeal was sensual at the same time as pitiful.[12]

In terms of historicising the sexual objectification of the poor it is impossible not to remark in passing upon the case of Victorian gentleman Arthur Munby (1828–1910). Munby was a collector, even an archivist, of representations of big working-class women. He preferred them dirty and rough, and preferably, deformed. He kept a huge record of his findings in photographs, diaries, letters, drawings and poems, material that has in itself fascinated scholars of the twentieth century. Munby's great personal experiment was his secret marriage to a maidservant Hannah Cullwick. The two lovers met when they were in their twenties in 1854. Although it is suspected that they never actually had sexual intercourse, the two built an erotic relationship in which Hannah would dress up (or rather down) in servant's rags for Arthur, who would fondle her, and preserve this image in drawings and photographs. The pleasures of voyeurism and fetishism in Hannah's degradation seem to be at least partly shared, although of course the couple were firmly located within the gender and class paradigms of their time. The Lancashire pit women who attracted Munby's prurience, for example, called him 'the Inspector'. Hannah frequently licked his boots, she seemed to gain erotic satisfaction from her humiliation, although the extent of her free consent in this play is impossible to establish. Attainment of nobility through servitude as practiced by working-class Hannah cannot be seen as totally disassociated from the articulate sacrifice of the philanthropic priests who flocked to the East End slums, the discourse was available to all via Christian worship. The photographs of Hannah denote a strong, self-knowing countenance and her recorded comments suggest she is far from a brainless drudge. To victimise Hannah is to see her as ignorant of, and complicit with, her own degradation; to deprive her of mindful consent is to reproduce the model of helpless passivity that so dominates views of the infantile underclass.

Munby also collected noseless women, he was excited by their corporeal abasement. Noses, in neo-classical cultures, were the *sine qua non* of rationality, judgement and beauty. In this phallic displacement onto the nose, to be without one was to be abnormally deformed; syphilis was the prime causation, and thus the lack of a nose connoted moral as well as sexual corruption. As Barry Reay remarks in his fascinating study *Watching Hannah* (2002) all of these specific photographs have vanished from the Munby archive, cleansed out subsequently by relatives. His fancy for the grotesque, for the Gothic deformities that populated the Victorian imaginary, was relished by Munby, and he clearly derived intense eroticism from his encounters with what, in the parlance of the time, were freaks and monsters. Reay asserts that Munby's enthrallment with such creatures was precisely to uphold his own values of extreme femininity:

> Conventions of the feminine – posture, a shapely body, attractive hair and clothes – framed this mask of death and disfigurement to make even more telling the horror of the essential femininity effaced and trapped within. My claim is that for Munby, these de-formations served, powerfully, to confirm their opposite: the feminine ideal. The very appeal of such subversions was the strengthening of their 'other'. (Reay 2002, 59)

We are constantly reminded of the crucial role of the face in shame and individuation. To dip into the seeming horrible savagery of another's existence is to be temporarily thrilled, but the voyager is safely returned to a normality reconfirmed, and newly appreciated. Many issues are raised here by the case study of Munby and his Pygmalions: how much of Munby's class transgression upheld conventional fantasies of working-class objects of desire; was Munby purely eccentric, or did he exemplify whole cultures of cross-class eroticism? Was it truly, subversively queer, or was Munby's archetypal fetishism merely one fine example of a diffuse cultural curiosity? What aspects of Munby's pleasure can be similarly reiterated in the audiences of *Shameless*? Representing the underclass is fraught with erotic projection, hence we need to reconsider the 'figurability' of the underclass with these historical, rather queer frames in mind.

Shameless the drama did inspire one or two twenty-first century journalists to do their own slumming in the West Gorton estate where the drama is filmed. Carole Cadwalladr of *The Observer* wrote a half page feature 'Down the Welly with the real Gallaghers' at the start of Series 3 in January 2006, based on a trip to The Wellington pub, the real life equivalent of The Jockey. On screen at The Wellington is the live feature length first episode of the new series, which has garnered a large, allegedly drunk audience from the estate. Cadwalladr is introduced by the landlord Steve to the 'real' Frank, John or 'Acky' and his family the Atkinsons. And sure enough the characters match their types: there is Frank/Acky, Sheila/Linda his wife, son Liam/Connor (an Irish name), and eldest daughter Fiona/Jo. The family agree the programme is just like their life, they joke with knowing familiarity about the comparison. Cadwalladr does make evaluative or surveillant comments like 'I'm trying to figure out how seven people sleep on a sofa-bed in the lounge and a couple of armchairs', an observation that would not be out of keeping with Edwin Chadwick's Victorian survey of the poor, overcrowding and hygiene (Chadwick 1842). What is most notable in this piece however is the style of writing, which mimics the fast edit, breathless sensory stream of the series:

> We can't leave because someone called Sharon is banging on the window and Steve is refusing to let her in. Not-Frank's telling me about the son who got done for 'tipping over a policeman', Connor shows no sign of going anywhere near a bed, Katherine 'the gypsy', has turned up and is getting boisterous. Howard tells me how it reminds him of being trapped inside a pub during the Moss Side riots, and Lynette has invited me back the next time there's a funeral. 'They're fucking brilliant.' (Cadwalladr 2006, 10)

Ethnic, colourful, vibrant – 'real good hearty vice' as the Reverend Holland might say. Journalist and the interviewees alike seem to share a consciousness of the anthropological or governmental gaze, and are keen to demonstrate a mutual playful irony, a class truce perhaps. One cannot help but wonder if this transaction was reciprocal, presumably the Atkinsons got free drinks for the night from *The Observer*.

Irish racism and the tribal cultures

Máirtín Mac an Ghaill reveals the 'current disavowal of anti-Irish racism' in British culture, he claims that some would call it a 'structuring absence', and an 'erasure' (Mac an Ghaill 2000, 138). Mac an Ghaill's work on Irish racism and migration is excellent, but I would go further, and argue that in the British imaginary, in the field of representation, there is a *displacement*, in which social exclusion, deprivation, and the ethnicising of an underclass is discursively Irish, and that an example of this structure can be seen in *Shameless*. There is a discursive correspondence between the figuration of the Irish and the figuration of the underclass as a dichotomous threatening/pet-like internal Other of British culture. Of course, seeing a tribal underclass as either ignorant savages or clowning children has a long pedigree that stretches back to feudal periods; it is a tried and tested device of eroticisation and political domination. Observe some mutual features:

1. Extreme appetites: exemplified in sexual, sensual, or addictive behaviours; association with greed for drugs, cigarettes, sugar, fats, and alcohol.

145

2. Carnivalesque humour, coupled with unlimited and unruly play, and teasing.
3. Emotion overwhelms reason, sometimes extreme; can be bipolar, manifest in hilarity or doom.
4. Tribal loyalty over-rules any external regulation; there is always one powerful family, whose head (matriarch or patriarch) is known as ruthless in maintaining 'order' or misrule.
5. Each individual is a real 'character', 'larger than life'; an ability to give a 'good story'.
6. An emotive bond to a specific 'place', a concomitant suspicion of 'outside'.
7. Display of distrust and ridicule toward strangers, who are undermined, often cruelly.
8. Criminality including the running of crooked 'Black economies', illustrative of primitive (to the observer), atavistic local systems and rules (eg. the scam).
9. Religiosity, blind faith and superstition; mysterious beliefs and a tendency to be 'lucky', to be blessed by fate.
10. Hedonistic sexuality, often perverse, including homosexuality and paedophilia.
11. Dirt and disease including Sexually Transmitted Diseases (eg. 'crabs', herpes).
12. Excess corporeality and bodily fluid incontinence manifest in 'gross' behaviour.
13. Behaviour that can be read as 'Black' – for example the nineteenth century scientific investigations of the Western Irish as the 'negroes of Europe'; the 'street' cultures of contemporary 'chavs', representing an ethnic 'scale' in which Black = worse.
14. The gendering of subjects as feminine irrespective of actual sex.
15. Unpredictable, extreme violence (the savagery of the hidden estates, the IRA).
16. The idea of 'simplicity', that they are closer to nature, animalistic or rawly human.
17. Sentimental or romantic attitudes.
18. Deviousness and cunning, the representation of which can be animalistic.
19. Lack of formal education or qualification but showing instinctual cleverness, and native creativity.

There are in addition obvious signifiers of Irishness in *Shameless* – the Gallaghers themselves have an Irish name, and so do the only other large family represented in the series, the wild and vicious Maguires, vicious sociopaths with Belfast accents. There are many signs of Catholicism in residents' homes, including the Gallaghers themselves and next door neighbours Carol and Veronica. Is it co-incidental that so many of the characters of *Shameless* are Catholic, (as is Stuart in *Queer as Folk*, and famously Stephen Gordon in *The Well of Loneliness*)? The overt Irish coding in *Shameless* serves to underline my interpretation here of ethnic ascription.

Anne McClintock, using a Foucauldian model of classification, observes how in Victorian times:

Racial stigmata were systematically, if often contradictorily, drawn on to elaborate minute shadings of difference in which social hierarchies of race, class and gender overlapped each other in a three-dimensional graph of comparison. The rhetoric of race was used to invent distinction between what we would now call *classes*. T.H. Huxley compared the East London poor with the Polynesian savage, William Booth chose the African pygmy, and William Barry thought that the slums resembled nothing so much as a slave ship. (McClintock 1995, 54)

It also worked in reverse: 'Similarly the rhetoric of *class* was used to inscribe minute and subtle distinctions between other *races*' (McClintock 1995, 55). The Zulu, she gives as an example, was seen as the 'gentleman' of the black race. What we see in contemporary British culture is this haunting heritage of co-implication read through Irishness and negritude, that results in an uncompromising racism toward our own underclass. The langue and the parole of this heritage are disavowed in an act of intentional forgetting, a momentous disavowal that can be seen in the diffuse hatred that is routinely directed toward those living within poverty, and exhibiting powerlessness. Take, as an indication of this, the demonisation of young single mothers in most Western countries right now. An anxiety of racial degeneration underpins these projections, misfounded upon a class/status-based fears of falling into debt, sexual risk, and having social privilege taken away. It is rooted in older myths of social collapse and decay. Often the newly promoted lower middle class or the respectable working class are the ones with most to fear in this respect, and therefore manifest the greatest aversion, as their capital is the least secure.

The underclass/Irish are of course desired as well as reviled. This interdependent mechanism of desire, disavowal and displacement is rooted within a dominant culture that is ashamed of its ongoing vilification: competitiveness, envy, and contempt are all types of shame-related behaviour, and Britons exhibit this behaviour toward the poor and the Irish alike, indeed indistinguishably. Blame and judgment are also behaviours closely related to shame, in a classic projection of fear of failure. So the curious position of *Shameless* is to be at one and the same time the repository of all the disgust and dissmell that embodies the repressed aspects of bourgeois norms, yet simultaneously to associate *pleasure* with that embodiment via an intense emotional engagement with the narrative. This narrative becomes a cathartic release for forbidden emotions. 'You are shameless, you!' is an Althusserian interpellation, a concept first coined by Marxist philosopher Louis Althusser to describe the process by which ideology addresses the individual subject, thus effectively producing him/her as an effect. In other words, the situation always precedes the (individual or collective) subject. Interpellation specifically involves the moment and process of *recognition*, of interaction with the ideology at hand (Althusser 1966). As Judith Butler explains:

> This turning towards the voice of the law is a sign of a certain desire to be beheld by and perhaps also to behold the face of authority, a visual rendering of an auditory scene – a mirror stage or, perhaps more appropriately, an 'acoustic mirror'. (1997, 112)

So, the *Shameless* cast of actors must at one and the same time recognise and represent this shame (they are there to *be shamed*), and yet rebut this shame using performative skills. This is how the series uncannily reinforces, confronts, and combats stereotypes concurrently. Coding the Gallaghers as Irish successfully distances the whole family as ethnic Other, a synthesis that has a convincing ideological and historical logic, thus rendering them visually safe to the non-Irish, middle-class viewer, the dominant audience segment.

In the unrelenting sexualisation of the Gallaghers and the Balls, the two main households in *Shameless*, each episode opens with fucking scenes. *Shameless* is also drawing on another historical discourse of representation, the eroticisation of the Irish. In 'Dismantling Irena: The Sexualizing of Ireland in Early Modern England' Ann Rosalind Jones and Peter Stallybrass (1992) point out that in 1188 Giraldus Cambrensis had described the Irish as 'entirely descended from beasts', a view that later fed into a sixteenth century typology of the Irish as itinerant barbarians, cannibalistic monsters, and virile warriors, 'Scythians'.[13] As the authors comment, this was a self-justifying ideology of war, so that: 'The imagined terror of the Scythians was met with the [real] terror of English colonialism' (Jones and Stallybrass 1992, 161). In an analysis of the contemporaneous poet Edmund Spenser, Jones and Stallybrass view as significant Spenser's selectivity from the Ancient Greek translations of the myth of the heroic Scythian adversary, notably his omissions from the original, including comments that the Scythians had had their male organs atrophied, that they were insane, possibly even pederasts, and perversely feminine. Hippocrates described them as moist, soft and chill, with lost manhoods caused from too much jolting from horse-riding. The authors argue that Spenser omits this feminisation of the Scythians to justify the brutal military oppression of the Irish. At the same time however the colonial English depicted Ireland in feminine terms as a virgin waiting to be penetrated, albeit one that is 'spotted'. Paradoxically, Irish women are also equated with prostitutes, they are the morally disordered progenitor of 'bastards'. This subjugation of the Irish, therefore, was imagined via emasculation, wherein the masculine resistance had to be brutally tamed, through rape, or enforced feminisation. The Irish were seen as class rebels too, in the Early Modern English view, they deliberately ignored appropriate class differentiations, which was read as a refusal to meet English standards of attire, indicating correct social categories. The men in Dublin in 1585 were being forced to wear trousers (Jones and Stallybrass 1992, 167). What we can glean from Jones and Stallybrass's study is that the glut of sex/gender projection being directed at the Irish via the colonial power, can only reflect the highly sexed, contradictory, and opportunistic confusion at 'home'.

Shameless can be considered part of the trend identified by Karen Bettez Halnon as 'poor chic':

> Poor Chic refers to an array of fads and fashions in popular culture that make recreational or stylish – and often expensive – 'fun' of poverty, or of traditional symbols of working class and underclass statuses... what is distinctive about Poor Chic today is that 'lower class' masquerade is now center stage in the historical theatre of downward impersonation, and is a phenomenon that takes place in the contexts of the increasing and extreme polarization of classes. (Bettez Halnon 2002, 501)

By deploying George Ritzer's McTourism as a guide she explains how Poor Chic protects its protagonist against sliding into poverty (or being mistaken for the 'real thing'), through the rational (controlled, efficient, predictable and calculable) consumption of it. Citing a range of examples from the USA from music and fashion to body-styling such as tattooing, Halnon says that Poor Chic symbols include mental illness, homelessness, starvation, 'shabby' refurbishment, drug addiction, 'white trash' culture, body augmentation, work clothes, slum and gang 'lifestyles', a 'code of the street' that is marked by anger, alienation, and delinquency. She argues that these stereotypes are distortions of reality, grounded in the real rather than complete simulation, that render the poor 'open' or de-privatised. She reminds the reader, using Erving Goffman's work on stigmatised identities that 'the extent to which an identity is open and accessible is a sociological gauge of its devaluation' (Bettez Halnon 2002, 509). The free association and dispersal of select signs taken from the cultures of the underclass however, does nothing, she maintains, to erase actual poverty, it just obscures it. She quotes Marx:

> 'The commodity form possesses the peculiar capacity of concealing its own essence and origin from the human beings who live with and by it.' The commodity fetishizes; it conceals its essence and replaces it with desires purchased for a price. The tourist (conveniently in this case) is estranged from what really lies behind the commodity: the haunting humanity of the poor and the fearful reality of poverty. (Bettez Halnon 2002, 508)

She concludes that the rational consumption of symbolic poverty is a class-distinguishing activity that controls against fears of decline by cultural ingestion, by its containment as a short, safe, socially-distanced and sanitised experience of symbolic commodification.

Let us reconsider the viewing of *Shameless*: it is on the independent Channel 4 Television, the professionalism of the writing, drama, production and hence identification evoked by *Shameless* is so powerful that it is sometimes hard to remember its *fictionality*. The actors in the series deal with this ascribed verisimilitude by either getting annoyed with the collapse, notably David Threlfall who plays Frank Gallagher, or like Jody Latham ('Lip), they seem to publically play with, and wish to gain street credibility from, the 'hardness' associated with their character. Goffman asserted how the impersonation of a disesteemed person evokes little concern (Goffman 1959). The viewer of *Shameless* is seduced into a cacophonic world that generically is not that different from a Dickensian novel, in its time the radical popular culture of its generation with a committed message of social reform from the author. Dickens also had that same hyper-realism (developed from the theatrical tradition of melodrama) that is typical of representations of Irishness. We love *Shameless* like the Victorians loved Dickens, and that is its moral contradiction.

Seeing the underclass

The underclass has only recently been defined as an entity by academics. Alan Buckingham's useful survey of approaches 'Is there an underclass in Britain?' in the *British Journal of Sociology* was only published in 1999. Skipping over his traditional neo-Weberian analytical frame (which unsurprisingly makes no allowances for a lesbian, queer or feminist viewpoint), one is still able to deduce a set of suppositions that go into identifying underclass norms; Buckingham summarises findings from three discrete socio-'logical' methods: the behavioural approach, the labour market approach, and critical approaches that oppose the definition.[14] Here he describes the behaviourial approach, which generates a set of key predictions:

(a) the underclass will consist mainly of welfare dependent lone mothers and 'workshy' males.

(b) Underclass members will hold a value system at odds with that of mainstream society.

(c) The underclass will be culturally homogenous; its members sharing similar values and behaviours.

(d) The cultural traits of the underclass will be transmitted across generations.

(e) Low work motivation and low cognitive ability will be powerful causes of underclass membership.

(f) There will be a clear distinction between the respectable 'moral' working class and the 'immoral' underclass (Buckingham 1999, 50).[15]

Labour market approaches contribute the following related typologies:

(a) The underclass will be culturally distinctive.

(b) Underclass members will reject institutionalised politics either by political withdrawal or through direct action.

(c) Common economic and spatial segregation of the underclass ensures membership is homogenous.

(d) Low occupational class, lack of skills and lack of educational qualifications will be powerful causes of underclass membership (Buckingham 1999, 51).

It is that spectre of the Victorian 'residuum' that Buckingham attempts to disprove, with the longitudinal National Child Development Study that was commissioned in 1958. One small part of this took place when their schoolteachers were asked to describe the children's behaviour, aged 11:

> When compared with children who later entered the lower working class [as opposed to the underclass] the 11 year olds destined for the underclass were significantly more likely to exhibit hostile, aggressive, restless, anxious behaviour [...] and withdrawn, depressive, inhibited behaviour... (Buckingham 1999, 64)

So there it is: the underclass, within that rigid Enlightenment frame of the socio-logical, are judged to hold too many bad emotions. I cannot not help but imagine the teacher filling in his report, looking at each child and in his or her mind's eye categorising that youngster with these improper emotions. Are these children shameful? Or are they being shamed?

There are many arguments of definition over what sociologists and politicians see as the 'underclass', but here I prefer Chris Haylett's explanation:

> 'Underclass' is generally held to refer to social groups at the base of the working class whose characteristics are those of long term unemployment or highly irregular employment, single parenthood and criminality, where some or all of those characteristics are tendentially if not causally related... The 'non-working' single mother and the young, unemployed male are central figures in this cultural landscape of amoral, anti-social council estate living. (Haylett 2000, 70)

Haylett continues:

> Nevertheless, the discourse of 'underclass' is not 'one thing' that has negative 'effects'. It is partly constituted by representations [that] make positive subject positions available to the working-class poor and new understandings available to mainstream audiences. (Haylett 2000, 71)

Haylett accurately signals the problem of sociological or cultural definition in that sometimes it is descriptive, but often it is *ascriptive*. However, in political sympathy with those scholars that are keen to avoid the trap of caricaturing underclass cultural consumers as couch potatoes, or as Stuart Hall put it 'cultural dupes' (Hall 1997 and 2003), she reads two films *L'Haine* ('Hate', Dir. Mathieu Kassovitz, 1995) and *Ladybird, Ladybird* (Dir. Ken Loach, 1994). Haylett draws attention to what she calls their resistant discourses of 'underclass', based on their subjugated knowledges of poverty. She reminds us that mythologies of class produced within popular culture can also be seen as a valuable strategic resource, of 'knowing differently'.

Haylett quotes from Black feminist writer bell hooks who over a decade ago put forward a strong ethical argument for an alternative regime of representations of the underclass:

> To change the face of poverty so that it becomes, once again, a site for the formation of values, of dignity and integrity, as any other class positionality in this society, we would need to intervene in existing systems of representations. (hooks 1994, 171)

Haylett argues that the two films chosen in her essay resist the objectifying point of view of the middle-class gaze, instead they enter into a filmic space of the underclass that produces 'a popular cultural cartography rather than a traditional ethnography' (Haylett 2000, 73). She claims that these films are representational spaces that offer possibility through a model of ethnographic poetics:

Indeed, particular non-traditional ethnographic forms – such as poetry, novels, and films – would seem to be well suited to the 'happening-all-at-once' quality that constitutes social life. That fullness of meaning creates complexity which refuses both the viewer and the director absolute control over the subject's story... As representational spaces these films express possibility, they complicate and defend what they show and they do not leave their subjects exposed. They also give a cultural presence to the working class poor that is not part of an injunction to tell. (Haylett 2000, 74)

This rationale has striking similarities to arguments made in the 1970s and 1980s, influenced by French Feminists such as Monique Wittig concerning the non-representability, or supra-representability of lesbian sexuality.[16] The Foucauldian compulsion for non-normative cultures to 'confess' their 'differences' within the language of the defining/dominant culture is highly resisted and challenged, this, coupled with popular resistance strategies of silence or antagonism, is a significant tactic in cultural politics. We have the conundra then, of the dense semiotic space of the 'unspeakable' that simultaneously grants a protected space of representation.

One of the pleasures of engagement in *Shameless* is the defamiliarisation of the middle-class perspective through the satiric deployment and/or challenge. In series 1, episode 2, Steve and Fiona start their cross-class romance; she initially mistrusts his advances, and Steve has to prove to her that he is for real and not just dallying. He rushes into a breathless explanation on his mobile:

Steve: 'You're dancing like there's nobody else in the room... You're life's not straightforward Fiona and a little bit of that travels with you but you don't stop it showing. You're not fake. You're not vain. You're not lost so you don't need finding. You're not trapped so you don't need springing... I swear to God Fiona, you're just... you make me want to enjoy my life.'

This can be read cynically as bourgeois pastoral gush for the authentic, but Steve takes Fiona to lunch and confesses that although a nice middle-class boy, he steals cars for a living. His mother, father, and sister are all doctors, but his mother is not above illegally prescribing Zopiclone, a short-acting hypnotic agent, for her son. Fiona finds this confession shocking and maddening, and she smartly puts down any of Steve's pretensions to 'slumming', shouting: 'Given your choices, its rich that you don't like other people living with theirs!' Fiona's rage exposes the cultural tripping of 'dumbing down' and the desire that lurks there for low-class sexual experience. In typical *Shameless* style the interlude is clever because it inverts the commonsense connotation of lower class criminality and child neglect/abuse, and reinscribes it as middle class.

The replacement of a (useless) bourgeois code with a creatively humane, local, spontaneous and folkish one is a thematic current playing through the series. Take episode 2 from series 2 (2005) that opens with a party in which all participants are scoffing a hash cake, and drunk, including Frank Gallagher's children. Next door, the neighbours Kev and Veronica are once again fucking violently upstairs, only to be upstaged sexually by her mother Carol and her young (bogus) continental 'toy-boy' Rico. During the post-party chill-down the next morning, Frank recalls vaguely that Kev had had a phone call the night before, and it turns out that their social worker intends to come round in the morning to bring around a new foster-child. The social worker Marissa is represented as an overwhelmed, hysterical middle-class do-gooder. Kev and Veronica are given a ten-year-old middle-class boy who has been abandoned by his parents. Marissa comments rather condescendingly: 'Give me *people like you* any day of the week'. The lad, Eric, is beautiful, bourgeois, and entirely a contrast to the Ball household's mayhem. Kev's sober observation is: 'He's a right miserable little twat!'. The next morning Eric is found unconscious and vomiting on the dining room table, causing another micro-dramatic, Keystone Kop-like rush to the hospital since Eric has scoffed the hash cake. Mortified Veronica says: 'We can do this Kev. We can be good parents. From now on, we just have to try, really hard, not to kill him.' Surreal sequences follow filmed in a golden light in which Veronica tries to be the perfect parent, producing meal after meal of fast food in the form of human faces. Eric declines, he is clearly used to middle-class food, and even shakes his head when offered ketchup. The generations are not alienated from each other by age, but by class. But later, in a heroic gesture, Kev drives into the school playground in the middle of lunch hour and snatches Eric away from some bullying girls, ensuring that Kev and Veronica are subjected to a middle-of-the-night raid by police ('restraint of the parents vital' reads the social worker/turncoat from her report). Eric is accused of being a 'fucking pansy' by the family, so Kev teaches Eric to box and Martin, Veronica's brother who has Tourette's Syndrome, trains him in extreme swearing. The inept social worker returns the child and apologises to Kev and Veronica the next day, claiming that they had got the address on the file wrong. All the agents of the state in the series are depicted as corrupt, hapless, and inept. The housing officer, the social workers that harass the Balls and the Gallaghers, the police – all of them are equally reproachable. Debbie however has psyched up Eric into viciously attacking the schoolgirls he is being bullied by. Debbie is possibly the most disturbing (and disturbed) Gallagher in her Jekyll/Hyde-like unpredictability, and sociopathic behaviours.[17] When Marissa comes to collect Eric from fostering she tactlessly asks the Balls 'How do you fancy a nice little Chinese girl. Long history of emotional abuse... but she's a cracking little cook' in an interesting inversion in which the underclass are seen as emotionally nuanced, and the middle-class bureaucrats the ones who are emotionally stunted.

What we see in these two episodes is a classic *Shameless* tropic inversion of good bourgeois norms and bad underclass stereotypes. Drawing on Raymond Williams' idea of the structure of feeling, Haylett argues that there are 'collective working-class subjectivities' that can rebut received wisdoms and stereotypes through an active engagement with the viewer. Here we see the Gallaghers and the Balls redeeming child abuse through specific strategies of empathy and empowerment that directly absorb the viewer's identification. Rather than pathologising underclass parenting, then, the programme invokes the subtlety and appropriateness of it, simultaneously implying that state interference damages – rather than protects – underclass families. Out of the two alien and competing systems of child-rearing the viewer witnesses, it is clear which is endorsed by *Shameless*, this competition is expressed through the convention of class conflict. The underclass aesthetic is seen as not only distinctive and appropriate, but is also a political and collective refusal of what is seen to be a damaging, irrelevant imposition of pedagogic norms. This is one example of how the series can be understood as offering a 'cultural cartography' to the viewer that radically resists the anthropological gaze. In *Shameless* it is the worldview of the middle classes that is continuously and repeatedly shamed by the narrative. Given that this group makes up the predominant audience share, one can only speculate that being (safely) exposed to this armchair ridicule forms a significant facet of viewers' masochistic pleasure, and for non-middle-class viewers, presumably, *Shameless* brings wry amusement.

Shamelessness

Representations of shamelessness are not new – think of the most famous working-class novelist of the twentieth century, D.H. Lawrence – his *Lady Chatterley's Lover* is a disputation on the subject. Shamelessness in sex is part of a classical literary tradition. As Frank says on the opening credits: 'But all of 'em, to a man, know first and foremost one of the most vital necessities in this life is they know how to throw a party!! Heh heh heh heh! Scatter!'.[18] *Shameless* does summon the carnival underclass, a stereotype of the poor since the Romans. So what does it mean to be literally 'shameless' – without shame? Or beyond shame? Is it possible, and if this has traditionally been seen as a 'bad' thing, would it now be appropriate to argue that it is a 'good thing'? The drama series *Shameless* is undoubtedly a cacophony of ethnicised stereotypes of the poor. However, it has also liberated grammars of shame by inducing an aesthetic of joyful exuberance that goes some way toward creating a text that is also 'open' to be read further for situated knowledges. The drama's intensity, its 'happening-all-at-once' hyper-realism manages to generate a cultural space for the articulation of underclass experience and vitality. It is this exuberance that captivates the viewer and allows for at least a temporary recodification of the underclass. This is undoubtedly Paul Abbott's hope and expectation.

Finally I want to bring to notice two episodes from the series that deliberately refigure shamelessness, following *Queer Attachments* major themes: the first example is of shame and homosexuality, and the second example takes up the issue of national pride/shame that I introduced in Chapter 2. In series 2, episode 6 of *Shameless* there is more trouble with the Maguires, as Mandy is pregnant. Everyone thinks that 15-year-old Ian is the father, but of course it is 'Lip, who is secretly fucking her as a mutually beneficial cover for Ian's closeted homosexuality. The Maguires menace Ian, telling him he must marry Mandy. Mimi Maguire makes it gothically clear with a large knife that he better not hurt her daughter or she will take off his testicles. Abortion is out of the question ('We're Catholics'). The Maguire men take Ian off to bond in a homosocial ritual that involves a lot of ridiculous drinking, fighting and watching football. Patrick Maguire, the sociopath, from Belfast (Britain's shamefully iconic 'frontier'), is clearly marked as the 'real' underclass of the estate (or the ruling class depending on your perspective). 'Lip and Ian have a bad fight about Mandy's pregnancy. The Maguires go ahead and arrange a tacky engagement party, hiring a white stretch limousine, and a pyramid fountain of champagne glasses. Ian is just too frightened to confess to being gay, the viewer is made to comprehend how it is for a young gay men to get inveigled into hopeless, closeted schemes. But tenderly it is Kash's wife who persuades Ian that he can't marry Mandy, that he can't 'live a lie'.[19] Also 'Lip enters the party shouting 'Call it off!' and 'The baby's mine!', which augurs a huge scrap between the families, as an enraged Patrick Maguire head-butts 'Lip. Sheila enters screaming and hallucinating now she is drug-free, which entitles Mimi Maguire to utter the immortal line 'Gallaghers – they're nothing but scum.' Patrick, now wired up for aggression, tells everyone to lace into the drink screaming 'Come on, we're the fucking Irish!' whilst beating his fists into the engagement cake. The soundtrack to this scene is 'The Wedding Singer' by 1980s band *Spandau Ballet*, which plays quietly in the background, only one line from it is audible: 'Oh I want the truth to be said'.[20] The narrative diegesis is clearly in sympathy with Ian's predicament, and it also manages to show in a completely touching way how much brotherly love exists between 'Lip and Ian. Interestingly, it is Veronica's mother who, back at the house, walks past 'Lip and tells him 'You should be ashamed of yourself.' The shame has passed from the homosexual association to the heterosexual, but what the viewer knows is that 'Lip has just done an heroic act by putting himself into blame for Mandy's pregnancy, he has excised shame in the name of loyalty.

The second example addresses Britain's colonial shame. Episode 10 of Series 2 opens with Kev's voice over saying that the Gallaghers make the rest of them on the estate feel lucky (the 'luck of the Irish'?). The local Labour councillor Bernie Creme turns up at The Jockey touting for votes; he bullies Kash Karib whose wife responds with righteous indignation, pushing Kash forward as his rival in the upcoming council elections. Bernie, typecast as 'Old Labour' is crude and clearly corrupt, taking backhanders for local planning and development projects.[21] Bernie makes a series of racist remarks about Kash such as that he is 'nothing but a third generation immigrant' and the crowd cheers like a Greek chorus. Then there is a verbal gladiatorial combat, and Kash retakes the crowd saying 'name a single other shop that takes milk tokens for booze!'. Next, Bernie lashes out in a racist tirade against 'the blacks, the chinks, the complete fucking leg-irons, the work-shy jobless scum, that bleed this fucking nation dry!' – which is, of course, exactly the multi-ethnic mixing that makes up the largely tolerant population of the estate, and the regular punters at The Jockey. Suddenly the audience goes quiet, and all in protest silently dump their red rosettes on the floor, exposing the supposed racism of the old style Labour Party, the representatives of the putative white working class. Thus the series ends by taking on the spectre of working and underclass racism, replacing it instead with a model of pluralism. The family comes together to sing the cod-nationalist hymn 'Jerusalem', all jubilantly singing in one voice the last line of the hymn: 'in England's green and pleasant land'. 'Jerusalem' is the hymn of choice for sentimentalists, such as rugby fans and the Women's Institute, provincial purveyor of cakes and jams. The utopian ending of series 2 of *Shameless* symbolises the nation state of Britain as inclusive, rejecting the cliché of the racist white poor. Difference and suspicion between groups is signified as superficial, part of the bad-tempered, shallow, curmudgeonly lack of grace that characterises 'community' for ordinary people. The Irish have a word for this – begrudgery – a concept that allows for gentility and affection to co-exist with complaint. This casual negativity is without malice, it is ignorant cant minus the hate, a disaffection that is disinterestedly applied to anyone and everyone, a democratic prejudice spread idly and evenly across the nameless, multiple irritants in life. Singing 'Jerusalem' is not really corralling national pride so much as sung sentimentally and ironically for enjoying the moment of brief communality itself. The truly British aesthetic is not pride, it resembles more of a national whingeing, it is beyond pride/shame, it is shameless. What Councillor Creme's tirade exposes is the insitutional expectation that white racism will respond to a rhetoric of victimhood, that votes can by mobilised by signalling a loss of British status. But the Chatsworth Estate residents have never had capital, status, or an investment in a greater force than themselves (other than, perhaps, Manchester United, or more likely, City). What they have been dealt is each other, and thus the greatest threat is from those that come in from outside with divisive intent.

In 2004 the British newspapers carried a story about the real-life council estate, West Gorton in Manchester, where *Shameless* is filmed, reporting that an 'ASBO' (Anti-Social Behaviour Order) had been served on a 17-year-old youth for 'the climate of fear' he brought to the estate.[22] This followed the crew filming the television series calling the Police on this offender, Stephen Birchall, for his alleged disruption and harassment of the 'set'. The press loved the irony. In January 2005 *The Guardian* newspaper carried an opinion piece by its Prisons Correspondent and long-term resident of the estate, Eric Allison, entitled 'Crying Shame'. Its tone is one of sadness for what has been lost: of the legend that the place is named after the bloody gore that flowed in the river after a battle between the Anglo-Saxons and the Danes, the decline of local heavy industry that earned Gorton the title 'the workshop of the North', the thriving worker-communities, now dissolved. Allison is rueful about the European city regeneration schemes that surround Gorton's boundaries, but don't include it. What characterises his piece tonally is a notable sense of pride that is not purely nostalgic; Allison takes the tiniest space to claim that he lives there by choice, in acceptance, and without shame. The last words of this chapter, speaking of West Gorton, should appropriately be his:

> For a start, I enjoy the racial mix. The saris and gowns bring a splendid colour, and I find it an inspiration the way the children mix happily. I also admire the courage and perseverance of the many parents who are bringing their kids up in a decent manner, encouraging them in their education and teaching them respect for others

– all in splendid defiance of the overwhelming odds they face on a daily basis. I enjoy the humour and the camaraderie I observe regularly.

Perhaps perversely, the place keeps me healthily angry about injustice and the way society demonises young people in deprived areas. There is little danger, I fancy, of feeling above my station in Gorton. (Allison 2005) [my emphasis]

Notes

1   Conversation with author at Brighton Unitarian Church, February 2006.

2   Anon. 'Paul Abbott' in *Media Guardian* Monday 12th July 2004. From the 'Guardian Unlimited' website archive at http://www.guardian.co.uk/Archive/0,4271,,00. html, searched January 2006. Abbott was number 90 in the annual chart the British 'Media 100', run by the newspaper. In 2005 he moved up to occupy number 25, and is the second highest writer in the list deposed from first only by the gay scriptwriter Russell T. Davies, author of *Queer As Folk* (see ch. 3).

3   http://www.channel4.com/entertainment/tv/microsites/S/shameless/

4   A thorough analysis of the figures of the primitive and the savage, especially in relation to women, Irish, and the working classes can be read in Stocking (1987).

5   Ironically the actress Duff who plays missing Fiona is playing the role of Queen Elizabeth I in a BBC classic costume drama adaptation for Sunday nights – a lovely bit of intertextual irony.

6   Anon. 'Paul Abbott' in the *Media Guardian* Monday 18th July 2005. From the 'Guardian Unlimited' website archive at http://www.guardian.co.uk/ Archive/0,4271,,00.html, searched January 2006.

7   Unpublished. These comments are taken from my own notes.

8   See http://www.screenonline.org.uk/people/id/975584/ for background on Carla Lane.

9   In series 1, episode 6 Monica, their mother, turns up with her girlfriend, a beautiful black butch truck-driving Geordie. The return of Monica causes emotional ructions for the whole family. There is an awkward dinner party during which Fiona loses her temper with Monica's endless narcissistic self-justification for abandoning the children, then a short scene which is striking for its blitzing of underclass stereotypes, in which Fiona stands up and gets the others to itemise their educational achievements: 'Lip is doing 10 GCSE's, Ian 7 or 8, Debbie has won four school prizes, Carl has built a model hovercraft. Fiona then walks out, shouting 'Over to you, Mum!' Norma's response is to play Patsy Kline's *Crazy* whilst Monica sobs. This scene of underclass credentials (as clever, as coping, as obtaining cultural value) confronts the viewer's assumptions. The Dickensian display of over-achieving libido is powerful in class terms, but when examined more closely you notice how stereotyped the butch/femme representation of the lesbian couple is, and how the whole scene is a vehicle for the narrative break with Fiona as the angel in the house.

10   Evans-Pritchard (1947); Mauss (1954).

11   See further Houlbrook, Matt (2005).

12   We only need to see Mel Gibson's film *The Passion of the Christ* (2004) to be convinced of the perverse eroticism of religious sacrifice performed through orgiastic suffering.

13   Elements of this typology linger in the racism directed toward Irish Travellers, Gypsies, or 'Pikeys' as they are derogatively tagged.

14   For an example of the latter 'critical theorists' of the underclass, I do recommend reading the article jointly authored by Bourdieu, P. and Wacquant, L. (1999). The first two paragraphs are fine examples of how to immediately alienate your reader via obscurantist gnomism, but persevere their bitter rant against American exceptionalism and hype is much more fun. They denounce Cultural Studies for being a marketing invention of Routledge, and are heavily snide about 'disciplines perceived to be marginal or subversive, such as Cultural Studies, Minority Studies, Gay Studies or Women's Studies' which take on 'the allure of messages of liberation' (p. 51). In elaborate terms the 'inanity' of the concept of the underclass is delineated further; the Gallic nose is impressively sniffed.

15   One clear and notable finding from Buckingham's study is his statement that 'the argument that intelligence is a predictor of underclass membership received no support.' (p. 70). Given the recent resurgence of academic claims regarding the innate intellectual inferiority of the 'lower' classes and certain ethnic groups, this finding could do with further dissemination and discussion.

16   For example Wittig, Monique (1981). There was also a more diffuse argument in lesbian feminism about the non-representability of Woman that followed Julia Kristeva's work.

17   In Series 1 Episode 4 there is an intimation that Debbie has been interfered with by a neighbour. It turns out that instead, Debbie is the 'criminal abuser' and has snatched a local toddler, Jody. Thus the narrative cliché of vulnerable pre-pubescent girl is instead rewritten as peculiar, deviant kidnapper. In order to protect Debbie from being found out and taken away by Social Services the family run an elaborate scam that fools the entire police force and surrounding estate, set to upbeat, jazzy music so that the whole rhythm of the programme is funny, fast, and febrile. Debbie is made to take the toddler back, and not realising that she is the perpetrator, residents throw money at her and the police give her a good citizen award. Instead of bringing in professionals such as child psychologists, the Gallagher family use the money raised by Debbie's award to build her a new bedroom complete with a cot and doll, as Steve says, 'Round here therapy was an unfamiliar word. Blackmail and bribery were tried and tested techniques.' But this mendicancy is undercut by the loving way in which Debbie is supported, protected and, in the Gallagher's own way, set right without state intervention.

18   It is a priapic metaphor: Frank scatters his seed, like all good Catholics, with his many children.

19   In the 2004 Christmas special there is a touching scene in the shop when Kash fends off soldiers from hitting his wife Yvonne; later he tells her that she means the world to him, as Ian walks in and hears it. It is this complex triangle that is so sensitively portrayed in *Shameless*, the subtle dexterity of the writing and portrayal of the versatile practices of love that pass between the three of them is

very impressive, setting up new paradigms of queer affection and familial bonds without being overtly sentimental or unrealistic.

20 Spandau Ballet (1998) 'The Wedding Singer' from the album *The Wedding Singer Vol. 2 Soundtrack*

21 Buckingham (1999) claims that the study finds the underclass to be the most homogenous politically, they vote overwhelmingly for the Labour Party. This finding also contradicts the stereotype of the politically alienated, stupid and apathetic underclass who don't vote.

22 In November 2006, in a classic move of cultural inversion the British press reported that ASBOS, far from shaming anti-social behaviour, were being vaunted by disaffected youths as a 'badge of honour'.

Chapter 6

A Queer Undertaking: Uncanny Attachments in the HBO Television Drama Series *Six Feet Under*

Six Feet Under and HBO

The USA television drama *Six Feet Under* ended after five successful seasons, in 2005. Created by Alan Ball, who also wrote and directed many of the subsequent episodes, the aesthetic of *Six Feet Under* manages to combine camp, dark humour with a contrasting tragic seriousness concerned with negotiating an ethics of love and death. This humour is manifest through the surreal content, for example in the bizarre and witty modes of death in the opening scene of each episode; the mischievously gothic representation of corpses and body parts; sentimentalism; musical and hallucinatory cameos; talking ghosts and sixpenny crooners; gruesome satire around death and the death industry; and an affectionately ironic melodrama. *Six Feet Under* has inscribed a gay aesthetic; this has much to do with its production context and with the programme's writers, producers, and directors. It is infused with the American experience of AIDS and death upon the gay aesthetic in the late twentieth century. *Six Feet Under* also deals with class in a complicated fashion – one might risk saying it has an uncanny, or *queer* rendition of class positions and relations.

The US television channel Home Box Office has produced a new kind of critical drama programme, recognisable for its high quality production, innovative scriptwriting, original complex structure and plot, explicit sex and violence, a liberal/democratic ideological tendency, clever narrative and characterisation, and fairly serious political contemporary theme. Typical products have been *The West Wing*, *The Sopranos*, and *24*, each aimed at adult entertainment audiences on cable or satellite television. Hence these televisual units are coded as writerly texts, programmes that require competent readers versed in a range of genres and institutional forms. Generically *Six Feet Under* is a hybrid: elements of family saga/soap opera, romance, American gothic, supernatural fiction, ribald tragi-comedy, Magical Realism, the grotesque, farce and pathos, experimental or avant-garde can be identified in the formal structure. The series is notable for both its intertextuality, and its 'knowingness', evident in the obvious dexterity of its makers to play with narrative and formal conventions, and expectations. HBO, although owned by global conglomerate Time Warner, sells direct to customers by subscription, thus the HBO stable's unique selling point 'USP', or appeal, is creative, quality television with a critical edge, an elite brand in a mass market industry.

Six Feet Under was first screened on Sunday June 3rd 2001 after the watershed at 10pm. US critics were slow to appreciate the show's talent, and early reviews were often lukewarm in judgement; British critic Kathryn Flett writing in the liberal broadsheet newspaper *The Observer* seemed more quick to realise the ethos of the product, calling it 'a genuinely entertaining and intelligent black comedy' (Flett 2002). The programme, not surprising given its central theme of death, also has a melancholic quality that gives it a perennial flavour of mourning, suffused with the multiple failures and losses of its primary characters. It is prevented from sliding into existential misery or indulgent annihilation by a real – I suggest 'post-AIDS' – emphasis on the continual need for re-evaluation and restitution in human relationships. The ethos of *Six Feet Under* is in that aphorism of Nietzche's: 'Human, All Too Human'.

Alan Ball, representing the middle-class American family in *American Beauty*

Alan Ball, an experienced television writer and producer on shows such as *Grace Under Fire*, and *Cybill*, is most well known for his screenplay for the film *American Beauty* (1999 dir. Sam Mendes) which won five Oscars including Best Picture in 2000. Ball himself won the Academy Award for Best Original Screenplay. As such, HBO contracted Alan Ball to be 'the auteur' for their proposed series *Six Feet Under*. The concept was from the start to be signalled by an industrial context of artistic creativity, and visionary cinematic 'authorship'. '*American Beauty* registers the death of the nuclear family' asserts Marcel O'Gorman, in a peculiarly presagic nod to *Six Feet Under* (O'Gorman 2004, 49). In the film *American Beauty* Lester Burnham, the middle-aged and middle-class anti-hero, throws off the responsibilities of the comfortable life he has come to despise when he begins to fantasise about having sex with his teenage daughter's best friend Angela. Lester's rebellion will ultimately bring about his murder by his homophobic next-door neighbour, but not before he redeems himself through an enlightenment regarding middle-class anxiety and repression. Katherine Rowe Karlin argues that *American Beauty* is a film about incest, and that Lester's real object of desire is his own daughter, transacted through another 'lower class' schoolfriend:

> The white middle class exorcises violence from its sons and precocious sexuality from its daughters by projecting these qualities onto nonwhites and the working class. While no more sheltered than working-class girls from sexual abuse at home, middle-class girls can afford, literally, to project sexual innocence. (Rowe Karlin 2004, 75–6)

It is important to acknowledge Alan Ball's history of incisively unraveling the perfect bourgeois 'American Family'. The film addresses middle-class audiences through the cultural capital of its 'art-house' appeal, stylishly persuading them to reject their neurotic and narcissistic attachments to material success. As Beverley Skeggs has described, this is of course a *cliché* of bourgeois preoccupation, namely that they are the comfortably educated, self-reflective class who rise *above* the common acquisition of capital and respectability (Skeggs 1997, 2004). The hero's rebellion is henceforth a predictable turn toward 'meaningfulness' and away from 'money', the underlying premise being that the luxury of finding an individual 'self' through denial and renunciation is always open to those wealthy enough to choose, and sly enough to present themselves sympathetically as a rebel.

The film does present a gay couple, Jim and Jim, who live opposite to Lester, and have a dog/child 'Bitsy', the fragment child. Vincent Hausmann comments:

> Though happy and represented as not hiding the kind of chaos barely hidden beneath the Burnhams' pristine lawn, Jim and Jim, as their names imply, are not, by virtue of their being gay, beyond investing in the numbing sameness that the film excoriates when such investments surface in heterosexual relations. In this, then, they appear no less guilty than the heterosexuals whom the film depicts (before their encounter with Ricky) as denying Otherness. (Hausmann 2004, 112)

This covetous delight in suburban propriety is played for laughs on these gay husbands. Jim and Jim the uncanny clones replicate in minute detail the unquestioned, aspirational fantasy of respectability. For the heteronormative viewer Jim and Jim are uncanny because of what is assumed to be their 'suburban' *gay* repression (Jim and Jim are also so hygienic and nice that the viewer is *compelled* to imagine what they do in bed); the couple are conjoined with a homophobic rendering of their desire for 'the same' that reverts to Freudian models of homosexuality as a narcissist stage. Ball is particularly good at ridiculing intense desires for conventionality, for intimating what lies beneath, and the parody of Jim and Jim is a dense sign that also works to send up the viewer's stereotypes, gay or straight. Jim and Jim's outrageous parody of suburban morés camply undermines heterosexual suburbia. Simultaneously it sends up the white gay bourgeoisie for their pallid investments in normality. Jim and Jim could never 'pass', and by implication, neither can the straights. In *American Beauty* the terror comes primarily from that staple of suburban gothic, the nuclear family, seen as the protagonist of the death drive. Whatever their surreal mimicry of suburban mores, though, les boys clearly dream of Jean Genet, les boys are *glad* to be gay.[1] *American Beauty* confronts normativity, sameness, and narcissistic conformity whether present in heternormativity, or its homosexual complement. This critique cannot be properly grasped without also accepting the *de rigeur* bourgeois condemnation of suburbia, and denunciation of lower middle-class conformity, that informs Ball's queer approach to class.

Hausmann writes that *American Beauty* 'explicitly affirms the importance of upholding the prohibition against incest' (Hausmann 2004, 143) – Lester's daughter is involved with their next-door neighbour's son, Ricky, son of Colonel Fitts. The Colonel manages Ricky through deploying punitive practices of extremely sexualised discipline and surveillance. The film depicts this severe paternal authority as rooted in Colonel Fitts' own repressed homosexuality, a symptom of his precarious, excessive masculinity and the implicit homo-sociality of military life. His attacks on his son's body are ritualistic, very stylised and fraught with longing looks. Whilst Colonel Fitts' eccentricity can initially be laughed at, Ball's film draws dramatic attention to the erotic, tender, yet murderous violence locked within suburban conformity. His work is a rebellious expressive intervention into bourgeois repression: this theme will be followed up in series 1, episode 6 of *Six Feet Under* 'The Room' which depicts Nate discovering a secret room his father rented. Like Ricky, Nate remains intrigued by that dissolute other life, the alternate space his father lived behind his stoic façade of respectability. In a sequence that hauntingly summons up the prior scene in *American Beauty* in which Lester is shot, Nate imagines his (phallic, naturally) father at a window shooting at passersby.

American Beauty sets up two parallel models of father/daughter and father/son incestuous desires, albeit with the former running through a displacement, the daughter's friend. The field of vision, the gaze, in the film, is structurally incestuous. In Hausmann's article he discusses scriptwriter Alan Ball's representation of Colonel Fitts in relation to Ball's perception of his own father's homo-erotic desires. He describes how, when Ball tells that he came out to his mother, his mother blamed his father for his homosexuality, saying that her husband was 'that way too' (Hausmann 2004, 127). Ball relates his own father's sadness and unhappiness to his unfulfilled desires (Chumo 2000 in Hausmann 2004, 148). In his subsequent fictional construction of Colonel Fitts, Ball apparently went through several anxious rewrites, each one procrastinating over the explicit content of Fitts' homosexuality. In this we might see something of a deferment of Ball's own patriarchal-incest fantasies. The film refuses to draw a clear definite line between heterosexual and homosexual [incestuous] desires, drawing attention instead to the violence latent in their prohibition. But, surely this is a troubling notion, that indeed incestuous longings *should* be denied? My point here is to signify how Ball's texts might generally be open to queer readings, his intention to expose the repressed in order to subdue it, or take the compulsive sting out by making it 'heard' as a form of therapeutic intervention.

Six Feet Under and the 'Death of the Father'

The first episode of *Six Feet Under* opens on Christmas Eve, traditionally the moment of celebration when the new King is born. But first the incumbent must die, and in a typically structuralist moment, the Father and patriarch of the Fisher Family Funeral Home, Nathaniel Fisher, is run over by a bus whilst rummaging for a cigarette driving his new hearse. There is clearly a Freudian (and maybe a Barthesian) joke in this moment: Nathaniel's grasp for his habitual phallus kills him rather more instantaneously and dramatically than the usual slow route of inhalation. In this narrative instant, the show heralds the new society, in which the old rules of tradition are destroyed, and the field becomes open for the resignification of new cultural identities and roles. Alan Ball sets up

Figure 6.1   From left to right: David Fisher, Ruth Fisher, Nate Fisher
Source: Getty Images/Getty Images Entertainment

the principal symbolic frame of the series – the phallus has gone, and traditional dominant heterosexual masculinity is no more: dead. It is to be replaced by the split phallus of the two brothers: aimless, promiscuous Nate, the heterosexual son who never resolves his own identity crisis, stumbling through relationships with a seemingly unlimited taste for sensation, experienced through a vague and foggy lens of New Age spiritual individualism. Nate's personality is of the quintessential bourgeois drop-out, he is the boy who took a gap year and never psychologically came back. And David, the closeted and anxious gay son, whose striving for bourgeois respectability seems to lead to ever more fretful conflicts with himself and others. This is a tale of sibling love and rivalry, an elegiac romance between brothers.

David's earnestness, his persistent desire for his own happiness (and his generally naïve and confused attempts to gain it), carries significant identificatory pleasures for the viewer of *Six Feet Under*, irrespective of their own sex/gender positioning. For the first time in mass broadcasting, gay David is the 'everyman' whose quest for love and self-acceptance inculcates the viewer. In the series, the deployment of gender orientations are also queerly fascinating: the women are all depicted as sexually robust, independent feminist characters who negotiate well through the complex morés of post-industrial sexualities. However the principal men, Nate and David, are depicted as mutually narcissistic, both having a problematically insecure, but dissimilar, masculinity. The main heroic foils to Nate and David are two men who are crucially not White: African American Keith, David's boyfriend, and Puerto Rican embalmer Federico Diaz. These two secondary men, both racially coded, are constructed as more at ease with their own masculinity. It is white masculinity (as ever?) that is in crisis. There are points in the series in which the representation of these two men borders on fetishism, the sexual difference-heterosexual economy becoming displaced onto a racial difference-homosexual economy. However, there is a determined anti-hegemonic strategy in evidence – especially in the overt, didactic way that the unconscious racism of Nate and David is exposed and challenged – that goes some way to sustaining a radical reading of the show.

David and Nate are sons suffering the loss of their father. In the partition of their grief, we require a Kleinian paradigm to fully understand the doubling, or symbolic counterpoint, of their respective positions (Klein 1975, Mitchell 1986). Nate is assigned to the depressive position. His burden is to embody poignant sadness, what Melanie Klein calls depressive anxiety, or 'pining'. Nate is melancholic, his series trajectory is to rediscover and re-experience loss, firstly through the breakdown of his relationship with Brenda, and then through the death (possible murder) of his wife. His final abandonment of Brenda in the last series for an immature affair with his step-sister, can only be understood if the viewer understands Nate's calamitous reaction to Brenda's miscarriage followed by her second 'abnormal' pregnancy as tests tragically confirm that she carries a potentially damaged child. Nate cannot countenance any more loss, he dreads it, and so he pre-empts more (or merely feared) loss by leaving Brenda and their expected child. It is a common reaction to fears of abandonment. He is already 'in loss' with the news of his less-than-perfect child; he is already mourning the demise of his ideal child, his redemptive child, the saviour of his marriage to Brenda. Nate is a man controlled by depressive grief, his occasional outbursts of manic joy only confirm this propensity to settle back into mourning, and exhaustion. Nate's role is to draw attention to dominant heterosexuality as fundamentally melancholic, based, as it is, on the realisation that the no-one can occupy or own the position of power manifest in its representation. There is also the concomitant loss of possibility. Alan Ball is a very knowing author and it is possible that he has read critic Judith Butler's writing on gender melancholy:

> In other words, heterosexual melancholy is culturally instituted and maintained as the price of stable gender identities related through oppositional desires. (Butler 1990, 89)

Homosexual desire is rendered unthinkable in dominant heterosexuality, however it is precisely this prohibition that maintains the tempting proximity of homoeroticism in the cultural unconscious. This ubiquitous repression results in an overwhelming hatred and fear, expressed through the discourse of homophobia, significantly, a discourse of *loss*.[2] As the heterosexual melancholic, Nate knows he has lost, but not what he has lost. What he has 'lost' is his loved father, but, as Butler goes on:

> The object is not only lost, but the desire fully denied, such that 'I never lost that person and I never loved that person, indeed never felt that kind of love at all.' The

> melancholic preservation of that love is all the more securely safeguarded through the totalizing trajectory of the denial. (Butler 1990, 88)

This disavowed homosexual love then, is preserved in aspic, and masculinity is firmly consolidated as a defence against it. Nate 'forgets' the gay imaginary, he never loved another man because he *is* a man, or as Butler puts it 'the love for the father is stored in the penis' (Butler 1990, 91). The taboo against homosexuality is also an incest taboo, a concern of Ball's manifested earlier in *American Beauty* and a tonal undercurrent present now in *Six Feet Under*, so we can read these mourning brothers as also lost to each other, because of this prohibition.

Homophobia, gay paranoia and the bourgeois subject

Homophobia, as a particular psycho-social formation and practice, is traumatic, and spatial. Homophobia displaces non-normative sexual practices into exile, its effects are productive as a territorialising force it creates both subjects and spaces. In the chief character of David, a middle-class white gay man, that exclusion puts him into a non-space in social terms, it negates his centralised selfhood, and he is right to fear and tremble at the loss of that security. Gay desires represent the metaphorical drop of blood that would make David a slave, and remove his automatic right to citizenship. His proximity to a bourgeois selfhood makes his homosexuality a special threat, but like the 'secret mulatto', David can also pass as straight. This generates a particularly potent anxiety for the liminal subject whose identity is so nearly, so very *almost* secure.

A further tension in David's identity is his petit-bourgeois aspirations, embodied in his Christian faith. The conflict resonant in David's shamed/ desired gay subjectivity is an internalised class struggle caught between aspiration and sexual 'slumming', typified by his relationship with his working-class bodyguard boyfriend and their negotiation of respectability through monogamy/coupledom. David, as the bourgeois subject and one of the two heroic brothers that anchor the narrative diegesis, has a self to find. It is his class location, securely established, that allows the text to posit gay subjectivity as central to narrative resolution, furthermore – heroic. (Indeed, through his acquisition of the status of *pater familias* in the final espisode, the opening crisis 'Father is Dead', five years earlier, finally resolves itself.)

Crucially this series interpellates the viewer in David's emergent homosexual self, through narrative conventions of identification. The character endures what might be termed as a classic bourgeois gay male trajectory, from shame and concealment, to exposure and attack. Ultimately though David achieves the heroic function, his trials and tribulations are rewarded, he gets his Prince [Keith], and the Gold [the Fisher family business]. Aspects of fairy tale make this story elemental, and as a gay narrative, utopian. Thus, it is David as the neurotic Queen who finally inherits the Fisher Family mantle in this serial drama, and the viewer's pleasure is satisfied by the intervening journey of televisual homo-tourism, the bildungsroman of David's emergent gay identity.

David's identity is depicted in a state of becoming, unusually for mainstream television this unstable *homosexual* orientation is resolved successfully, through the convention of marriage and reproduction. What makes the series give a representational twist to this romantic cliché however is its social authorisation of queer families.

The homosexual subject is wounded, paranoid – but paranoia itself is an 'other place' full of historical truth. I will go on to explain how homophobia as a social practice is internalised and causes an architectronic schizophrenia. David Fisher, within the dualistic world of Kleinian thought, is ascribed in his grief and mourning to the paranoid position. What makes this assignment of paranoia creative, in the sense of teaching us something about the development of a narrative subjectivity, is his homosexuality. There is an absolute logic to David being returned, again and again, to the paranoid position. Ultimately, David's grief is resolved only by him appropriating the phallus for himself, in the very last episode, but significantly, his is a queer *pater familias*, an uncanny mimicry. David's anxiety is of the more visible, hysteric, queenly variety. This gay voyager ventures out from the closet in Series 1; he only partially negotiates through his own homophobia to then to be assailed by a homophobic mugger. His effeminate masculinity and agrophobic panic attacks make his attempts at respectability fraught with misfires. His queerly phallic mothering of his adopted sons confounds the all-American heroic, so that David's rendition of the classic bourgeois (neurotic) self manages to be both feminine and masculine simultaneously. Indeed, David's engendering is something the show likes to have fun with, in the series he incarnates a range of gay possibilities: bitter self-hating closet queen, disco diva, pleasure addict, neurotic mother's boy, anxious annie, beautiful boy, upstanding member of the community, gay conservative, paranoid queer, complacent assimilationist couple, angry young man, searcher for daddy's approval, and lesbian. (Yes, the latter based on an interpretation of David's curled claw-like hand, a hysterical symptom that appears suddenly after Nate's death. Hands, as Mandy Merck has so cogently explained, are the symbols *sine qua non* of lesbian sex (Merck 2000, 9).) This is *Six Feet Under* at play: David as a castrated lesbian is just one of the many twisted turns the series makes with his character.

To begin with, David is depicted as in the closet, and desperate to maintain an image of hetero-normativity. He does this in first series with a number of minor but accumulative moments and actions that, through repetition and banality, recreate for the viewer the daily imperative of the gay closet. In this way the viewer is being inculcated in the suffusion of invisibility and cloaking that constrains a gay person's sexuality, and, therefore his concomitant anxiety. David must maintain his uptight appearance of hetero-normativity in order to ensure his respectability. This is in direct contrast to Keith's openness, Keith – despite being a police officer with the Los Angeles Police Department – is out of the closet. His blue collar positioning, first as a police officer, then as a security guard and bodyguard, gives Ball an opportunity to play mischievously with middle-class gay men's projections of men in uniform. They are assumed to be the object, never the subject, of gay desire. This is an old assumption that can be traced back at least to Victorian times. Morris B. Kaplan in *Sodom on the Thames* describes how young working-class men were exempt from the accusation of sodomy, as one trades union spokesman put it in 1890 'Working men are free from the taint' (Kaplan 2005, 188). Diligent sons of the working class were vulnerable to corruption as randy young males, and Kaplan elucidates how homosexual desire between working-class men for each other was seen as ridiculous, rather, the popular conception was always that an active, older sodomite from the middle or upper classes would exploit them. Returning to the contemporary, typically Tom of Finland's erotic drawings communicate this flavour of make-believe, of dressing-up to be in uniform, a working-class drag, an uber-masculine masquerade made acceptable by the playful bourgeois subject. Manual labourers especially are rendered as gay phantasmagoria in the bourgeois imagination, think check shirts and Levis, rippling forearms and tanned necks. The appropriation of working-class style by middle-class gay men and lesbians in Western 1970s subcultures in order to communicate both conviction and allure was a folly I think we are still too historically close to, to fully notice. In this structure, working-class homosexuality is read *through* bourgeois appropriation, not in and for itself as a desiring subject. Middle-class gay men see themselves as being more tolerant, open-minded, educated and accepting of their homo-desire, something they munificently bequeath to, bestow on lower class men; traditionally an easeful gay identity belongs to them.

Keith, in a challenge to received understandings of working-class gay sexuality, fully inhabits the space to operate as a gay person in the world. Hence, in the economy of repression, Keith is coded as physically and psychically 'freer' than David, his body movement is more fluid and graceful, his progress through social space more assured. There is a constitutive opposition between David and Keith: David is white, middle class, closeted, anxious and repressed – a victim; Keith is black, blue collar, 'out', relaxed and expressive – an agent. The tension this creates between them in series 1 drives the viewer's curiosity, investing the viewer's romantic longings with the need for David to resolve his gay shame. This is typified in an incident in episode 4 when the couple are at the supermarket buying food. A man in a truck is impatient to take their parking space, intolerant of David and Keith's delay as they pack the groceries into the boot of the car, he hails them as 'fucking fags' before attempting to drive off. Keith gives chase and confronts the man and challenges his homophobia, angrily standing up for himself. David's response is panic, shame, and disapproval of Keith's reaction. Crucially, Keith demands in response 'Do you hate yourself that much?'

In *Six Feet Under* the dead speak. Ghosts/spectres commonly engage with major characters in surreal sequences in which the characters negotiate critical moments in their subjectivities. These scenes usually presage the emergence of shifts in selfhood in the key characters, and hence often concomitant changes in the plot, as these sensibilities are carried through into actions that drive the narrative. One such instance in series 1, episode 4 'Familia' is when David is working on the body of Mexican-American gang member Manuel Pedro

Antonio Bolin, or 'Paco'. Paco has been murdered by rival LA Latino hoods, and his shot-up body requires detailed reconstruction by David. The scene is interesting in that its manifest content contains the working through of David's homophobia to the point where he can see Keith's rage, its enactment a justifiable rebuttal to homophobic bullying. Paco persuades David to comprehend that Keith's furious response has a healthier purpose in exposing harassment, and that he was defending their right to a peaceful public space. Paco does this by quoting the Bible, using the example of Peter's denial of Jesus, his Catholicism becomes the vehicle for David's comprehension of his incapacitating shame, his Catholicism *enables* David to be gay, through the structure of the sodomitical sublime. It brings David's private, shameful homosexuality into a public, gay embodiment. The dead in *Six Feet Under* return as angels, oracles, phantoms and apparitions that progress the diegetic frame of liberal humanist fulfilment. The dead prise open possibilities for the living, and impart deliverance, unshackling *jouissance*.

It takes an underclass, Latino gang member such as Paco to interpret David to himself; the classed other is the site/sight of David's epistemological homosexuality. Paco himself is constructed as unrelentingly macho, he has a street masculinity that makes David appear even more emasculated. But Paco commands David to 'be a man'. This man that David is travelling toward is intrinsically gay *and faggoty*; in that sense then the series proffers the model gay citizen as embodying camp masculinity, a manliness yet to be properly understood as a popular culture form. The shift in David is underscored when he faces his own bully, this time from a corporate takeover by rival undertaking behemoth Kroehner. Their agent is threatening the Fisher Brothers family firm with incorporation by the Kroehner chain ('kroner' – the Germanic march of death industry capital, presumably). Kroehner's representatives' menacing encroachment on the Fisher autonomy lasts for several episodes, and is only brought to an end by David (following Paco's prompting), issuing the following counter-threat 'One day... I will find you or someone you love... There are tragedies worse than death. Things you couldn't even dream of you spineless candy-ass corporate fuck.' David finds his spine, refuses to be 'a bitch',[3] he is his own bitch, and enters the first turning point of the sequence of events that leads to his gay equilibrium. David's words are a ventriloquism, Paco is speaking through him, this challenge is articulated in the diction of a gang member, not a nice middle-class boy from a suburban home. But Paco's ghostly voice gives David an agency that he is unable to find on his own.

But he is not there yet. Series 1 continues with David trying to equivocate between his bourgeois aspirations for respectability – typified by his strait-laced ambition to become a Deacon in the Episcopalian Church – and the pressure he experiences in the concealment of homosexuality that this social elevation will require. In terms of consolidating his position in the Church, we can read this as David's compensatory reassurance – that is to say he may be gay, but in all other respects his rigid personal conformity and veneration of convention compensates for the sexual error, and, perhaps, sin. The series continues with a number of vignettes in which David continues to be put in comprising positions by the Church. In each instance the requirement is that David is mandated to closet his homosexuality, whilst at the same time his gayness is maintained by Church authorities as an 'open secret' (D.A. Miller 1985). So long as compulsory heteronormativity is outwardly maintained, then David's active closetry, his sexual 'deviance' may be tolerated. This, as the viewer will recognise, is a historically prevalent strategy of ecclesiastical, military and state hypocrisy that has generated a schizophrenic malaise in its protagonists and victims. As his deaconate progresses, David tells Keith he cannot come to Church with him on Sunday. This move is instructive as it educates the viewer in an understanding of how contagious homophobia is, how easily transferred across subjects. Homophobia can thus be seen as viral, infecting those closest (closetest) to us. David's prohibition provokes rage in Keith, and indeed it is this accumulation of petty internalised homophobia that in the end splits them up.

The pace of queer pedagogy in the series is relentless: in episode 11 of series 1, 'A Private Life', the homophobic killing of a gay man forces David to confront his own fears and gay shame. In series 2, Keith loses patience with David's fixated closetry and dumps him. David, once single again, learns to be a 'gay about town', allowing the programme to explore facets of gay life, and to demonstrate David's playful queer adolescence. At the end of this season though the romance between the two men remains focal. In series 3, episode 29, appropriately named 'The Eye Inside', David and Keith go to a vacation resort together. In the first scene as they drive toward Los Lamos on the LA Freeway, Keith and David are singing their way to the couples holiday in the sun. By contrast the next scene cuts to Nate masturbating alone in his car, he is the one trapped in a small and lonely space, claustrophobic and unfulfilled.

David and Keith, now relaxed, enter the hotel pool area, but instantly David begins to hallucinate that everyone is laughing at them; he anticipates public condemnation. In the HBO official DVD edition of the series each disc has a version in which the Directors comment in real time throughout on the diegesis as it unravels. Episode 29, written by Kate Robin, is directed by Michael Engler, and his narrative commentary on the show is continuously suffused with a psychotherapeutic vocabulary, for example in describing how 'this very repressed family [the Fishers] is being forced to confront themselves'. Engler explicitly mentions David's paranoia ('the eye within'), and comments on David's projection of how the two of them must be seen by the world. David is seen adjusting his behaviour 'appropriately' – that is to say defensively – rather than perceiving the rather more neutral reality of the poolside colony. Engler comments on how David is trying to be as invisible as he can, his paranoia causes him to efface their gay charisma. On the pool patio they find two sunbeds, Keith tries to wrap his arms affectionately around David, who tries to shrug him away. Keith comes back teasingly with 'God, no – they will really think we're gay, and we can't have them thinking that!' In the next scene in their hotel room David and Keith are kvetching about visibility as they wash and dress for dinner in a rather sweet domestic intimacy. As David tries to set limits on their participation in the hotel's activities, Keith reminds him that their couples counsellor has told them to be less isolated. Then after their evening at the hotel party, presumably following a rare moment of pleasurable integration, we see David and Keith making love. They are blissfully happy, and David shouts out 'Hey we're gay in here! … And we're having some hot man on man love action!'. It contrasts so strongly with Nate's onanism, and anomie.

This high point of their mutual harmony and delight is temporary, a respite space, as travelling back to the city the pressures upon them begin to pull them back and apart. They are returned, as Engler comments, to the 'more externally defined construction of themselves and their relationship'. Going back to LA in the car David plays a tape of himself singing, Keith tells David that it bugs him when David sings 'at me', so they go on to sing together as they are stuck in a traffic jam. The song is 'Rocket Man' by that middlebrow gay icon Elton John, 'a song about feeling like an alien, like you don't belong in your own life, and gaining the awareness of that, and knowing you have to get back to your own life and not knowing how to do that' (Engler 2005).[4] Somehow this moment of unity they have found is lost so quickly, and the episode ends in their uneasy silence as they drive back to LA in the car, as the soundtrack fades back up. Theirs is an alien existence, however this is not necessarily *alienated*, as Luce Irigaray writes:

> In the relationship between two subjects, in the constitution of intersubjectivity, one must take into account a nothingness in common – 'an almost absolute silence', as I wrote in *I Love to You* – in order to begin to speak to each other. (Irigaray 2000, 51–2)

Several dimensions are being communicated here: firstly through an identification with David the viewer is sympathetically inculcated into experiencing the homophobic *logic* of his fear of public censure. Secondly, through domestic intimacy, those fears are expressed and reasoned with in a safe, enclosed space, they are brought close. This opportunity for social integration and acceptance is enabled through their own mutual care, importantly it is the *couple* who are able to manage this transition from private to public together, which can then be celebrated in sexual joy. Remember that the Greek meaning of paranoia is to be 'beside oneself', a perspective that is not altogether delusional. We can also read David's anxiety as a symptom, a message of truth from the Real. We can also see David and Keith 'beside each other' in the car (unlike Nate) travelling in the same direction. Irigaray talks about how to *conceive* silence, a silence which is at least three territories, which is becoming (Irigaray 2000, 62–3). The necessity of these 'other spaces' – like the holiday, extraordinary to everyday life (in Foucauldian terms, the 'heterotopia') – is that they are restorative, and allow them to return, to travel back revivified, to an urban homophobic reality (Foucault 1986).

David, as I have shown, occupies the paranoid position, a position of peculiar illusory clarity. Klein argues that the paranoid-schizoid position is so called because it is dominated by the processes of splitting, a practice lucidly represented in the visual representation of David's inner life throughout the whole series.[5] However I would also argue that this should be qualified further as the *paranoid schizophrenic* position. Here I am acknowledging Gilles Deleuze and Felix Guattari, whose argument in *Anti-Oedipus: Capitalism and Schizophrenia* advocates the liberation of desire by making evident the generally concealed split in human subjectivity, thus freeing the unstructured unconscious libido to live out its unconstrained polymorphous perversity. We can see in *Six Feet Under* how the character of David is spatially relocated through his gay desire from a non-place to the actively desiring boundless, limitless place of schizophrenia (Deleuze and Guattari 1977). Losing contact with 'reality' can be seen as a strategic necessity for non-normative sexual persons to find the impetus to live a hopeful life.[6] As Marx once said 'To call on [men] to give up their illusion about their condition is to *call on them to give up a condition that requires illusions*' (Marx 1975/1844, 244. Italics in the original).

In series 4, episode 44 'That's My Dog', David's paranoid homosexuality can be read as a necessary precaution to the urban threat, as his liberated (schizophrenic) desire causes him to make a classic dangerous mistake of overconfidence. Now the city has become the space of urban eroticism, he foolishly picks up an attractive young male hitchhiker, who carjacks and then viciously assaults him. David's ordeal is graphic: he is terrorised and humiliated, his suffering is extreme and very hard to watch. He spends the rest of *Six Feet Under* haunted by Post-Traumatic Stress Disorder, enduring panic attacks and flashbacks. Despite this being the serial drama fictionalisation of the old adage 'Just because you're paranoid it doesn't mean people aren't out to getcha!', gay paranoidal anxiety has a useful protective function. When David's sexual desire supercedes and over-reaches his secure bourgeois enfoldment, he leaves the safety of his vehicle behind, and takes an erotic risk, on the street. But by trying to live out his liberated desire David is viciously imprisoned and dehumanised ('my dog'), as his resultant agoraphobia will demonstrate. Having gradually led the viewer into a trajectory of the gay desire for acceptance (through an identification with David and his love for Keith) s/he is now powerfully wrenched back into the grim social and political reality of the spatial restraints of that expression. David's psychic states are directly related to his homosexuality. That the homosexual, as a desiring subject, is placed under the sign of paranoid schizophrenia, is a valenced prospect: on the one hand he can live the metaphor as a liberation. On the other hand, the pathology is a prison.

Race, class and masculinity

The secondary characters of Keith Charles, an African-American, and Federico Diaz, a Latino, play with and confront racial stereotyping. Although only a low-level police officer, Keith has a degree in criminology, as does Federico, in mortuary science. They are what we might describe as 'upper working class', or 'educated proleteriat'. By the end of the series we see both of these characters becoming their own businessmen, as they break into becoming petit bourgeois themselves. However, for the duration of the five years these men are employees, and act as foils to the capital self- discovery of the Fisher brothers. Diaz has aspirations that are to some extent caricatured, especially through the figure of his wife Vanessa. Her job as a nurse is seen as dissatisfying, and Vanessa continuously prods her husband to earn more money, and get more status. Her aspirations are ridiculed; she doesn't know her place, as illustrated in the programme in which she tries to hire day care for her sons, employing a nanny in episode 57 in series 5, 'The Rainbow of her Reasons'. Her failure in cultural capital ensures that these attempts at bourgeois independence will provide narrative opportunities for humour. She doesn't have the skills to employ appropriate staff, and hence she is thrown back on her own devices and has to ask Federico to move back in with her as she cannot cope on her own with the labour of the household. In this rather anti-feminist storyline then, the wife of an employee must know her place. By the end of the series Federico and Vanessa have renegotiated their marriage, through pain and concession; it is instructive that successful heternormativity becomes embodied in a Latin-American Catholic family.

Moving on from the inability of the Diazs to accept their social positioning, we also might recognise the extent to which Keith is coded as the virile male. David's partner Keith is Black; leaving aside for the moment the strong historical taboo against inter-racial sexuality in US culture, and hence its relative obscurity within American popular representation, a feminist analysis should consider exactly how Keith is manifested on the screen. As a working-class man, a Black ex-policeman now security officer, his uber-masculinity is counterpoint to David's fey/faux respectability. The queer feelings evoked in this subnarrative of gay normativity involve the displacement of race onto class, a structure that collapses the viewer into a complex series of identifications. Keith is the 'totty' on the programme, his body is filmed as such, and he is first observed by Ruth in episode 1 (with a sneer) as 'that cop. The black man'. Keith's large, sculpted body affords the viewer with an uncomplicated erotic spectacle, but Keith's desirability is much enhanced by his almost continuous self-ease. He is the 'gay icon' of *Six Feet Under*, and the viewer his voyeur. But his main function in the series is to be the lover-of-David, rather than a character in and for himself, and so not only do we look at Keith, we look *through* Keith, to David. Partly this is because of the structure of narcissism that has historically bedevilled cultural opinions of homosexuality and gay identity, and repeatedly infantilised/neutralised them. The iconic axis of sameness/difference which organises sexual relationships is notably visual, and scopic. Whereas in *American Beauty* Ball satirises gay bourgeois coupledom with Jim and Jim (they are 'the same'), in *Six Feet Under* the effect of an eroticising racial and class difference in Keith/David serves to internally dynamise their union, making it more fascinating for the viewer. That Keith occupies the lower terms of the cultural/ social hierarchy, and is somatically enchanting, merely reproduces conventional economies of desire. However, this is strongly mitigated by the depiction of Keith as an *aspirational figure*, simply put: he has a self, and David wants it.[7]

The closet of respectability

The closet [the grave] is perennially waiting to recapture David, even whilst he is struggling toward a fuller acknowledgment. *Six Feet Under* will go on, over the five years of the programme, to thoroughly explore the import of homosexual prejudice for contemporary Americans. However, the closet is not always simply homosexual: there is also a sense in which Nate's heterosexuality can be read as a gay coming out story. The first time that David comes out to his brother as gay and with Keith is also simultaneously a moment in which Nate and Brenda are acknowledged as 'an item'. The two couples bump into each other having Sunday brunch (that quintessentially couple moment) at the same restaurant in series 1. It is elder brother Nate that first nervously ventures out with 'This is Brenda… my uh… my girlfriend.' Brenda gloriously parries with this alternative 'I prefer the term "fuck-puppet".' The parameters of Nate's sexuality are perpetually returned to in the programme, however it is not so much his sexual practice as his *preference* that drives the narrative momentum. His marriage to Lisa is a classic heroic narrative function of displacement, the viewer, fully cognisant of the conventions of romantic fulfilment, 'knows' that Nate's destiny is to be with the much more interesting, sympathetic and attractive Brenda. Using a Victorian convention, loosely speaking Brenda is the whore and Lisa is the angel in the House, *Six Feet Under* plays with these character functions, so by the end of the series Brenda's crisis is her subsummation from the former into the latter. Brenda is a senior character to Lisa – she is a major persona in a complex, sustained way that outdoes Lisa's rather one-dimensional rendition of the whining eco-hysteric. In a daring hiatus of two whole series, Nate's relationship with Brenda is suspended whilst he digresses down 'the wrong path' in diegetic terms. His sexual journey, though apparently more liberated than David's, is actually more constrained by sexual dissatisfaction, emotional loneliness and frustration. Nate's heterosexuality is teased out over the five years so that at the end his momentary satisfaction is gained in the adulterous arms of his stepsister.[8] The betrayal of Brenda (heroic stalwart, the narrative's Princess function, however ironically rendered), results post-coitally in Nate's annihilation, and death. Nate's yearning for respectability via his marriage to Lisa is disastrous. It seems that the 'proper wife' was having a long-term affair with her brother-in-law, and possibly was murdered by him. Hence, Nate's own attempt at bourgeois respectability is also viciously undercut, and exposed for its ultimate sham/shame. There is no happy ever after for Nate. *Six Feet Under* sticks to the 'underside' of suburban desires, – hardly a narrative endorsement of individualistic self-aggrandising male heterosexual masculinity.

David's character is repetitively straining for respectability – he is the good son, the faithful Protestant, and by the series denouement he is the one who happily marries (Keith), their adopted children inherit the family mantle. He is a good man who is rewarded. It is the gay family who become significantly 'Fisher and Sons' within the last instalment, and the future dream sequence finale of the series. The 'closet' becomes redundant as a metaphor as the whole family 'becomes perfectly queer'. In terms of heroic narrative, viewer identification and resolution, David is central to the momentum, the ending is utopian in its representation of final assimilation/closure. David, crucially, moving into the Fisher home with his nuclear family, presides at the family table, marries Keith, and lives to a ripe old age to pass on his capital to his descendants. *Six*

Feet Under in one sense then is absolutely queer – the future is not only gay, it is also multi-racial – a liberal utopia. There is a whole subplot made clear in the final sequences when the viewer realises that the younger adopted son Anthony will become a gay man, seen in the snapshotted future holding hands with an Asian-American partner. David's recognition of the child Anthony in the playground during the Adoption Picnic, in series 5, episode 56 'Eat a Peach', is clearly the fulfilment of David's right/wish to find his own 'gay son', (coded so by Anthony's outsider status, his gentleness and beauty). In another twist to the queer doubling of the new generation of the Fisher family, Anthony comes with a 'difficult' straight, older brother, Durell.

The last episode of *Six Feet Under*, containing the final sequences that show the accelerated lives of the main characters rushing toward their deaths, is unique in serial drama. These mini-narratives have no dialogue, they are staccato, dream-like scenes that depend on the interpretation of a knowing viewer who can interpret the visual shorthand. They also address an audience who will record and replay the images in slow-mo on VHS or DVD, lingering on those speedy glimpses of the Fisher family futures. This is a unique breaking of form, showing the yet-to-be uncanny future, the future anterior, breaking the temporal frame of the series, opening up the future space, and the pluperfect tense. And with the death of *Six Feet Under* the viewer dies with it, her only enduring hope is to join HBO's community forum, on bulletin boards like 'David and Keith'; the thread is still live, and the fans are still touching their imaginary friends.[9]

The end sequence offers the completion of the American Dream, in which everyone becomes middle class. *Six Feet Under* is resolutely underpinned by American ideals of individual fulfilment, and the accruement of the riches of personality, family, and history, by commitment and hard work. The reward of self-authenticity, is a place to belong, literally and figuratively. That the centre holds for David Fisher is simultaneously sexually radical but in class terms securely conventional. Economically the series – right until the very last episode – shows the class mobility of non-Whites to be static. Keith starts off as an LAPD policeman, conferring conventional approval if not actual status, but he loses this job and subsequently becomes an itinerant bodyguard or personal security guard, with little employment security. Federico and Vanessa are skilled working class, and their economic position remains entirely static until the very last show in which they are seen to acquire their own funeral home through an elusive 'endowment' from a dead relative. Their capital is acquired through that classic nineteenth century novelistic staple of fate: an inheritance. Keith, in the final episode, realises he has enough money saved (presumably from his LAPD pension) to buy out Brenda's portion of the Fisher empire, thus acquiring sole ownership status with partner David. This development endows credibility to the 'gays will inherit the earth' theme of the utopian ending.

Although the Fisher family retains its status, its 'mom and pop' operation, that staple small town American model economy is under threat from Kroehner, the ruthless industrialist. The business is threatened by bankruptcy because of the frail state of the drains; Ruth has gambled Nathaniel's legacy or given it away to her Russian lover, leaving Nate and David in financial crisis and debt. This is only resolved by bringing Federico in as a co-owner, albeit with a 'minority' share. There is not much of a safety net for the petit bourgeoisie. This is how *Six Feet Under* indeed could be said to 'work' as economic realism – it critically reflects back to the viewer the subtle reality of how capital works, of risk versus complacency in middle America. The incident of the drains is of course metaphorical as well as real: as the drains back up and the blood and human effluvia spurts up from the basement into the household plumbing system, this gothic analogy reminds the viewer of the series fascination with 'what lurks beneath'.

Queer love and death

Six Feet Under, unusual for a mainstream programme, has fraternal love as its central structure. Familial love, including the long and touching story of the incestuous relationship between Brenda and her younger brother Billy Chenowith, is the core quandary of the narrative, more broadly – how to love without the phallus. We are reminded that in the Celtic myth of the Fisher King, he sustains a knee or groin wound which is typically interpreted as castration.[10] The radical theme of how to love differently, and even queerly, weaves through the series in multiple guises; loving without the phallus is its defamiliarising aim. What does it mean to turn away from the phallus, to refuse to cathect to its dictats, to turn away from it and reject shame? Love relationships are depicted as diffuse, difficult, and often unredemptive, there is an unambiguously ethical imperative though: the principal qualities of loyalty and perseverance are represented as vital. In *Six Feet Under* we must learn to love again in spite of loss, without the gaze of the loving father and in sight of the prospect of death. The wound of the series is the direct historical and demographic loss due to AIDS, but the show also infers a diffuse cultural loss that marks the homosexual subject: that s/he has lost that place in society that s/he imagines heterosexuality would grant. That chimeric loss of social belonging is six feet under, buried and unconscious, impossible to exhume (but leaving a ghostly depression in the soil nevertheless). This trauma of non-belonging is a broader 'human condition' that locks the viewer into gender melancholy, but s/he is released via its utopic finale. *Six Feet Under* bestows a satisfying closure, the panoramic future that opens up in the last episode is a joyful bricolage of the deaths of the characters we have loved for five years. The surreal spatio-temporal grammar of this ending, or 'death' is to gift to the viewer a ritual of 'successful' mourning, ensuring that the melancholic homosexual subject position is averted.

Heterosexual Nate's death displaces him as the proto-paternal heir, the potential replacement father/phallus. His demise frees gay David to take his own place, at the centre of the family. In the last series, at the moment in the hospital when Nate dies, we see a merging of the two brothers' imaginary. Nate falls unconscious and starts to dream his own death, in which his brother David collects him at the Fisher home in a hearse. This fantasy is Nate's final journey, uncannily though, David is almost unrecognisable to the viewer, he appears as a surf bum, presumably in the guise of Nate's ideal soulmate. This inversion of David is shocking to the viewer, he is the antipathy of the David we have known: he is exultant, unbound, enlightened. Toking on a joint, the boys share a giggling journey in the hearse of perfect intimacy; they enter the sublime. Nate realises they are being driven by their father, Nathaniel, to the ocean, the primordial sea, the symbolic location of a peaceful death throughout the series. The father has returned to collect his sons. When Nate throws himself into the Pacific waves, there is a joy and liberation that signifies that for Nate, this is his relief and fulfilment. At this point David is metamorphosed back to his 'normal self', as he stands on the beach in his suit, watching his brother run to his death. In the primary narrative David awakes from his own sleep alongside Nate's hospital bed, and – as though this dream was now *his* – he realises that Nate has gone. Their final connection is therefore psychic, rapturous, and queerly feminine.

The cultural history of homosexuality has been linked to death, negation, the embodiment of morbidity, corruption, futility and stasis; queer theorists have been remarking on and reworking this association for many years, following Leo Bersani's classic essay 'Is the Rectum a Grave?' (1995).[11] What *Six Feet Under* radically achieves is an inversion of that association, so that the endearingly positive message of the series becomes 'homosexuality=life'. Jonathan Dollimore has discussed the importance of homosexuality as it becomes invested with 'extraordinary redemptive potential, even as it is also the focus of intense cultural, psychic and political anxieties about degeneration and death' (Dollimore 1998, 77). *Six Feet Under* then, fabricates a popular gay aesthetic that refigures the traditional equivalence between death, desire and loss, in which the figure of the homosexual now can stand for the 'future', impelling the viewer toward hope. Whereas in the predominantly pessimistic narrative of Western Culture, death is found inside desire, in this series – this small corner of popular culture – desire is found instead, inside death.

Notes

1   *Les Boys* (1980) Dire Straits from *Making Movies* album Warner Bros/WEA.
2   Of course the corollary to this dynamic is the melancholy created in gay/lesbian subjects that is a direct effect of their unacknowledged mourning for their heterosexual desires.
3   The gendering of the slur 'bitch' is not simply misogynistic. The term in USA slang can also connote strength of purpose and expression. Its use in the specific instance by Paco can be read as an injunction to David not to 'bend over' and capitulate to his oppressors, but simultaneously to grasp his gay effeminacy as a genuine gay manliness. David is made out to be a *gay bitch* – an empowering masculinity, in this context.
4   Engler, Michael (2005) Episode 29 [series 3, episode 3]. DVD edition. HBO.

5   Klein (1975) reprinted in Mitchell (1986). Also for a concise critical definition of the paranoid-schizoid position see Hinshelwood, R.D. *A Dictionary of Kleinian Thought* Free Association Books, London, 1989.

6   The DSM-IV criteria for schizotypal personality disorder offers a definition followed by nine characteristics or symptoms that appear to me to be utterly logical steps for the creative maintenance of a subjectivity which has been damaged by social, or psychic contempt. See DSM-IV: American Psychiatric Association (1994) *Diagnostic and Statistical Manual of Mental Disorders*, 4th Edition, American Psychiatric Association, Washington D.C.

7   We assume, incidentally, that Keith fucks David, not the other way around. The reasons for this are inevitably coded in racial and class terms.

8   This event in plot terms can also be read as Nate's failed attempt to regain the love of the father, even if this is via his stepfather's daughter, the transitional object.

9   http://boards.hbo.com/thread.jspa?threadID=300000286andtstart=0andstart= -1 'David and Keith' chatroom. Web page accessed December 2005.

10   Thanks to Michael O'Rourke for making this connection.

11   For example Ellis Hanson 'Undead' in Fuss, D. (1993), Patricia White 'Lesbian Spectre' in Fuss, D. (1993) Sue Ellen Case (1991) 'Tracking the Vampire', Judith Butler's writing on melancholia (1993, 1994), also much of the critical work from the 1990s concerning gay men, representation, mourning and AIDS.

Chapter 7

After the Fall:
Queer Heterotopias
in Philip Pullman's
His Dark Materials Trilogy

Michel Foucault was deeply interested in the imaginative potential of space, seeing, like other Marxist critics such as Henri Lefebvre, how space generates conditions of possibility. In his project to inventively redefine the human he also understood how linguistic elements regulate prospective outcomes, and how extraordinarily implicated sexuality continues to be in the creation of these new forms of self. In a close reading of Philip Pullman's *His Dark Materials* trilogy, in this chapter I argue how such radical concerns are not only to be found in the academic reaches of philosophy. Popular culture – in its most derisory form of teenage fantasy fiction – can push open new spatial-textual realms, and can come very close to exemplifying Foucault's radical philosophical project of re-inventing the human. By also bringing in the work of Adriana Cavarero I clarify how narrative and story must be integrated into this model of spatial-textual possibility. Popular culture, far from being a denigrated simulation of canonic literature or even a distortion of Great Ideas, provides us with new cultural fora for challenging the political. *His Dark Materials* is an apt choice for several reasons: because of Philip Pullman's avid public opposition to organised Christianity, its myth of the Fall and concomitant notions of original sin and sexual shame; the fantasy genre allows the reader to 'think differently' through cognitive estrangement; because narrative is fundamental to ideas of selfhood and this epic in three, long volumes allows a nuanced emotional world to unfold, encompassing its own psychological and theological parameters. *His Dark Materials* leads the reader forward through powerful empathetic identifications into a deliberate reinscription of the narrative of the Fall, a rewriting of shame. What Pullman has created is a queer heterotopia, as I shall go on to explain.

Foucault: Non-human spaces beyond shame

Foucault's œuvre is replete with spatial analysis, from the banishment of the lepers and the journeying of the Ship of Fools in *Madness and Civilisation*, to the spatial distribution of disease in *The Birth of the Clinic*, to the visual and territorial practices of punishment in *Discipline and Punish*. Foucault, by grounding his writings in the material and metaphorical operations of space, could be described as a spatial historian.[1] Stuart Elden describes how Foucault has deployed spatial language throughout his works, drawing from Heidegger, that:

> Rather than conceive of historical changes as a linear development, Foucault suggests that the 'domain of the modern *episteme* should be represented rather as a volume of space open in three dimensions... [an] epistemological trihedron'. These examinations lead Foucault to one of his most celebrated formulations, suggesting that 'the human is an invention of recent date. And one perhaps nearing its end.' (Elden 2001, 98, original source is Foucault 1970, 346–7)

Here Foucault is embarking on a project to redefine the human as a spatial invention, the narrative shift of his writing is to move away from subjection through spatial regulation, he was keen to communicate a concept of space that engendered hope. Foucault, in his later work, turned from a focus on subjection to revitalise agency and play, indeed his own life and later interest in sadomasochism could be read as a determined, even dedicated, reinscription of the entrenched shame of sodomitical practice. In the later writings, Foucault brings in his notion of 'technologies of the self', specifically in the second and third volumes of *A History of Sexuality* (1985, 1986). Foucault saw these elaborate and rigorous cultivations of self as agentic, not just for the individual, but also importantly, for the communal, social body too. He spoke about the technologies of the self as producing a 'space of freedom', the site of a radical alterity, which, as David Halperin puts it: 'is the space within each human being where she or he encounters the not-self, the beyond' (Halperin 1995, 75). To clarify, this self is not a private interiority to be explored/discovered, but an attempt to realise oneself by cultivating a kind of transcendence of origins, something that is achieved relationally through multiple interventions with the present and imagined futures. This now familiar figure is the one whom has been shamed, who has turned away and been released, whose gaze is momentarily free to look around and make new, propitious connections. Literature and culture are powerful imaginative spaces where this self progresses with an expansive movement, through the readerly impetus of desire, to places that are simultaneously 'here' and 'nowhere', 'other spaces' that enable the self to reconfigure the 'real' of her own life in a dialogic relationship to her individual and the collective imagination. Think of the etymology of the word 'novel' – every time this reader engages with a 'revolution-ary' text or textual fragment, s/he is subtly repositioned within the specific cultural 'episteme' – she is *moved* emotionally and imaginatively, through that consumption, to new prospects.

Being non-intelligible means more potential for new identities to form, in the moment of radical indecypherability, when the subject is turned, s/he is lost from view and undefined. Foucault saw the homosexual as peculiarly positioned to maximise this radical potential, specifically because s/he has historically been indeterminate, and thus discursively more open to resignification.

Foucault indicts us to invent new freedoms, through collective self-fashioning. He argued that it is our culture, our way of life, our *savoir-faire* that poses a threat to heteronormativity, more so than our sexual acts. He argues:

'No! Let's escape as much as possible from the type of relations which society proposes for us and try to create in the empty space where we are new relational possibilities'. By proposing a new relational *right*, we will see that non-homosexual people can enrich their lives by changing their own schema of relations. [Original emphasis] (Quoted in Elden 2001, 100)

Leaving aside for a moment Foucault's rhetorical invocation of an 'empty space' – as if a thing were possible – we need to recognise the utopian motif for such an impulsion, as he says, for *all* people. Within the visible economy of being, the space of representation, there are powerful stencils for predetermining selfhood. However, and this is a key principle, those subject positions, through their own precarious repetition, create spillage, slippage, blurs. The creative arts understand the importance of the mistake, the error, the accidental eruption, the beautiful flaw, and Foucault is gesturing to these and adding an injunction to imaginative and deliberate intent: to actively *queer* aesthetics, whatever your sexuality, leaving shame behind. Foucault, of course, argued that the acquisition of intelligible selfhood in the modern era is distinctively imbricated with sexual identity, and that the varied techniques deployed are not without cost. But it remains an important principle to search around for these interventions promiscuously, as it were, in all types of cultural forms and practices.

The active reflection that Foucault espouses contains comparative spatio-temporal dimensions, where the self both projects (future) and introjects (past). The self negotiates both the spatial and the temporal in order to have a sense of individuation; indeed, 'losing one's bearings' through insanity or mental illness is symptomatic of the temporary 'loss' of this self, or identity. The modern bounded self has to manage intelligibility of itself through time, and it achieves this through *narrative*, through becoming the 'hero' of its own story. This self is very durable: techniques of the self such as writing (confession, diary, autobiography) render the self visible and plausible to itself, and to others.[2] The folding of the outside into the inside creates intelligible interiority; over time, this gathering accrues the force of a plot, it is retrospectively submitted to a sense of ordering, it is made to mean, it contains narrative devices such as cause and effect, heroes and villains, major themes, disruptions, and the emplotment of random events. These elements cohere into the thing we call 'a life'. This is not to say, incidentally, that the 'self' being produced is a fiction, in the pejorative sense of the word, nor is it simply a sum of habits. This is, I think, what hero Lyra Belacqua is musing upon in one of the last pages of *His Dark Materials*:

This was the very thing she'd told Will about when he asked if she missed God: it was the sense that the whole universe was alive, and that everything was connected to everything else by threads of meaning. When she'd been a Christian, she had felt connected too; but when she left the Church, she felt loose and free and light, in a universe without purpose. [TAS 473]

She has a profound confidence in connection and proliferation, rather than the more conventional separation and individuation inflicted by God, through the concept of sin, shame and The Fall. Crucially this optimistic worldview escapes the Calvinist doctrine of predestination, the idea that our future is already predetermined by the Authority, or in a more secular, contemporary version: the hegemonic stare of the state.

Recent critical theory has to some extent fetishised the spatial dimension, yet it is through time, and specifically through the narrativisation of the temporal dimension, that a sense of self and agency occurs.[3] We have seen, after Foucault, the importance of understanding the *genealogy* of the subject, that any negotiation of agency requires an understanding of the historical vicissitudes of power:

> Three domains of genealogy are possible. First, an historical ontology of ourselves in relation to truth through which we constitute ourselves as subjects of knowledge; second, an historical ontology of ourselves through which we constitute ourselves as subjects acting on others; third, an historical ontology in relation to ethics through which we constitute ourselves as moral agents. (Foucault 1982, 237)

Roughly following the three phases of his own writing, then, these three domains of enquiry stress the co-implication of time with agency: we need to know where we have come from (spatially/temporally), in order to facilitate the future. The emergence of enunciation, the self to claim, must be understood processually. Foucault sees these 'enunciative modalities' as sites/spaces of emergence in which political identities are formed (Foucault 1972, 50–56). Certainly Foucault attempted to describe the limits of what could be said through discursive intervention, drawing attention to how resistance is made intelligible to its protagonists and adversaries alike, in a dynamic, dialectical movement. Through the meticulous mechanism of spatial regulation such as enclosure, partitioning, and rank, the subject is provided a place to speak; through the calibrated truths of temporal discipline such as timetabling, seriating, and the imposition of clock-time, the subject is accorded a moment to speak in. Docile bodies indeed. Except, here we have Foucault the optimist: 'I firmly believe in human freedom' (Foucault 1984, 5), a freedom, he claims, that is made possible by the use of counter-memory. Counter-memory liberates us from particular subjectivities by a process of reflection and recognition, we begin to know that that which is posed as truth, is an optional way of being. Thus counter-memory becomes a deliberate process of forgetting who we are, a state of continual self-transformation, of loosening the bonds of shame. The opportunity to imaginatively transform the self is achieved through a network of relations; one self is positioned in reciprocity to many other selves, some more influential than others, all circulating within certain fields of force. Thus, through interaction and repetition, incitation and struggle is continuously a possibility; in spite of – because of – identity ascription, there is always the prospect of refusing what we are, or perhaps more appositely 'named and shamed'. Narrative formations embedded in time provide us with crucial material for this self-fashioning.

Thinking about selfhood inevitably leads to a consideration of consciousness, and, as David Lodge claimed, to literature – 'the record of human consciousness, the richest and most comprehensive we have.' (Lodge 2002, 9). Popular culture is not where the Humanities generally goes to answer that sort of quest, and emphatically not in teenage fantasy, a genre already labelled as 'adolescent' in scope and commonly regarded as puerile kitsch. Fantasy novels are a feminised sub-genre of science fiction, the latter being distinct from the former by the stipulation that SF must depict that which is technologically or scientifically possible, something that is in a vague sense 'reasonable'. Fantasy is by definition unreasonable; historically it hails from the traditional excesses of Gothic, and Baroque, it is allied to unconscious desires, and is the textual exploration of the strange, the gigantic, the elemental, and the boundary between human and non-human, themes more prevalent in the Middle Ages. Fantastic writing provokes readers to think differently, it reveals the silent truths of hegemony by painting Bosch-like pictures of chaotic alternatives. It 'breaks up bourgeois syntax' and rebels against cultural order (Foucault 1986). Even as a kind of vital consolation for the limits of a mundane existence, its form demonstrates a formidable 'if only'. The monstrous revelations of fantasy extrapolate the human within a space of contingency, its stories collide the self with the not-self, perhaps the fantasy genre at best could be a Foucauldian episteme that pushes open human knowability.

Cavarero: Beyond the Other, to the You

Following post-colonialism, the self must have an Other to project onto and appropriate. In confounding the spatialised estrangement of Self/Other I want to turn now to the work of Italian feminist philosopher Adriana Cavarero. Her book *Relating Narratives: Storytelling and Selfhood* engages with current – one might say forestalled – Anglo-American work on identity, principally returning us to look back at the idea of a self, and through it an appreciation of what she prosaically calls the 'you'.[4] Cavarero writes generically complex tales of the narratable self, reviving the writerly tradition of Roland Barthes, and echoing his emphasis on eros, love and desire. Drawing also from Hannah Arendt, Cavarero is keen to revivify notions of individual 'who'ness, in recalling the uniquess of each human story. Cavarero doesn't reproduce the Cartesian remoteness so preponderant in modern versions of the self. Her self is distinctive, but entirely dependent upon the love, recognition, and *narration* of the other, the person she calls 'you'. This is an intimate relation, a fragile one, a consensual exchange of knowing/being that does not depend on the spatial economics of projection and displacement. Kottman describes this structure in Cavarero's work by imagining a dialogue between her and Judith Butler: Butler, as we have seen in *Bodies That Matter*, described the formation of the subject as structured by the constitutive outside, the excluded and abjected other. Despite repudiation, precisely because the other is constitutive, it thus becomes the necessary folded 'inside' of the subject. Whereas in Butler's work this relationship is fundamentally one of subjection, in Cavarero this is figured more along the lines of the 'gift', the gift of narratability that is bestowed in the generous recognition of another, not an Other in a distantiating sense, but another in the sense of a singular living human relationship (such as a parent, a lover, a friend, indeed Cavarero uses all of these examples). Whereas Butler begins by insisting that subjection is the prerequisite for intelligibility, which in turn is the precondition for speaking as individuals, rather '[f]or Cavarero, as for Arendt, the intelligibility of the unique existent is not "first established in language", but rather he/she is a flesh and blood existent whose unique identity is revealed *ex post facto* through the words of his or her life story.' (Kottman 'Translator's Introduction' in Cavarero 2000, xiii)

Both Butler and Kottman, when commentating on Caverero, point out the circular paradox of the subject, noting Butler's observation that the subject has to create its own estranged and ghosted third person 'other' in order to tell its own story. However, Caverero, in a gesture that underlines sociality and generosity, prefers instead to argue that the narratable self desires this story from the mouth of another (person). Rather than stressing the wish for intelligibility in this self-story, instead Caverero emphasises the longing for familiarity, and for ownership of one's story through the essential uniqueness of each person's *storia* told within the dwelling-time, the existence of the life itself:

> It is this *sense* of being narratable – quite apart from the content of the narration itself – and the accompanying sense that others are also narratable selves with unique stories, which is essential to the self, and which makes it possible to speak of a unique being that is not simply a subject. (Ibid., xvi) [original emphasis]

Through the linguistic interpellation of the subject, alienation is produced due to the inhuman indifference of the process, producing 'the feeling that *who* one is, is *not* being addressed, and indeed has no place in the name [shame]-calling scene at all'(Ibid. p xix). As Foucault has said, 'Discourse is not life; its time is not yours' (ibid. p xx). Cavarero articulates this gap, between life and language (the one that Butler allows for resignificatory practices), between life and the tale, as being filled with desire. This allows Caverero to reconfigure the political:

> If one understands 'politics' in Arendt's sense, argues Cavarero – that is, as a 'plural and interactive space of exhibition' – then the scene of narration, of telling each other life-stories, takes on the character of political action. Moreover, through such a suspension of the disjunction between discourse and life, it becomes possible to imagine a relational politics that is attentive to *who* one is, rather than *what* one is. (Ibid., xxiii, citing Cavarero 2000, 71)

Cavarero uses the model of the lover to help us understand the interdependence of agency and selfhood, noting the way that lovers engage in reciprocal narrations to empower each other, to bring each 'to be' in co-appearance.[5] Cavarero's argument demands a much closer reading, as she summarises in the title of her last chapter: The World is Full of Stories Just Waiting to be Told. Even though Cavarero's work would most logically therefore be illustrated in life-stories such as biography or autobiography, I think it pertains more closely to the types of fantastic literature that produce the extrapolated or expanded selves that have something 'real' to say, and that only imaginative writing can truly put this across.

What Cavarero's idea of the 'you' transforms is an entirely pessimistic view of the self/other dyad that implicitly accords any imaginative projection or story of others as colonial, abusive and poisoning. Her concept is profoundly feminist and egalitarian, Cavarero rejects the split subjectivity inaugurated by shame. Taken together with Foucault's technologies of the self – which can be (mistakenly) read as endorsing a muscular individuation – we can instead rethink selfhood as ethically pluralistic and interdependent. Crucially, in order to inaugurate these new selves, narrative and story become elemental. In 'thinking the beyond' in this way Foucault famously saw heterotopias:

> [as] something like counter-sites, a kind of effectively enacted utopia in which the real sites, all the other real sites that can be found within the culture, are simultaneously represented, contested, and inverted. (Foucault 1986, 24)

Heterotopias are kinds of mirrors to utopias, a counterpoint of the real to the unreal, in which the utopic glance returns to reconstruct the real, in a new way of seeing. Heterotopias are the conceptual space in which we live, they allow a slippage of meaning, they produce a kind of imaginative spatial play, out of which can emanate a new kind of semiotic, new practices, and by extension, new kinds of identities and subjectivities. They are simultaneously, and paradoxically, here, and nowhere; perhaps they can be best described as an enabling idea that permits the imagination to reconfigure space, rather than affording a real place we can actually go to. In that latter sense there is a powerful argument for examining the fiction of 'alternative worlds', of which Pullman's trilogy is a prime contemporary example. Seeing *His Dark Materials* as a heterotopic textual space permits the reader precisely the kind of discursive, semiotic reflection that Foucault advocates. Cavarero's emphasis on the power of the story, and Foucault's idea of the heterotopia, are sympathetic. Both models offer a reflective dimension that is identical in two key aspects: they are spatial, and they are textual, and they reject the dominant account of self-formation in Western Culture, via shame. Both discursive structures offer a protensive folding in which the imaginative projection can dynamically return to a mutable self, through a loving and ethical process of reader reception. This process is durational, and contained within narrative (or its corollary, anti-narrative). Furthermore, as I shall show, queer sexuality is at the core of this new human self.

Daemonic heterotopias

Philip Pullman's trilogy is a substantial investigation of the Christian, Western self.[6] He is, like Foucault, convinced that the self is produced as fundamentally sexual, and like Cavarero, dependent upon narrative – a story that is a gift from another. In Philip Pullman's novels selfhood is profoundly sexual, spatial and textual, illustrated in his distinctive proposition of a self that is not an 'I', but a rather Irigarayan 'we'.[7] The first novel, *Northern Lights*, takes place in a single parallel world, a heterotopia based on an extrapolation of our own. It is an uncanny fantasy, in which one 12-year-old girl, Lyra Belacqua, goes on a quest to rescue her friend Roger from the 'Gobblers' (in Pullman's post-Christian theology: the General Oblation Board). Pullman establishes the strangeness of this world by granting each person a daemon, which can be variously interpreted as the individual soul, spirit, emotional expression, unconscious, child, companion, or perhaps the irreducible 'it-ness' of a particularised life. Daemons take the shape of an animal, and cannot be separated far from their person's body. Until puberty, daemons self-determine their shape, their animal form changes in relation to external events and the emotional state of their human; they are highly mutable. When the human reaches sexual maturity (around the age of 12/13), the daemon fixes constantly as one specific animal, its typography then permanently alluding to the 'who-ness' of the person it emulates, usually a bird, reptile or mammal, for example a poodle, a snake, or an eagle (fish obviously present practical difficulties, and are rare). The vividness of the self/daemon relationship is impossible to convey here: daemons can talk, usually conversing with their human out loud, although thoughts can also be shared, and communication is instinctive.[8] They sleep and die simultaneously[9], their life is lived as one breath, a shared consciousness that is dialogic. Lyra's daemon is Pantalaimon, who is effervescently playful, he also protects, advises, and at times, sulks. Most daemon/human selves are heterosexually paired, although same-sex combinations do appear occasionally.

The intricacy of the human/daemon union is developed throughout the trilogy, in the second book, *The Subtle Knife*, two new worlds are introduced. Firstly, Pullman presents Will Parry (also aged 12), the second hero of the trilogy, who comes from 'our reality', a kind of palimpsest Oxford, whose daemon, Kirjava, Lyra claims to recognise as being inside of him.[10] Secondly he designs a third world, entered through the city of Cittàgazze, which is haunted by soul-eating vampiric Spectres who kill *sexually mature* adults, their victims are made into pallid zombies by having their consciousness 'eaten'. Spectres are a kind of purgatorial undead; this is what it feels like to be attacked by one:

> She felt a nausea of the soul, a hideous and sickening despair, a melancholy weariness so profound that she was going to die of it. Her last conscious thought was disgust at life: her senses had lied to her; the world was not made of energy and delight but of foulness, betrayal and lassitude. Living was hateful and death was no better and from end to end of the universe, this was the first and last and only truth. [TSK, 329]

**Figure 7.1   Philip Pullman with a monkey-daemon, London Zoo
Source: Getty Images/Getty Images Entertainment**

It is an extremely effective description of ontological shame. The evil Mrs
Coulter, the trilogy's anti-hero and high-ranking envoy of the Church, is able to
command the spectres because 'They know I can give them more nourishment
if they let me live. I can lead them to all the victims their phantom hearts desire'
[TSK, 324]. De facto, it is the Church that renders sexually mature adults into
spectres, and sub-human wraiths. In *The Subtle Knife* the author hones his post-
Christian theological precept of 'Dust', preparing the reader for the republican
war in Heaven that becomes more fully delineated in *The Amber Spyglass*. But
it is in the second volume that we begin to understand empathetically the
human/daemon relationship, through a secondary character Lee Scoresby and
his daemon Hester. Lee is introduced in the first book as a Texan aeronaut
and explorer. He is the archetypal lone adventurer whose role in the novelistic
structure is of 'helper' and 'good father'. His plot function is twofold: to protect
Lyra, and to find Will's father, although the latter results in the death of both
fathers, symbolic and real. The two protagonists Lyra and Will, in common
with classic fairy tales, share the same psychic orphanage, of mad/dead
parents.[11] Lee is cast as an alternative, loving, heterosexual masculinity, richly
demonstrated through his relationship with Hester, first described in *Northern
Lights* as 'a shabby hare, as thin and tough-looking as he was' [NL 192]. When
Lee is travelling, he tucks his daemon Hester into his coat ('with Hester secure
in his breast' [SK, 302]) – but she is far from infantilised – it is often Hester
who warns or curtails Lee, she is dry, wise, and alert. In this queer marriage they

share an intimate ambience: 'He was used to her silence, and she to his. They spoke when they needed to' [SK, 217]. In the depiction of Lee/Hester the author has rendered a most ideal intimacy, in which profound knowledge and acceptance occurs between elements of the 'us', making visible 'the necessary "inside" of the subject'. In Cavarero's terms, Hester is that Lover/Other that is part of the self:

> Lee looked for Hester in alarm, and found her sleeping, which never happened, for when he was awake, so was she; so when he found her asleep, his laconic, whip-tongued daemon looking so gentle and vulnerable, he was moved by the strangeness of it, and he lay down uneasily beside her... [SK, 304]

When Lee/Hester are faced with their personal Alamo, a gunfight with the soldiers of the Magisterium Guard who are chasing them in order to capture to Lyra, Lee becomes mortally wounded:

> As he reloaded he felt something so rare his heart nearly failed; he felt Hester's face pressed to his own, and it was wet with tears... Another crack, and this time the bullet went deep somewhere inside, seeking out the centre of his life. He thought: it won't find it there. Hester's my centre... Then she was pressing her little proud broken self against his face, as close as she could get, and then they died. [SK 317–19]

This passage, depicting an idiosyncratic love relationship between a man and a rabbit, is incredibly moving; partly this is generic because children's fiction can be powerfully direct in expression, but principally it is because in the daemon/human structure Pullman has invented, there is displayed something queerly profound regarding our internal spatiality: that it is a kind of compound-gendered private collectivity, dependent upon love, sometimes non-human love. It is this difference in perspective, choosing to creatively emphasise an inter- and intra-subjectivity, which echoes the optimism of Cavarero, it also forms the premise of much of Luce Irigaray's philosophy too, '[t]o love together with her, porous to a multiple familiarity' (2000, 114). Rather than the gloomy aggrandising self/other preponderant in contemporary critical approaches, then, it challenges us to radically reconfigure the split subject of shame.

There is a queer attachment, a physical 'space of containment' for this self; the daemon cannot be separated too far from the human without extreme physical pain. In an early scene reminiscent of Freud's *fort-da* game, Lyra and Pantalaimon try to rescue the bear-king Iorek Byrnison:

> Pantalaimon looked at her, and then became a badger.

> She knew what he was doing. Daemons could move no more than a few yards from their humans, and if she stood by the fence and he remained a bird, he wouldn't get near the bear; so he was going to pull.

> She felt angry and miserable. His badger claws dug into the earth and he walked forward. It was such a strange tormenting feeling when your daemon was pulling at

the link between you; part physical pain deep in the chest, part intense sadness and love. And she knew it was the same for him. Everyone tested it when they were growing up: seeing how far they could pull apart, coming back with intense relief. [NL, 194]

It is a stirring visualisation of the compelling vagaries of emotional attachment. Throughout the trilogy appears another haunting notion of disattachment, 'intercision', a torture that separates daemon from person, either by the internal evisceration of the daemon by the Spectres, or in the mechanistically sadistic guillotining deployed by the General Oblation Board, a wing of the Church. This forced division, or metaphorical castration, is tested upon pubescent children in a prison camp in a parallel Siberian-like world. The first book, *Northern Lights* has its plot driven by this horror of intercision: 'They have no daemons, so they have no fear and no imagination and no free will, so they'll fight till they are torn apart!' claims Marisa Coulter [SK, 209]. More often, the daemon-less just wither and die, but either way they self-destruct as this disconnection is spiritual, and permanent. The *His Dark Materials* trilogy is immersed thematically with the various perils of separation, isolation, and seclusion, the daemon-less are detached from the collective good and existentially lost, in loops of shame, unable to reconnect.

At sexual emergence intercision becomes no longer possible because at the point where the daemon defines its shape, the self becomes settled into. In this Pullman could be criticised for sentimentalising actual childhood for its endless potential, which is something nostalgically deluded adults tend to do. Pullman has described the Blakeian movement in the novels as from innocence to experience,[12] it is through experience the self becomes integrated as a moral, accountable entity, chiming with Foucault's late injunction for building an ethical self. The daemon/human self is a social structure, but it is demonstrably a symbolic psychic split, split in a Kleinian sense of projection (1975).[13] However, unlike in classical psychoanalysis, this splitting is not pathologised: Pullman makes materially visible a modern, multiple self underpinned by association, negotiation and cooperation, rather than rejection, fragmentation and alienation. In that sense, Pullman creates a synergy between the Enlightenment Man of Reason, linked inexorably to the rise of the Church, a self formed through the exercise of will, choice, and accountability, and the postmodern decentred self that is founded upon doubt, diversity, and narrative. The taboo against touching someone else's daemon unless the humans are lovers clearly indicates the erotic intimacy of this self-daemon bond. Each real-world sexual self, of course, is multiply intersected by social discourses. Beverley Skeggs has argued that the construction of selfhood is inevitably classed, and linked to cultural property (Skeggs 2003). That the self is produced through status, that only some persons are created with interiority, dimensionality, and that the ability to propertise oneself depends on one's value as proscribed by others, are all conditions of the emergence of the bourgeois subject. Experience – of the right kind – accrued through the methodical operation of history and memory, is interpreted critically to form a concept of personal depth and interiority, of reflexive selfhood. This selfhood, which is intrinsically spatial and accrues through sexual experience, is then 'possessed' by the individual as a form of 'authorisation'. This model of middle-class selfhood is also carved out via appropriation, and accumulation, defined against the working class as the limit-site; they form the constitutive outside that is sexually excessive, abject and immoral. Selfhood can thus be perceived as a kind of appetite.

In order to be hegemonically acceptable, discursively readable, working-class narratives of selfhood are frequently rendered through a rhetoric of redemption, of moral correction/aspiration. Skeggs has argued that '[t]he self then becomes an ethical imperative: it has to be displayed as a sign of one's social responsibility, one's morality' (Skeggs 2003, 33). Fantasy fiction for children and young adults is heavily strewn with these social and moral signifiers, think, for example, of the remarkably classed signifiers of the *Harry Potter* series, or the overbearingly repressive class politics of J.R.R. Tolkein's *Hobbit* and the *Lord of the Rings*. Elements of typecasting all too familiar to this genre are also present in Pullman: Lyra is a resoundingly upper-class orphan who sets out to 'find' herself in a tale teeming with moral messages. Certain working-class stereotypes are plentiful within the epic: servants have rather plain daemons that are usually dogs, as Lyra explains, daemons express 'something like your real nature' and hence:

> Like if your daemon's a dog, that means you like doing what you're told, and knowing who's boss, and following orders, and pleasing people who are in charge. A lot of servants are people whose daemons are dogs. [TAS, 483]

These types always seem to be grammatically challenged in the novel's dialogue; there is a Traveller group or pseudo-Gypsy tribe called Gyptians who are jolly folk who perform the function of rosy-cheeked helpers who have lots of cheerfully ungovernable children. If Lyra – with the innocence of a child – claims that servants' 'real nature' is to be dogs, then we are seeing here the hoary animalisation of the lower classes.[14] Fantasy as a genre is replete with strictly hierarchical societies, it is often the most intransigent of representations in otherwise quite radical novels. This seems to be a political slip by Pullman, who is otherwise very careful to challenge received notions. The middle/upper-class characters in *His Dark Materials* seem to be either more mendacious, or more honourable, or just more individuated, in that classic economy of accumulative interest. Even Will, despite his single-parent-family status, has a missing heroically masculine father who is a famous explorer and ex-marine (officer class, we presume). *But* even though the novels do deploy some clichéd class representations, there is also some visible effort directed into challenging them.

Angelic sodomites

Principally Pullman's remaking of the Christian self is pictured through the pairing of characters, with the self/daemon as described, but this coupling structure is present elsewhere and powerfully communicated in *The Amber*

Spyglass with the story of two male angels, Balthamos and Baruch. Angels are 'huge structures composed of intelligence' [TAS, 147], but they are envious of human bodies. Balthamos and Baruch are two aged homosexuals, and in spite of these creatures' fearsome intelligence they are also humorously familiar: the Muscle Mary (Baruch) and the Biting Queen (Balthamos). Pullman has some fun with these gay stereotypes: we recall that they would be very familiar images to teenagers, whose chat is peppered with anti-gay cliché. Balthamos, already charming the reader with his trenchant sarcasm, his sour sulking, his disdain and physical ineptitude, is every angelic inch a reluctant, rescuing hero. Pullman takes these worn out typologies and resignifies the homosexual in a creative rewriting of Foucault's imperative to remake ourselves. Balthamos and Baruch become the archetypes of love, a love that is transcendental and eternal, but not at all sentimental. What is striking in this pairing in *His Dark Materials* is that Baruch and Balthamos are the perfect, passionate lovers ('we feel as one, though we are two' [TAS, 24]), and when Baruch dies, the representation of Balthamos' grief is profound. These two aged sodomites love without shame, they are 'advanced democratic beings' who benefit from an ancient wisdom, as the angel Balthamos comments on the origins of the Authority who is 'formed of Dust as we are, and Dust is only a name for what happens when matter begins to understand itself' [TAS, 31]. Attaining self-consciousness is perhaps a more prosaic, universal formulation of Foucault's injunction to galvanise an 'aesthetics of the self' (1985, 1986). Baruch and Balthamos are rogue angels not obedient to the Authority, they are unbound militants who have escaped the shame-ties of convention and their function in the novel is to aid the revolution in Heaven. These two angels are in fact a perfect visualisation of the sodomitical sublime. In producing an anti-religious polemic, what purposeful irony to make one of the most aspirational love relationships of the text revolutionary, anti-authoritarian, and heroically homosexual, – and all this for teenagers.

Of 'Other spaces'

To return to the Cavarero's literary model of the self, explained as 'a flesh and blood existent whose unique identity is revealed *ex post facto* through the words of his or her life story' (Kottman 2000, xiii). Pullman's fiction exemplifies this, for example in this scene in *The Amber Spyglass* where Lyra descends to the land of the dead, a purgatorial wasteland of abandoned souls. Chapter 23 is entitled 'No Way Out', however, its epigram is taken from the Gospel of St John 'And ye shall know the truth, and the truth shall make you free'. The *truth* of the self is contained in the life-story, embodied by Lyra as she journeys down through the spatial/spiritual land of the dead in order to liberate Death, to end the rule of the Authority. Lyra tells her story to the evil harpy called 'No-Name'; it becomes clear that the appointed role of No-Name has been to torment the souls that were sent there, to fill them with fear, remorse, and self-hatred by reminding them of their life's worst and wicked deeds, for eternity. They are the damned, castigated by perpetual guilt and condemned to eternal shame.

However the harpies have a kind of warped sincerity, in that they can detect truth from fiction: when Lyra spins a tale in order to deflect them, they attack her. Lyra redeems the harpies by giving them the task of hearing the true tales or life-stories of the recent dead, in exchange they promise to lead them out from death; as these ghostly souls emerge into a new pastoral world in which their atoms disperse, they become one with nature, transformed into life again. When this new treaty for the dead is reached, Lyra kisses No-Name, and in an act of love she gives the harpy a name: 'Gracious Wings', and hence, a self. The whole scene evokes a Foucauldian aim to distinguish truth, but also woven through are Western Christian principles of oral confession and absolution.[15]

Critic Millicent Lenz has drawn attention to how Pullman deploys storytelling in *The Amber Spyglass* to enable children to come to terms with the idea of death, by appropriating Platonic and also Romantic sources from Keats and Percy Bysshe Shelley, 'providing a kind of armor for the psyche' (Lenz 2003, 48). Lenz claims that 'Escape from the Land of the Dead can be won only by those who have lived aesthetically and soulfully, who have enjoyed the gift of life through their intellects and senses. Only then, it is implied, will they have stories to tell.' (Lenz 2003, 52). Plato expressed the hope that stories could provide a way of salvation, through their power to transform, to imagine a way out from suffering. It is this act of storytelling, demanded by the harpies, that releases the dead, but it is also effortless to read this as a metaphor for release from despair and shame. Stories nourish the soul, but only if the storyteller has an active listener who is able to receive the gift. This quality of mutual listening is an extended sensibility of openness, the role of the You, in Cavarero's terms, the one who gives the subject her story.

In Pullman's trilogy everyone has their own personified death, a spirit-world character similar to a shadow, an unseen companion who ensures that life and death have their proper resolution. An old woman's Death says this to Lyra:

> You must call up your own deaths. I have heard of people like you, who keep their deaths at bay. You don't like them, and out of courtesy they stay out of sight. But they're not far off. Whenever you turn your head, your deaths dodge behind you. Wherever you look, they hide. [TAS, 264]

Death is an internal entity that must be negotiated with, kindly. The model is integrative, it is anti-psychoanalytic in the sense of Freud, offering instead a philosophical construct located historically with the nineteenth century Romantic's concept of a 'sympathetic imagination', Lenz relates it to empathy, another critic Naomi Wood calls it 'a Coleridgean distinction between fancy and imagination' (Wood 2001, 253). In Pullman's trilogy this quality of listening and telling depends not upon a superficial, fanciful whimsy, it is a redemptive extrapolation sourced from a kind of deep consciousness, from the emotional integrity of self-acceptance. It is an authorisation of self-narrative, with a reflective understanding of dependency as connectivity, rather than subjectivity. Lenz quotes Mary Watkins as saying that what this active imagination offers is a capacity for visualising 'what the Romantic poets called 'a heterocosm – a world other than this one – which, once alive imaginally, can inspire action' (Watkins 1987, in Lenz 2003, 53). This seems very akin to Foucault's heterotopic imagination, his idea of the enabling 'other space'.

The title of *His Dark Materials* is taken from Milton's *Paradise Lost*, Book II, line 915, from the passage on chaos. Satan is just getting his ticket out of hell from Sin in order to go off and make trouble for mankind. The reference to 'dark materials' is to two kinds of controversy: firstly the *ex nihilo* problem, which wonders what there was before God made the world, whether He made the world out of something, or out of nothing. But what would 'nothing' be, and how can any 'thing' come from it? The second controversy is the 'other worlds' problem: might God have made a multiplicity of worlds, or could He make new ones if this one goes wrong? Would the Fall take place in all of these worlds, would Christ be incarnated in all of them, would He be the same in each? These theological questions had a long history in Milton's day.[16] Pullman is investigating the potential for the creation of a self that is complicated by the indeterminable freedoms of human will, and that lives beyond/after shame. Seeking the domicile of the Authority, Mrs Coulter makes this observation in *The Amber Spyglass*:

> It reminded her of a certain abominable heresy, whose author was now deservedly languishing in the dungeons of the Consistorial Court. He had suggested that there were more spatial dimensions than the three familiar ones; that on a very small scale, there were up to seven or eight other dimensions, but that they were impossible to examine directly. He had even constructed a model to show how they might work, and Mrs Coulter has seen the object before it was exorcised and burnt. Folds within folds, corners and edges both containing and being contained: its inside was everywhere and its outside was everywhere else. [TAS, 415]

In this heresy there is no longer an interiority that is a site of injury formed through shame, and in shame. Instead there is a less rigid, more playful sense of the layerings of potentially joyous intersubjectivities. This idea of space as dynamic possibility emerges out from under Newtonian physics, following Da Vinci, with Kant's 'island universes', it consolidated in the twentieth century with the theory of the expanding universe popularised by Hubble's telescope, and is epitomised in Einstein's theory of relativity, and more recently, in quantum physics. Thus – in what Pullman so wittily describes as experimental theology – we can envisage a dynamic cosmic architecture with its own organic history: a Big Bang that produced curved, expanding space. This space seethes and ripples and produces any number of space-time dimensions, most famously in the form of 'strings'. Cyber-idealism is one contemporary casualty of this free-floating, Gnostic, disorienting swarm. Dizzying as these possibilities are for human potential, Pullman insistently grounds his figures in a self-space that is clearly collective and accountable, presenting his characters with moral choices that are old-fashioned and fleshly. He retains an idea of shame that is closer to guilt, less of an ontological separation and more so an internalised ethic that is reached through the Foucauldian exercise of self, something profoundly optimistic. In his models of other- and same-sex couplings, whether human-daemon, human-human, or angelic, the 'dark materials' of self-making are irrepressibly and dynamically anti-heteronormative and queer.

After the Fall

The trilogy is centrally concerned with a Blakeian rewriting of the story of the Fall of Adam and Eve, from innocence to experience. Pullman describes Milton as being one of the two other sources for *His Dark Materials*, the third being an essay written in 1812 by Heinrich von Kleist called 'On the Marionette Theatre' that offers three metaphors for the Fall. In an interview when asked how important is this central conceit Pullman calls it:

> Completely essential. It's the best thing, the most important thing that ever happened to us, and if we had our heads straight on this issue, we would have churches dedicated to Eve instead of the Virgin Mary. That's basically it. (Parsons and Nicholson 1999, 118)

In *Northern Lights* the Genesis story is reworked, the serpent tells Eve that if she eats the fruit:

> Your eyes shall be opened, and your daemons shall assume their true forms, and ye shall be as gods, knowing good and evil. [NL, 372]

The end of shame brings knowledge, once their eyes are opened Adam and Eve can fully see themselves and each other, their selves are formed through recognition and accountability, two themes I shall go onto explore further in the last chapter. Pullman declares that they have the capacity to become gods, in non-theological terms they are able to claim full agency only through this act of radical disobedience. Rejecting authority/repression brings the responsibilities of free will ('Will' Parry[17]), and consequently the gifts of discernment and ethical discretion. As Wood has claimed 'Pullman argues that storymaking should not be an escape from the world but a way to reinvent it,' she continues, 'Mary Malone's role [in *The Amber Spyglass*] as "serpent" in this new Garden of Eden is to tell her own true story of her "deconversion" from celibacy to joyful sexuality.' (Wood 2001, 255). Anne-Marie Bird analyses Pullman's reworking of the myth of the Fall and points out that the original creation story is charged with naming, making distinctions, classification, and articulating opposites; she helpfully observes that the Judeo-Christian creation story opens with the concept of division and separation: God dividing the light from the darkness, the heaven from the earth, the day from the night. Bird points out that by appropriating William Blake's concept of the 'Contraries': 'Pullman attempts to synthesise the opposing principles that lie at the core of the myth while leaving the innocence-experience dichotomy firmly in place' (Bird 2001, 112). Because Adam and Eve opt for knowledge rather than paradise, Satan can be said to have liberated Man 'from a place of temporal and moral stasis with no opportunities for growth or development... Adam and Eve were trapped in a preconscious state'

(Bird 2001, 121). Adam and Eve are not trapped in immovable shame, shame impels them away from God toward an allegorical journey we call 'the human condition'. The appearance of shame is thus imbricated with the revelation of sex and death, it is synonymous with becoming fully human, with *becoming*. This is what Deirdre F. Baker calls Pullman's metaphysical map (Baker 2006, 243), as Will says: 'We have to build the Republic of Heaven where we are' [TAS, 488]. *His Dark Materials* is an extended dissertation on human limitations and moral accountability.

Bird asserts that Pullman is reworking a story of disobedience and punishment into a narrative of self-development, based on his theory of interconnectedness and the necessary interplay of opposites. Dust is the matter that unites all that is known and unknown. Pullman's worlds and the subjects within them are predicated on this mutual, affective energy. Dust links sexuality to the life-force, to the reproduction of selves, and in this association of Dust with Original Sin, as the General Oblation Board claims, Pullman tries to reinvigorate an argument of sex-as-biological drive that Queer Studies has often tried to refute. However, it is not too different from the more Deleuze and Guattarian preconceptions of sex as proliferating desires, Dust as the precondition for desire, a 'desiring-machine' (1977). The conflation of sex with possibility, sex with life, depicted in its magnificent complexity, is something that stories can explore with imaginative impunity. Pullman tries to remake sex as a foundational principle of life, as something to positively embrace as mystery.

We recall that the original Fall also inaugurated the creation of sexual differentiation. In an early scene from *Northern Lights*, when Lyra is first installed in the home of her mother in London, Mrs Coulter tries to, like a 'good mother' install femininity in Lyra:

> In Mrs Coulter's flat, everything was pretty... Charming pictures in gilt frames, an antique looking-glass, fanciful sconces bearing anbaric lamps with frilled shades; and frills on the cushions too, and flowery valances over the curtain-rail, and a soft green lea-pattern carpet underfoot; and every surface was covered, it seemed to Lyra's *innocent* eye, with pretty little china boxes and shepherdesses and harlequins of porcelain. [NL, 76] [my emphasis]

Pullman associates seductive femininity with the horrors of the upwardly mobile suburban boudoir, indeed, '[t]he bathroom was another wonder', all rose-pink and fragrant, in which Lyra sees in the mirror 'a softly illuminated figure, quite unlike the Lyra she knew' [ibid]. Later:

> Then a bath, with thick scented foam. Mrs Coulter came into the bathroom to wash Lyra's hair, and she didn't rub and scrape like Mrs Lonsdale either. She was gentle. Pantalaimon watched with powerful curiosity until Mrs Coulter looked at him, and he knew what she meant and turned away, averting his eyes modestly from these feminine mysteries as the golden monkey was doing. He had never had to look away from Lyra before. [NL, 78]

The passage is densely significant: on the one hand Lyra, as the 'new Eve' is being auto-seduced by femininity, something to which she retains ambivalence toward in the later books. Secondly, Lyra is surprised by a sensuality that is rather perversely tendered by her mother. Then thirdly, and principally, this scene epitomises how essentially the spatial self is a sexual self, illustrated here through the mechanism of shame. I have written in Chapter 3 about how shame instigates a state of uncomfortable self-knowledge that becomes an internal consciousness of differentiation. This is Pullman's rendering of Francis Broucek's 'keystone effect' (Broucek 1989, 369), which can substantiate a recursive moment of recognition of our place in the social world. Shame is based upon separation and loss, in this instance, it presages the excision of self/other that constitutes Lyra's loss of her daemon in the final volume. Yet, it is this separation from Pantalaimon that ensures the radical success of Lyra's redemptive narrative. In this depiction Pullman is suggesting that even in selfhood, desire for the other internal self must be spatially negotiated.

His Dark Materials is a secular humanist attack on institutionalised religion, and its role in war. The Roman Catholic Church has perceived the trilogy as an attack on itself, Pullman's archaic and apocalyptic version has certainly annoyed conventional Christians. But Pullman's aim is wider than that, for example he has also roundly attacked fundamentalist Protestantism in public debate, and he notoriously hates the Narnia books of C.S. Lewis. *His Dark Materials* focuses upon the Old Testament Judeo-Christian origins in Genesis because that is what Pullman sees as the core falsehood. In his project of critiquing and remaking the model of the shamed Christian self, Lyra is a central conceit. Her destiny as the new Eve (or 'Eve again' as the witches call her) is explicit, and it is her function in the fable to eat from the tree of knowledge and thus gain true consciousness through sexual experience. In *His Dark Materials* Eve's tragic disobedience in eating the forbidden fruit makes her a hero, not a villain, it inaugurates a new era of sexual love without guilt forcing religion to relinquish its power. The symbolic re-enactment of the Fall is written from the perspective of 'what if' the serpent was right, it is a heresy that has fascinated literature from Marlowe to Milton to Blake. The dark matter of Dust – the creative erotic force of the Universe – brings consciousness, and through it the agency to resist the religious tyranny of the Church. Lyra is a nascent little savage who is never really tamed, indeed her stubborn mutineering provides redolent identifications for the teenage reader targeted by the trilogy. Pullman is adamantly opposed to religious fundamentalism, as his public comments attest.[18] Rewriting *Paradise Lost* for teenagers allows the author to radically dissent from the ideologies of the Christian Right in their popular mobilisation of teenage celibacy in such campaigns as 'True Love Waits'. It is fair to say though that the Calvinistic, Talibanesque Church of *His Dark Materials* is a parody, an ironic intensification, albeit one constructed out of the ecclesiastical scaffolding of our own Roman Catholic Church. The trilogy structure depends systematically upon the grand narrative forms and logic of Christianity, not just the Fall but also the pilgrim's journey, temptation and redemption, the descent into Hell, the resurrection after death. The author has repeated the convention and turned away from it, only to be reconnected in a new way.

The queer spatiality of *His Dark Materials*

I have described aspects of sexual subjectivities in the trilogy that can be interpreted as non-normative or 'queer'. Experimentation with gender includes for example Will's father turning out to be a celibate shaman, a healer and spiritual figure who integrates the feminine and masculine, and Lyra is the consummate tomboy who likes to climb over College roofs spitting plum stones on passing scholars and hooting like an owl. Nevertheless, the narrative imperative of the series might still be read as heteronormative, in that the plot is resolved by the emerging sexual knowledge and experience of its two main heterosexual protagonists. The climax of the trilogy comes at the end of book three, *The Amber Spyglass*, when Will and Lyra re-enact the Fall. They become Adam and Eve in the Garden of Eden, reunited with their daemons, and make love. In the stage adaptation, Lyra is seen kissing Will as a stream of gold pours over them, and the witch Serafina declares 'two children are making love in an unknown world'. Pullman has taken the classic narrative convention of Western culture but given it a characteristic twist. Firstly, we recall that Lyra and Will, the archetypal heterosexual couple that anchor the novel, are with their daemons, who also cavort with each other sexually, they are *more than* a pair, their sex is explicitly not 'private' in a traditional sense, they are 'to be two' (Irigaray 2000). Secondly, the couple do not end up together in romantic wedlock at the conclusion of the books, they remain apart in separate yet parallel worlds to become more fully themselves (Russell 2003). Thirdly, at this point in their lives, Lyra and Will are still *children*; its hard to imagine a more radical gesture in the current climate of paranoia about child sexuality and paedophilia than to depict under-age sex, in a teenage novel and a play at the *national* theatre. Fourthly, Lyra is a firmly feminist action hero, and it is Will who out of the two of them is the most introspective, troubled and sensitive. Their re-enactment of the Fall is all the more powerful for its insistence upon the full agency of the two/four sexually charged participants, and its outcome is their joy, spiritual knowledge and accountability, not their shame. Original Sin becomes transformed in *His Dark Materials*, so that '... your eyes shall be opened, and your daemons shall assume their true forms, and ye shall be as gods, knowing good and evil' [NL, 372].

Pullman's trilogy is a queer heterotopia in that it insists upon a self-fashioning, or self-work that is achieved through being responsive to the collective good, and by holding fast to ethical truths, achieved dialectically in many forms. By presenting this narratable self as an ethical and accountable self, Pullman gives a moral map to agency by dispensing with the sovereign, split, subject forged through shame. He optimistically reworks the Fall of Man into the rise of the posthuman, an ascent to adulthood via sexual experience. *His Dark Materials* is a very Foucauldian project, by looking to spatial and textual realms of the imagination Pullman attempts to redefine what it is to love as a human. His writing fulfils the Foucauldian injunction to actively queer aesthetics; he asserts that techniques of the self are intrinsically narrational ['tell them stories'], and therefore intertextual. He is gnomic, Foucaldian even, when he comments upon his aims, contending that his trilogy 'is not fantasy. It's a work of stark realism. I don't read fantasy' (Parsons and Nicholson 1999, 131). These self-stories are an effort to form different truths: Pullman gives us a moral accountable self, accrued by means of a diversity of sexual experience and pleasure, and the rejection of shame. Pullman's self is one stirred toward connectivity, of fundamental openness and vulnerability, aligned with Cavarero's faith in the non-shaming You, and the Irigarayan 'to be two'.

Michel Foucault saw his last work, the three volume *History of Sexuality*, as a project that returned to the precepts of the Enlightenment that he had spent his previous career refuting. His modern ethics of the self is infused with emancipatory potential, it is opposed to the idea of split, alienated subjectivities that are trapped in cycles of shame and rejection, and it eschews large-scale belief systems that demean and restrict the ordinary person. Pullman's fiction is engaged with a similarly trenchant criticism of religious orthodoxy, and an extended refutation of the Biblical theology of sexual shame. Instead, he offers us in creative story-writing what Foucault couldn't: the reimagination of queer heterosexuality, of prelapsarian opposite-sex love that is outside of the phallic economy. Foucault rebuked Christianity for its heteronormativity, for its contrived values, and its subordination of individuals, posing instead a locally emergent ethic, what he called the 'autonomous aesthetics of the self', a Kantian attitude of critical self-awareness, the person as a 'work of art' (which I will go on to elucidate in the next chapter). It is in fantasy fiction then, that we can find clues to Foucault's project of the constructive reworking of Enlightenment self-fashioning. This genre opens up more fluid spaces where alternative truths of the imagination – thinking and being in the world – can be invented:

> ... the critical ontology of ourselves... has to be conceived as an attitude, and ethos, a philosophical life in which the critique of what we are is at one and the same time an historical analysis of the limits that are imposed on us and an experiment with the possibility of going beyond them. (Foucault in Rabinow 1994, 49–50)

This torque of possibility is reminiscent of the elastic tendon binding self and daemon, and of the twisting and turning dynamics of shame.

Notes

1   Elden argues that Foucault was influenced by Martin Heidegger who insisted that time and space be more integrated as time-space, understood as dwelling in the present presence, the 'moment-site' [*Augenblicksstätte*] (Heidegger 1999).

2   These techniques are resources not equally accessible to all. See further Byrne (2003) on how some women do not narrate.

3   See Grosz (2004, 2005).

4   Translated by Paul A. Kottman who includes an excellent introduction to Cavarero's thinking.

5   The term is Jean-Luc Nancy's see further Derrida (2005).

6   *His Dark Materials* is enormously dense in terms of its size, literary complexity and narrative richness and in this chapter I can only skim the surface of notable material. I recommend two useful introductory secondary texts for readers wishing a more detailed overview: Squires (2003) and Tucker (2003).

7   This idea is at the core of the work, illustrated when the stage version performed at the National Theatre in two separate three-hour plays in January 2004. The first play opened with a scene that immediately addressed this conjunction by deliberately foregrounding the main characters' interdependence:

     'The first person to speak a line of the new play was Anna [playing Lyra]. 'Will?' she said… The second person to speak was Dominic [playing Will]. 'Lyra?'. Dominic playing Will, told Anna playing Lyra, that he missed her, and he missed Pantalaimon too. In fact, he missed Pantalaimon as much as he missed Lyra, 'because he *is* you.' Butler, Robert (2003, 9).

8   I am writing this in Autumn 2006 before the release of the film *Northern Lights*, the first novel of the trilogy to be adapted for screen. The ability to use Computer Generated Imagery to illustrate the human/daemon relationship will hopefully give us new possibilities for imagining its meaning. The dramatic production at the National Theatre in 2004 used translucent puppets with little lights inside controlled by the hand of the actor. See Butler (2003) for more detail.

9   Like favourite slaves in the Viking era – thanks to Noreen Giffney for this observation.

10   'You *have* got a daemon,' she said decisively. 'Inside you.' Pullman, Philip *The Subtle Knife* Scholastic Ltd. London [1997] 1998, p. 26.

11   This is a standard trope for children's fiction, but also for crime fiction, another genre preoccupied with the heroic search for ontological security for an 'unanchored', free-floating self. In children's fiction it is particularly obvious that this structure is also a wish-fulfilment for children's ambivalent feelings for their parents: the fear of separation ('don't leave me!), and the rage of individuation ('I wish you were dead!').

12   Pullman is evoking nineteenth-century poet, artist and philosopher William Blake, whose epigrams open many of the chapters in the trilogy.

13   For a fascinating psychoanalytic interpretation of the trilogy see the three consecutive journal articles by authors Margaret and Michael Rustin (2003).

14   Dogs, however, don't escape being classified into hierarchical fractions either, as I indicated in my Introduction with reference to hunting hounds. Further, I was told yesterday about a woman from a local council estate who walks her own dogs only in middle-class areas, as her expectation is that her pets will be safer there (finding a better class of dog).

15   In common with the theme of Lyra as the 'New Eve', Pullman's feminist agenda is to have her, rather than 'Adam', name the creatures of creation.

16   This explanation was given to me by Brian Cummings, University of Sussex.

17   'Will' is of course also short for 'William', and there must be an allusion here to William Blake.

18   Pullman has given many interviews at which he has been explicit about his political aims in writing *His Dark Materials*. Useful sources include: De Bertodano (2002); Parsons and Nicholson (1999); Sharkey (1998); Tucker (2000). For an enjoyable twist on this see Minette Marrin's comments in the week following the Archbishop of Canterbury's suggestion to a group of theologians at 10, Downing Street [the home of the British Prime Minister] that the trilogy be taught in Religious Education classes in schools (Marrin 2004).

Chapter 8

A Queer Feeling When I Look at You: Tracey Emin's Aesthetics of the Self

In *Queer Attachments* I have been rereading shame through a Foucauldian perspective. I see shame as operating as a field of force and a field of legitimacy (and hence, delegitimacy). Shame is a force that acts upon the self, constituting social subjects who are marked and shaped by its interpellating propensities of recognition, misrecognition and refusal of recognition. We know from Foucault that where there is power there is also resistance, and in that vein shame also is *productive*, in socially unpredictable ways. Shame circulates in an acute form throughout our public cultures, in shame scenarios or moments that punctuate social spurning, or more diffusely in veiled strings of shame that worm themselves through the social imaginary, attaching to groups or individuals like wet spaghetti, puncturing wormholes in the social fabric as they go. Insiduously, shame can cling, mildew-like, to certain bodies, detectable on them like a clammy smell. These few people that suffer in states of profoundly visible shame seem to emit an aura/odour of shamefulness that causes avoidance in those near. Shame is perceived as contagious, contaminating – viral even – and in this extreme mode its victim can be collectively averred and ostracised. Shame has an opposite tendency toward effacement and disguise, mutating into other more visibly expressed emotions like disgust, envy, antagonism and contempt. Shame is a chameleonic emotion, adapting to the colour of its psychic host, exercising/exorcising tendencies within that host, hence a depressed person who is shamed will turn destructively inward, and an extrovert will extrude vocal contempt. To a significant extent then, shame can persecute the individual, who in turn can project his internal persecution, spreading it over his network of peers. Shame that goes unacknowledged is most often the culprit and source of this damage. In the peculiar mutations of shame we can begin to understand that shame as an affect can be alternately hyper-sensive, semiotically embodied, and yet also seep invisibly like a gas, sucked into a hospitable host's unconscious often without his awareness, experienced merely as a vague psycho-somatic discomfort, hunched deportment, or sickly habitus.

Tracey Emin – The work of art of shame

Shame has a plasticity that lends itself toward creative and critical exploration. One British artist whose art is vitally concerned with the effects of shame, who reworks public and private shame as a critical engagement with the self, is Tracey Emin. In Carl Freedman's complete works of *Tracey Emin* (2006), Jeanette Winterson's Introduction claims that:

> 'Arguments that begin, *But is it art?* Miss the point. The point is that Tracey Emin has done more for public awareness of art, both as a force in its own right and as a necessary part of life, than any other living artist' (Winterson in Freedman 2006, 6).

Emin's art has crossed over into popular and public culture, she is presently the British Council's chosen artist for the 52nd Venice Biennale 2007, the world's longest running art exhibition. Emin has a cultish celebrity or notoriety, she is known for her strikingly creative reworking of shame, disgust, and sexuality, particularly of the female body. Omnipresent themes include fucking, anal sex, masturbation, drunken excess, excretion, self-hatred, her art is a visceral revelation for the spectator. Stylistically, her art ranges from the deceptive immediacy of crude, scratchy and instant monoprints, to large sculptural wooden structures using images drawn from British seaside iconography like rollercoasters, and beach huts, to living installations that include herself as a nude, vibrant neons, raw digital videos, and also carefully sewn fabric quilts strewn with quasi-religious messages wrought with felt letters in primary colours cut out with scissors, and individually stitched. Her two most famous pieces are installations: *Everyone I Have Ever Slept With 1963–1995* (sometimes referred to as *The Tent*) (1995) which was part of the famous Royal Academy *Sensation* exhibition of that year, and *My Bed* (1998) which was shortlisted for the 1999 Turner Prize. Both of these achieved notoriety, the first because of Emin's alleged promiscuity, although in fact its premise is rather sweet (it is not about fucking, but about *sleeping*) – and the second because of the dirty bed sheets, menstrual-stained knickers, used condoms, empty vodka bottles and fag-ends... and the rest of the well-documented, disgusting detritus strewn around that desolate bed.

Summer 2005, in Siena: as cultural migrants we had wandered around the teeming tourist traps in the August weather, rotating sun and torrential rain, eating local cake in the famous shell-shaped Piazza del Campo, and being bemused by the Italian penchant for rude pasta shapes. The football club A.C. Siena, was playing a loud, loyal, typically Italian game at the Stadio Artemio Franchi and their exultant cheers wafted over the cobbled streets. Siena is known for its cult of the Virgin Mary, and also for being the home of St. Catherine of Siena, whose head and right thumb we visited (her body is in Rome, and her foot in Venice). In about 1366, St Catherine experienced what she described in her letters as a 'Mystical Marriage' with Jesus, then her charitable mission began to tend the sick and serve the poor. In 1370 she received a series of visions of Hell, Purgatory, and Heaven, after which she heard a command to leave her withdrawn life and enter public life. Her major work is the *Dialogue of Divine Providence*, her letters, political pleas for peace and mystical writings are considered one of the great works of early Tuscan literature. In 1970 Pope Paul VI bestowed on Catherine the title of Doctor of the Church, the first woman,

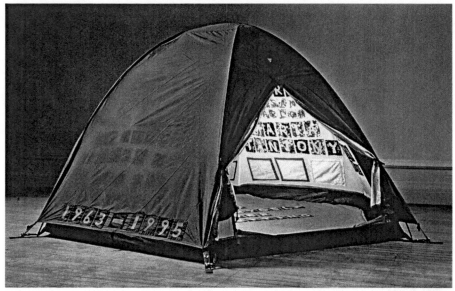

**Figure 8.1   Tracey Emin, 'Everyone I Have Ever Slept With 1963–1995'
(1995). Appliquéd tent, mattress and light. 48 × 96½ × 84½
in (122 × 245 × 215 cm)
© The Artist. Photo: Stephen White. Courtesy Jay Jopling/
White Cube (London)**

with Saint Teresa of Ávila, to ever to receive this honour. In this devoted
Catholic city, dominated historically by legendary spiritual women, I had my
first encounter with Emin's art, at an exhibition 'Identity and Nomadism', held
in the Palazzo delle Papesse.

It was defamiliarising, walking up and down the stairs of this palazzo, built
by order of Caterina Piccolomini, sister of Pope Pius II, between 1460 and
1495. In typically imposing Florentine Renaissance style, the palazzo is on
three floors, with the ground floor sheathed in studded stone and mullioned
windows opening up on the floors above. Following a meticulous restoration, in
November 1998 the palazzo was reopened to the public as a contemporary arts
centre, financed by the Siena town council. Up and down the stairs, following the
labyrinthine crossing and recrossing of the exhibitors' space appeared familiar
British and American contemporary political artists of the Left such as Ajamu
or Chantal Akerman, juxtaposed with strangers (to me) such as Chen Zhen's
houses/altars made from candles, or Medhat Shafik's multicoloured jute bails.
The exhibition frequently references Michel Foucault in its guide, to whom
curator Lanfranco Binni claims 'we owe the capacity to lead the great dynamics
of social power back to the fundamental terrain of the "microsphysics of
power"' (Binni 2005, 25). It is that unpredictable tension between hegemonic
forms and individual identities that cements the exposition. At the end of one

Figure 8.2 Tracey Emin, 'My Bed'. Installation Turner Prize Exhibition, Tate Gallery, London, 20 October 1999–23 January 2000 © The Artist. Photo Stephen White. Courtesy Jay Jopling/ White Cube (London)

route I entered a dark and empty room, at once a digital video began to play, projected vibrantly across the entire wall. It was Tracey Emin's *Why I Never Became a Dancer* (1995), her favourite piece, filmed on grainy Super 8, the cheap medium of amateur film-makers and students. The film's soundtrack has a solo voice-over, narrated by Emin herself.

Why I Never Became a Dancer was made in an edition of ten. It encapsulates the artist's early teenage years, spent kicking against the boredom of the working-class English seaside town, Margate, where she grew up. Following experiences of sexual abuse including a rape aged 13, the young Emin experimented with sex until she became disillusioned with the older men she was shagging, and turned instead to dancing. The film opens with the title words written large on a wall, then the camera pans around to snapshot views of Margate significant to Emin's past: the school she attended, the sea front, shopping arcades, cafés, and a clock tower. These images are also familiar clichés of a British seaside resort, they are cultural icons of working-class leisure. The scenes are overlaid with the voice of the artist narrating her story of sexual emergence (more realistically though, the child Tracey was hauled out of sexual innocence). The story climaxes with her attempt to win the finals of the local disco-dancing competition, an escape-attempt from Margate for London, to compete in the 1978 British Disco Dance Championship:

> And as I started to dance
> people started to clap
> I was going to win
> and then I was out of here
> Nothing could stop me
> And then they started
> SLAG SLAG SLAG[1]

Shamed and humiliated by a group of local young men (most of whom she'd slept with), Emin discovers their vicious hypocrisy as their cat-calls noisily annihilate her dreams of escape. The film then shifts scene to the artist as an adult, twirling around in a large sunlit and empty room, to the song *You Make Me Feel (Mighty Real)* by Sylvester.[2] Emin's voiceover continues with a reeling off of their names, a list of shame: 'Shane, Eddy, Tony, Doug, Richard ... this one's for you' as she then spins joyfully out of their orbit, like a Whirling Dervish, liberated and ecstatic. The lines 'You make me feel/Mighty real/I feel real' are sung over and over again; they are moving prayers, meditative mantras set to joyful beats. The film is deeply spiritual, its central message – the transformation of shame into joy – is corporealised in the viewer through sound as s/he views it in the enclosed space in Siena, the vivid colour in the darkened room coupled with the reverberating sound, becomes a participatory, physical experience of transformation. Emin's art has this shamanic quality, to lead the viewer into sacramental spaces of redemption. I sat on the hard wooden floor captivated, and watched this movie repeatedly through several times, until the meaning of Emin's metamorphosis of shame entered my own psyche, and healed something.

Barry Schwabsky, commenting in *Artforum* observed:

> Emin's art is fundamentally based on talking. She is a monologuist. A few of her videos present this storytelling in raw form, but most of her production – cartoon-like drawings in which the captions are more prominent than the images, patchwork blankets blazoned with seemingly arbitrary conglomerates of phrases, and so on – consists of stabs at pruning her anecdota down to some more contained quasi-iconic form. In the process the work suffers twofold: Not only do we miss the speaking person behind the language -the tone, the hesitations, the accompanying facial expressions and gestures that convince us of the speaker's honesty – but more important, we miss the narrative development at which the artist excels. Emin simply doesn't draw, sew, sculpt, or anything else with the same adroitness with which she speaks. (2003)

Whilst this critic's judgment on Emin's visual art seems harsh, he has a point: that she is predominantly skilled as a narrator, a storyteller, and it is this very

Figure 8.3   **Tracey Emin, 'Why I Never Became a Dancer' (1995). Single screen projection and sound shot on Super 8**
© The Artist. Duration: 6 minutes 30 seconds. Courtesy Jay Jopling/White Cube (London)

Cavareroan emphasis on breaking down the space between the self/other, the drawing close of the You, that powerfully characterises Emin's artistic production (as Sylvester would say it: '*You* make me feel (mighty real)'). Andrea Rose, Director of Visual Art at The British Council and Commissioner for the British Pavilion at the Venice Biennale said recently: 'Tracey's work goes from strength to strength. She's a storyteller with an extraordinary ability to scratch away the surfaces to what lies below,' Jon Pratty, in writing this article, describes how 'Emin's work draws with ineffable candour on her life and times'.[3] Such is the intimacy of her work, that it implicates the viewer in a Foucauldian confessional mode (often very somatically emphasised), and then interpellates her – via the abjection – into a transcendent deliverance. The artist and the viewer together experience a kind of collective or mutual release from abasement, this is extremely ritualised in Emin's art, drawing upon long established structures of religious expression. She has the perspective of the insider within: Emin's biography, growing up poor and of mixed ethnicity in 1960s provincial England, often homeless and hungry, with unmarried parents and a sporadically present Turkish Cypriot father, Enver Emin, a man with very dark skin who explains he is descended from the Ottoman Empire's Sudanese slaves (Barber 2001). Emin was subjected to racism and childhood sexual assault and abuse, traumas that stimulate her art of angry alienation. Emin is perhaps the contemporary Foucauldian artist *par excellence*, experimenting with extreme forms of living, making of her own life a work of art, rhetorically implicating the practice of self-making with the politics of representation.

Emin loves words, as she says:

> ... I don't think I'm visually the best artist in the world, right? I've got to be honest about this... it's my words that actually make my art quite unique. (Quoted in Barber, 2001)

Her most well known pieces are appliqué and embroidery involving the attachment of individual cloth cut-out letters in bright colours sewn onto blankets, appropriating the women's arts of craft, needlework and quilt making. Critics have commented upon how Emin's work has been influenced by traditional Western women's artistic production, commemorated in the 1970s by feminist artists such as Judy Chicago and others, but it is also the art of the poor and dispossessed, of artists using what has been trendily called 'found objects' but more prosaically could be described as free materials. The gaudy playground, primary colours of Emin's word-images are reminiscent of children's expression; their childlike directness is underlined by her apparent dyslexia, so that many of the words appear mis-spelled according to convention, giving an uncanny, infantilising quality to the work. Given that many of the expressions are shocking and sexualised, the pieces are profoundly complex statements of inappropriate sexual harm, they are brutal declarations, somehow tainted with innocence and protestations of love. These 'queer attachments' onto that quintessential object of ordinariness and symbol of poverty – the blanket – also connotes Emin's origins on the 'wrong side of the blanket'.

Emin's childhood was characterised by ill-health, homelessness, and assorted fears of the dark, of ghosts. She was a sickly awkward child, rather (to use a cruel word from the time) 'uncouth', and peculiar. In her most major publication before *Strangeland* (2005), *Exploration of the Soul* (1994) she included a 'postscript', a narrative poem written in free verse:

> *I was seven –*
> *Mummy I said – one of the girls in my class*
> it's her birthday – and this evening she's having
> a party – can I go –
> I put on my favourite party dress – Mum
> carefully wrapped up some cheap Turkish jewelry
> in a piece of tissue paper – for my gift –
> And up the road I went – outside school five
> or six girls stood around – the girl
> whose birthday it was arrived with her dad
> in the car – and as everybody went to get

in – the girl said to me – you can't come – and her father sternly followed by
    saying
I'm afraid you're not invited – you don't
have an invitation –
I waited outside school for as long as I
could – and after hiding the jewelry – I went home –
Mum – asked 'did you enjoy the party' – yes I said
    it was lovely –
That night – I laid in bed and cried – I cried
myself to sleep – and in the morning I asked –
Mummy – what's an invitation.

The movement in the poem, suggested by its arrhythmic breathless punctuation, is like a child sobbing, taking burning breath after breath as she relates this truly mundane yet appalling tale of playground humiliation. Rejected by the nice, normative girls and their families (that harsh suburban father with his car), the young girl protects herself and her own Mother from further social injury and shame by pretending that she had had a 'lovely' time. Even at aged seven we see her making the necessary jump in identification and perspective to ensure their mutual protection from her social indiscretion. This is the same year that Tracey's family are bankrupted and made homeless, the young girl crashing from living 'like a princess' in the Hotel International, to squatting in the staff cottage (Emin, in Barber 2001). The child's shame musn't be seen; that young Tracey Emin was a misfit, a freak, queerly disattached from her peers and living in ignomy, prematurely learning the cruelty of ostracism.

Extraordinarily for a contemporary conceptual artist, Tracey's fan base includes enthusiastic young women who follow her around shouting 'A'right Tracey?!!', 'We love you Tracey!'. Emin has commented herself upon the importance of role modelling an independent female sexuality, her autobiographical novel *Strangeland* even includes a didactic (strangely maternal) comment on 'The Proper Steps for Dealing with an Unwanted Pregnancy' (2005, 147–150), presumably consequent of her own disastrous, emotionally ruinous, experiences of abortion. Emin has communicated her frustration that her only feature film *Top Spot* (2004), which follows the lives of six teenage girls living in the seaside town of Margate and deals rawly with teenage pregnancy and suicide, was certificated '18' by the British Board of Film Censorship. The film, using an inter-subjective, mosaic effect in which each of the six girls are facets of the teenage 'Tracey', clearly has a moral pedagogy aimed at young women, and it has a didactic message concerning shame. Songs on the soundtrack include Shirley and Co.'s disco hit from the 1970s – *Shame, Shame, Shame*.[4]

Shame shame shame hey shame on you
If you can't dance too

– a neat intertextual reference to her *Why I Never Became a Dancer*. 'Top Spot' has an elegiac feel that intersperses teenage sexual abuse and angst with emblematic shots of pretty wildflowers against urban fences, dancing in the wind. The film is quite grim until the humorous finale in which the Director, Emin herself, jumps into a helicopter, chuckling joyfully, to be 'e-vacced' out of Margate, whilst a cartoon-like World War II aeroplane flies overhead, bombing the town. The rudimentary filmic style of this barrage suggests that Emin's escape is a witty commentary on her own compulsive returns to her childhood site/scene of abuse and shame in her art. This is Emin's endearing charm, that she can laugh at her own excesses.

The Tart with a Heart

One of the reasons that Tracey Emin is so popular is because of the mischievous humour in her work, humour that is often exceedingly queer. 'Reincarnation' (2005) is a short, affectionate, lingering film of a golden Alsation mixed-breed dog pleasurably, and leisurely, licking its own genitals, it is accompanied by a series of rather beautiful watercolours of the same dog in action.[5] The film is shot in poor quality, grainy bleached-out stock, it is a home-movie video on the beach, complete with only one sound, the cliché for orgasm: waves crashing on the beach. Interspersed with the live action film of the 'hot dog' licking itself are superimposed handrawn monoprint comments such as 'To know your smile', 'The touch of your skin', 'I love your soul', 'I kiss you deep inside' 'LOVE I LOVE YOU'. This visual meta-commentary is in Emin's trademark handwriting, so the viewer assumes that this is about dog-human desire and love, but equally it could also be onanistic, the dog's body is curled, swirled into a circle. The dog is ungendered.

A similar short (2–3 minutes) narrative is contained in 'Love is a Strange Thing' (2000) a single screen projection shot on Mini-DV in which another large, beautiful butch dog, a Bull Mastiff, offers sex to Tracey:

As I walked to the bridge I could see him sitting there.
Suddenly he said: 'Alright Trace' in a very deep voice.
What? Weird, a dog talking to me! He said: 'Alright Trace. How 'bout it then?'
'How 'bout what?'
'D'you fancy a fuck?'
'Aherm, pardon?'
He said: 'Well, d'you fancy a fuck?'
I said: 'Umm, I'm erm sorry...'
He said: 'Well, what's wrong? Don't you find me attractive? Don't you think I'm good looking?'
I said: 'Well, it's not that, it's just that, well, you're a dog.'
He looked hurt. His big, sad eyes. He looked wounded. And as I walked away, he looked back at me and he said: 'Tracey, Tracey you of all people. I never expected you to be prejudiced.'

This humour is also aligned somewhat to the working-class custom of mobilising self-respect in the face of shame through 'taking the piss', discussed earlier in my analyses of *The Office* and *Shameless*. Emin's perfectly formed visual anecdote conforms tightly to narrative conventions of the joke, whilst also retaining affection for the 'dog-like' masculinity it spoofs. This lesser known piece can also be read as a gently mocking counterpoint to the popular characterisation of 'Tracey the slag', the artist's rendition of herself (sometimes traumatically, sometimes ironically) that has reverberated in the mass media surrounded by the iconic collapse of the artist with her work.

Emin is synonymous with the autobiographical, confessional genre, she continuously experiments with authorial roles or persona making her own life, especially her interior life, its chief subject. Splattering her emotional truths across mixed media, her careful renditions appear deceptively naive, the works are produced by a professional artist and are inevitably more technically skilled and sophisticated in design than the ostensibly screaming content would belie. Emin presently holds the title of 'Professor of Confessional Art' at the quite eminent European Graduate School. However she retains a romantic, disinhibited honesty in her work, as Neal Brown recently commented 'It is poeticised truth – arrived at through the vehicle of mediated autobiographical truth – that defines Emin's work' (2006, 10).[6] It contains themes of spiritual anguish, debasement, and revelation, appropriating many religious traditions of art and representation that intimates the soul-searching quality of its purpose. It shares a theological premise with the anti-psychiatry movement initiated by R.D. Laing in the 1960s: madness-as-divine-revelation. Looking further back, it is also influenced by powerful, often somatically distorting, painters such as Pablo Picasso, Vincent Van Gogh, William Blake, and tortured Expressionists such as Egon Schiele or Edvard Munch. Emin has a personal affinity with Munch's *The Scream* (1893), honouring him in her own video shorts *Homage to Munch and All My Dead Children* (1998) a reference to her two abortions.[7] Her preoccupation with memory is rendered formally in her art by the use of actual souvenirs, plus her constant visual reiteration of icons from Margate. The collection of these totemic items of memorabilia can be read as autistic, but it also a habitual symptom of a person who needs to externalise their history in order to remind themselves that they have 'a self', i.e. whose self-existence has been previously threatened.

The contemporary autobiographical aesthetic has been discussed by Christine Fanthome, who quotes Susanna Egan on the role of the addressee in autobiography's recent, more dialogic form:

> Writer and reader in sequence create the narrator and subject of such autobiography, and this sequence, furthermore, can become an ongoing dance as the reader rereads or as the writer produces more autobiographical work. (2006, 32)

The subject of this new autobiography then, is quite complex and unclear given the compound transactions of production and consumption involved;

s/he becomes 'permeable, unstable, essentially in distress'. This 'unresolved crisis' is seen as negative by Egan, and Fanthome goes on to suggest a less draconian intersubjectivity, but this reading fails to give sufficient recognition to the narrative impulses of joy, resolution, healing and respite that are frequent characters in Emin's art. In *Hot Spot* one of the six teenage protagonists fantasises about her lover who is supposedly in Egypt (although the other girls insist he is in fact in Borstal), and the film contains dreamlike sequences in which she goes to Cairo to look for him. Emin claimed in an interview that Helen is the character she would like most to be (in Fanthome 2006, 36), and it is Helen who near the end of the film packs her suitcase for Egypt but in fact then throws it off, spinning, over a Margate jetty, into the cold sea. This young woman dumps her dreams, but also her 'baggage', and it is a peculiarly liberating moment in the diegesis. Fanthorne comments: 'The notion of dumping baggage and moving on is ironic, given that Emin can never really escape her own past' (2006, 36), as Bryan Ferry croons on the film's soundtrack:

> I've been thinking now for a long time
> How to go my own separate way
> It's a shame to think about yesterday,
> It's a shame...

There is a growing sense of equilibrium in the song though, in its idea of acceptance:

> ... We've been running round in our present state
> Hoping help would come from above
> But even angels there make the same mistakes
> In love.[8]

The 'rags to riches' story of a girl from the proverbs – sorry suburbs – country, or seaside, coming up to the nation's capital naked, holding nothing but her talent, then making it big, has become somewhat of a romantic cliché of capitalism: Emin has fulfilled Dick Whittington's dream. However, envy and resentment about her flagrant success comes from many quarters, reactions include those who freely judge her to be a sensationalist charlatan, an opportunistic 'chav', and those whose fond response has tended more toward condescending affection, as though she is simply 'our girl Tracey' from Margate.[9] Response to her art is often very classed... the particulars of Tracey's biography are unimaginable for most of her constituent audience, undoubtedly there is a voyeurism to be found in its reception, some sense of the class tourism of sensation, a disagreeable echo of nineteenth century slumming, perhaps. Emin's 'eminence' must be understood as part of the general cultural shift toward confession and disclosure typified by the popular television genres that mediate everday life which have exploded in the past decade, creating multiple 'folk celebrities' from the working classes. Fanthorne reminds us of Anthony Giddens' 'project of the self':

> Autobiography – particularly in the broad sense of an interpretative self-history produced by the individual concerned, whether written down or not – is actually at the core of self-identity in modern social life. Like any other formalised narrative, it is something that has to be worked at, and calls for creative input as a matter of course. (Giddens 1991, 76, quoted in Fanthorne 2006, 39)

The raw 'material' of that self that is to be creatively 'worked upon' is most often – in life as in the sphere of art and representation – pain. The growth of therapy culture enabled in the past three decades by the availability of leisure and its parallel economy of 'self-improvement', has been driven by socially produced desires for personal transformation as a practice of consumption. Previously in the Judeo-Christian tradition emotional pain was seen to be quietly ennobling, something to be worn mutely, like a badge of honour to be rewarded posthumously in heaven; in our now secular, late capitalist societies suffering is seen rather more shamefully, as raw matter that must be alchemically transformed by acts of self-exposure into the manifest content of 'personal development'. This contemporary compulsion for 'healing' must also be discretely enacted and privately congratulated. Working-class celebrities, on the other hand, have become our modern fallen plaster saints, their trials and tribulations have become mass voyeuristic spectacles of emotional pilgrimage that appeal for armchair arbitration. Not only is the modern subject asked to expunge unhappiness from her own life, it being so much shameful 'baggage', but s/he is also expected to pass judgement frequently on the 'acting out' of others, on their seeming inability to 'manage' their own pain 'appropriately'. Emin falls foul of these new rituals of bourgeois respectability, seemingly she has 'too much self' to uncover.[10]

Art and literature are a symbolic conduit for the reorientation of emotional states, the intensification of existing emotions or the movement from one affective condition to another is what characterises the very process of aesthetic consumption, indeed it is the function of a work of art to induce sensation. Emotions seem to 'lock on' to the spectator, and artworks can be understood as psychic interpellations that can rhetoricise sets of feelings. Horror, shame, anguish and abjection form a dominant presence in the pantheon of Western art, particularly religious art. This ubiquity infers the pervasiveness of shame narratives, it can also be read as evidence of the human desire to *transcend* shame symbolically; hence such art has a sacramental impulse, to invoke the ritualistic desire for sanctification and release, to provide a cultural and aesthetic vehicle for entering (or re-entering) shame, as a rite of expiation. Art and religion are the two domains in which shame-transcendence rituals are most present in our culture, indeed Emin's autobiography *Strangeland* (2005) can hardly be read without the reader's cathection into shame, as Jeanette Winterson declared in

The Times newspaper concerning *Strangeland* that 'some of it should have been edited out by someone who loves her' (2005).[11]

'My ironic art'[12]

Emin's art is often criticised for being too autobiographical, as incessantly authentic, or as Neal Brown describes it rather more kindly, as 'disinhibited honesty' (2006, 10). Her fountainhead of anguish seems to require its own release, according to prevalent opinion, like an old-fashioned 'hydraulic model' of creativity. This view is taken irrespective of the artist's evident technical artifice, and her specialised training in fine art practice. Despite Emin's canonic knowledge of art and philosophy, her emerging playfulness and subtle absurdity, she is rarely read aesthetically by others as a conscious satirist. Irony can be understood historically as a very middle-class sensibility, an indulgence perhaps, of Puritanical contempt for what it perceived to be sentimental excesses. The hypothetical emotional refinement of the bourgeoisie depended upon taking dry distance from too much expression: classic irony instils a vision of a cartoon-like Victorian gentleman raising his lace handkerchief to his nose, nostrils peeled to protect against an undignified glut of sensation. The middle classes, remember, invented *schadenfreude* – the pleasure taken in the misfortune of others – surely a shameful desire to escape the threatening destabilisation of self that 'too much' feeling might dangerously incite? To cover one's face or avert one's eyes in order to evade communicating emotional passions is of course a shame gesture. We have already learned about shame and its infectious propensity to inculcate further or intensify shame in those who testify to it, or those who witness it. The bourgeoisie seem to project onto, resent, and scorn the perceived extensive emotional ranges available to the 'lower classes', and become pricked into a series of dull, mean-spirited shame gestures, dragged seemingly from their own shadowy, pale repetoire of excitation. Emin is judged too harshly (particularly by the high cultural establishment) because she is regarded as naively lacking the requisite amount of masculine iron-y and self-control deemed essential for classical artistic genius. Such responses are typified in the language of *The Times* newspaper review of *Strangeland*, written by Henry Hitchins; his phrases include: 'unabashedly autobiographical [i.e. 'unashamedly', implying she probably should be...], 'a flair for noisy hyperbole', 'strident... an unresisted urge to trumpet metaphysical profundities', 'gimcrack philosophy/platitudinous guff', 'unctuous self-communion', '[r]estraint is not a part of her creative vocabulary', 'self-portraiture slides into self-disgust' (Hitchins 2005). One can almost hear the corset elastic snapping in his faux-Victorian idiom. It could be this deficit of cultural capital that explains Emin's unnerving failure to display appropriate *hubris*, at times so proud of her disclosure, then again, perhaps it is her deliberate working-class *habitus*. A conscious practice of her own aesthetics of existence is a strategy of Emin's that Henry *The Times Literary*

Supplement reviewer has wilfully or naively missed. These elements include bold sexual statement, vitality in language, uncensored attitude, candour about money, gleeful drinking and partying, respect for family, curiosity for religion, spirituality and the paranormal, moral firmness, repentance, flagrancy of the juicy body, imaginative use of found objects (recycling 'junk'), and loudly voiced irritation with restrictions and taboos. As another critic, this one a feminist academic (herself from a working-class childhood) once commented:

> ... perhaps for those of us who have learnt silence through shame, the hardest thing of all is to find a voice: not the voice of the monstrous singular ego but one that, summoning the resources of the place we come from, can speak with eloquence of, and for, that place. (Kuhn 1995, 103)

Hence perhaps: 'Mad Tracey from Margate'.[13]

The spirit of shame

Shame has a metaphysical energy, it can generate abasement, abjection, and soulless despair. It can also stimulate an energy that has a restorative, creative force, it can mobilise the self and communities into acts of defiant presence, in cycles of disattachment and reconnection. Whilst we may commonly accept that joy contains an attribute that can seem to make us rise above our immediate circumstances, that it has some immaterial, indefinable quality of transcendence, it seems perverse to claim the same for shame. And yet, throughout this book I have encountered examples of just that potential within diverse public and popular cultures, in which shame acts as a solvent or catalyst for transformation. Some have taken the annihilating desperation of shame and turned it into something beautiful, surprising agents of this change have included television writers such as Ricky Gervais, Stephen Merchant, Alan Ball, Paul Abbott, Jane Turner and Gina Riley. Tracey Emin has produced one of the most powerful œvres of shame in Western art, and, in doing so, she has demonstrated how shame can be intensely inhabited, and reworked into elation. In shame a range of related emotions can become intensified, it is like a dark crystal that attracts rays of affect, separating and refracting and sending them out again, spinning into the social atmosphere. It is a magnet for pain and exclusion and a channel for passion and integration; we might wonder how or why it is that some impressionable individuals show an affinity or propensity toward shame, that unlikely crucible of the self, but we might also wish to marvel at shame's mutations, shame's surprising potential for strategic disengagement and reinvention.

Emin has described a lonely epiphany following a black depression:

> I was walking along the beach [at Margate] a couple of years ago and I looked out to sea. The tide was going out and it was winter and the tide was blue. I thought 'this is so beautiful'. With a piece of chalk I wrote on the sea wall 'I Need Art Like

I Need God'. And when I had written it I knew it was the strongest declaration I had ever made.[14]

She has previously complained during interviews that 'People think my work is about sex, but actually a lot of it is about faith' (quoted in Brown 2006, 50). She claims that her work is just as equally concerned with mysticism, 'The only thing I am really well read in.' (Morgan 'Story of I' p.56, quoted in Vara 2002, 172). Both Renée Vara and now four years later Neal Brown have written about spirituality in Emin's art, the former concentrating upon Emin's family tradition of female spiritualism, and influences from art history such as Munch, the latter concerned more with drawing out the enchanting, esoteric qualities of the art itself. Actually I don't think the sexuality and spirituality of Emin's output are at all detectable or detachable as discrete themes, rather, the inscribed viewing position demands a visceral, almost masochistic spectator whose visual consumption synthesises both responses concurrently, and sometimes rhapsodically. As Lynn Barber asserted in an interview in 2001:

> Her art demands a sort of *subservience* to an Eminocentric vision of the world that feels like *surrender*. That is why, I think, people often resist her art for a long time and then suddenly *fall* for it... (Barber 2001) [my emphasis]

Frances Broucek, discussing the legacy of Christ in art and representation, suggests a polarity of shame/humiliation-glory/triumph that has shaped the Western psyche; he makes connections between fame, narcissism, and what he calls the 'shame-glory complex' (1991, 78). Audiences might suspect something of this swing in Emin's art, but this is to be too cynically dismissive. Emin's art takes us beyond her 'self' to open up contemplation of other dimensions: think, for example, of the ecstatic dancing at the climax of the shame narrative depicted in *Why I Never Became a Dancer*, or the alchemic memorial that is dedicated to the death of her beloved *Uncle Colin 1963–93*, or the soaring plaster gulls of *In My Family When Someone Dies They Are Cremated And Their Ashes Are Thrown Across The Sea* (1997). Neal Brown discusses the cultural shifts of value between religion and art in Western aesthetics since the Enlightenment, contextualising Emin as she tries to dissolve some of the distinctions between secular and religious art, he goes on to say that:

> This creates new challenges, especially for the intellectual elite of cultural life, who cannot praise art's valuable function as a quasi-religious practice without surrendering back to religion some of its power (thus diminishing their own status as being, through art, at the moral centre of society).

(Perhaps this may also account for the hostility and contempt that academics usually have for religion – but I digress) – Brown continues:

> Traditional connoisseurship, which should have the vocabulary to deal with Emin's relationship with religion, is also unable to do so, since its representatives are not

equipped to make an estimation due to their distaste for, or incomprehension of, her contemporary [spiritual] style. (2006, 118)

He draws attention to how unacceptable it is to talk about spiritual feeling in critical discourse, but yet how common those feelings or experiences are in those people (such as Emin) that have undergone extremes of suffering. She demands a certain lyrical suspension from the viewer, some of her more ascetic critics resist this pull. We need not patronise Emin by according her individual religious faith automatic respect or deference by virtue of its intensity alone, however Brown is right to address how:

... whether dealing with the spiritually debased or the exaltedly sanctified, Emin's work constitutes a demand that she be entitled her most intimate feelings – and we, by extension, ours. (2006, 119)

'Spinoza I like because of all the lines connecting'[15]

How can we untangle these queer, twisted, affective attachments that weave through the social body, our bodies, our selves? Art and creativity bring lucidity to these bonds. Perhaps it is easier to distinguish the threads if we consider suicide, an unambiguously violent way of cutting those lines completely. Kirsty Wark, when interviewing Emin in November 2006 asked Emin to compare her own autobiographical art, based similarly as it is on personal trauma, to Mark Rothko's. Rothko described seeing his own paintings as intimates, until they were finished, after which he felt no relationship to them, as if they were estranged. Wark asked Emin how her own art was different. Emin paused, and then remarked poignantly:

'The difference between me and Rothko is that Rothko committed suicide. He could distance himself from everything... he had a cut off point with everything, even with the world, whereas I haven't got a cut off point with anything. [smiling] Everything for me is totally engaging and I hold onto everything for as long as possible.'[16]

Perhaps we need a new category for the 'ex-shamed', for whom re-attachment is such a priority. Lines of love, lines of hate, lines of deliberate apathy, of studious indifference, of revulsion, envy, curiosity, delight, regret, jealousy, joy, empathy, guilt, fury, and disgust. Such feelings bind us imperceptively to each other, and to the collective worlds we live in, in intimacy or abandonment. Over years those feeling threads accumulate as we truss ourselves more firmly to ourselves, sometimes regretfully, cohering into a particular life-story, a historical identity, a set of residual memories and somatic associations that we nominate as the woolly entity 'myself'. Histories of human creatures will always contain some shame, minor shame is a good thing, it is what homeopathically prevents us from committing major acts of shame, giving us a moral key to living collaboratively and empathetically with others, and often, we want to talk about these slights. Confession is one of the most dominant genres in contemporary culture, we invented religious ceremonies that ritualise the expiation of shame, such as the Prayers of Penitence in the Eucharist. The shamed are required to internalise this gaze, to turn its scrutiny inward toward themselves, as Jean-Paul Sartre once said:

> Shame is the feeling of an *original fall*, not because of the fact that I may have committed this or that particular fault, but simply that I have 'fallen' into the world in the midst of things and that I need the mediation of the other in order to be what I am. (Sartre 1943, 288–9)

We confess our shame to another, whose disapproving gaze can render us static and petrified, as the routine of shame is to objectify the self, and the medium of shame is (asymmetric) transference. Conventionally the marginalised self cannot return this gaze with full force, because society is a poorly reflective mirror, it is more often a one-way glass that selectively confers the light of social visibility on some, but not on others. Shame is an affect that entails communal effort, sometimes shame is enacted specifically *as* a collective rite, intended to re-attach those who are alienated to a communal bond. The following Anglican prayer is a public oral rite spoken by all (congregation and minister together) prior to Holy Communion, it is only a part of an extended oral ritual of public and private shame, repentance and forgiveness:

> Almighty God, *our* heavenly father,
> *We* have sinned against you *and against our fellow men*,
> In thought and word and deed,
> Through negligence, through weakness,
> Through *our* own deliberate fault.
> *We* are truly sorry,
> And repent of all *our* sins
> For the sake of your Son Jesus Christ, who died for *us*,
> Forgive *us* all that is past;
> And grant that *we* may serve you in newness of life
> To the glory of your name. *Amen*.[17]

Theologically the Eucharist, the focal Christian rite, could be said to be as much concerned with reattaching a community to each other as to God.[18]

We have looked at ways that shame modifies the self, and how it manifests in subcultures, stimulating energies of attachment and disattachment. How can we conduct an ethics of shame, or perhaps more accurately, an aesthetics of shame, so that shame ricochets within the self and converts into joy? Gilles Deleuze (1988), in his study of seventeenth century Jewish philosopher Spinoza, makes a differentiation between Spinoza's term *affectio* (affection), which can be understood as the passive state of the affected body (implying the presence of another who is affecting upon it) and *affectus* (affect), which can be understood as the passage or active energy itself transforming from one state to another. Spinoza wrote about the passions as energies of the social body, in our terms best understood as electrical charges that pass through and also 'charge up' specific corporeal hosts. This energy is conductive, as Genevieve Lloyd says '... if we imagine someone like us to be affected with some affect, we will necessarily be affected with a like affect' (Lloyd 1996, 76). This is not dissimilar from my own description in chapter 3 of the Newtonian mechanics of shame – the equal and opposite force – 'shame's reactive turn' if you will. Spinoza described how the body-mind provides parameters for these interconnections of affect and affections, noting how certain passions become distilled. Some passions seem to linger longer, like shame, sedimenting into a body, or, as Spinoza would have said, a soul. His central concept was the *conatus essendi*, a right to existence, the striving for being, the affirmative life force, a flourishing gladness that continuously renews, a core aspect of his vision for an ethics based on joy. As Judith Butler comments:

> Spinoza writes in *The Ethics* that the desire to live the right life requires the desire to live, to persist in one's own being, suggesting that ethics must always marshal some life drives... (2004, 140)

Lloyd claims that Spinoza's philosophy is as much about attachment and detachment, about love and acquiescence, as about anything else. The ethics of joy, as Deleuze goes onto elucidate, are based on building powerful affirming unions with other bodies, collectively enhanced, that go on to generate further endlessly joyful capacities for harmony. If Susan Miller is correct then, in defining shame as 'displeasure about the status of the self' (1985, 167), we might speculate that what Spinoza calls *conatus* is like a spur that aggravates this displeasure into a vital urge to renew its attachments to others.

Aesthetics of shame

Michel Foucault's later writing on technologies of the self still seem less popular with scholars and students than his major studies on the repressive regimes of the prison, the asylum, and the hospital. And yet his final books are so much more optimistic, concerned, as they are, with how human subjects actively fashion their own identities *in spite of* regulation, prohibition, and subjugation. Generally the academy likes to fixate upon defeat; maybe this emphasis speaks volumes about a nostalgia for or preoccupation with loss of status, because it would seem to me that by contrast the Foucauldian later, more elastic model of power-as-vitality, power-as-protest, is pragmatically applied across the globe, by ordinary people as popular resistance, every day. Foucault argued that power nestles in the body, the body being the locus of social power relations in their most concrete form. Remembering that shame is the most embodied of emotions, and that shame is also intrinsically relational, correlative, and associative, perhaps we can imagine an aesthetics or technology of the self that reinscripts the bio-power of bodies, that builds ethical futures out of shame, that perceives shame as a sort of muscle, an energy that can make things happen. Foucault claimed that there are no relations of power without a multiplication of resistances, and thus, to stay with the gym analogy, sometimes a muscle must be 'ripped' in order to extend; perhaps shame must be intensely endured in order that individuation, and hence new thoughts and feelings, can occur. In his last two volumes on the history of sexuality Foucault developed an ethics of the self, describing practices or techniques by which the citizen would order his life, and understand its meaningfulness in spiritual terms. He advocated the constitution of selfhood as a poetics:

> I am referring to what might be called the 'arts of existence'. What I mean by the phrase are those intentional and voluntary actions by which men not only set themselves rules of conduct, but also seek to transform themselves, to change themselves in their singular being, and to make their life into an œvre that carries certain aesthetic values and meets certain stylistic criteria. (Foucault 1985, 10–11)

He underscores the historical context of this self-formation:

> In a way that may be surprising at first, one sees the formation, in Greek culture and in connection with the love of boys, of some of the major elements of a sexual ethics that will renounce that love by appealing to the above principle: the requirement of a symmetry and reciprocity in the love relationship; the necessity of a long and arduous struggle with oneself; the gradual purification of a love that is addressed only to being per se, in its truth; and a man's enquiry into himself as a subject of desire. (Foucault 1985, 245)

What is relevant here, of course, is how intrinsic sexuality, desire, and bodies are to the creation of this reflective ethics, a critical ontology of attachment. Indeed, psychotherapy, done ethically, must support the subject to practice precisely this method: a reflective engagement not just with the self but a reorientation toward taking responsibility for one's effects upon others, distal and proximate, so that we become self-governing not according to neurosis (and neurotic prejudices), but according to principle: an ethos. Foucault requires us not so much to uncover our hidden needs but to deconstruct the stimuli for those needs by expanding solipsistic perceptions through experience with others, he exhorts us to think intuitively, and feel 'beyond the self'. We must sustain enough subjective coherence for political action, and continue to remain critically, stoically, engaged with the social. Perhaps this model is just too abstract and elitist for some, implying a Nietzschean beautification of the will, an aggressively narcissistic justification for moral buck-passing... I sincerely hope not, and I believe not: according to Foucault all care of the self must incorporate care of the other, it cannot become a retreat into a privatised, sanitised realm. Regrettably he died before he was able elaborate further on these ideas, before they could be dialectically engaged with the explosion of feminist, postcolonial and queer theory that followed him in the 1990s.

In her most recent book *Giving an Account of Oneself* feminist political theorist Butler reminds us of how Nietzsche in *On the Genealogy of Morals* (1887) gave an explanation of how we become reflexive:

> He remarks that we become conscious of ourselves only after certain injuries have been inflicted. Someone suffers as a consequence, and the suffering person, or, rather someone acting as his or her advocate in a system of justice seeks to find the cause of that suffering and asks us whether we might be that cause. (2005, 10)

In seeking out who is responsible for this injurious action upon another, and in exacting punishment, we are required to examine ourselves for accountability, thus interiority occurs. Butler states that this may be done out of revenge, in fear and terror of the outcome, but it may also be done honourably, in a spirit of concern for the harm allegedly caused. What emerges out of this shame scenario is the 'subject of conscience' (2005, 15). She then goes onto elaborate the dilemma of 'how am I going to treat you back?' if ethics are already predetermined within a sphere of normativity in which the other is recognisable only as exterior and separate to the self. Conferring recognition of selfhood upon another is fraught with difficulty, as the terms are already configured, 'I am, as it were, dispossessed by the language that I offer' (Butler 2005, 26). Butler also reconsiders the Hegelian subject of recognition that vacillates between loss and ecstasy (*ekstasis* – to be out of place), always exceeding its position, perpetually moving. In her discussion of accountability she comes back to Adriana Cavarero, who advocated the direct and ethical question of recognition 'Who are you?':

> In a sense, this theory of the 'outside' to the subject radicalizes the ecstatic trend in the Hegelian position. In her view, I am not, as it were an interior subject, closed upon myself, solipsistic, posing questions of myself alone. I insist in an important sense for you, and by virtue of you. If I have lost the conditions of address, if I have no 'you' to address, then I have lost 'myself'. In her view, one can tell an autobiography only to an other, and one can reference an 'I' only in relation to a 'you': without a 'you' my own story becomes impossible. (Butler 2005, 32)

Butler and Cavarero are underscoring our fundamental sociality: without you I do not exist, without me you do not exist, we are irreducible to each other and utterly dependent on each other. My exposure as a (constantly) emergent self depends on your recognition. This dyadic acknowledgement is perhaps the primary human experience, and as such, if you shame me, or I shame you, that encounter will feel annihilating: to both.

Recognition would seem key to soothing shame, an agenda focussed upon recognition tries to resolve the injurious abjection caused by the withdrawal of the gaze of social acceptance.[19] But we should pause and remember that not everything can or even should be seen: Butler goes on to argue that an ability to acknowledge what is incoherent and contingent in oneself enables the other or in Cavarero's term the You, to become acceptable and non-threatening:

... we might consider a certain post-Hegelian reading of the scene of recognition in which precisely my own opacity to myself occasions my capacity to confer a certain kind of recognition among others. It would be perhaps, an ethics based on our shared, invariable, and partial blindness about ourselves. (2005, 41)

An acceptance of our own opacity can lead to greater humility, patience and generosity toward unformed and confused elements in others:

By not pursuing satisfaction and by letting the question remain open, even enduring, we let the other live, since life might be understood as precisely that which exceeds any account we might try to give it. (2005, 43)

So, the question 'Who are you?' doesn't expect a full answer, a complete account, there is always a gap or a space left there for unknowability, for questioning, for a suspension of disbelief or for listening without prejudice; in other words, we should undoubtedly hesitate and take a breath before we are tempted to shame, as we often shame what we don't understand. As she says '[c]ondemnation, denunciation, and excoriation work as quick ways to posit an ontological difference between judge and judged, even to purge oneself of another' (2005, 46). Condemnation, Butler claims, works toward purging and externalizing one's own opacity, wasting that strangeness within ourselves that is also a potential to transform. Condemnation leads to punishment in the name of a public ethics, but if we shame and banish those whom bring us discomfort, then we also commit violence upon ourselves; we lose something. Hence, we should mitigate the desire to shun those who are 'other-to-oneself' and replace with an outlook of open curiosity. This practice, of course, would extend to giving closer attention to our own internal world of psychic complexity, in order to gain greater mindfulness of its propensity to harm.

This gap, the space of unknowability, returns us to the concept of the sublime that I introduced in the first chapter. Edmund Burke's concept of the sublime in *A Philosophical Inquiry into the Origin of Our Ideas of the Sublime and Beautiful* (1756) obliterates the sight of an object, it is unrecognisable because it 'goes beyond'. The imagination is moved to awe and instilled with a degree of horror by what is 'dark, uncertain, and confused.' The sublime may even inspire horror, as well as anxious pleasure, it has the capacity to instil feelings of intense emotion. In his *Critique of Judgment* (1790), Kant investigated the sublime, stating 'we call that sublime which is absolutely great', distinguishing between the 'remarkable differences' of the Beautiful and the Sublime, noting that beauty 'is connected with the form of the object', having 'boundaries', while the sublime 'is to be found in a formless object', represented by a 'boundlessness'. Kant considers the Sublime 'indefinite', one's inability to grasp the enormity of a sublime event reveals the inadequacy of one's rational perception. The sublime was revived recently within postmodernist theory in the work of Jean-François Lyotard (1994), for whom the sublime's significance is located in the way it points to an *aporia* in human reason; it expresses a puzzle or an impasse, bringing us to the periphery of our conceptual powers. Lodged in the experience of the sublime is a consciousness that provokes a crisis in representation, but crucially we have some sense of it, we *know* there is something more to be sought. For Lyotard in *Lessons on the Analytic of the Sublime* this is ethical, what one witnesses in the sublime is the *differend* – the straining of the mind at the edges of itself. The *sodomitical sublime*, therefore, is a symbol of desires that cannot be foreclosed, that provoke mystery, that can evoke a musical resonance in oneself for stretching out what is possible to endure, and perhaps, enjoy.

It was Foucault (1993) that first posited that a subject can only recognise itself within a regime of truth, and that it was possible, indeed desirable, to try to get further than this 'truth' through elaborate and rigorous cultivations of the self. Technologies of the self, as I have described in the previous chapter, can produce 'spaces of freedom', sites of a radical alterity, that allow 'the space within each human being where she or he encounters the not-self, the beyond' (Halperin, 1995: 75). Realising oneself by cultivating a kind of transcendence can be achieved dialectically within the queer heterotopic, but the ways in which we respond to injury, the threat of injury, or the 'insult', say, of homosexuality, is crucial. Judith Butler quotes from Adorno's work on becoming-human, in *Minima Moralia* (1969):

> Someone who has been offended, slighted, has an illumination as vivid as when agonizing pain lights up one's own body. He becomes aware that in the innermost blindness of love, that must remain oblivious, lives a demand not to be blinded. He was wronged; from this he deduces a claim to right and must at the same time reject it, for what he desires can only be given in freedom. In such distress he who is rebuffed becomes human. (2005, 101–102)

Is not shame – the affect most closely affiliated with sight, with the expression of the face and the eyes, with the conference and consequent withdrawal of the approving gaze of loving acceptance – the principle axis of this discursive injury? In literary metaphor we remember that blindness is oft symbolic of castration. In casting down one's eyes in shame one in fact 'blinds' oneself, one turns away from the gaze and in doing so, in that fragment of time, s/he is turned into one who compelled to be ashamed and impotent. But s/he need not be: at that moment-site a claim to seek reprisal ought to be rejected, for the blindness that is inflicted may also augur a break in perspective, a fresh view, and so in that agonising, burning distress of being turned away, and then turned back, s/he can seek miscellaneous queer, non-phallic attachments that reform social bonds, making space for supplementarity and the ineffable. I am thinking here of Plato's *Republic* in which he exhorts us to 'turn the soul around', to shift one's perception in order to bring about a change in life, a rupture.[20] Becoming 'unhinged' is British slang for madness, but we could take lessons here from Tracey Emin's aesthetics, wrought from the suffering of extreme shame from within her own dark night of the soul. The damaged humanity she shapes is not so much fixated upon, or foreclosed by, the 'divine' art of retribution, but is passionate for the release of diffuse joy, for *conatus*. Although her insight into shame is often profound, Emin is not acting as a lone genius, she articulates and intensifies through her art a collective awareness of queer shame. She is an artisan of the self, and in doing so Emin brings forth into public culture an ethical challenge to think otherwise about shame, inciting us to risk entering shame and make insanely joyful, dancing sodomites of us all.

Shame is the shawl of Pink
In which we wrap the Soul
To keep it from infesting Eyes –
The elemental Veil
Which helpless Nature drops
When pushed upon a scene
Repugnant to her probity –
Shame is the tint divine.

Emily Dickinson (1877)

From Emily Dickinson: *The Complete Poems* ed. Thomas H. Johnson (London: Faber & Faber 1975) p. 603.

Selected works by Tracey Emin

Emin, Tracey (1994) *Exploration of the Soul* (London: Counter Gallery).

Emin, Tracey (1995) *Everyone I Have Ever Slept With 1963–1995* Appliqué tent, mattress and light 122 X 245 X 215 cm.

Emin, Tracey (1995) *Why I Never Became a Dancer* Single screen projection and sound (shot on Super 8). Duration 6 mins. 30 seconds.

Emin, Tracey (1998) *Homage to Munch and All My Dead Children* Single screen projection and sound (shot on Super 8 transferred to DVD). Duration 2 mins. 10 seconds (looped).

Emin, Tracey (1998) *My Bed* Installation: mixed media. Dimensions variable.

Emin, Tracey (2000) *Love is a Strange Thing* Single screen projection and sound (shot on mini-DV). Duration 2 mins. 42 seconds.

Emin, Tracey (2004) (Director) *Hot Spot: A Film by Tracey Emin* BBC Productions (62 mins.). Distributed by Tartan Video, London 2006.

Emin, Tracey (2005) *Strangeland* (London: Sceptre, Hodder and Stoughton).

Emin, Tracey (2005) *Reincarnation I-V* Paintings: watercolours, gouache, and pencil. Series of five.

Emin, Tracey (2005) *Reincarnation* Single screen projection animation, transferred to DVD.

Notes

1 Emin, Tracey (1995) Why I Never Became a Dancer © Courtesy of the artist, Lehmann Maupin gallery NY and Jay Jopling, White Cube, London.

2 © Sylvester/ Wirrick 'You Make Me Feel (Mighty Real)' Lyrics from the album *Step II* (1978) Fantasy Records.

3 Pratty, John (2006) 'Tracey Emin to Represent Britain at the 2007 Venice Biennale' in *24 Hour Museum News* 25th August. http://www.24hourmuseum.org.uk/nwh_gfx_en/ART39671.html, accessed 28th November 2006.

4 Shirley and Co. (1975) *Shame, Shame, Shame.* Words and music by Sylvia Robinson.

5 Available on-line at http://www.lehmannmaupin.com/past/?object_id=153, 5 November to 17 December 2005.

6 Readers wishing to acquaint themselves with Tracey Emin's work would do well to read Neal Brown's (2006) excellent critical introduction.

7 My mother kept a copy of this print at home when I was a child, its unnerving quality will always be associated, for me, with her. Munch's figure is conventionally taken to be a man, but actually the gender of the human figure is quite indistinct, it could easily be a woman.

8 Ferry, Bryan (1972) 'Sea Breezes' from the album *Roxy Music* © Roxy Music 1972.

9 A place, presumably, that most of those commenting have never been to. Margate is a 'downmarket' seaside resort for working-class Londoners and the labourers of Kent. 'Chav' is British slang. For definitions of 'chav' see the infamous http://www.chavscum.co.uk/. Wikipedia defines 'chav' as follows:

> Refers to a subcultural stereotype of people fixated on fashions such as flashy 'bling' jewellery (generally gold) along with designer clothing in the Burberry pattern (most famously a now-discontinued baseball cap) and from a variety of

other casual and sportswear brands. They often wear tracksuits/shellsuits and 'hoodies'. The Baseball caps usually consist of the MLB baseball team New York Yankees. Musically, chavs tend to like rap, Rave dance, and RnB. Response to the term has ranged from amusement to criticism that it is a new manifestation of classism. The term has also been associated with delinquency, the 'ASBO Generation', and 'Yob culture'.
Accessed Monday November 6, 2006.

10 In my unscientific personal survey British colleagues who chatted to me about writing this chapter felt free to express their own opinion on Tracey Emin: academics from middle-class backgrounds would express loathing of her/her work, and academics from working-class backgrounds would express their delight. This pattern was absolutely uniformly observed.

11 Article is accessible at http://www.jeanettewinterson.com/pages/content/index. asp?PageID=357.

12 This anagram belongs to Tracey Emin. From 'Tracey Emin Talks to Kirsty Wark' BBC4 Television, Sunday 19th November 2006.

13 'Mad Tracey from Margate' has become Emin's public moniker, it is also the title of one of her 1997 monoprints. There is also an allusion here to a 1980s Thatcherite stereotype of the 'Essex girl', at that time 'Sharon' or 'Tracy' were both used as symbolic names in the political and public sphere, intended to conjure up an idea of thick, gormless and slaggish young women from outside London who were intent on destroying English femininity. It was a classed stereotype of extraordinary spitefulness.

14 In an exhibition in a branch of the chain store Habitat in 1997 of a series of eight monoprints of birds, an accompanying sheet included an interview that Tracey Emin had undergone with the gallerist and friend Carl Freedman. Two of the bird drawings are reproduced, alongside this text from the interview, in Brown, Neal (2006) pp. 30–35, p.33.

15 Tracey Emin, quoted in Brown (2006, 50).

16 'Tracey Emin Talks to Kirsty Wark' BBC4 Television, Sunday 19th November 2006. 'Tragedy,' as writer Joseph John Campbell explains, 'is the shattering of forms and of our attachment to the forms.'

17 Extract from The Order For Holy Communion, The Alternative Service Book, Church of England, 1980.

18 The theology of shame in the Christian tradition is more valenced than perhaps secular humanism would suspect. In conversation with Reverend Kit Gray she pointed out to me that although the supplicant experiences shame and turns her face away, God's loving gaze remains unfaltering. So, theologically, the person turns from God, not the other way around.

19 Readers will recall the exchange between Judith Butler and Nancy Fraser in New Left Review (1998, 2000) on the 'economic turn' in gender and sexuality studies, and the politics of recognition.

20 See Plato's Republic 518d.

Bibliography

Adams, Tim (2003) 'Making a Drama Out of a Crisis' *The Observer* newspaper (London) Sunday 21st December.

Adams, Tim (2005) 'Second Coming'. Interview with Ricky Gervais, *The Observer* newspaper, (London) Sunday 10th July.

Adorno, Theodor (1974) [1969] *Minima Moralia: Reflections from Damaged Life* Trans. E.F.N. Jephcott (London: Verso).

Aesop, *The Complete Fables* Trans. Temple, Olivia and Temple, Robert (London: Penguin Books, 1998).

Ahmed, Sara (2004) *The Cultural Politics of Emotion* (Edinburgh: Edinburgh University Press).

Akass, Kim and McCabe, Janet (2005) *Reading Six Feet Under* (London and New York: I.B. Tauris).

Allen, Theodore W. (1994) *The Invention of the White Race Vol. 1: Racial Oppression and Social Control* (London and New York: Verso).

Allison, Eric (2005) 'Crying Shame' *The Guardian* newspaper (London) Wednesday January 12th.

Althusser, Louis (1966) '*Ideology and Ideological State Apparatuses (I.S.A.) (Notes towards an Investigation)*' Published in English in *Lenin and Philosophy and Other Essays*, available online for free at http://ptb.sunhost.be/marx2mao/Other/LPOE70ii.html#s5

Anderson, Benedict (1991) *Imagined Communities* (London and New York: Verso).

Anon, 'Sparks Fly Over Queer as Folk', *Pink Paper* 5th March 1999, p.4.

Anthony, Andrew (2003) 'Bearing the Full Brent' *The Observer* newspaper (London) Sunday 14th December.

Baker, Deirdre F. (2006) 'What we found on our journey through fantasy land' *Children's Literature in Education* 37, 237–251.

Banks-Smith, Nancy (2004) 'The Estate We're In' *The Guardian* newspaper (London) Wednesday 14th January.

Barbalet, J. M. (1998) *Emotion, Social Theory, and Social Structure* (Cambridge: Cambridge University Press).

Barber, Lynn (2001) 'Show and Tell: An Interview with Tracey Emin' in *The Observer* newspaper. (London: Sunday 22nd April).

Barrin, Jean (1683) 'Venus dans la Cloitre' Trans. Samber, Robert (1725) 'Venus in the Cloister; or, the Nun in her Smock'. Text from Dialogue 1 reprinted in McCormick, Ian (ed.) (1997) 187–197.

Beckett, Francis and Hencke, David (2004) 'Regular at Mass, Communion From Pope. So why is Blair Evasive about his Faith' *The Guardian* newspaper, Tuesday 28th September.

Bennington, Geoffrey (1994) 'Postal Politics and the Institution of the Nation' in Bhabha (ed.) 121–137.

Berlant, Lauren (1997) *The Queen of America Goes to Washington City: Essays on Sex and Citizenship* (Durham and London: Duke University Press).

Berlant, Lauren (ed.) (2004) *Compassion: The Culture and Politics of an Emotion* (London and New York: Routledge).

Berlant, Lauren and Freeman, Elizabeth (1993) 'Queer Nationality' in Warner, Michael (ed.) 193–229.

Bersani, Leo (1995) *Homos* (Cambridge, MA: Harvard University Press).

Bettez Halnon, Karen (2002) 'Poor Chic: The Rational Consumption of Poverty' in *Current Sociology* 50:4, 501–516.

Bhabha Homi (1997) 'Dissemination: Time, Narrative, and the Margins of the Modern Nation' in Bhabha, Homi (ed.) 139–170.

Bhabha, Homi (1994) *The Location of Culture* (London: Routledge).

Binni, Lanfranco (2005) 'Identità' in *Identità Nomadismo* (Milano: Regione Toscana, Palazzo Delle Papasse, Silvana Editoriale Spa) 13–26.

Binnie, Jon (2004) *The Globalisation of Sexuality* (London: Sage Publications).

Bird, Anne-Marie (2001) "Without Contraries is no Progression': Dust as an All-Inclusive, Multifunctional Metaphor in Philip Pullman's 'His Dark Materials" *Children's Literature in Education* 3: 2, 111–123.

Bisagni, Francesco (2002) 'The mother's hatred and the ugly child' Mann, David (ed.) (2002) *Love and Hate: Psychoanalytic Perspectives* (London: Routledge) 186–195.

Bodhan, Zachary (1999) 'Politically Incorrect Queer Folk' *The Advocate*, 8th June (New York: Liberation Publications Inc.) 65.

Bourdieu, Pierre and Wacquant, Loïc (1999) 'On the Cunning of Imperialist Reason' *Theory, Culture and Society* 16: 1, 41–58.

Bourdieu, Pierre *The Logic of Practice* (Cambridge: Polity Press).

Brennan, Teresa (2004) *The Transmission of Affect* (Ithaca: Cornell University Press).

Broucek, Francis (1989) 'Shame and Its Relationship to Early Narcissistic Developments' *International Journal of Psycho-Analysis*, 63, 369–78.

Broucek, Francis (1991) *Shame and the Self* (New York and London: The Guilford Press).

Brown, Neal (2006) *Tracey Emin* (London: Tate Publishing).

Brown, Wendy (1995) *States of Injury: Power and Freedom in Late Modernity* (Princeton NJ: Princeton University Press).

Buckingham, Alan (1999) 'Is there an underclass in Britain' *British Journal of Sociology* 50: 1, 49–75.

Butler, Judith (1990) *Gender Trouble: Feminism and the Subversion of Identity* (London and New York: Routledge).

Butler, Judith (1993) *Bodies That Matter: On the Discursive Limits of 'Sex'* (New York and London: Routledge).

Butler, Judith (1997) *Excitable Speech: A Politics of the Performative* (New York and London: Routledge).

Butler, Judith (1997) *The Psychic Life of Power: Theories in Subjection* (Stanford, CA: Stanford University Press).

Butler, Judith (1998) 'Merely Cultural' in *New Left Review* 227, 33–44.

Butler, Judith (2004) *Precarious Life: The Power of Mourning and Violence* (London: Verso).

Butler, Judith (2005) *Giving an Account of Oneself* (New York: Fordham University Press).

Butler, Robert (2003) *The Art of Darkness: Staging the Philip Pullman Trilogy* (London: National Theatre/Oberon Books).

Byrne, Bridget (2003) 'Reciting the Self – Narrative Representations of the Self in Qualitative Interviews' *Feminist Theory* 4:1 April, 29–49.

Cadwalladr, Carole (2006) 'Down the Welly with the Gallaghers: Life shamelessly imitates TV art – but at least the car didn't get nicked.' *The Observer* newspaper, Review section, Sunday 8th January, 10.

Case, Sue-Ellen (1991) 'Tracking the Vampire' in *Differences* 3:2, 1–20.

Castle, Terry (1993) *The Apparitional Lesbian* (New York: Columbia University Press).

Cavavero, Adriana (2000) *Relating Narratives: Storytelling and Selfhood* Trans. Kottman, Paul A., (London and New York: Routledge).

Chadwick, Edwin (1842) *Report on the Sanitary Condition of the Labouring Population of Great Britain* (Edinburgh: Edinburgh University Press).

Chinn, Sarah (1994) 'Queering the profession, or just professionalizing queers?' in Garber, L. (1994) 243–250.

Chumo, Peter N. (2000) '*American Beauty*: An Interview with Alan Ball,' *Creative Screenwriting* January-February, 33.

Cohen Ed (1994) *Talk on the Wild Side* (London: Routledge).

Collins, Michael 'There's a Queer Thing on TV', *The Guardian* newspaper web page (archives), accessed Sunday 24th January 1999. http://www. guardianunlimited.co.uk/Archive/Article/0,4273,3811928,00.html

Conrad, Katherine A. (2004) "We Are Home': ILGO and the Public Sphere' in *Locked in the Family Cell: Gender, Sexuality and Political Agency in Irish National Discourse* (Madison, WI: The University of Wisconsin Press).

Cronin, Michael and Adair, Daryl (2002) *The Wearing of the Green: A History of St Patrick's Day* (New York and London: Routledge).

Damasio, Antonio R. (1994) *Descartes' Error: Emotion, Reason and the Human Brain* (New York: Grosset/Putnam).

Damasio, Antonio R. (2000) *The Feeling of What Happens: Body and Emotion in the Making of Consciousness* (New York: Harcourt Brace).

Damasio, Antonio R. (2003) *Looking for Spinoza: Joy, Sorrow, and the Feeling Brain* (New York: Harcourt Brace).

Darwin, Charles (1999/1872) *The Expression of Emotions in Man and Animals* Introduced by Ekman, Paul. (London: Harper Collins/Fontana).

Davies, Russell T. (1999) *Queer as Folk: The Scripts* (London: Macmillan).

De Bertodano, Helena (2002) 'I am of the Devil's Party' *Sunday Telegraph* (London) 27th January.

Deleuze, Gilles (1988) *Spinoza: A Practical Philosophy* Trans. Robert Hurley. (San Franscisco: City Lights Books).

Deleuze, Gilles and Guattari, Felix (1977) *Anti-Oedipus: Capitalism and Schizophrenia* (New York: Viking Press).

Derrida, Jacques (2002) 'The Animal That Therefore I am (More to Follow)' Trans. David Wills in *Critical Inquiry* 28:2, 369–418.

Derrida, Jacques (2005) *On Touching, Jean-Luc Nancy* (Stanford CA: Stanford University Press).

Dillon, Sam (2006) 'Law to Segregate Omaha Schools Divides Nebraska' in *New York Times*, 15th April.

Doan, Laura and Prosser, Jay (eds) (2001) *Palatable Poison: Critical Perspectives on The Well of Loneliness* (New York: Columbia University Press).

Dooley, Brian (1998) *Black and Green: The Fight for Civil Rights in Northern Ireland and Black America* (London: Pluto Press).

Douglas, R.M. (2002) 'Anglo-Saxons and Attacotti: the Racialization of Irishness in Britain between the World Wars' *Ethnic and Racial Studies* 25:1, 40–63.

Duberman, Martin (1993) *Stonewall* (New York: Dutton).

Dyer, Richard (1997) *White: Essays on Race and Culture* (London and New York: Routledge). Evans-Pritchard, E.E. (1947) *The Nuer: A Description of the Modes and Livelihood and Political Institutions of a Nilotic People* (Oxford: The Clarendon Press).

Edge, Simon (2002) review of *The Office* Series 2, quoted in *The Media Guardian* (London) Tuesday 1st October.

Egan, Susanna (1999) *Mirror Talk: Genres of Crisis in Contemporary Autobiography* (Chapel Hill: University of North Carolina Press).

Ekman, Paul and Friesen, Wallace (1975) *Unmasking the Face* (New Jersey: Prentice Hall).

Elden, Stuart (2001) *Mapping the Present: Heidegger, Foucault and the Project of a Spatial History* (London and New York: Continuum).

Eliot, George (1986/1871) *Middlemarch* (ed.) Carrol, David (London: Clarendon Press).

Eribon, Didier (2004) *Insult and the Making of the Gay Self* (Durham and London: Duke University Press).

Fanthome, Christine (2006) 'The Influence and Treatment of Autobiography in Confessional Art: Observations on Tracey Emin's Feature Film *Top Spot*' in *Biography* 29.1, 30–42.

Flett, Kathryn (2002) 'Drop Dead Wonderful' *The Observer* newspaper (London). 16th June, 20.

Flett, Kathryn (2003) 'Last Bow in Slough' *The Observer* newspaper, Sunday 28th December.

Flett, Kathryn (2004) 'Once Upon a Time in the North' *The Observer* newspaper, Sunday 18th January.

Foucault, Michel (1970) *The Order of Things- An Archaeology of the Human Sciences* Trans. Alan Sheridan. (London: Routledge).

Foucault, Michel (1972) 'The Formation of Enunciative Modalities' *The Archaeology of Knowledge and the Discourse on Language* Trans. A.M. Smith, Sheridan (New York: Pantheon Books).

Foucault, Michel (1979) *A History of Sexuality: An Introduction, Volume One* Trans. Hurley, Robert (Harmondsworth: Penguin Books).

Foucault, Michel (1982) 'On the Genealogy of Ethics: An Overview of Work in Progress' in Dreyfus, H. and Rabinow P. *Michel Foucault: Beyond Structuralism and Hermeneutics* (Chicago: Chicago University Press).

Foucault, Michel (1984) 'What is Enlightenment?' in Rabinow P. (ed.) *The Foucault Reader* (Cambridge: Polity Press).

Foucault, Michel and Baker, Catherine (1984) 'Interview with Michel Foucault' in *Actes* 45–46, June.

Foucault, Michel (1985) *The Use of Pleasure: The History of Sexuality, Volume 2* Trans. Robert Hurley. (Harmondsworth: Penguin).

Foucault, Michel (1986) 'Of Other Spaces' in *Diacritics* Spring, 22–7.

Foucault, Michel (1986) *Care of the Self: The History of Sexuality, Volume 3* Trans. Robert Hurley, (Harmondsworth, Penguin).

Foucault, Michel 'Politics and the Study of Discourse' in Burchell, Graham et al. (ed.) (1991) *The Foucault Effect: Studies in Governmentality* (Chicago: University of Chicago Press).

Foucault, Michel (1993) 'About the Beginning of the Hermeneutics of the Self' Trans. Thomas Keenan and Mark Blasius. In *Political Theory* 21:2, 198–227.

Fox, Pamela (1994) *Class Fictions: Shame and Resistance in the British Working Class Novel, 1890–1945* (Durham NC: Duke University Press).

Fraser, Nancy (1998) 'Heterosexism, Misrecognition and Capitalism: A Response to Judith Butler' in *New Left Review* 228, 140–149.

Fraser, Nancy (2000) 'Rethinking Recognition' in *New Left Review* 3, 107–120.

Freedman Carl (ed.) (2006) *Tracey Emin* (New York: Rizzoli).

Freud, Sigmund 'Creative Writers and Day-dreaming' (1908) *The Standard Edition of the Complete Psychological Works of Sigmund Freud Vol. 2* Trans. Strachey, James (ed.)(1973) (London: Hogarth Press) 141–53.

Freud, Sigmund (1915) 'Mourning and Melancholia' *On Metapsychology: The Theory of Psychoanalysis* Trans. (ed.) Strachey, James (1991) (London: Penguin Books, Penguin Freud Library Vol. 2) 247–68.

Freud, Sigmund (1922) *Group Psychology and the Analysis of the Ego* Trans. James Strachey (London and Vienna: The International Psycho-Analytical Library, No. 6).

Freud, Sigmund (1989/1930) *Civilisation and Its Discontents* (New York: W. W. Norton and Company).

Fuss, Diana (1993) *Inside/Out: Lesbian Theories, Gay Theories* (New York: Routledge).

Game, Ann and Metcalfe Andrew W. (1996) Passionate Sociology (London: Sage Publications).

Garber, Linda (ed.) (1994) *Tilting the Tower: Lesbians/Teaching/Queer Subjects* (London and New York: Routledge).

Garrett, Paul Michael (2005) 'Irish Social Workers in Britain' *British Journal of Social Work* 35, 1357–1376.

Geertz, Clifford 'Description: Toward an Interpretive Theory of Culture,' in *The Interpretation of Culture* (NY: Basic Books, 1973) Chapter 1.

Gellner, Ernest (1983) *Nations and Nationalism* (Oxford: Blackwell).

Gibson, Janine (1999) 'Gay programme upsets viewers', Tuesday 22nd June 1999. Accessed on the *The Guardian* newspaper web page archives http://www.guardianunlimited.co.uk/Archive/Article/0,4273,3877108,00.html

Giddens, Anthony (1991) *Modernity and Self-Identity* (Cambridge: Polity Press).

Glasgow, Joanne (1990) 'What's a Nice Woman Like You Doing in the Church of Torquemada? Radclyffe Hall and Other Catholic Converts' in Jay, Karla and Glasgow, Joanne (eds) (1990) 241–254.

Goffman, Erving (1959) *The Presentation of Self in Everyday Life* (Garden City, NY: Doubleday).

Goffman, Erving (1990) [1963] *Stigma – Notes on the Management of Spoiled Identity* (London, Penguin Books).

Goleman, Daniel (1995) *Emotional Intelligence: Why it can Matter More than IQ* (London: Bloomsbury Publishing).

Gooderham, David 'Fantasising It As It Is: Religious Language in Philip Pullman's Trilogy, *His Dark Materials*' *Project Muse* http://muse.jhu.edu 155–175.

Gray, Breda (2002) ''Whitely Scripts' and Irish Women's Racialized Belonging(s) in England' *European Journal of Cultural Studies* 5:3, 257–274.

Gribbin, Mary and Gribbin, John (2003) *The Science of Philip Pullman's His Dark Materials* (London: Hodder Childrens' Books).

Griffin, Gabrielle (ed.) (1995) *Feminist Activism in the 1990s* (London: Taylor and Francis).

Grosz, Elizabeth (1994) *Volatile Bodies: Towards A Corporeal Feminism* (Bloomington: Indiana University Press).

Grosz, Elizabeth (2004) *The Nick of Time* (Durham NC: Duke University Press).

Grosz, Elizabeth (2005) *Time Travels* (Durham NC: Duke University Press).

Hall, Stuart (2003) 'Encoding/Decoding' in Nightingale, Virginia and Ross, Karen *Critical Readings: Media and Audiences* (Cambridge: Open University Press) 51–64.

Hall, Stuart (ed.) (1997) *Representation: Cultural Representations and Signifying Practices* (Milton Keynes: Open University Press) 15–30.

Halperin, David M. (1995) *Saint=Foucault: Towards a Gay Hagiography* (Oxford: Oxford University Press).

Haltunnen, Karen (1995) 'Humanitarianism and the Pornography of Pain in Anglo-American Culture' *American Historical Review* April.

Hann, Michael (2001) 'Leave My Town Alone' in *The Guardian* newspaper (London) Tuesday 7th August.

Hanson, Ellis (1993) 'Undead' in Fuss, Diana (ed), 324–340.

Hausmann, Vincent (2004) 'Envisioning the (W)hole World 'Behind Things': Denying Otherness in *American Beauty*' *Camera Obscura* 19.1, 112–149.

Haylett Chris (2000) 'This is about us, this is our film!' in Munt, Sally R. (2000) 69–81.

Hazlitt, William (2004/1826) 'On the Pleasure of Hating' *On the Pleasure of Hating* (London: Penguin Books)104–120. [First published in *The Plain Speaker*].

Heidegger, Martin (1999) *Contributions to Philosophy: From Enkowing* Trans. Emad, Parvis and Maly, Kenneth (Bloomington: Indiana University Press).

Hindle, Steve (2004) 'Dependency, Shame and Belonging: Badging the Deserving Poor, c.1550–1750' in *Cultural and Social History* 1, 6–35.

Hitchins, Henry 'Tracey Emin in the Raw' in *The Times* newspaper (London: 2005). Available at http://www.timesonline.co.uk/uk/ accessed June 2006.

Hoare, Stephen (2004) 'Laugh and Learn' *The Guardian* newspaper, Tuesday 6th January.

Hobsbawm, Eric J. *Nations and Nationalism Since 1780* Cambridge University Press, 1990

Hochschild, Arlie Russell (1985) *The Managed Heart: Commercialization of Human Feeling* Berkeley CA: University of California Press).

Hoggart, Simon 'Gorgeous and Gay', *The Spectator* 19th February 2000, 52.

hooks, bell (1994) *Outlaw Culture: Resisting Representations* (London and New York: Routledge).

Houlbrook, Matt (2005) *Queer London* (Chicago: Chicago University Press).

Hughes, Christina (2004) 'Perhaps she was having a bad hair day! Taking issue with ungenerous readings of feminist texts – an open letter' *European Journal of Women's Studies* 11 February, 103–109.

Ignatiev, Noel (1996) and Jacobson, Matthew Frye (1999) *How the Irish Became White* (New York: Routledge).

Irigaray, Luce (2000) *To Be Two* (London: The Athlone Press).

Jacobson, Matthew Frye (1999) *Whiteness of a Different Color: European Immigrants and the Alchemy of Race* (Cambridge MA: Harvard University Press).

Jay, Karla and Glasgow, Joanne (eds) (1990) *Lesbian Texts and Contexts: Radical Revisions* (New York: New York University Press).

Johnston, Jill (1974) *The Lesbian Nation* (New York: Touchstone Books/Simon and Schuster).

Johnston, Lynda (2005) *Queering Tourism: Paradoxical Performances of Gay Pride Parades* (London and New York: Routledge Studies in Human Geography).

Jones, Ann R., and Stallybrass, Peter 'Dismantling Irena: The Sexualizing of Ireland in Early Modern England' in Parker et al. (1992) 157–171.

Kant, Immanuel (1951) *Critique of Judgment* Trans. J.H. Bernard (London: Macmillan) 1951.

Kant, Immanuel (2003) *Observations on the Feeling of the Beautiful and Sublime* Trans. John T. Goldthwaite (Berkeley: University of California Press).

Klein, Melanie (1975) *The Writings of Melanie Klein Vol 1: Love, guilt and reparation and other works 1921–1945* (New York: Free Press).

Klein, Melanie (1975) *The Writings of Melanie Klein Vol. 3: Envy and gratitude, and other works, 1946–1963* (London: Hogarth Press).

Kolodny, Annette (1980) 'Dancing Through the Minefield: Some Observations on the Theory, Practice, and Politics of a Feminist Literary Criticism' *Feminist Studies* 6.

Kottman, Paul A. (2000) 'Translator's Introduction' in Cavarero, Adriana *Relating Narratives: Storytelling and Selfhood* Trans. Kottman, Paul A. (London and New York: Routledge).

Koven, Seth (2004) *Slumming: Sexual and Social Politics in Victorian London* (Princeton and Oxford: Princeton University Press).

Krause, Donald G (ed.) (1996) *The Art of War for Executives* (London: Nicholas Brealey Publishing).

Kuhn, Annette (1995) *Family Secrets: Acts of Memory and Imagination* (London: Verso).

Lacan, Jacques (1991) *The Seminar of Jacques Lacan Book I.* Jacques Alain-Miller (ed.), trans. John Forrester (New York: W. W. Norton).

Lacan, Jacques (1992) *The Ethics of Psychoanalysis 1959–1960, The Seminars of Jacques Lacan Book VII* (ed.) Miller, Jacques-Alain, trans. Potter, Dennis, (New York: Norton).

Lane, Harriet (2004) 'Real-life Romance' *The Observer* newspaper (London) Sunday February 8th.

Lansky, Melvin R. and Morrison, Andrew P. (eds) (1997) *The Widening Scope of Shame* (Hillsdale NJ and London: The Analytic Press).

Lefebvre, Henri (1974) 1991 *The Production of Space* Trans. Nicholson-Smith, Donald (Oxford: Blackwell).

Lenz, Millicent (2003) 'Story as a Bridge to Transformation: The Way Beyond Death in Philip Pullman's *The Amber Spyglass*' *Children's Literature in Education* 34:1 March, 47–55.

Lewis, Helen Block (1971) *Shame and Guilt in Neurosis: Volume One* (New York: International Universities Press).

Lingis, Alphonso (2000) *Dangerous Emotions* (Berkeley CA: University of California Press).

Lloyd, Genevieve (1996) *Spinoza and the Ethics* (London: Routledge).

Lodge, David (2002) *Consciousness and the Novel* (New York: Secker and Warburg).

Luongo, Michael (2002) 'Rome's World Pride' *GLQ: A Journal of Lesbian and Gay Studies* 8:1–2 , 167–181.

Lyons, Tom (2006) 'Ireland 'a country of sodomite dandies'' *The Irish Independent* newspaper Wednesday 26th April.

Lyotard, Jean-François (1994) *Lessons on the Analytic of the Sublime* Trans. Elizabeth Rottenberg (Stanford CA: Stanford University Press).

Mac an Ghaill, Máirtín (2000) 'The Irish in Britain: the Invisibility of Ethnicity and Anti-Irish Racism' *Journal of Ethnic and Migration Studies* 26:1, 137–147.

Maggenti, Maria (1991) 'Women as Queer Nationals' *Out/Look* Winter 20–23.

Maguire, Anne (2006) *Rock The Sham!* (New York: Street Level Press).

Mann, David (ed.) (2002) *Love and Hate: Psychoanalytic Perspectives* (London: Routledge).

Manzoor, Sarfraz (2006) 'Stereotypes? It's 'chavs' not black people who really get a raw deal', (*The Observer* newspaper, Review section: 27th August, p.7).

Marrin, Minette (2004) 'Oh Lord, Even the Archbishop is Clutching at Atheist Straws.' *The Sunday Times* newspaper (London) 14th March.

Martin, Lorna (2006) 'Cracker creator blasts 'chav' TV', (*The Observer* newspaper 27th August, p.5).

Marvin, Garry (2005) 'Disciplined Affections', Knight, John (ed.) *Animals in Person: Cultural Perspectives on Human-Animal Intimacies* (Oxford: Berg Publishers) 61–77.

Marx, Karl (1844) Introduction to *A Contribution to the Critique of Hegel's Philosophy of the Right*. Reprinted in (1975) *Karl Marx: Early Writings* (Harmondsworth: Penguin Books) 244–57.

Masson, Jeffrey (1996) *When Elephants Weep: The Emotional Lives of Animals* (New York: Vintage).

Masson, Jeffrey (2003) *The Nine Emotional Lives of Cats: A Journey into the Feline Heart* (London, Vintage).

Masters, Robert (2000) 'Compassionate Wrath: Transpersonal Approaches to Anger', *Journal of Transpersonal Psychology* available on-line at: http://robertmasters.com/ESSAY-pages/Compassion-Wrath.htm accessed September 14th 2006.

Mauss, Marcel (1954) *The Gift: Forms and Functions of Exchange in Archaic Societies* Trans. Cunnison, Ian. Introduction by E. E. Evans-Pritchard. (London: Cohen and West).

McClintock, Anne (1995) *Imperial Leather: Race, Gender and Sexuality in the Colonial Contest* (London and New York: Routledge).

McCormick, Ian (ed.) (1997) *Secret Sexualities: A Sourcebook of 17th and 18th Century Writing* (London and New York: Routledge).

McNulty, Amy, University of Salford, Manchester (2005) 'Postmodern Style, Realist Intent: The Internal Contradictions of *Shameless*'. Paper given at the

'Cultures of British Television Drama' conference, University of Reading 13th–15th September.

Meissner, William W. (1978) *The Paranoid Process* (New York: Jason Aronson).

Merck, Mandy and Townsend, Chris (2002) *The Art of Tracey Emin* (London: Thames and Hudson).

Merck, Mandy (2000) *In Your Face: 9 Sexual Studies* (New York: New York University Press).

Miller, Susan (1985) *The Shame Experience* (Hillsdale, New Jersey and London: The Analytic Press).

Mitchell, Juliet (1986) *The Selected Melanie Klein* (London: Hogarth Press/ Penguin).

Moran, Leslie J. (2000) 'Homophobic Violence, the Hidden Injuries of Class' Sally R.Munt (ed.) (2000) 206–18.

Morris, Herbert (ed.) (1971) *Guilt and Shame* (Belmont CA: Wadsworth).

Morrison, Andrew P. (1989) *Shame: The Underside of Narcissism* (Hillsdale NJ: The Analytic Press).

Mosse, George L. Mosse (1988) *Nationalism and sexuality : middle-class morality and sexual norms in modern Europe* (Madison: University of Wisconsin Press).

Mullen, Kenneth, Williams, Rory and Hunt, Kate (1996) 'Irish Descent, Religion, and Alcohol and Tobacco Use' *Addiction* 91:2, 243–254.

Munt, Sally R. (1992) 'Sex and Sexuality', Hargrave, Andrea Millwood (ed.) *Sex and Sexuality* in *Broadcasting Standards Council Annual Review 1992* (London: John Libbey and Company Ltd.).

Munt, Sally R. (1997) "I Teach Therefore I am": Lesbian Studies in the Liberal Academy *Feminist Review* 56, Summer 85–99.

Munt, Sally R. (1998a) *Butch/Femme: Inside Lesbian Gender* (London and Washington: Cassell Academic/ Contemporary Studies).

Munt, Sally R. (1998b) *Heroic Desire: Lesbian Identity and Cultural Space* (New York: New York University Press).

Munt, Sally R. 'Orifices in Space: Making 'the Real' Possible' in Munt Sally R. (ed.) (1998a) 200–9.

Munt, Sally R. (1999) 'Power, Pedagogy and Partiality' *Feminism and Psychology* 9:4, 422–425.

Munt Sally R. (2000) *Cultural Studies and the Working Class: Subject to Change* (London and New York: Cassell).

Myers, Joanne (2003) *Historical Dictionary of the Lesbian Liberation Movement: Still the Rage* (London: Scarecrow Press, Religions, Philosophies, and Movements Series).

Nathanson, Donald L. (1997) 'Shame and the Affect Theory of Silvan Tompkins' Lansky, Melvin R. and Morrison, Andrew P. (eds) (1997) 107–38.

Newton, Isaac *Principia* in Humphrey D. (1949) *Intermediate Mechanics: Dynamics.* (London: Longmans, Green and Co.).

Ngai, Sianne (2005) *Ugly Feelings* (Cambridge MA, Harvard University Press).

Nietzsche, Friedrich (1989) [1887] *On the Genealogy of Morals: A Polemic* (New York: Vintage Books).

O'Connor, Thomas H. (1995) *The Boston Irish: A Political History* (Boston: Northeastern University Press).

O'Gorman, Marcel (2004) 'American Beauty Busted: Necromedia and Domestic Discipline' *Substance* 33:3 pp. 34–51

O'Rourke, Rebecca *Reflecting on The Well of Loneliness* (London: Routledge, 1989).

Parker, Andrew, Russo, Mary, Sommer, Doris, and Yaeger, Patricia (eds) (1992) *Nationalisms and Sexualities* (London and New York: Routledge).

Parsons, Wendy and Nicholson, Catriona (1999) 'Talking to Philip Pullman: An Interview' *The Lion and the Unicorn* 23:1, 116–134.

Piers, Gerhart and Singer, Milton B. (1971) *Shame and Guilt: A Psychoanalytic and a Cultural Study* (New York: W.W. Norton and Co.).

Pullman, Philip (1998) *The Subtle Knife* (London: Scholastic Children's Books).

Pullman, Philip (2000) *The Amber Spyglass* (London: Scholastic Children's Books).

Pullman, Philip [1995] 2001 *Northern Lights* (London: Scholastic Children's Books).

Rampton, James (2004) 'Paul Abbott: My Shameless Life' *The Independent* newspaper, (London) 20th December.

Reay, Barry (2002) *Watching Hannah: Sexuality, Horror and Bodily De-formation in Victorian England* (London, Reaktion Books).

Renan, Ernest (1994) 'What is a Nation?' reprinted in Bhabha, H. (ed.) 8–22.

Roof, Judith and Weigman, Robyn (1995) (eds) *Who Can Speak: Authority and Critical Identity* (Urbana and Chicago: University of Illinois Press).

Rose, Jacqueline (2003) *On Not Being Able to Sleep: Psychoanalysis and the Modern World* (London: Chatto and Windus).

Rowe Karlin Kathleen (2004) "Too Close for Comfort': *American Beauty* and the Incest Motif' in *Cinema Journal* 44:1, 69–93.

Rule, Jane *Lesbian Images* (Garden City, New York: Doubleday 1975) reprinted in Doan, Laura and Prosser, Jay (eds) (2001) 77–88.

Rushbrook, Dereka (2002) 'Cities, Queer Space, and the Cosmopolitan Tourist' *GLQ: A Journal of Lesbian and Gay Studies* 8:1–2, 183–206.

Russell, Mary Harris (2003) 'Ethical Plots, Ethical Endings in Philip Pullman's *His Dark Materials*' *Foundation: The International Review of Science Fiction* 32:88, Summer, 68–74.

Rustin, Margaret and Rustin, Michael (2003) 'Learning to Say Goodbye. An Essay on Philip Pullman's *The Amber Spyglass*' *Journal of Child Psychotherapy* 29:3 December, 415–25.

Rustin, Margaret and Rustin, Michael (2003) 'Where is Home? An Essay on Philip Pullman's *Northern Lights*, in *Journal of Child Psychotherapy* 29:1 April, 93–105.

Rustin, Margaret and Rustin, Michael (2003) 'A New Kind of Friendship – An Essay on Philip Pullman's *The Subtle Knife*' *Journal of Child Psychotherapy* 29:2, August, 227–34.

Ryan, Louise (2004) 'Family Matters: (e)migration, familial networks and Irish women in Britain' *The Sociological Review* 52:3, 351–370.

Said, E. (2000) Reflections on exile and other essays (Cambridge: Harvard University Press) 173–186.

Sartre, Jean-Paul (1943) [1958] *Being and Nothingness :a phenomenological essay on ontology* Trans. Hazel Barnes (London: Methuen).

Sayer, Andrew (2005) 'Class, Moral Worth and Recognition' in *Sociology* 39:5, 947–963.

Scheff, Thomas J. and Retzinger, Suzanne M. *Emotions and Violence: Shame and Rage in Destructive Conflicts* (Santa Barbara CA: Lexington Books).

Schulman, Sarah et al. (1993) *The Lesbian Avenger Handbook: A Handy Guide to the Revolution* (New York).

Schwabsky, Barry *Tracey Emin* in *ArtForum*, (Amsterdam: Stedelijk Museum – Reviews, Gale Group) February, 2003. Available on-line at http://www.findarticles.com/p/articles/mi_m0268/is_6_41/ai_98123169

Sedgwick, Eve Kosofsky (1991) *Epistemology of the Closet* (Hemel Hempstead: Harvester Wheatsheaf).

Sedgwick, Eve Kosofsky (1993) 'A Poem is Being Written' in *Tendencies* (Durham and London: Duke University Press) 177–214.

Sedgwick, Eve Kosofsky (1993) 'White Glasses' in *Tendencies* (Durham and London, Duke University Press).

Sedgwick, Eve Kosofsky and Frank, Adam (eds) (1995) *Shame and Its Sisters, A Silvan Tomkins Reader* (Durham and London: Duke University Press).

Sedgwick, Eve Kosofsky (2006) 'Teaching/Depression' in *The Scholar and Feminist Online* 4:2 Spring.

Sharkey, Alex (1998) 'Heaven, Hell, and the Hut at the Bottom of the Garden' *Independent on Sunday* (London) 6th December.

Showalter, Elaine (1985) *The Female Malady: Women, Madness, and English Culture, 1830–1980* (New York: Pantheon Books).

Showalter, Elaine (1997) *Hystories: hysterical epidemics and modern media* (New York: Columbia University Press).

Signorile, Michelangelo (2003) *Queer in America: Sex, the Media, and the Closets of Power* (Madison WI: University of Wisconsin Press, 3rd Edition).

Skeggs, Beverley (1997) *Formations of Class and Gender: Becoming Respectable* (London: Sage Publications)

Skeggs, Beverley (2004) *Class, Self, Culture* (London: Routledge).

Slouka, Mark (1995) *War of the Worlds: The Assault on Reality* (London: Abacus).

Smyth, Ailbhe (1995) 'Haystacks in My Mind – or How to Stay SAFE (Sane, Angry and Feminist) in the 1990s' in Griffin, G. (1995) 192–207.

Solomon, Robert C. (2004) *Thinking About Feeling: Contemporary Philosophers on Emotions* (Oxford: Oxford University Press).

Squires, Claire (2003) *Philip Pullman's His Dark Materials Trilogy: A Reader's Guide* (London and New York: Continuum Contemporaries Series).

Stevens, Anthony, and Price, John (2000) *Evolutionary Psychiatry: A New Beginning* (Hove: Brunner-Routledge).

Stimpson, Catherine (1981) 'Zero Degree Deviancy: the Lesbian Novel in English' *Critical Enquiry* 8:2, 363–379; reprinted as 'The Lesbian Novel in English' in Stimpson, Catherine (1988) *Where the Meanings Are: Feminism and Cultural Spaces* (London and New York: Methuen) 97–110.

Stocking, George W. (1987) *Victorian Anthropology* (New York: Free Press/ Macmillan).

Stychin, Carl F. (1998) 'The Nation's Rights and National Rites' *A Nation by Rights: National Cultures, Sexual Identity Politics, and the Discourse of Rights* (Philadelphia: Temple University Press).

Sun Tzu (2005) *The Art of War* (Boston/San Francisco: Shambala Publishing).

Tavuchis, Nicholas (1991) *Mea Culpa: The Sociology of Apology and Reconciliation* (Stanford: Stanford University Press).

Taylor, Gabriele (1985) *Pride, Shame and Guilt: Emotions of Self-Assessment* (Oxford, Clarendon Press).

Tomkins, Silvan (1995) 'SHAME-HUMILIATION CONTEMPT-DISGUST' reprinted in Sedgwick, Eve Kosofsky and Frank, Adam (eds) 133–178.

Tucker, Nicholas (2000) 'Paradise Lost and Freedom Won' *The Independent* newpaper (London) 28th October.

Tucker, Nicholas (2003) *Darkness Visible: Inside the World of Philip Pullman* (Cambridge: Wizard Books) 87–186.

Valentine, Gill (1998) '"Sticks and stones may break my bones": a personal geography of harassment' *Antipode* 30:4, 305–332.

Vara, Renée (2002) 'Another Dimension' in Merck and Townsend op. cit. 172–194.

Warner, Michael (ed.) (1993) *Fear of a Queer Planet: Queer Politics and Social Theory* (Minneapolis: University of Minnesota Press).

Watkins, Mary (1987) 'In dreams become responsibilities: moral imagination and peace action,' *Facing Apocalypse* (eds) Andrews, Valerie, Bosnak, Robert, and Walter Goodwin, Karen (Dallas TX: Spring Publications) 70–95.

White, Patricia (1993) 'Female Spectator, Lesbian Spectre: *The Haunting*' in Fuss, Diana (ed) 142–172.

Williams, Raymond (1975) [1961] 'The Analysis of Culture' in *The Long Revolution* (Harmondsworth: Pengiun) 57–88.

Williams, Simon J. (2001) *Emotion and Social Theory: Corporeal Reflections on the (Ir)Rational* (London: Sage Publications)

Wittig, Monique (1981) 'One is not born a Woman' *Feminist Issues* 1:1 Winter.

Wood, Naomi (2001) 'Paradise Lost and Found: Obedience, Disobedience, and Storytelling in C.S. Lewis and Philip Pullman' *Children's Literature in Education* 32: 4, December 237–259.

Yalda, Christine A. (1999) 'Walking the Straight and Narrow: Performative Sexuality and the First Amendment After Hurley' *Social and Legal Studies* 8:1, 25–45.

Index

abjection xiv, 23, 26, 45, 92, 94, 95, 98, 103, 185, 192, 208, 214, 216, 222
academia – ivory tower xiii, xiv, 1, 106, 108, 110, 112, 114-117
ACT-UP 77
Adorno, Theodore *Minima Moralia* 224
Aesop's Fables 90, 97, 102
affect economy 11, 13
affective computing 8
Ahmed, Sara xvi, 3, 12
Allison, Eric 156
American Beauty 162-4, 167
American Civil Liberties Union 57, 71, 77
Ancient Order of Hibernians 56-7, 60-2, 64, 70-74, 76-7
Anderson, Benedict xiii, 55, 60, 229
Anti-Social Behaviour Orders [ASBOs, UK] 156, 159, 226
anxiety xvii, 2, 96, 108-9, 112, 119, 124, 147, 162, 166-8, 172, 173

Barbalet, J. M. 11-12
Bennington, Geoffrey 59
Bentham, Jeremy 46-7
Berlant, Lauren 30, 66-7, 76, 115
Bettez Halnon, Karen 148-9
Bhabha, Homi 55, 58-60, 74, 76, 131
Bird, Anne-Marie 196-7
Bisagni, Franscesco 111
Blair, Tony 20, 29
blushing 5, 6, 9, 38, 46, 49, 83-4, 99
body dysmorphic disorder 2
Bourdieu, Pierre xiii, 16, 29, 158
Bowers v. Hardwick (fn) 49, 53

Bray, Alan 38-9, 47
Brennan, Teresa 12-14
Broucek, Francis 30, 99, 100, 114, 198, 217
Brown, Neal 212, 215, 217, 218, 226
Brown, Wendy xiii, 24-6, 75
bullying 112, 124, 125, 129, 153, 170
Burke, Edmund v, xvii, 18
  on sympathy 40-53
  speech to the House of Commons 1780 27, 28, 31, 37, 40-53
  Treatise on the Sublime and Beautiful 40, 41, 42, 81
Butler, Judith
  gender melancholy xiii, 76, 166, 167, 179
  injurious speech 25, 30, 224
  performativity 129
  queer citationality and the constitutive outside 87, 94, 100, 105, 185, 186, 223
  recognition 102, 113, 147, 220-2, 227n

Cavarero, Adriana xiii, 186
Chinese medicine 13
Chinn, Sarah 107, 129, 230
Christianity xiv, 143, 181, 198, 200
  blasphemy 82, 90
  Christ, imagery of 68, 81, 82-4, 88-9, 91, 143, 157, 217
  Eden vii, xiv, 45, 72, 79, 80, 82, 84, 85, 90, 127, 134, 141, 142, 157, 196, 199
  forgiveness and ritual 120, 143, 194

in *Holy Communion* 4, 143, 219
martyrdom and suffering,
    mortification 2, 46, 64, 81, 83,
    85, 89
Protestantism 1, 15, 20, 36, 37,
    40, 47, 60, 68, 175, 198
religious art 214, 217
Roman Catholicism 63, 68, 74,
    198, 234n
    and invisibility 29, 37
    and sodomy 37, 81, 99, 103,
        170
    clergy 37, 60, 73
    Irish Catholicism 18, 39, 47,
        60, 62
        diaspora 16, 137
        racism and eugenics 19, 20,
            36, 145, 158n
        stereotypes 15, 20, 22, 28,
            30, 37, 38, 68, 134, 137,
            138, 146, 154
    Latino Catholicism 170, 174
sectarianism 60, 68
sin xiv, 4, 41, 80, 85, 89, 90, 123,
    127, 181, 195, 199
the Fall of Adam and Eve 45, 71,
    79, 80, 181, 184, 195, 196, 198,
    199
theology, experimental theology
    68, 80, 81, 90, 143, 181, 188,
    195, 200, 212, 219, 227
The Holy Bible 45, 53, 75, 80, 82,
    170
class
    and representation 26, 58, 73-4,
        104, 137, 138, 143, 145, 151,
        157n, 192
    and the Anthropological gaze
        136-145
    class tourism and class voyeurism
        14n, 133, 134-145, 148, 213
    classed affects 11, 14, 16, 25, 27,
        128
    cross-class desire 16, 38, 43, 98,
        142, 144, 174

manners and fear of
    embarrassment 19, 121, 122,
    124, 147, 172
bourgeois / middle class norms 1,
    25, 27, 64, 76, 99, 162-7, 169,
    191, 215, 226n
read as ethnicity 21, 23, 55, 133,
    134, 147
respectability 97, 124, 125, 147,
    150, 240n
suburbia 1, 27, 123, 163, 164, 170,
    175, 197, 210, 213
underclass, the 3, 133
    aesthetic of 27, 95, 104, 137,
        140, 145-6, 149-54
    as Irish 18-28, 31, 58, 73-4,
        134, 145-9
    as Dickensian 21, 133, 145,
        149, 157
    'poor chic' 148, 149, 230n
    Victorian 'residuum' 21, 136,
        141, 150
working class humour 26, 27, 122,
    212
closet 1, 20, 23, 115, 154-5, 165, 168-
    71, 174, 175
coffee houses 44, 45
confession, confessional art 81, 93,
    96, 152, 155, 183, 194, 208,
    212, 213, 218, 219
contempt 2, 26, 27, 43, 45, 51, 89,
    103, 109, 112, 114, 123, 147,
    179, 203, 215, 217
Crompton, Louis 46
cultural studies xv, 11-16, 24, 158

Damasio, Antonio 7-8, 29n
Darwin, Charles 5-7, 29, 46, 83, 136,
    141
Denton, Denice, late Chancellor of
    UCSC 116-121, 130n
Derrida, Jacques 9, 201n
Dickinson, Emily
    'Shame is the Shawl of Pink' 225
Dollimore, Jonathan 65, 178

Douglas, Lord Alfred
  In Praise of Shame 52, 86, 104
  as anti-Irish 19, 20

Ekman, Paul 7
Elden, Stuart 182-3, 200n
Eliot, George 115
Emin, Tracey xvi, 17, 203-28
  Love is A Strange Thing 211
  Reincarnation 211
  Strangeland 201-10, 214-15
  Top Spot 210
  Why I Never Became A Dancer 205-
    6, 208, 210, 217
emotion, definitions of xvi, 4-5, 7, 8,
    11-14, 40, 46, 47, 214
  and/between non-human animals
    9-10
  embodiment of, xiii, 1, 5-6, 7, 23,
    29n, 112, 114, 123, 147, 170,
    178, 220
  transmission and contagion 12-14,
    47, 106, 112
envy xvi, 2, 5, 26, 27, 36, 84, 105,
    106, 108-13, 116, 118, 127,
    128, 147, 203, 213, 218
  penis envy 127
  see also Nietzsche *ressentiment*
Eribon, Didier 25, 30
ethnicity 6, 18, 20-2, 55, 57, 60, 73-
    4, 117, 135, 137, 146-7, 155,
    158
evolutionary psychiatry 7

Fanthome, Christine 212-13
fethishism 18, 87, 97, 143, 144, 149,
    166, 184
Foucault, Michel
  on governmentality xiv, 103, 203,
    205, 224
  on sexuality xiii, 4, 15-16, 39, 50,
    200
  on spatiality 172, 181-4, 187, 195,
    199
  on discourse and genealogy 58,
    146, 152, 184, 185, 186, 208

technologies of the self, ethics of
    the self xiv, 93, 187, 191, 193-
    4, 220-1
Freud, Sigmund
  'Civilisation and its Discontents'
    29n
  'Creative Writers and Day-
    dreaming' 101
  'Group Psychology' 128
  jokes 190
  'Mourning and Melancholia' 101
  on psychoanalysis 106
Gallop, Jane 111,130n
Garrett, Paul Michael 20
gay paranoia 167-73
Gellner, Ernest 58, 74
Goffman, Erving
  stigma xiii, 23, 149
Goldberg, Jonathan 30, 38
Goldman, Daniel P. 11
Gray, Breda 19
grief xv, 9, 59, 79, 84, 101-2, 166,
    168, 193
Grosz, Elizabeth (fn) xiii, xvi, xvii, 8,
    29, 200

Hall, Radclyffe vii, 10, 81, 85
Hall, Stuart xv, 24, 151
Hausmann, Vincent 163, 164, 166
hate 27, 47, 55, 101, 105-6, 109-10,
    112-3, 116, 123, 151, 156, 180,
    190, 218
Haylett, Chris 151-3
Hazlitt, William 113, 130
Herrup, Cynthia B. 32, 36-7, 52n
Hoggart, Simon 92
homophobia 1, 55, 57, 68, 71-2, 80,
    95, 99, 113, 115, 118, 166, 170
Human Rights Commission (USA)
    and homophobia 53, 71-3

incest prohibition 64, 162-4, 167, 177
Ireland 18-22, 29, 34, 36, 40, 47, 56-
    61, 63-4, 71-2, 74-5, 128, 137,
    148
  as sodomitical 75, 148

Mother Ireland 64
multiculturalism and the Celtic
Tiger 74, 75
the Irish 'Scythians' 148
Irigaray, Luce 172, 188, 190, 199, 200
Irish Lesbian and Gay Organization
[ILGO] 56, 68-75, 77

joy 4, 9, 28, 129, 143, 154, 166, 172,
178, 195, 196, 199, 207, 211,
213, 216, 219, 220, 224

Kaplan, Morris B. 169
Klein, Melanie
depressive position 109, 116
envy 118
grief 166, 168
paranoid/schizoid position 109,
118, 172, 178n
projective identification 108, 114,
191
Koven, Seth 141-3
Kuhn, Annette 216

Lacan, Jacques 106, 110, 116
Le Vay, Simon 7
lesbianism
and butchness 1, 90, 104n, 157n,
211
in Cork, Ireland 74
Lesbian Avengers 67-8
lesbian fetish
hands 82, 168
scars 87
lesbian novel 81, 88
Lesbian Studies 26, 105-16, 121,
130
Lloyd, Genevieve 219-20

Mac an Ghaill, M. 18, 20, 22, 145
Masaccio 'Expulsion from the
Garden of Eden' 79
marches and parades
Gay Pride [LGBT Pride] 23, 57,
62-3, 66

on St Patrick's Day 18, 53, 56-8,
61, 68, 70-4
Macbride, Ernest William 19-20, 61
Manchester 53, 91-2, 97, 99, 104,
136, 156
Masson, Jeffrey 8-9
Masters, Robert 5
Meissner, William xiii, 102
Merck, Mandy 168
McClintock, Anne 19-20, 63
McNulty, Amy 137-8
Milton, John
Paradise Lost 195-6, 198
Mosse, George 64-5
Munby, Arthur, and Culwick,
Hannah 143-4

narcissism 9, 26, 74, 101, 109, 115,
116, 157, 163, 165, 217, 221
narcissism and homosexuality
120, 163, 174
nations/nationalism, definitions of
55-8, 60
and gender 19, 21, 46, 63
as heteronormative 36, 56, 57, 64,
66
as homosocial, homo-erotic 57,
64-6, 75, 91
as sentimental 58, 129, 155, 156
Irish-American nationalism 55,
57, 64
Lesbian Nation 67, 76
Queer nationalism 66-7, 94 [see
also sodomitical]
Neurophysiology 7-8, 13
Ngai, Sianne 128
Nietzsche, F.
On the Genealogy of Morals 128,
162, 221
ressentiment 11, 21-6, 128

paedophilia 7, 93, 146, 199
pillory 27, 31-2, 42-51
phallus 53, 60, 81, 84, 126, 129, 144,
164-5, 168, 177, 200, 224

Pullman, Philip
   His Dark Materials 181-202
projection and introjection 13, 43,
   55, 84, 89, 101, 109-10, 116,
   144, 147, 148, 168, 171, 185,
   187, 191
queer
   definitions of 12, 21-3
   queer aesthetics 199
   queer animal love 8-10
      daemons 188-201
   queer desires 103, 142
   queer discipline 15, 107, 197
   queer ethnicity 18, 64-7
   queer families 159n, 168
   queer representation 27, 43, 50,
      66, 93, 99, 103, 104, 120, 157n,
      161, 164, 166, 179, 193
   queer shame 22, 38, 39, 43, 103,
      224
Queer As Folk 80-100, 104, 146, 157

Radel, Nicholas F. 37-8
Red Nose Day (UK) 51, 124-5, 131n
Renan, Ernest 58
ritual 4, 10, 32, 39, 46, 60, 67, 86, 96,
   177, 219
Rose, Jacqueline 106
Rothko, Mark 218
Russell Hochschild, Arlie 11
Ryan, Louise 21
Said, Edward 56
same-sex intimacy
   in seventeenth century 38
   in eighteenth century 39-40, 43-4,
      46, 50
St Catherine of Siena 204
St Patrick's Day – see marches and
   parades
Sartre, Jean-Paul 218
Sayer, Andrew 14
Scheff, Thomas & Retzinger,
   Suzanne 3, 28n
Schwabsky, Barry 207
Sedgwick, Eve Kosofsky xiii, 23, 30,
   65, 103, 109

shame, definitions of
   and abasement 85, 144, 208, 216
   and attachment/disattachment 4,
      12, 22, 23, 24, 26, 66, 71, 83,
      89, 94, 95, 100, 103, 163, 190,
      191, 209, 216, 218, 219, 220,
      221, 224
   and class transgression 28, 31, 144
   and colonialism 63, 148, 155
   and embodiment on the face 18,
      42, 46, 82-3, 85, 89, 103, 125,
      141, 144, 212, 215
   and gender transgression 38, 39,
      47, 84
   and nations/nationalisms 3, 55-
      76, 154, 165
   and poverty 133, 137-8, 141-2,
      148-9, 151, 209
   and pride, binary opposition of
      4, 55, 56, 71, 74, 82-3, 87, 113,
      156
   and recognition 3, 8, 11, 15, 21,
      37-40, 42-3, 48-9, 75, 99, 102,
      107-8, 112-5, 129, 147, 184-6,
      196, 198, 203, 222, 224, 227
   and sadomasochism 4, 7, 46, 82,
      86, 182
   and sexual transgression/
      homosexuality 4, 36, 43, 45,
      49, 83-5, 88, 90, 92, 95, 96,
      142-3, 155, 166, 168, 171, 200
   and separation/ splitting 4, 9, 24,
      45, 80, 88-114, 184, 190-1,
      195, 196, 198-9, 216, 222
   and toilets 95-7
   as pleasurable 4, 43, 45-7, 81, 128-
      9, 147, 154, 165, 220, 223
   communities of 4, 15, 128
   cultural politics of 6, 14, 32
   exile and banishment 32, 56, 57,
      59, 60, 71, 74, 79, 84, 98, 181,
      223
   in organisations 105-32
   interspecies shame 9
   Newtonian model – the 'turn of
      shame' 13, 102-3, 195, 219

origins in Western culture 23, 45,
80, 90, 99, 181, 197-8, 199, 218
public/private 4, 15-6, 18, 27, 31-2,
39-40, 43-51, 63, 66-7, 70, 72,
76, 103, 116-8, 141-2, 170-2,
198, 203-4, 219, 223, 224, 227
sexual shame 83, 181
shame binds, shame loops, shame
spirals 24, 26, 28, 55, 86-7,
105, 108, 121, 191, 218
Shameless 133-59
Simpsons, The 23, 30, 134
Six Feet Under 161-80
Slough, England 27, 121-3
John Betjeman on, 123
Ted Hughes on, 123
Slouka, Mark 8
slumming 139, 141-4, 152, 213
queer slumming 142, 167
Smith, Adam *Theory of Moral
Sentiments* 5
socio-biology 7
sodomy/sodomites 27
and class 32, 37, 38, 169
and nations 36-7
emergence of, 31-53
as foreign pollutant 36, 39
sodomitical angels 192-3
sodomitical nuns 81
sodomitical sublime 28, 43, 75,
170, 193, 223

soul, the 2, 38, 84, 88-9, 177, 188,
193-4, 209, 211-2, 216, 220,
224-5
Spinoza, Baruch xvi, 7, 8, 218-20
spirit/spirituality 36, 64, 65, 79, 80,
84-5, 89, 116, 141, 165, 191,
193, 199, 204, 212, 215, 217,
218, 220
Stone of Shame, Padova 32-4

The Office 121-30
therapy culture 11, 158n, 164, 214,
221
Tomkins, Silvan 104, 114
Touchet, Mervin – Second Earl of
Castlehaven v, vii, 18, 31-7, 52
Toynbee Hall 142

uncanny, the 80, 88, 119, 135, 137,
147, 161, 163, 168, 176, 177,
188, 209

Well of Loneliness, The 80-103, 146
West Riding Pauper Lunatic Asylum
6
Whiteness 18, 19, 85, 134, 137
Wilde, Oscar 32, 37, 52, 86, 142
Williams, Raymond, 'structure of
feeling' xv, 15-8, 23, 153
Winterson, Jeanette 130, 204, 214
Woolcock, Penny 138-40